Cannibalism ar

In *Cannibalism and the Colonial World*, an international team of specialists from a variety of disciplines – anthropology, literature, art history – discusses the historical and cultural significance of western fascination with the topic of cannibalism. Addressing the image as it appears in a series of texts – popular culture, film, literature, travel writing, and anthropology – the essays range from classical times to contemporary critical discourse. *Cannibalism and the Colonial World* examines western fascination with the figure of the cannibal and how this has impacted on the representation of the non-western world. This collection of literary and anthropological scholars analyses the way cannibalism continues to exist as a term within colonial discourse and places the discussion of cannibalism in the context of postcolonial and cultural studies.

FRANCIS BARKER is Professor in Literature, University of Essex. With Peter Hulme and Margaret Iversen he edited *Literature, Politics and Theory* (1986), and *Colonial Discourse/Postcolonial Theory* (1994). He is author of *The Tremulous Private Body* (1984) and *The Culture of Violence* (1994)

PETER HULME is Professor in Literature, University of Essex. He is author of *Colonial Encounters: Europe and the Native Caribbean, 1492–1897* (1986), and has edited *Wild Majesty: Encounters with Caribs from Columbus to the Present Day* (1992).

MARGARET IVERSEN is Reader in Art History and Theory, University of Essex. She is author of *Alois Riegl: Art History and Theory* (1993).

Cultural Margins

General editors

Timothy Brennan
Associate Professor of Comparative Literature and English, University of Minnesota

Abdul JanMohamed
Department of English, University of California, Berkeley

The series **Cultural Margins** originated in response to the rapidly increasing interest in postcolonial and minority discourses among literary and humanist scholars in the US, Europe and elsewhere. The aim of the series is to present books which investigate the complex cultural zone within and through which dominant and minority societies interact and negotiate their differences. Studies in the series range from examinations of the debilitating effects of cultural marginalisation, to analyses of the forms of power found at the margins of culture, to books which map the varied and complex components involved in the relations of domination and subversion. This is an international series, addressing questions crucial to the deconstruction and reconstruction of cultural identify in the late twentieth-century world.

1 Ann Marie Smith, *New Right Discourses on Race and Sexuality: Britain, 1968–1990* 0521 459214

2 David Richards, *Masks of Difference: Cultural Representations in Literature, Anthropology and Art* 0521 47972x

3 Vincent J. Cheng, *Joyce, Race, and Empire* 0521 478596

4 Alice Gambrell, *Women Intellectuals, Modernism, and Difference: Transatlantic Culture, 1991–1945* 0521 55688

Cannibalism and the Colonial World

Edited by

Francis Barker, Peter Hulme, and Margaret Iversen

CAMBRIDGE
UNIVERSITY PRESS

PUBLISHED BY THE PRESS SYNDICATE OF THE UNIVERSITY OF CAMBRIDGE
The Pitt Building, Trumpington Street, Cambridge CB2 1RP, United Kingdom

CAMBRIDGE UNIVERSITY PRESS
The Edinburgh Building, Cambridge CB2 2RU, United Kingdom
40 West 20th Street, New York, NY10011–4211, USA
10 Stamford Road, Oakleigh, Melbourne 3166, Australia

First published 1998

Printed in the United Kingdom at the University Press, Cambridge

Typeset in Palatino 9.5/12pt [CE]

A catalogue record for this book is available from the British Library

Library of Congress cataloguing in publication data

Cannibalism and the colonial world / edited by Francis Barker,
Peter Hulme, Margaret Iversen.
p. cm. – (Cultural margins)
Includes bibliographical references and index.
ISBN 0 521 62118 6 (paperback). – ISBN 0 521 62908 x (paperback)
1. Cannibalism. 2. Cannibalism in literature.
I. Barker, Francis, 1952– . II. Hulme, Peter. III. Iversen, Margaret. IV. Series.
GN409.C35 1998
394′9 – dc21 97–44368 CIP

ISBN 0 521 62118 6 hardback
ISBN 0 521 62908 x paperback

Contents

Illustrations

Notes on editors and contributors

WILLIAM ARENS is Professor of Anthropology at SUNY, Stony Brook. He is the author of *The Man-Eating Myth* (1979).

FRANCIS BARKER is Professor of Literature at the University of Essex. He is the author of *The Tremulous Private Body* (1984/1995) and of *The Culture of Violence* (1994). He is writing a book on artificiality, with the working title *Breathing Simulacra*.

CRYSTAL BARTOLOVICH is an Assistant Professor of English and Textual Studies at Syracuse University. She is currently completing a book entitled *Boundary Disputes: Land-Surveying Discourse and the Culture of Capital in Early Modern England*. She has published essays on topics in Marxism, cultural studies, and early modern culture.

SÉRGIO LUIZ PRADO BELLEI is Professor of Anglo-American Literature and Literary Theory at the Universidade Federal de Santa Catarina, Brazil. He is the author of *O Cristal em Chamas* (1986) and *Nacionalidade e Literatura* (1992), and is currently completing a book of essays entitled *Monstros, Indios e Canibais: Ensaios de Crítica Literária e Cultural*.

GRAHAM HUGGAN is Professor of English at the University of Munich. He has written on Caribbean literature and postcolonial theory, and is currently completing an edited book on cannibalism in a Latin American context.

PETER HULME is Professor of Literature at the University of Essex. He is the author of *Colonial Encounters: Europe and the Native Caribbean, 1492–1797* (1986), and editor of *Wild Majesty: Encounters with Caribs from Columbus to the Present Day* (1992). He is currently completing a book entitled *Visiting the Caribs: Travellers to Dominica, 1877–1992*.

MARGARET IVERSEN is a Reader in the Department of Art History and Theory at the University of Essex. She is the author of *Alois Riegl: Art History and Theory* (1993). She has written extensively on topics in art theory, particularly on psychoanalytic theory and modern art. She is at present writing a book provisionally entitled *Objects of Anxiety: Art and the Unconscious Spectator.*

MAGGIE KILGOUR is an Associate Professor of English at McGill University. She is the author of *From Communion to Cannibalism: An Anatomy of Metaphors of Incorporation* (1990) and *The Rise of the Gothic Novel* (1995), and is currently writing on water. She likes to have people for dinner.

JOHN KRANIAUSKAS is Lecturer in Latin American Cultural History at Birkbeck College, University of London. He is co-editor of *The Journal of Latin American Cultural Studies (Travesía)*, and is completing a book entitled *Mexican Approaches: Latin-Americanist Perspectives on Cultural Studies.*

LUÍS MADUREIRA is Associate Professor of Comparative Literature at the University of Wisconsin-Madison. He has recently completed a book called *The Aesthetics of Post-Colonial Emancipation.*

GANANATH OBEYESEKERE is Professor of Anthropology at Princeton University. He has written several books, most recently *The Work of Culture: Symbolic Transformation in Psychoanalysis and Anthropology* (1990) and *The Apotheosis of Captain Cook: European Myth-Making in the Pacific* (1992)

JERRY PHILLIPS teaches American literature at the University of Connecticut. He is currently completing a book on the theme of adventure in Herman Melville.

MARINA WARNER is a writer of fiction, criticism, and history. Her studies of female myths and symbols include *Alone of All Her Sex: The Myth and the Cult of the Virgin Mary* (1976), and *Monuments & Maidens: The Allegory of the Female Form* (1986). She gave the 1994 Reith Lectures, published as *Managing Monsters: Six Myths of Our Time*; and her most recent book is *From the Beast to the Blonde: On Fairy Tales and their Tellers.* Her study of fear, *No Go the Bogeyman,* will be published in 1998. She is currently a Fellow Commoner at Trinity College, Cambridge, where she is working on a new novel.

Preface

In 1972 André Green opened his long essay in the landmark issue of the *Nouvelle Revue de Psychanalyse* called *Destins du cannibalisme* by remarking on what he called the 'paradoxe du cannibalisme': that while anthropophagy was disappearing amongst the cultures which practised it, our culture's interest in the phenomenon continued to grow (Green 1972: 27). More than two decades later the paradox seems even more acute. 'Cannibalism' has continued to disappear, not just in Green's sense of cannibal barbecues being slowly replaced by McDonald's franchises even in the most 'remote' parts of the world, but also because anthropologists and cultural critics have become – on the whole – more sceptical about the existence of cannibalism as a social practice even in earlier times and in other places. Meanwhile, our interest in the phenomenon seems insatiable, as witnessed by popular films and books, and by a variety of scholarly studies, including the one to which this is the Preface, or *hors d'oeuvre*.

Cannibalism is a topic that unnerves and fascinates. No subject horrifies more than the cannibal serial killer with body parts in his refrigerator, no subject intrigues more than the beneficiary of survival cannibalism; yet cannibalism has proved an endless source of puns and black jokes, and has provoked a lengthy, if intermittent, scholarly debate. Walter Benjamin's invitation to 'seize hold of a memory as it flashes up at a moment of danger' (1992: 247) captures our sense, during discussions in 1992, that the figure of the cannibal, present in popular culture and the language of finance, as well as in anthropological and postcolonial discussions, was worthy of concentrated interdisciplinary and historical attention at one of the Essex Symposia.

Preface

Regularly held since 1989 under the general heading of 'Literature/Politics/Theory', the Essex Symposium series follows on from the Sociology of Literature conferences at Essex, which provided during the 1970s and 1980s an important forum for those interested in left literary and cultural theory in Britain. The Symposium operates by asking around ten invited participants to prepare a draft paper on the announced theme. At the Symposium the pre-circulated papers are discussed in detail. Papers are then rewritten in the light of the discussion, ensuring greater coherence, though not necessarily internal agreement, than a collection of commissioned essays. The Symposium at which early versions of these papers were first discussed took place at the University of Essex in July 1995 under the title 'Consuming Others: "Cannibalism" in the 1990s'. For financial assistance, we thank the University of Essex Research Promotion Fund, and the Departments of Literature and Art History and Theory. For organisational assistance, we thank Elizabeth Weall.

Papers from earlier Essex Symposia have been published as *Uses of History: Marxism, Postmodernism and the Renaissance, Postmodernism and the Rereading of Modernity, Colonial Discourse/Postcolonial Theory* (all in the references under Barker, Francis *et al*, eds.), and as the first volume of the journal *Studies in Travel Writing*, no. 1 (1997).

1

Introduction: the cannibal scene

Peter Hulme

> Weapons hung against the walls – long spears, strangely shaped knives, a couple of narrow shields. In the center of the room was a cooking pot, and at the far end a litter of dry grasses covered by woven mats which evidently served the owners as beds and bedding. Several human skulls lay upon the floor. (Burroughs 1990: 84)

The story of *Tarzan of the Apes* begins in 1888. Tarzan – the orphaned son of Lord Greystoke and his young wife – has been raised among apes and actually kills the first human being he sees, the African Kulonga, in revenge for Kulonga's killing of Tarzan's 'mother', the ape Kala. After the killing, Tarzan examines Kulonga's body carefully, admiring the tattooing on the forehead and the sharp filed teeth. He investigates and appropriates the feathered head-dress, 'and then he prepared to get down to business', because he was hungry and what Edgar Rice Burroughs calls 'jungle ethics' allowed him to eat the meat of the kill: Kulonga seemed just another of the 'countless wild things of the jungle who preyed upon one another to satisfy the cravings of hunger'. However, 'of a sudden, a strange doubt stayed [Tarzan's] hand'. From the children's books he had found in his dead parents' hut, Tarzan had learned that he was a man; and Kulonga – he recognised – was a man too. This produced a dilemma: did men eat men? Tarzan didn't know, but the doubt wells up inside him and a 'qualm of nausea' prevents him from tasting Kulonga's flesh: '[H]ereditary instinct, ages old, usurped the functions of his untaught mind and saved him from transgressing a world-wide law of whose existence he was ignorant' (79–80).

Just what Burroughs means by 'hereditary instinct' remains

temporarily unclear, although the obvious reading would seem to be that Tarzan 'realises' on an instinctual level that, as a human being rather than an animal, he is subject to a law that forbids cannibalism. However, in the next chapter he enters the African village, emptied by the uproar following the discovery of Kulonga's body, and slips through the door of a low thatched building, where he observes the scene described at the top of this page.

This scene is archetypal in a number of ways, and its variants provide one of the threads to this introduction. Like its ultimate precursor – Dr Chanca's 1493 description of a Carib village on Guadeloupe – and like many of its analogues, Burroughs' scene is bereft of actual cannibals: the primal scene of 'cannibalism' as 'witnessed' by Westerners is of its aftermath rather than its performance. At the centre of the scene is the large cooking pot, essential utensil for cannibal illustrations; and surrounding it is the 'evidence' of cannibalism: the discarded human bones.

But the scene also serves to answer the question about the nature of Tarzan's 'strange doubt'. Although the Africans are 'of his own kind' (89), they are clearly not held back by any hereditary instinct from their cannibalistic inclinations. Tarzan's difference is in part racial – he is a white man – and in part a matter of breeding. This is clarified later when he has Jane in his power for the first time and is unsure whether to take her by force since that is the order of the jungle which is all he knows, but which he again vaguely suspects is inappropriate to the human world. He gives her his parents' locket and, when she kisses it, he presses his lips to it where hers had rested:

> It was a stately and gallant little compliment performed with the grace and dignity of utter unconsciousness of self. It was the hall-mark of his aristocratic birth, the natural outcropping of many generations of fine breeding, an hereditary instinct of graciousness which a lifetime of uncouth and savage training and environment could not eradicate. (189)

The repetition of the phrase 'hereditary instinct' brings together cannibalism and rape as the twin aspects of a savage voracity which Tarzan manages to avoid. Not because he is human, but because he is a gentleman. Cannibalism is inseparable from considerations of difference and distinction, here highlighted precisely because, since that difference is in no sense perceptible, therefore it must be innate.

There will be other cannibal scenes in this Introduction, but

Tarzan's offers itself as an archetype: there is no more typical scene in the writing about cannibalism in whatever genre than that in which a witness stumbles across the remains of a cannibal feast. The repetition of that scene can be read in a number of ways, from confirmation that cannibals are cannibals, wherever you find them, to evidence of a deep-rooted cultural obsession in need of analysis. Tarzan's scene also incorporates a good number of the topics that this book will engage through its analyses of the discourse of cannibalism: race, class, genealogy, species, gender, imperialism.

1

For many years histories and analyses of cannibalism were written from firmly within the European or Western tradition, which saw itself as fully civilised. For this tradition, cannibalism was a feature of life in many non-European parts of the world: pre-Columbian America, the Pacific, Africa. If cannibalism featured prominently in accounts of those parts of the world, it was because it was so prominent a practice that accounts could not ignore it. It forced itself upon our attention, and we merely registered our horror and buckled down ever more robustly to the civilising mission. According to this history, cannibalism marked the world beyond European knowledge and was, by the second half of the twentieth century, found only in isolated communities in places like New Guinea and the Amazon, though it elsewhere might remain below the surface, ready to reappear when civilisational influence showed signs of waning.

Like many imperial verities, this story has been comprehensively reversed in recent years. The full counter-narrative is sometimes proposed: cannibalism is merely a product of the European imagination, it was never practised anywhere, it was a calumny imposed by European colonisers to justify their outrages, it had its origins in the disturbed European psyche, it is a tool of Empire. Like many counter-narratives, this version is in danger of oversimplifying almost as much as the once hegemonic story it seeks to overturn. But, as with other counter-narratives, it is actually proposed and defended in this form much less frequently than sometimes supposed, especially by those who seek to expose its presumed oversimplifications while defending some version of the earlier story.

On this vexed question of the reality of cannibalism as a social practice, the views of the contributors to this book can probably be classified as occupying different points on the sceptical part of the spectrum, and as therefore closer to the counter-narrative than to its original. But two points should be emphasised. Firstly, even for the sceptics, cannibalism does exist: it exists as a term within colonial discourse to describe the ferocious devouring of human flesh supposedly practised by some savages. That existence, within discourse, is no less historical whether or not the term cannibalism describes an attested or extant social custom. And second, what marks the concerns of this book and its contributors is the recognition that the really interesting questions about cannibalism begin rather than end with the statement of scepticism, however modulated. For us, the overriding questions remain, why were Europeans so desirous of finding confirmation of their suspicions of cannibalism? and why does cannibalism feature so insistently as a contemporary trope in different forms of writing? The chapters in this book offer a variety of approaches to these questions.

So, for the most part, the 'reality' or otherwise of cannibalistic practices is a question sidestepped rather than directly confronted by our emphasis on the discourse of cannibalism. After all, the starting point for this book is that the imperial narrative about cannibalism has no way of explaining why our fascination for the subject seems to grow in inverse proportion to the amount of cannibalism which that narrative assumes to be (or to have been) practised in the world. Even the most fervent believer in cannibal rites would have to acknowledge that cannibalism is now primarily a linguistic phenomenon, a trope of exceptional power. So, despite the variety of disciplinary backgrounds represented in this book, we approach cannibalism first as cultural critics rather than as anthropologists, historians, or literary analysts. There are no fine distinctions offered here between, say, survival cannibalism, ritual cannibalism, and mortuary cannibalism. An argument does exist – perhaps too purist to gain much acceptance – that anthropophagy should remain as the general term, reserving 'cannibalism' for the ideology that constitutes itself around an obsession with anthropophagy. However, such sophisticated distinctions have been eschewed here, as for the most part has the holding up of the term in sceptical inverted commas. The whole endeavour of this book has been to interrogate the term cannibalism and the phenomenon it purports to describe. Cannibalism is in question throughout; and some of the witnesses called belong to the rich metaphorical hinterland in which the term flourishes: appetite, consumption, body politic, kinship, incorporation, communion.

The general direction travelled by *Cannibalism and the Colonial World* is, then, from elsewhere to here, from the sense that cannibalism is practised over the seas and beyond the hills to the inkling that we need to look within to understand why the cannibal scene means so much to us. That looking within can take many forms: from the psychoanalytical gaze to attention to the vocabulary of cannibalism within our cultural practices, from the analysis of cannibals and vampires in popular culture and film to the self-reflective analysis of imperialism as itself a form of cannibalism.

That movement has a geographical correlate: from two of the classical Pacific sites of cannibalism, New Guinea and Fiji, through the equally classical American sites, Brazil and the Caribbean, eventually arriving back at what is 'home' to the majority of the book's contributors, the cultural 'centres' of Western Europe and North America. But the journey is far from being that simple. To arrive home is to realise – as Marina Warner's chapter shows – that cannibals have been with us for a long time, crucial figures of myth and fairytale; and to remember that supposed cannibals have been brought back to Europe ever since the end of the fifteenth century, as part of the slave trade which Columbus established (Sued Badillo 1992). However, if – as many of the chapters here suggest – cannibalism needs to be understood as a topic within the dialogue between Europe and its others, and therefore within the context of the colonial world, then our symbolic starting point must be the historically resonant appearance of the Tupinambá who disembarked at Rouen in November 1562, where they conversed with the young French king, Charles IX, and with Michel de Montaigne. Montaigne's conversation with the Tupinambá, and the reflections it produced in his essay 'Des cannibales', reverberate through all subsequent cultural debates about cannibalism – and are a frequent reference point in this book.[1]

Montaigne's famous essay brings America back to Europe: a conjunction which has recently been recognised as crucial not just for the development of European colonialism but for that of capitalist modernity itself (a point which we have recovered rather than arrived at fresh, since it was a commonplace for Adam Smith and Karl Marx). The modern Cartesian subject of that capitalist modernity depends for its sense of self as independent entity on an image of a clearly differentiated 'other' who destroys boundaries, the kind of 'other' so powerfully figured in the cannibals who threaten Robinson Crusoe: modernity enters the world's stage attached to its cannibal shadow. One of our contributors quotes Stallybrass and White's formulation:

> The bourgeois subject continuously defined and redefined itself through the exclusion of what it marked out as 'low' – as dirty, repulsive, noisy, contaminating. Yet that very act of exclusion was constitutive of its identity. The low was internalized under the sign of negation and disgust ... But disgust always bears the imprint of desire. (below, p. 223)

Disgust, but also desire; loathing, but also fascination. Montaigne's cannibal scene is a dialogue, albeit fraught by the difficulty of bad interpretation; a dialogue which offers itself as a model for much of the work of this volume.[2] To concentrate on the notion of dialogue is to insist on two emphases, not always present in discussions of cannibalism: on the agency of those described as cannibals – difficult to access but necessary to posit; and on the relationship between describer and described, between Europe and its others. The figure of the cannibal is a classic example of the way in which that otherness is dependent on a prior sense of kinship denied, rather than on mere difference. At least from Peter Martyr onwards, cannibals have been compared with their describers, comparisons which tend to undermine the strong sense of difference carried by the surface argument. Brazilian cannibalism was immediately drawn into the religious controversies of sixteenth-century Europe, with papist theophagy denounced as by far the worse practice of the two (see Lestringant 1982). Jean de Léry – Montaigne's most important source, and one of the key European witnesses of Tupinambá cannibalism – makes the same point about the European usurers who eat everyone alive, especially widows, orphans, and other poor people (Léry 1990: 132). For Marlow in *Heart of Darkness* the thrill was in the thought of his kinship – however remote – with the cannibals of the Congo (Conrad 1967: 244).

2

Another way of describing the trajectory of this book would be through reference to the work of the authors of its opening and closing chapters, William Arens and Maggie Kilgour respectively, taking us from the historical scepticism of Arens's influential 1979 polemic, *The Man-Eating Myth*, which marks the beginning of the contemporary debate about cannibalism, through to the broader literary and cultural concerns of Kilgour's *From Communion to Cannibalism* (1990), a book which took on cannibalism as a metaphor, reading it in conjunction with its associates, incorporation and communion.

The nature of Arens's argument has been so often misrepresented, especially by its association with Holocaust denial (which I come to below), that it's worth reiterating his fundamental project: 'First, to assess critically the instances of and documentation for cannibalism, and second, by examining this material and the theoretical explanations offered, to arrive at some broader understanding of the nature and function of anthropology over the past century'. The actual question as to whether or not people eat each other is taken as 'interesting but moot'; and less interesting than the fact that the idea that they do so is commonly accepted without adequate documentation (1979b: 9). Arens considers several of the well-known historical cases, reports his efforts to track down eyewitnesses, and looks in detail at the most famous contemporary case of cannibalism, as supposed transmitter of the disease of kuru among the Fore of New Guinea, a thesis that won a Nobel Prize for its proponent – and which Arens returns to in the first chapter of the present volume (and cf. Arens 1990). Arens's conclusions are actually directed less at the evidence for cannibalism – about whose customary practice he remains sceptical – than at the relationship between cannibalism and anthropology. The pattern of that relationship ('comfortable and supportive' (1979b: 162)) seems highly suspicious to Arens:

> Once having made the proper excuses for the benighted natives' former moral transgressions, the anthropological fieldworker is also able to report ... that contact with Western civilization has immediately resulted in the demise of this custom which our culture views with such fascination and horror. Fortunately, but strangely enough, this is often the only trait which has been abandoned by the indigenes with such ease. Other customs which the agents of Western morality also fail to appreciate, but which have actually been encountered, somehow manage to remain a vital part of the culture, in spite of determined attempts by others to stamp them out. (168)

For Arens the association between cannibalism and Western imperialism is impossible to ignore: cannibalism was supposedly the trait that characterised those parts of the world into which the torch of civilisation had not yet shone. That such areas of darkness were by definition unobserved by the torch-bearers did not dent their confident description of the practices that flourished there. Yet to shine the torch of civilisation into these dark spots immediately caused the practice to wither. Such patterns are enough for the suspicious cultural analyst to turn the spotlight back onto the way in which cannibalism contains and transmits 'significant cultural messages for those who maintain it' (Arens 1979b: 182).[3]

The good humour and mild tone in which Arens conducts his investigations present a remarkable contrast to the outrage his book provoked, with wild charges of 'slur' and 'scandal' thrown around, along with liberal doses of adjectives such as 'dangerous', 'mischievous', and 'offensive'. *The Man-Eating Myth* clearly touched a raw nerve and drew any number of 'refutations', most of which missed the point.[4] Here, for the first time, in 'Rethinking Anthropophagy', Arens responds to some of his critics, reassesses the nature of the debate nearly two decades on, and brings the story of the vexed relationship between kuru and cannibalism up to date, a story newly topical given that Creutzfeld-Jacob's Disease is a variant of kuru. In particular, Arens demonstrates how the impression of Fore cannibalism is conveyed through self-referentiality and inference in citation and photography.

Kilgour's book, though less controversial, has been an equally important influence, offering as it does what is little short of a full re-reading of the Western literary tradition through the trope of cannibalism, paying substantial attention to major authors such as Homer, Ovid, Augustine, Dante, Rabelais, Jonson, Milton, Coleridge, and Melville.[5] This canonical literary tradition features in the present book, though often in supplementary or shadowy ways: the stories of Hesiod and Ovid retold in the fifteenth or nineteenth centuries; the Prospero-Caliban relationship from Shakespeare's *The Tempest* echoed in a Guyanese novel of the 1950s. Conrad's *Heart of Darkness* is the one indispensable canonical reference point. But it is often other, perhaps less well-known genres, that come to prominence here: nineteenth-century ethnographic adventure stories treading the narrow line between fiction and travel-writing; sailors' yarns, sometimes transcribed into would-be best-sellers, sometimes acting as the explicit model for the literary patterns of Melville and Conrad; cinematic examples from the black humour of *The Cook, the Thief, his Wife and her Lover* and *Cronos* to the tacky images of *Dawn of the Dead*; the hallucinatory world of late colonial and postcolonial fiction in the Caribbean; the provocative and witty texts of Brazilian *modernismo*;

the psychological macabre of children's stories; the dark American gothic, fictional and real, of Thomas Harris and Jeffrey Dahmer. Through it all emerges the figure of the cannibal: ferocious, innocent, threatening, playful, Rabelaisian, Hobbesian, postmodern, postcolonial, paranoid, rational: Hannibal Lecter sums up that overdetermined figure for the 1990s, and it's therefore appropriate that this book ends with Maggie Kilgour's careful and perceptive analysis of the modern cannibal at the centre of *The Silence of the Lambs*.

In Kilgour's book, Freud features as constant commentator on cannibal concerns, and he is inevitably a key figure on the cannibal scene, as Hannibal Lecter, analyst, himself suggests. Postcolonial counter-narratives will seek support from the language of psychoanalysis to argue that the figure of the cannibal is a projection of European fantasies, a screen for colonial violence (see Bucher 1979). However, psychoanalysis – at least in its classical Freudian model – offers only ambivalent support for this view. After all, Freud had his own cannibal narrative, as fully developmental as – and very much of a piece with – imperial stories; and that cannibal narrrative is part of a universal story of psychic development, not one which is interested in distinctions between the colonisers and the colonised. That narrative has its own cannibal scene, too, visualised as the beginning moment of all human culture:

> One day the brothers who had been driven out came together, killed and devoured their father and so made an end of the patriarchal horde. United they had the courage to do and succeeded in doing what would have been impossible for them individually... Cannibal savages as they were, it goes without saying that they devoured their victim as well as killing him. The violent primal father had doubtless been the feared and envied model of each one of the company of brothers: and in the act of devouring him they accomplished their identification with him, and each one of them acquired a portion of his strength. The totem meal, which is perhaps mankind's earliest festival, would thus be a repetition and a commemoration of this memorable and criminal deed, which was the beginning of so many things – of social organization, of moral restrictions and of religion. (Freud 1983: 141–2; cf. Kilgour, below, pp. 244–5)

More precisely, the Freudian narrative offers a powerful encoding of the 'development of the self' in what Kilgour (in this volume) calls his quest-romance of sexual development, in which the individual recapitulates the development of the species. During this development the oral or cannibal 'stage', in which the infant has no sense of its separation from the world, is left behind – yet never completely sloughed off, since what Freud calls the 'final structure' of the self often contains 'vestiges of earlier fixations' (quoted below, p. 244). Regression is feared as pathological, yet erotic desire is a notoriously 'consuming passion' which threatens to dissolve the boundary between ego and object in a way that has often led poets to use cannibalistic imagery to describe the actions of lovers. This allows cannibalism to appear as a form of nostalgia, offering a restoration of social wholeness, which may account for some of the relatively benign assessments of the phenomenon during the early modern period, most notoriously Montaigne's, and which Kilgour suggests may explain our current fascination with the topic: 'a sign of our culture's refusal to let go of the idea of the natural, the wild, the savage, at the very time in which it is disappearing in the external world' (below, p. 247). Less an idealisation of the cannibal, then, than an attack on our own rapacious egos. The man-eating myth is still with us – but as a story about ourselves.

3

Why cannibalism fascinates us at the end of the second millennium is a difficult question that several of the later chapters of this book address, in cultural analyses that draw on the language of ideology and psychoanalysis. Why cannibalism interests scholars of cultural process is easier to answer: few topics seem to concentrate so effectively so many key cultural issues, especially those that cluster around the questions of relativism and scepticism that have played such a large part in the 'culture wars' of recent years. In some ways cannibalism might seem an unlikely topic to generate much heat: after all its contemporary political resonance is rather small and its range of potential application distinctly limited. Nevertheless, beyond our perennial fascination with the topic, two related issues have put it in the forefront of current debates: the comparison made between those sceptical of cannibal stories and those who deny the Holocaust; and the whole question of Western attitudes towards and understanding of non-Western cultures. The first issue can be introduced and disposed of; the second simply introduced.

Defenders of traditional cannibal stories have raised the stakes by repeatedly associating Arens's revisionism with the denial of the Holocaust. The initial linkage goes back to an exchange in the *New York Review of Books* even before *The Man-Eating Myth* was published, when Arens intervened in a debate between, on the one hand, Marshall Sahlins, and on the other Marvin Harris (1977) and Michael Harner (1977) (Arens 1979a). Harris and Harner were proponents of the so-called 'materialist' theory of cannibalism, which saw cannibal motivation as arising from the need for protein; on the contrary, Sahlins (1978) saw cannibalism as a deeply symbolic ritual. Arens wrote to the *NYROB* with a summary of the arguments of his forthcoming book in an attempt to undermine the assumption shared by Harris, Harner, and Sahlins that cannibalism was a common feature of 'primitive' cultures. Concentrating on the Aztec case, he concludes by suggesting that what he has analysed as an 'anti-intellectual process' can in part be explained by the evidently felt need of our culture's anthropologists and historians 'to create and relocate savagery in its most gruesome form by calling into existence man-eaters at the fringes of our time and space' (Arens 1979a: 46). Sahlins's response to Arens's letter engages with his arguments, puts forward what he sees as eye-witness accounts, but then ends by generalising the argument from Arens' imputation of 'an "anti-intellectual" conspiracy' involving Harris and himself to what he sees as 'a familiar American pattern of enterprising social science journalism':

> Professor X puts out some outrageous theory, such as the Nazis really didn't kill the Jews, human civilization comes from another planet, or there is no such thing as cannibalism. Since facts are plainly against him, X's main argument consists of the expression, in the highest moral tones, of his own disregard for all available evidence to the contrary. He rises instead to the more elevated analytical plane of ad hominem attack on the authors of the primary sources and those credulous enough to believe them. All this provokes Y and Z to issue a rejoinder, such as this one. X now becomes 'the controversial Professor X' and his book is respectfully reviewed by non-professionals in *Time*, *Newsweek*, and *The New Yorker*. There follow appearances on radio, TV, and in the columns of the daily newspapers.[6]

Sahlins is a formidable polemicist, but he himself is not above (or beneath) *ad hominem* arguments and attributing guilt by association. 'I am a scholar, you are a journalist' doesn't exactly address the issue at hand; 'conspiracy' is a word used by Sahlins, not by Arens; and 'there is no such thing as cannibalism' is quite clearly not the thesis of Arens's letter, or indeed of his book, which Sahlins had already read. However, despite the evidently offhand and unconvincing nature of Sahlins's paragraph, the association of Arens's argument with Holocaust denial was almost immediately picked up by the French historian, Pierre Vidal-Naquet, in his essay 'Un Eichmann de papier', published in the journal *Esprit* in September 1980.[7] The target of Vidal-Naquet's essay is Robert Faurisson and his work of Holocaust denial. Cannibalism features only as a launching pad, one that Vidal-Naquet borrows from Marshall Sahlins, quoting with approval (in translation) the passage above, as well as two other extracts, one from Sahlins' letter and one from the earlier piece reviewing Harris's and Harner's work. There is no indication that Vidal-Naquet has read Arens's book: certainly there are no quotations from it and no references to its pages, and the brief summary he offers is drawn almost verbatim from Rodney Needham's review in the *Times Literary Supplement* (1980). The only characterisations he offers of its argument – 'les cannibales n'existent pas' (1987: 17) and 'il n'y a jamais eu de cannibales' (18) – are blatantly inaccurate. The point of the exercise is to establish what he calls 'deux formes extrêmes et opposées du délire sur les cannibales: le délire réducteur de Harris et le délire négateur d'Arens' (20), which enables him to launch the analogous distinction between the 'materialist' reductionism of the ultra-leftist arguments of *Auschwitz ou le Grand Alibi* and the pure negation of Faurisson. The shoddiness of the comparison should perhaps lead to its dismissal with the same speed that Vidal-Naquet wants to dismiss Arens's book. However, the deserved eminence of Sahlins and Vidal-Naquet as scholars demands that the comparison is taken with a greater seriousness than it would otherwise merit.[8]

Looking beyond the assertions of a relationship (evident in the work given by the analogists to terms like 'reminiscent'), there would seem to be three conceivable points at which the two matters could come together into the same field of vision. A secondary tactic of the Holocaust deniers is to assert moral equivalence: for example, there may have been some killing of Jews (even if not six million), but the bombing of Dresden by the Allies was just as bad. Likewise, commentators on the cannibal question, from Léry to Melville and beyond, have asked whether the eating of human flesh – even if it happens – is any worse than some of what passes for acceptable practice in Europe, from usury to the forced feeding of geese. But then such questions about moral equivalence have become the staple of most contemporary debates about morality, without anyone having seen it necessary to associate, say, cannibal sceptics and those who refuse to equate abortion with murder.

Potentially more convincing is the point that both arguments can flourish in the current climate of scepticism and uncertainty, underpinned by the kind of academic relativism associated with names such as Stanley Fish, Richard Rorty, and Jacques Derrida. This is one of the explanations that Deborah Lipstadt gives in her *Denying the Holocaust* for the 'success' of Holocaust denial in recent years. But in very much the weakest part of her excellent history of the phenomenon, she ends up associating Holocaust denial with Oliver Stone's theory about the assassination of Kennedy and with Leonard Jeffries' Afrocentrism (1993: 18–19). As even these examples show, credulity is no less prevalent than scepticism, and arguably much more of a problem for our intellectual world: after all, Holocaust deniers are wrong not because of their sceptical attitude towards evidence but because of the weight and substance of the testimony they try to deny, while Holocaust denial has gained some small degree of acceptance because, firstly, of continuing anti-semitism, and second, of widespread credulity towards almost all bizarre claims, from the landing on the moon being mocked up in a Hollywood studio to an epidemic of abductions by alien spacecraft. If academic relativism has any connection to all this, then it would presumably be found in Jean Baudrillard's infamous denial that the Gulf War ever took place, a denial which – even those unsympathetic to the claim would admit – operates at a level of philosophical abstraction totally removed from Holocaust denial (see Norris 1992). The radical scepticism common in very different ways to Arens, Baudrillard, Derrida, and the Holocaust deniers is also shared by scientists who look at the evidence for UFO landings, but such 'similarities' actually tell us nothing of interest about the phenomena being debated.[9] One can only conclude that the danger involved in rejecting the prevalent climate of intellectual questioning in favour of believing what we're told is considerably greater than any inconvenience caused by having to filter out the bizarre from the plausible.

That leaves one final area of possible comparability: both cannibal sceptics and Holocaust deniers move into the area of textual scholarship, sometimes calling into question the 'authenticity' of particular texts – Anne Frank's diary being the best-known example. Here, as Lipstadt is able to point out, Holocaust denial has merely mimicked the methodology of orthodox scholarship (1993: 229–35). It's true that some of the cannibal stories have been put under pressure by textual scholarship, but then so have some of the old 'certainties' about Shakespeare's plays, without anyone suggesting – yet – that to question the orthodoxy of a single *King Lear* is equivalent to denying the Holocaust (see Holderness et al. 1995). The textual 'scholarship' of Holocaust deniers can only pay dividends through forgery, fraud, and wilful misreading. For all the bitterness of the polemics around cannibalism, none of these charges have been made against the scholars involved: inability to see what's in front of their noses or to read a paragraph of simple prose is usually as serious as the allegations get.[10] Indeed, the difficult questions about textual scholarship and use of evidence are posed by the sceptics – as Arens' chapter here demonstrates.

A reading of Lipstadt's book makes clear the fundamental differences between cannibal scepticism and Holocaust denial. Lipstadt herself distinguishes Holocaust denial from other forms of historical revisionism, including the work on which the deniers have drawn. Vidal-Naquet uses the term 'revisionism', but Lipstadt rightly points out that all historians are to a degree revisionist; and 'denial' has as a term the merit of distinguishing from proper scholarship what she calls 'a purely ideological enterprise' (26) which only gives the 'illusion of reasoned inquiry' (28). Holocaust denial is driven by a motive (anti-semitism) and associated with a political programme (fascism) which can rarely be spelled out and which must therefore be concealed by its proponents: its agenda is always obfuscated. Even where it mimes the scholarly forms, it falsifies quotations and information: it is, in Vidal-Naquet's proper phrase, an assassin of memory. None of this is true of Arens's arguments, or of those who have supported those arguments. The sceptical approach to the prevalence of cannibalism is certainly revisionist, but it denies nothing.

Lipstadt does not stress denial (disavowal) as a psychoanalytic term, but if denial enters the cannibal scene it does so, according to the sceptics, through the denial of colonial violence – which is one of the roots of the projection of cannibalism onto the victims of that violence: denial is a facet of the proposal of cannibal stories, at least in their early forms, when legal or moral justification was being sought for campaigns of slavery or extermination. Two resonant literary images also speak to this connection. When Robinson Crusoe first confronts what he takes to be the cannibal scene on the beach of his island, his second response – after self-protection – is to think of 'nothing but how I might destroy some of these Monsters' (Defoe 1975: 132). Cannibalism and mass murder are associated here

– but in the mind of the European who directs his destructive fantasy at the supposed cannibals.[11]

Nearly two centuries later, the figure of Kurtz in *Heart of Darkness*, seen by Marlow, offers a frightening representation of the way in which European cannibal fantasies have taken on a physical dimension: 'I saw him open his mouth wide – it gave him a weirdly voracious aspect, as though he wanted to swallow all the air, all the earth, all the men before him' (quoted below, p. 189). Africa's 'real' cannibals are put in the shade by this fantasy of total incorporation, which is a not inaccurate metaphor for Kurtz's relationship to 'his' territory. There is little distance from here to 'Exterminate all the brutes': as Jerry Phillips remarks, 'in one respect, genocide is the logical destination of totalizing infantile egoism' (below, p. 190). The comment made to Marlow by a colleague of Kurtz's – 'He would have been a splendid leader of an extreme party' – serves to associate Kurtz with European fascism (and allows Phillips, in his chapter, to imbricate the discourses of cannibalism and anti-semitism (p. 201 below)).

When Jean de Léry begins his relativistic defence of the Brazilian cannibals (in his *History of a Voyage to the Land of Brazil*, published in 1578), asking his horrified readers to bear in mind the things that go on every day over here among us, his first example plays, without much subtlety, on the stereotype of the Jewish usurer:

> In the first place, if you consider in all candor what our big usurers do, sucking blood and marrow; and eating everyone alive – widows, orphans, and other poor people, whose throats it would be better to cut once and for all, than to make them linger in misery – you will say that they are even more cruel than the savages I speak of. And that is why the prophet says that such men flay the skin of God's people, eat their flesh, break their bones and chop them in pieces for the pot, and as flesh within the cauldron. (Léry 1990: 132; referring to *Micah* 3.2–3)

It comes as no particular surprise to learn that Léry was, in Lestringant's words, 'un chaud partisan de la chasse aux sorcières' and that he cites Jean Bodin's *Démonomanie* to the effect that Brazilian women and European witches are 'conduites d'un mesme esprit de Satan' (1994: 127–8). Indeed, witchcraft – for so long part of the 'truth' of European history – makes a much more obvious point of comparison with cannibalism than the Holocaust. To make that connection, however, is to begin to recast the terms of the discussion, with cannibals joining witches and Jews as what

Norman Cohn (1975) refers to as Europe's 'inner demons', sharing a set of images which include the dissolute orgy and the Thyestean feast. In other words, if there is an association to be made between cannibalism and the anti-semitism which motivates Holocaust deniers, it's to be found in the fact that cannibalism is one of the practices anti-semites associate with Jews.

Spurious analogies are made with the speed of a hare, but take time to discredit since scholarship can only move at the pace of a tortoise. The Holocaust is denied; reports of cannibalism are put into question through careful reading of textual evidence, a process that can proceed only serially, at least until there are sufficient cases for the emergence of the kind of patterns that piqued Arens's interest in the topic. Let me offer just one example from my own area of interest by way of a final rejection of a connection that does no credit to its proponents, and as a demonstration that cannibal scepticism operates according to a hermeneutics of suspicion and not through irrational denial.

Inasmuch as the topic of this present book is the discourse of cannibalism, rather than cannibalism itself, another of its beginning moments can be traced to 4 November 1493, a moment recounted, not more than several weeks later, by the pen of Dr Diego Alvarez Chanca, who sailed with Columbus on this second voyage to the Caribbean. These are Chanca's words, often taken as the earliest modern account of cannibalism, and certainly the first account of cannibalism in the Americas:

> When we came near, the admiral ordered a light caravel to coast along looking for a harbour. It went ahead and having reached land, sighted some houses. The captain went ashore in the boat and reached the house, in which he found their inhabitants. As soon as they saw them [our men] they took to flight, and he entered the houses and found the things that they had, for they had taken nothing away, and from there he took two parrots, very large and very different from all those seen before. He found much cotton, spun and ready for spinning, and articles of food; and he brought away a little of everything; especially he brought away four or five bones of the arms and legs of men. When we saw this, we suspected that the islands were those islands of Caribe, which are inhabited by people who eat human flesh. For the admiral, in accordance with the indications as to the situation of those islands which the indians of the islands which they had previously discovered had given to him on the former voyage,

> had directed his course to discover them, because they were nearer to Spain and also because from there lay the direct route by which to come to Española, where he had left people before. To these islands, by the goodness of God and by the good judgment of the Admiral, we came as directly as if we had been sailing on a known and well-followed route. (Translated in Hulme and Whitehead 1992: 32; Spanish in Gil and Varela 1984: 158)

This is one of the primal scenes of Early America: indigenous savagery observed and reported on by a European eyewitness, with Chanca's status as a medical doctor equipping him with the kind of knowledge and approach which supposedly mark him as an appropriate forerunner of the objective historian. On closer inspection, however, the 'horrors' that Chanca reported turn out to have been four or five human bones collected – that is to say, stolen – by one of Columbus's officers from a deserted hut on the island, along with some cotton, some food, and two large parrots.

To be stressed here is that Dr Chanca's testimony, far from being, as sometimes claimed, a 'matter-of-fact' description, is a highly mediated piece of prose deeply embedded in the assumptions which governed Columbus's second voyage. To begin with, what Chanca offers is not a description at all: he was not a member of the landing-party and therefore not an eyewitness to anything. He reports second-hand what was told to him, probably by the captain of the caravel. Chanca had not been on the first voyage, so he himself had no expectations, let alone any knowledge: 'We suspected that ...' can only refer to a collective view promulgated principally by Columbus himself as source of authority and as main conduit of information and opinion between first voyage and second. In writing this sentence Chanca places himself grammatically, through his use of the first-person plural, within the 'official version' propounded by Columbus. In no way can he be seen as an independent or fresh witness who 'just' reports what he sees. The official working assumption is that the second expedition has arrived at islands inhabited by cannibals: the sight of four or five human bones is enough then to confirm the suspicion 'that the islands were those islands of Caribe, which are inhabited by people who eat human flesh', however short such a sight might fall of anything that could be called eyewitness testimony, and however probable it was that such bones were part of the funerary rituals commonplace in the native Caribbean. In other words, in this one instance – the primordial – Arens's argument seems vindicated:

some historians leap to conclusions on inadequate evidence and careless reading.[12]

The cannibal scene reported to Chanca has an interesting history, illustrative of the augmentative process that often marks the passage of ethnographic description from one context to another. Chanca's cannibal scene passed into the European imagination via the graphic description offered by the influential humanist scholar Peter Martyr, who never got nearer the Caribbean than Andalucía. To the handful of bones in one hut reported by Chanca, Peter Martyr pluralised the location, gave the houses kitchens, added pieces of human flesh broached on a spit ready for roasting and, for good measure, threw in the head of young boy hanging from a beam and still soaked in blood.[13] This Caribbean barbecue was disseminated not only through the many reproductions of Peter Martyr's own writings, but also through the vastly influential collection put together by Montalboddo, and called *Mondo Novo e Paesi novamente retrovati da Alberico Vespuzio* (1507), which added for good measure the feverish cannibal fantasies that the pseudo-Vespucci had interpolated into the original 'Letter to Bartolozzi' written by the distinguished Florentine navigator.[14] One particular consequence of this intervention was that the term 'cannibal' spread in European usage down the coast of South America into what is now Brazil.

A further elaboration of the scene Chanca describes is found in one of the celebratory volumes produced for the Columbian quatercentenary: *Columbus and Columbia: A Pictorial History of the Man and the Nation* (Blaine et al. 1892). A drawing containing the requisite icons of cooking pot and scattered limbs is framed by a descriptive paragraph which draws out its implications:

> It was in this village of Guadaloupe that they first discovered the ravages and wrecks of cannibalism. Human bones were plentifully scattered about the houses. In the kitchens were found skulls in use as bowls and vases. In some of the houses the evidences of man-eating were still more vividly and horribly present. The Spaniards entered apartments which were veritable human butcher-shops. Heads and limbs of men and women were hung up on the walls or suspended from the rafters, in some instances dripping with blood, and, as if to add, if that were possible, to the horror of the scene, dead parrots, geese, dogs and iguanas were hung up without discrimination or preference with the fragments of human bodies. In a pot some pieces of a human limb were boiling, so that with these several evidences it was manifest that canni-

> balism was not an incidental fact, but a common usage, well established and approved in the life of the islanders. (172)

A handful of bones – which might have had nothing to do with cannibalism – has now been transformed into 'veritable human butcher-shops', a kind of mass-production line for cannibal delicacies. Martyr's own addition of a child's head hanging from the rafters has multiplied. And the inevitable pot makes its appearance, with limbs boiling away. In two easy stages we move from a second-hand report of a few human bones to 'several evidences' that it was 'manifest' that cannibalism was 'a common usage'. Chanca's report does not provide – as often stated – evidence for cannibalism in the Caribbean islands. However, the history of its transmission, elaboration, and embroidery provides evidence of a fascination which requires more analysis than it is usually given.

How to understand non-Western cultures is a question obviously fundamental to anthropology. The set-piece debate for the 1990s has been between Marshall Sahlins and Gananath Obeyesekere over the degree of 'difference' that should be accorded to one particular non-Western culture, that of the native Hawaiians who were responsible for the death of Captain Cook in 1779. In short, Obeyesekere (1992a) argues that Sahlins invents cultural differences which remove from the Hawaiians the capacity for rational behaviour. Sahlins (1995) counters that Obeyesekere removes from the Hawaiians their own standards of behaviour, which may well not correspond to what Obeyesekere regards as rational. The debate is overdetermined by the antagonists' respective historical placements and backgrounds, although – in an echo of the equivalent set-piece of the 1970s between Claude Lévi-Strauss (1992 (1995)) and Jacques Derrida (1976) – the charge of ethnocentrism is countered with that of anti-anti-ethnocentrism. These are murky waters, indeed, in which I shall swim only a few strokes further in order to investigate how cannibal questions are interlaced in the debate.

The body of Captain Cook, dismembered and parts of it possibly eaten, is the graphic image at the centre of the set-piece. Sahlins has already appeared as an early critic of Arens's work and Obeyesekere has almost inevitably turned to the cannibal question in his reading of South Seas materials, referring in his chapter in the present book to one of the examples Sahlins had quoted against Arens. In a very minor key, the Obeyesekere/Sahlins debate is played out in the specifically cannibal register in a recent exchange in *Critical Inquiry* where Myra Jehlen puts the kinds of questions asked by Sahlins to the argument of my book, *Colonial Encounters*, which is deeply sceptical about the accounts of Native Caribbean cannibalism, for some of the reasons spelled out in the previous section (Jehlen 1993 and Hulme 1994). Cannibalism is – as practice or accusation – quite simply the mark of greatest imaginable cultural difference and therefore the greatest challenge to our categories of understanding.

The danger of these set-piece debates is that they tend to exacerbate relatively small (though important) differences into major intellectual gulfs. Jehlen and myself, like Sahlins and Obeyesekere, actually share much more by way of general intellectual approach than such disagreements suggest. And, in fact, Obeyesekere's recent work on cannibalism in *Critical Inquiry* (1992b) actually offers a significant way forward from the antinomies that so easily take over the cannibal scene. It can be outlined here, as having been a further impetus to *Cannibalism and the Colonial World*, offering an example of how to go beyond the existing terms of the cannibal debate.

4

One of the significant new emphases in postcolonial work has been in the area of cultural contact. In place of the 'frontier', for so long the defining concept, with its implications of expansion and contraction, there is now envisaged a 'contact zone', a phrase Mary Louise Pratt uses, as she explains in her book *Imperial Eyes*, to refer to the space of colonial encounters, the space in which peoples geographically and historically separated come into contact with each other and establish ongoing relations of some kind, even if these are often marked by conditions of coercion, radical inequality, and intractable conflict. 'Contact' is a term that Pratt takes from linguistics, where contact languages refer to improvised forms of communication that develop among speakers of different native languages who need to communicate with each other, and which become 'creoles' when they have native speakers of their own.[15]

The emphasis on contact zone can help clarify the role of the cannibal. That cannibal questions have arisen from cultural contact may seem a truism. However, the shift from 'frontier' to 'zone' asks us to conceive of an encounter in which the two (or more) cultures inevitably and immediately begin to adapt as a result of the inevitable and immediate dialogue between them – which may not, of course, take place on terms of equality. This perspective – antagonistic to the supposedly objective language of observation and description that marks much colonial discourse – encourages careful attention to the circumstances of the cultural exchange in which reports of cannibalism are found.

Nor is it necessarily the case that the idea of cannibalism is even introduced by Europeans. In the South American context, for example, the important work of Neil Whitehead has stressed that 'Europeans and Amerindians shared a passionate interest in the idea of cannibalism, reflected in the doctrinal strictures of both Catholic transubstantiation and the divine hunger of the Amerindian pantheon' (1997: 80). That shared interest then provides the basis both for the development of the trope of cannibalism ('for it was the Spanish who had come to eat out the native inhabitants' – as those inhabitants clearly perceived) and for the actual practice of cannibalism as a communicative act in the exchange between European and Amerindian. In this approach – as in Obeyesekere's – cannibalism ceases to be regarded as a determining social practice (which is not to say that it never was) and becomes an element in cultural contact, an 'entangled object' in the resonant title of Nicholas Thomas's book (1991).

In '"British Cannibals": Contemplation of an Event in the Death and Resurrection of James Cook, Explorer' (1992b), Obeyesekere concentrates on a particular 'scene' which took place in November 1773 during Cook's second voyage to the South Seas, when the *Resolution* had anchored off the New Zealand coast for repairs. Bored by the delays, some of the officers went on shore 'to amuse themselves among the Natives' (Cook's words). There they saw the head, bowels, and heart of a youth who had apparently been killed in a skirmish with other Maori. One of the officers, Richard Pickersgill, bought the head for two nails and brought it on board. There, Cook writes, 'a peice of the flesh had been broiled and eat by one of the Natives in the presince of most of the officers' (Cook 1961: 293). This is not, as it happens, an eye-witness account: Cook makes it clear that he returned on board after the 'incident'. However, behind Cook's words is an account that is by an eye-witness, indeed rather more than an eye-witness, from the journal of Lieutenant Charles Clerke, which J. C. Beaglehole has correlated with Cook's in his monumental edition of Cook's journals. Clerke gives us what Beaglehole calls 'the circumstantial details':

> ... I ask'd him if he'd eat a peice there directly to which he very chearfully gave his assent. I then cut a peice of carry'd [it] to the fire by his desire and gave it a little broil upon the Grid

> Iron then deliver'd it to hin – he not only eat it but devour'd it most ravenously, and suck'd his fingers 1/2 a dozen times over in raptures. (293, n.2)

There are several aspects to this 'scene'. It is certainly an eye-witness account, and needs to be dealt with as such. On the other hand, it leads to questions about the status of the 'eye-witness', a key factor in much of the discussion of cannibalism, whether by those who are affirming or denying the existence of the practice. The term 'eye-witness' belongs to a very particular discourse, partly scientific, partly legal, and carries with it the suggestion of somebody whose evidence can be accepted because they saw what happened without them being involved in what happened. This is both the protocol of scientific experimentation and the assumption of legal witness. If Cook's journal was all we had, then his officers would have remained eye-witnesses in this sense. Everything happened in their presence (which implies lack of participation), with the flesh 'broiled and eat by one of the Natives'. Only when Clerke's entry is read alongside this does the ambiguity of Cook's phrasing become apparent: its implied meaning is that one of the Natives had broiled and eaten the flesh; but it could also be read as 'had been broiled' – with no agency indicated, followed by 'eaten by the Native'. 'Had been broiled by one of my own officers' – though more accurate – would have certainly complicated the story.

When first told of what had happened, Cook reacted just like Robinson Crusoe and other predecessors when confronted with the signs of cannibalism: 'The sight of the head and the relation of the circumstances just mentioned struck me with horor and filled my mind with indignation against these Canibals', but Cook quickly lived up to his reputation as an experimenter by insisting on replication:

> but when I considered that any resentment I could shew would avail but little and being desireous of being an eye wittness to a fact which many people had their doubts about, I concealed my indignation and ordered a piece of the flesh to be broiled and brought on the quarter deck where one of these Canibals eat it with a seeming good relish before the whole ships Company. (293)

Note the upper case 'C' as the 'Natives' become 'Canibals': eating human flesh always erases any other possible ethnic or national identification. James Boswell's response to Cook's story – related over dinner at the Mitre in April 1776 – indicates the unproblematic way in which it was taken as revealing a truth: 'He gave me a distinct account of a New Zealander eating human flesh in his presence and in that of many more aboard, so that the fact of cannibals is now certainly known' (Boswell 1963: 341).[16]

Most striking, however, about the whole scene is the extent to which it involves a fully interactive relationship between English sailors and the Maori: we are very far from Columbus's captain stumbling on bones in a Guadeloupian hut, or Crusoe finding the remains of a cannibal picnic on the beach, or Tarzan's observation of a cooking pot and human skulls. The Western 'observer' has traditionally come afterwards. Clerke and Cook were both actively involved, commissioners of the act they so deplore. It is their evident fascination with cannibalism that allows Obeyesekere to conclude that

> What is called cannibalism at this period is a British discourse about the practice of cannibalism, rather than a description about its practice. This discourse is initiated by British ethnological inquiry and stimulated in turn by the demands of their reading public. The discourse on cannibalism tells us more about the British preoccupation with cannibalism than about Maori cannibalism. (1992b: 641)

Perhaps the most important issue raised by Obeyesekere's discussion is what the Maori thought they were doing. To even raise the issue of agency in the context of discussions of cannibal scenes is to run counter to the observational ethos which still dominates much anthropological work, and which clearly governs Cook's thinking and writing. He conducted an experiment in which a Native proved himself a Canibal by eating human flesh: the Native ate human flesh because that is what Canibals do. Since his very identification depends upon that trait, the question of motivation doesn't arise, or at least no motivation which is local to the event described, no motivation which would place the Maori in a social situation, as participating in a dialogue with his British 'observers'.

Obeyesekere's argument is too detailed and complex to be spelled out here but, in outline, he suggests that the British discourse on cannibalism produced the Maori practice of cannibalism; that the British fascination with and horror of cannibalism was perceived by the Maori, who responded by admitting to and exaggerating their own cannibalism, sometimes in play as part of a dialogue with the Europeans, sometimes for real as a weapon of terror, one of the few weapons they possessed in an unequal contest. If Maoris ate white sailors – for which Obeyesekere is prepared to admit 'reasonable evidence' (651) – then that was a new practice, a response to European presence. The crucial point is that cannibalism defies simple formulation as an ethnographic category. Obeyesekere's essay builds on the perception that cannibalism needs to be understood not just as part of the discourse of alterity, confirming the already established picture of the ferocious savage, but also – and arguably more importantly – as belonging to a discursive exchange between native populations and European interlocutors.

As to why the British were so obsessed with cannibalism, Obeyesekere's brief answer to the question looks to the

> terms of a larger pervasive fantasy of cannibalism resulting from European socialization of that period and, more narrowly, from a subculture of sailors with a tradition of the practice of cannibalism that in turn gets locked into the primordial fantasy and then, cumulatively, produces shipboard narratives and ballad literature on the subject. (641)

It might be noted here that from the very first, European colonisers were denied food by Native Americans (their most effective weapon), and therefore resorted not infrequently to eating each other (Sued Badillo 1984), and that there was – not surprisingly – a long Western tradition of shipboard and other survival cannibalism (Simpson 1986; Savigny and Correard 1986). Cannibalism was intimately connected with imperial and colonial ventures – as part of the experience and mythology of Europeans. One of the earliest Virginian scandals involved an Englishman eating his wife, and several plays of the period feature a good deal of 'cannibal talk' – all involving Europeans eating each other.[17]

Although the cannibal butchers' shops of European fantasy suggest an almost charming bourgeoisification of the eating of human flesh, cannibals are usually allowed a slightly paradoxical sense of occasion, marked by the 'cannibal feast'. This allows an inkling of the sacred to accompany the consumption, read either as a pleasantly sedate ritual cannibalism (by anthropologists), or as an orgy of limb-tearing violence, possibly accompanied by excesses of other sorts, from infanticide to sodomy. This Thyestean feast – attributed to Christians by Romans, to Jews by Christians, and to savages by Europeans – is a powerful element within cannibal imagery, and seems to have had a particularly strong hold during the nineteenth century, perhaps as antonym to the exaggerated table manners of the European haute bourgeoisie. Jules Verne offers a good South Seas example:

> The sacrifice completed, the whole mass of natives, chiefs, warriors, old men, women, and children, without distinction of age or sex, and all seized with a bestial fury, threw themselves upon the lifeless remains of the victims. In less time than it takes to tell, the smoking bodies were torn to pieces, divided, dismembered, cut not only into morsels, but into crumbs. Of the two hundred Maoris present at the sacrifice, each had a share of the human flesh; they disputed and fought over the least scrap, and drops of hot blood bespattered these horrible creatures: it was the delirium and the rage of tigers, infuriated over their prey. (Verne 1964: 131–2)[18]

Obeyesekere's chapter in this volume says more both about shipboard cannibalism as a firmly rooted tradition of the sea and about the 'primordial fantasy' of Europeans, although he now focuses on Fiji, the nineteenth-century cannibal islands, par excellence, at least – as Obeyesekere points out – after the Treaty of Waitangi (1841) had 'settled' the Maori question. As with the cases of Chanca and Cook glanced at above, Obeyesekere's approach to what he calls the 'impeachment' of some of the texts fundamental to the construction of Fijian cannibalism is based upon a hermeneutic of suspicious reading which, in this case, depends upon the recognition of genre. In a word, Obeyesekere questions what have been read as the authoritative texts of genuine travellers (by, for example, Fergus Clunie 1977). This takes Obeyesekere into the difficult area of travel-writing which is still struggled over by literary critics, historians, and anthropologists (see, for examples relevant to this area, Rennie 1996 and Edmond 1997). He looks closely at the narrative of John Jackson, known as Cannibal Jack (Jackson 1967), an example used by Sahlins (1979) in his response to Arens, and at William Endicott's 'A Cannibal Feast in the Fiji Islands by an Eye-Witness', originally published in 1845, which contains graphic and detailed accounts of such a feast, although Obeyesekere demonstrates that Endicott couldn't – on his own evidence – have attended this particular occasion. Since there is no mention of cannibalism in Endicott's journal (the basis for his book), Obeyesekere suggests that Endicott fabricated his account thirteen years later to meet the growing European demand for stories of savage cannibalism – somewhat in the later manner of Henry Stanley (see Rigby 1992; cf. Youngs 1994: 151–81). Here Obeyesekere works to distinguish between the conventions of shipboard journalism and those of the seaman's yarn, both active within the same text.

Obeyesekere compares John Jackson's narrative with the seemingly autobiographical *Cannibal Jack*, written when Jackson (also known as William Diapea) was seventy. The significant differences between the two accounts of the 'same' event remove any possibility of ethnographic verity, and Obeyesekere ends up by seeing *Cannibal Jack* as an adventure story in the manner of Defoe, marked by Jackson's relatively sophisticated manipulation of romance tropes, but with 'the aura of verisimilitude' (below, p. 80).

5

Cannibalism and the Colonial World properly begins with questions historical and ethnographic, of the kind this Introduction has so far focused on, and those questions have a ghostly afterlife in all the subsequent chapters. However, there are two further shifts to be noted. The first of these retains the geographical area that was the focus of the first wave of modern cannibal descriptions – the extended Caribbean, from the islands south of Cuba down the Atlantic littoral of South America through to the area around Rio de Janeiro; but moves into the twentieth century to look at literary and cultural appropriations of the cannibal scene.

From the south of this region stems one of the most original cultural movements of the century, Brazilian *modernismo*, which had as its centrepiece the positive re-evaluation of the cannibal idea as a cultural norm (*antropofagia*). *Modernismo* has analogies with the better-known négritude movement, but is distinguished by its own complexities, not least in its relationship to notions of indigeneity, which remain a problematic aspect of attempts to construct a Brazilian national culture. *Antropofagia* has been a cultural constant in twentieth-century Brazil, but has recently attracted wider interest as possibly adding a dimension to postcolonial cultural strategies, a witty and self-reflective response increasingly seen as a model for imitation; although within Brazil the current success of *modernismo* is often criticised as having to do 'with its integration into the discourse of conservative modernization' (Schwarz 1992: 109). The chapters by Sérgio Luiz Prado Bellei and Luís Madureira introduce *antropofagia* to a wider readership, analyse its development, and add some cautionary notes.

Traditionally dating from Modern Art Week in the city of São

Paolo in February 1922, Brazilian *modernismo* shares the annus mirabilis of its European counterpart, but operated to a different agenda, at least according to the influential cultural historian of Brazil, Robert Morse: 'In São Paolo the purpose of the week was not to mystify a parochial bourgeoisie with Europe's latest divertissements but to use these as explosives to demystify the foundations of a class-based system of literary production and to achieve artistic expression of national scope' (Morse 1995: 17; and cf. Johnson 1987 for a good introduction in English).

Two of the most significant documents of the movement were the Brazilwood Manifesto (1924) and the Anthropophagic Manifesto (1928), produced by the leading *antropofagista,* Oswald de Andrade (1890–1954), documents sometimes seen as merely imitative of European models, a view Robert Morse again contests, following here the influential arguments of the de Campos brothers and Benedito Nunes:

> In 1920 Francis Picabia had even published a 'Manifeste Cannibale Dada' in Paris and co-founded the review *Cannibale* with Tristan Tzara. But Oswald's Anthropophagy was far from imitative. For Brazilians cannibals were a historical reality, not a divertissement. That is, once one accepts the Tupi as the original Brazilian, his cannibalism is no longer savage, exotic, or an anthropological curiosity. It now becomes the Indian ritual ingesting of the strength and power of enemies and eventually of European invaders ... They could now repudiate the clumsy binomial between mimicry of Europe and a 'native' culture cut from whole cloth. Cannibalism recognized both the nutritive property of European culture and a transformative process of appropriation. (Morse 1995: 18–19; and cf. Andrade 1991b for an English translation of the second manifesto)

Primitivism was very much a dimension of European modernism, but the supposed primitive was very definitely elsewhere – the Congo, the Pacific, Mexico. For Oswald de Andrade, however, the figure of the cannibal was part of a possible national past, an authentically Brazilian figure which offered the possibility of a defined national tradition, an anti-colonial critique, and a communitarian ideal. As Roberto Schwarz puts it:

> pre-bourgeois Brazil, almost innocent of puritanism and economic wiles, assimilates the advantages of progress in a judicious and poetic manner and so prefigures post-bourgeois humanity, unrepressed and fraternal; aside from this, it provides a positive platform from which to attack contemporary society. (1992: 111; cf. below, p. 105)

The usual paradoxes apply, as Bellei's and Madureira's papers demonstrate. Oswald's literary forms – simple elements, unorthodox combinations, provocative manifestos – derive from the European avant-garde; the innocent cannibal comes from Montaigne. Even at the level of influence, however, these paradoxes can mislead: after all, Montaigne and his chief source, Léry, took their ideas in part from Brazilian Tupi sources, and the example of cannibalism had helped illuminate some fine points of Christian doctrine in the early sixteenth century: imitation and borrowing are hardly one-way affairs. But in any case the cannibal metaphor renders irrelevant such niceties. What through the colonial optic might appear as mimicry or derivation comes to be celebrated as the triumph of the cannibal's digestive juices, making its materials new: a regenerative cannibalism. What is new to us is that this tributary aesthetic has moved into the mainstream, this offbeat notion of cultural process has now become the norm, belatedly succeeding what seem like irredeemably antiquated notions of cultural 'purity' and 'influence'. As the contemporary Brazilian critic, Haroldo de Campos, has written: 'In Latin America as well as in Europe, writing will increasingly mean rewriting, digesting, masticating' (quoted below, p. 100).

Oswald de Andrade's two best-known anthropophagous catchphrases are deeply revealing of the cultural complexities of the movement, and give some indication of the reasons for contemporary attention. 'Tupi or not Tupi, that is the question' – supposedly spoken at a famous banquet during Modern Art Week, poses the conundrum of Brazilian nationalism in English, in a parodic version of a famous quotation from an English writer, invoking one of the major indigenous groups to occupy the part of the American continent that eventually became the Portuguese colony of Brazil. The humour disarms almost any critical analysis that might be offered. Equally knowing, this time in its use of Freud, Andrade's reference to 'transforming the taboo into a totem' implies, according to Bellei's reading, 'legitimating anthropophagy by transforming the taboo of the primeval father's parricide (the father being in this case the European coloniser) into the acceptable eating (by the colonised) of the totemised animal that symbolically replaced the primeval father' (below, p. 93).

Bellei is, on the whole, rather sceptical of the claims made for *antropofagia*, seeing its contemporary revaluation as conducted at the expense of the broader historical context of a Brazilian cultural ethos, which his chapter is concerned to identity and analyse as the dream of the abolished frontier. Against the de Campos's and Nunes's emphasis on the radical and revolutionary aspects of the movement, Bellei counterposes the arguments of Antonio Candido and Roberto Schwarz. Crucial to Bellei's argument is the point that the contemporary revindication of the anthropophagic project involves a reduction to the aesthetic of what – seen in the light of Andrade's life-long project – was a fully social and political programme. The language of postmodernism, so apparent in Haroldo de Campos's 'an open multilinguistic hybridisation, a carnivalised transencyclopedia' (quoted below, p. 102), where the distinction between who eats and who gets eaten simply doesn't apply, involves an occlusion that, as Bellei points out, is bound to appear anomalous in the context of this volume's concerns.

Madureira looks particularly closely at one of the central texts of *modernismo*, the extraordinary novel *Macunaíma*, written by Mário de Andrade in 1928, and at its relationship – or not – with *antropofagia*. The hero's final transformation into a constellation in the sky and the book's version of the formulaic ending of Tupi oral narratives are both subject to close, deconstructive analysis, which involves an extended comparison with Nietzsche. But Madureira's main focus is actually on the brief period at the end of the 1960s and beginning of the 1970s which saw both the decisively anthropophagic film version of *Macunaíma* directed by Joaquim Pedro de Andrade (none of the three Andrades are related) and the popular success *How Tasty Was My Little Frenchman*, a film which recasts some of the classic texts of Brazilian beginnings, notably Hans Staden's cannibal classic, *The True History of His Captivity*, 1557. Against this refreshing cannibalisation of the colonial archive, Madureira sets some telling remarks about the absent presence of the indigenous population, their 'cultural death' being finally remarked in the appearance of 'spectral Anthropophagi upon a silver screen' (below, p. 125).

The development of imperial histories has ensured that the only connections between Brazil and Guyana are indigenous in nature. Nevertheless, the Guyanese 'cannibal countermemory' with which Graham Huggan's chapter deals, belongs alongside its Brazilian counterpart, though speaking in different tones. Although Oswald's *antropofagia* is invoked with humour and beneficence, the figure of the cannibal is ultimately inseparable from the threat of violence, in however attenuated and metaphorical a form. Huggan's phrase 'uncanny cannibals' – in reference to the works of Edgar Mittelholzer and Wilson Harris – restores the sense of that figure's unease, only intermittently present in the Brazilian case. Here, the cannibal features (along with the ghost) as a textual mediator through which these Caribbean writers can reimagine their European literary ancestry and set up what Huggan (following Foucault) calls a countermemory to the hegemonic European record of Caribbean history. Unease, even trauma, is inseparable from process and conversion: in Huggan's examples there is a re-membering, a putting together of what was torn asunder: countermemory enacts a process 'whereby a history of exploitation is estranged even as it is confronted, and a pattern is established for the transformation of individual trauma into the inspiring recollective force that bonds a whole community' (below, pp. 129–30).

The racial dimension of the discourse of cannibalism was never far from the surface during the colonial period: the tendency was to associate cannibalistic practice with darkness of skin, so the Caribs and Melanesians were more likely to be accused than the Arawaks or Polynesians – although, in a familiar colonial trope, suspicion of cannibal practice could land native groups in those supposedly descriptive categories and miraculously darken their skin. Mittelholzer's *My Bones and My Flute* has a strong racial dimension, superficially similar to the pathology underlying one of the most powerful cannibal stories, Edgar Allan Poe's *The Narrative of Arthur Gordon Pym*. Huggan shows, however, how the racial fantasies of Guyanese plantation owners in Mittelholzer's work are situated with respect to the region's complex cultural history and made finally to recognise the subaltern past they had once disclaimed.

The bones and flute are both European, belonging as they do to the murdered Dutch planter whose parchment diary dictates the novel's action. Huggan's original reassessment illuminates Mittelholzer's work through the intertextual effect of the Carib bone flute that Wilson Harris invoked so powerfully in his note on the genesis of *Palace of the Peacock*:

> The Carib flute was hollowed from the bone of an enemy in time of war. Flesh was plucked and consumed and in the process secrets were digested. Spectres arose from, or reposed in, the flute ... In parallel with an obvious violation ran therefore, it seems to me, another subtle force resembling yet differing from terror in that the flute became the home or

> curiously mutual fortress of spirit between enemy and other, an organ of self-knowledge suffused with enemy bias so close to native greed for victory. (Harris 1985: 9–10)

Palace of the Peacock is quest narrative as well as ghost story, alchemical romance as well as cannibal fiction, national allegory as well as symbolist prose poem, a rich tapestry of influences that Huggan's analysis does much to illuminate. An ancient Arawak woman features prominently as a reminder of the country's Amerindian past (and present) but, as in *Heart of Darkness*, another of the novel's intertexts, the cannibal violence belongs to the Europeans, especially to the expedition leader, Donne, whose relentless greed and cruelty amount to 'an incalculable devouring principle' (quoted below, p. 137), against which the cannibal/ghost alliance establishes a beneficent alchemical transformation.

In terms of the development of *Cannibalism and the Colonial World*, John Kraniauskas's chapter is a hinge. On the one hand it provides the fourth paper with an American focus – this time Mexico (with cross-references to the Andes), after Brazil and Guyana. On the other hand, it moves us into the themes of contemporary culture and global capitalism which are the focus of two of the final chapters.

Kraniauskas's essay introduces vampires into the cannibal scene, a connection that will also be important in the later papers by Jerry Phillips and Crystal Bartolovich, all three drawing on Marx's extensive use of vampire imagery. There is another progression of a kind articulated here: from the ferocious man-eating of mythic borderlands and colonial fantasy to the more refined and civilised sipping of the blood. Is vampirism a simultaneously aristocratic, modern, and popular European form of cannibalism, asks Kraniauskas, recoded through the displacements of the 'civilising process'? And can the symbolic cannibalism of the Catholic liturgy provide a connection between cannibalism and vampirism? Guillermo del Toro's intriguing vampire film, *Cronos*, the subject of Kraniauskas's paper, certainly suggests affirmative answers to these questions, with its pivotal cannibal scene where the protagonist (named Jesús) licks blood from the floor of a bathroom.

Bram Stoker's *Dracula*, like its near-contemporary *Heart of Darkness*, has been the object of much recent re-reading, some of which Kraniauskas triangulates with Marx's *Capital* and James Ellroy's *American Tabloid* in order to provide an initial context for *Cronos*, one which stresses sexual threat, the piercing of the body, and the circulation of capital. *Cronos* is, however, a film made and set in Mexico; and Kraniauskas gives himself the more difficult challenge of producing a set of intertexts that will illuminate the Latin American dimension of the film.

These intertexts include Nathan Wachtel's study of the modern vampire stories of the Andes, in which members of peasant communities are accosted and put into a deep sleep while their blood or body fat is extracted, stories that Wachtel reads as a narrative response to the often sudden intrusion of modernity into the region, threatening the roots of established identities and causing a traumatic process of social and cultural restructuring; and later stories from the Peruvian coast in which blood, fat, or often – in this case – eyes are removed by white doctors to be sold abroad, a fantasy which emerged in the place of violent protests or strikes in the midst of a massive national crisis. Interestingly – given the proto-cyborg device that features in *Cronos* – both sets of stories involve a machine ('a transparent box ... two wires stuck on to the head by the nose and ears, and a button which, when pressed, popped the eyes out into a round receptable' (below, p. 152)). There are connections here to older African stories of European cannibalism; and it is hardly surprising that the 'endangered' indigenous communities whose blood samples have been targeted for collection have seen the Human Genome Diversity Project as the 'vampire project' (Cunningham and Scharper 1996).

6

Despite its ethnographic and historical concerns, *Cannibalism and the Colonial World* finds the most insistent and difficult question relates to our own (the 'Western') continuing fascination with cannibalism. The last four papers all bravely address this issue, although in very different ways. Marina Warner's essay could have been placed as the first chapter since it addresses cannibal origins in myth and psyche, and their continued existence in children's stories, lengthening our historical record and decoding the genealogy of our appetites. According to Warner, 'the motif of cannibalism, in its earliest mythological expression, enfolds a threat to children, above all, and appears to dramatise the struggle for survival of the family – mother, father, and infant' (below, p. 168). The naked cannibal with his cooking pot gives way, in Warner's representative scenes, to an ogre of monstruous appetite deceived by the young boy he aims to eat, behind which – as ultimate progenitor of many contemporary narratives – stands the figure of Cronus in the founding Hesiodic myth, told that one of his children will supplant him, devouring them one by one, but fooled by Zeus's mother into swallowing a stone instead of Zeus.

Cannibalism was an active cultural sign of tyranny, brutality, and excess, in the mainstream tradition of the early travellers. Cannibalism remains a sign of evil to be defeated and undone; much of the ancient and medieval imagery of devouring is recycled to portray new world cannibals when they begin to appear; and the genres cross, with fascinating results, in a story (and film) like *King Kong*, briefly discussed by Warner. But there are new concerns too. For example, behind the ogre stands Satan, all orifice; and Warner reminds us of the extensive Christian imagery which uses ingestion, digestion, and regurgitation as a potent way of conveying eternal suffering – in counterpoint to the whole body of the resurrected faithful.[19]

The topoi of mythology and fairytale also extend the hinterland of cannibal metaphor since the imprisoning and devouring ogre may, seen or read from the perspective of young women, represent confinement, conception, and pregnancy, experiences also fraught, as Warner says, with widespread fears of extinction. Cannibalism here operates as family romance, its stories engaging with the fundamental enigmas of kinship: what is the relation between identity and origin?; how can doubleness of origin (from mother and father) be expressed?; how does biological origin convert into social relation? The relationship between the generations is, to put it mildly, important to the Freudian narrative and Warner reminds us of Freud's own confusion of the myths of Ouranos and Cronus, and his analysis of that confusion in *The Psychopathology of Everyday Life*, where both confusion and analysis of confusion tend to point in the same direction – towards the vulnerability of the father.

The ogre is, then, however threatening, largely a figure of fun and, perhaps therefore ultimately less productive of anxiety than the cannibal: Robinson Crusoe shoots his cannibals dead with bullets; Odysseus is confident enough to fool the ogre Polyphemus with word-play before poking his eye out. Fairy tales are comic, giving cunning and high spirits a heroic role, as opposed to the more straightforward aggression characteristic of adventure stories. Somewhere in many of these ogre stories, Warner suggests, is the confidence of the young, with time on their side: 'allegories of time and resignation' as she calls them (below, p. 181). These themes of genealogy and gender ensure a revisionary tradition, perfectly embodied in the work of Angela Carter.

The chapters by Jerry Phillips and Crystal Bartolovich both return our attention to 1492, seen not as the year of American discovery, but rather as a key moment within the development of capitalist modernity. Phillips's essay moves with assurance through the discourse of cannibalism, analysing the metaphorical deployment of the term as a motif, metaphor, and ideologeme, concerned with the way in which the language of cannibalism 'imprisons the Jew or the colonised native in an exotic mythology of the dangers proffered to the "universal" subject – dismemberment, ingestion, castration, the measures of bestial appetite' (below, p. 184). *Heart of Darkness*, *The Jew of Malta*, and *The Merchant of Venice* provide Phillips's sites of analysis, but his paper begins with some striking examples of cannibal imagery deployed by Marx in his analysis of the depredations of capitalism, 'that hideous pagan idol, who would not drink the nectar but from the skulls of the slain' (quoted below, p. 184). Although the chapters here have moved in disciplinary terms from ethnography to cultural critique, Marx's language serves to press home the point implicit in Arens's and Obeyesekere's chapters: that the imagery of cannibalism stems in part from a denial of the very violence underlying colonising (and other similar) relationships, a violence which is then projected onto its victim. The logic, which Marx certainly comes close to following, is that primitive accumulation would frequently 'cannibalise' its labour forces, entering modernity, in Marx's stunning image, 'dripping from head to toe, from every pore, with blood and dirt' (quoted below, p. 186), while capitalism in its 'classic' form would function vampirically, living off the blood (labour) of its victims, who would be reduced to zombies, but not bodily ingested (a point made in Bartolovich's chapter (below, p. 224)). Primitive accumulation is usually associated with primary capital formation, but Phillips thinks 'it should be regarded as the permanent destination of capitalism, in its aggressive imperialist mode' (below, p. 187). Bartolovich will draw on yet further examples of Marx's cannibal imagery to discuss Marx's swerve away from the metaphorical equivalence of capitalism and cannibalism (below, p. 224): cannibalism, she suggests, represents the necessary but impossible desire of capitalism. The

Marxian imagery offers no anthropological analysis. Indeed, as Bartolovich notes, Marx manages to combine in spectacular fashion anthropological ignorance with numerical specificity in claiming the existence of 4,000,000 cannibals in the world in 1857. It might, however, be noted that the commonest explanation for cannibalism – vengeance – could associate cannibals with the aristocratic code of honour that passed as a social relationship under feudalism, facilitating the analogy between conspicuous consumption and savage cannibalism.

In Africa in the nineteenth century, in keeping with Marx's metaphors if not with his anthropology, the fear of cannibalism ran both ways, with Africans often convinced that whites were buying them in order to eat them. As William Piersen concludes: 'As a mythopoeic analogy it does not seem farfetched to portray chattel slavery as a kind of economic cannibalism; and in that sense, a mythic sense, stories of white man-eaters were true enough'.[20]

Against this background, Phillips offers his reading of *Heart of Darkness* as a moral fable in which capitalist expansionism is seen as little more than a cruel farce with, as Conrad writes, 'no more moral purpose at the back of it than there is in burglars breaking into a safe' (below, p. 189). Kurtz is the embodiment of this farce, beginning as a proponent of the 'civilising mission', ending as an advocate of genocide. As Phillips puts it, in his analysis of the psychopathology of the capitalist imaginary: 'The sheer insanity of capitalist desire is pointedly expressed in the totalitarian fantasy that marks Kurtz's discourse' (below, p. 189). There is, then, a kind of poetic logic in the setting of *Heart of Darkness*, a darkness which contains the African cannibals about whom Marlow shows such insouciance, but where Kurtz is the 'real' cannibal – metaphorically real because of his insatiable appetite for ivory and power but also possibly, depending on one's reading of the 'abominable rites', really real. At the heart of Phillips' argument is the idea that the cannibal feast to which Kurtz regressed is figured within the moral theatre of the colonial capitalist world as a truly infantile pleasure – to which Marlow feels drawn but which he knows he must resist: any longing for the pre-industrial world becomes an ethical impossibility as carnival makes that small lexical shift to cannibal (below, p. 276 n. 11).

Like Phillips, Bartolovich is concerned with the relationship between the cannibalism motif and capitalist modernity. Like Phillips, her reference points are the present day, the writings of Marx, and the 'moment' that Marx referred to as 'primitive accumulation'. But where Phillips looks to literary texts as sites of analysis, Bartolovich focuses on Hakluyt's collections of travels and voyages as the appropriate archive to illuminate the rampant (metaphorical) cannibalism of corporate capitalism as witnessed in the language of the business journalism she analyses early in her paper and whose presence she is attempting to explain via a forced encounter of the Benjaminian kind.

The nub of Bartolovich's connection is the notion of appetite: her argument is that the cannibals summoned by the early modern European imaginary provided both an example of and a limit text for European proto-capitalist 'appetite', which was tending in its mercantile and colonial forms toward the limitlessness which the logic of capital requires (below, p. 215): 'The cannibal appetite is the self-consolidating other of capitalist appetite as well as European civility' (below, p. 214). In class terms this serves to link absolute consumption (cannibalism) with the aristocracy: capitalism needed the accumulation that came about from 'restraint' and investment. This 'restraint', however, is not a moral quality of the individual capitalist (the view of bourgeois historians Marx is attempting to refute), but rather a limit imposed by capitalism itself, since the capitalist must engage in constant competitive accumulation and investment if he is to survive. As much as the capitalist may long for absolute consumption, he cannot satisfy this desire. At the same time, cannibal appetites abroad also needed retraining to desire the goods that were on show, while the many-headed monster back home produced a parallel threat as the proto-proletariat – primary producers already separated from the means of production (peasants driven from the land) – were starved sufficiently to be, in Hakluyt's own words, 'redie to eate upp one another' (quoted below, p. 223).

A key concept for Bartolovich is what she calls the supplementary logic of capitalism, explained via the contrast between the zero sum culture of the feudal mode – marked by the military contest for territory – and the accretive view of worlds yet to be discovered. In Montaigne's words: 'I wot not whether I can warrant my selfe, that some other [world] be not discovered hereafter, sithence so many worthy men . . . have so many ages beene deceived in this' (below, p. 227). This leads her to the cultural connotations of accumulation, for which Hakluyt's collections provide a fine example. In Hakluyt there is a rhetorical fortification of the English position, but at the same time an exhortation to follow the Spanish and Portuguese examples since, in John Locke's influential words, 'enough, and as good' has been left by them in the 'vacant places of America' (Locke 1965: 329, 335). Where that supplementary logic reaches its limits, the figure of the cannibal reappears as the threat: the preoccupation with cannibalism read as one of the morbid symptoms of capitalism in crisis, an insight Bartolovich brings back to the language of contemporary business journalism and to the striking tableau that concludes Peter Greenaway's film, *The Cook, the Thief, his Wife and her Lover* (1989), where the thief is presented with the lovingly roasted remains of his wife's lover, and ordered to eat them. After tasting a morsel, the thief is shot by his wife, who then speaks the film's final word, 'Cannibal', while looking directly at the camera. The implication of the reader / critic suggested by that word spoken in that way leads directly into Maggie Kilgour's invocation of Arnold and the function of the critic as cannibal in the volume's final chapter. Something of the fluidity of cannibalism as a trope – and something of the playfulness with which it must, at times, be treated – can be gauged from its substitutive qualities in these last two essays: replacing capitalism in Bartolovich's 'The Logic of Late Cannibalism', and now criticism in Kilgour's 'The Function of Cannibalism at the Present Time'. Fredric Jameson would probably be no more amused than Matthew Arnold.

Interestingly, the cannibal scene from Thomas Harris's *The Silence of the Lambs* which provides Kilgour with her central image is the dialogue between the cannibal Lecter and the detective Starling, a version of the psychoanalytic scene, and of the conversation between critic and work. Starling and Lecter are both detective and detected, both analyst and patient, in doublings not unfamiliar to the thriller genre. But, as Kilgour points out, at the beginning of Starling's story is no guilty secret. Instead, in a family romance for the 1990s, Starling's childhood traumas culminate in her coming to know the workings of the slaughterhouse – hence the novel's title. Cannibalism is 'certain and direct' in *The Silence of the Lambs*, while sexual difference is always hard to determine.[21]

Kilgour helps the book end on a self-reflexive note. If, as the chapters in this book suggest, the function of cannibalism lies in its utility as a form of cultural criticism, Kilgour wants – in a move which echoes Arens' original impulse in *The Man-Eating Myth* – also to suggest 'how the figure of the cannibal reveals some of the contradictions with our own reimagining of this function of criticism'. Again, as the movement of interests within the book suggests, 'where in the past the figure of the cannibal has been used to construct differences that uphold racism, it now appears in projects to deconstruct them' (below, p. 242). As these words indicate, Kilgour is especially concerned with the role of the cannibal in matters of boundary formation and exclusion, where cannibalism can function as a 'dark double' for what Kilgour sees as our critical predicament: simultaneous desires for autonomy and identification, for subversion of boundaries and their reinforcement: our recourse to the cannibal read as a materialist refusal to see a distinction between sublimation and repression. In other words, Kilgour ends by raising the kinds of critical questions about boundaries and difference which, since Montaigne, Western thought has grappled with through the topic of cannibalism.

2

Rethinking anthropophagy

William Arens

Mais, je ne suis pas un cannibale
(Emperor Bokassa I, *Echoes From a Somber Empire*)

In *Religion and the Decline of Magic* (1971: 338), Keith Thomas informs us that astrologers of an earlier age were often wrong in their predictions but rarely embarrassed by this outcome. He provides the instructive case of Jerome Cardan, a mid-sixteenth century Italian practitioner of the art, who upon arrival in England publicly announced that the boy-king Edward VI would live to be fifty-five if not older. Shortly thereafter, at the age of fifteen, the royal lad died. Undeterred by this temporary set-back to his career, which he concluded was preferable to having predicted the early demise of a ruling monarch, Cardan actually published the erroneous horoscope, together with an apologia entitled, 'What I Have Thought Afterwards on the Subject', thus garnering two publications from one egregious error.

Minus the admission of error, what follows are my own further, somewhat revised thoughts on the subject of cannibalism, since the publication of *The Man-Eating Myth* in 1979. This commentary is offered with posthumous apologies to Sir Edmund Leach (1966) for having adapted the title of his 'Rethinking Anthropology', since in considering my original effort he was of the opinion: 'Montaigne writing about cannibals in the 16th century is still far more convincing then W. Arens writing about the same topic from Stony Brook in 1979' (Leach 1989: 141). Yet, in the same literal breath he also argued that ethnographers are less concerned with the factual truth than with convincing readers of their authority by the way they write.

On this point we are in agreement, for I continue to maintain that the ever-present cannibals on the horizon of the Western world are the result of intellectual conjuring – including the anthropological variety. Thus, I see no reason to revise my original premise concerning the mythological nature of these creatures. This lack of repentance requires some elaboration, including an attempt to reclaim my original argument from its other interpreters.

Without denying the value of deconstruction – for *The Man-Eating Myth* itself was just such an exercise – the argument I initially advanced developed two primary concerns. The first involved a relatively detailed evidential examination of some well-known 'cannibal' cultures, staples of popular literature and introductory anthropology textbooks. The second, and to my mind the more complex and interesting, was an attempt to provide an explanation for the existence of cannibals on the frontiers of our time and space. This threatening idiom extends from the onset of recorded thought to the latest television documentary, my own efforts to the contrary not withstanding. As a result, the newly-minted Microsoft CD-Rom encyclopedia *Encarta* will take us into the twenty-first century with a fairly typical nineteenth-century view of the matter. Thus, 'The Binderwurs of central India ate their sick and aged in the belief that the act was pleasing to their goddess Kali' (Anon. 1994).

The ethnographic sites chosen for the cannibal tour through time were the fifteenth-century Caribbean, sixteenth-century Meso-America, nineteenth-century Africa, and finally, mid twentieth-century New Guinea Highlands. Each in its time served as the latest outpost of Western expansion and its cannibal denizens were identified by the then-prevailing institutional creators of knowledge, beginning with the conquistadors and missionaries to the New World and culminating in the recent researches of medical and social scientists in New Guinea. In response to these choices, some commentators faulted me for consciously, if not nefariously, avoiding the literature on various islands of the South Pacific and the far reaches of Amazonia which allegedly harboured the truly well documented man-eaters who continued their customary anthropophagy to this day (see Sahlins 1979).

Although each era and area was more problematic in its own way than originally anticipated, as demonstrated by the subsequent analyses of others on both sides of the argument, upon reconsideration I see no reason to recant my original conclusion: that the evidence for these test cases was insufficient to justify labelling them as cannibals. The pattern was, and still is, to document – in a literal sense – the existence of cannibalism after the cessation of the presumed activity, rather than to observe and describe it in the present tense. (In direct response to *The Man-Eating Myth,* two exceptions are noted for Papua New Guinea, where the credibility stakes for a number of contemporary disciplines are high. These instances are considered below in some detail.)

Thus, in terms of the particulars, I continue to aver not only that the Caribs, Aztecs, Pacific Islanders, and various African, Native American, and New Guinea 'tribes' have been exoticised, but also – and equally importantly – that Western culture has congratulated itself for putting a stop to this cultural excess through colonial 'pacification' and introducing Christianity to once-benighted natives.[1] Equally relevant, the commentator, typically an explorer, missionary or anthropologist, is self-romanticised by the experience of a sojourn among a once cannibal people.[2] In effect, most others have been consistently traduced by the cultural agents of our civilisation past and present. This conclusion is not meant to imply some peculiar feature of Western thought, since the accusation of cannibalism against others is pandemic. Yet this feature of our thought does point to an unsettling contradiction between avowals of scholarly objectivity and a prefigured outcome, particularly within the discipline of anthropology, which has laid claim to a demythologising project.

From my perspective it is important to note that in recognition of the logical and methodological difficulties involved in proving a negative case, I avoided any hard and fast conclusion in *The Man-Eating Myth.* To wit: 'the question of whether or not people eat each other is taken as interesting but moot' (1979b: 9); and later, 'I have stated my reservations on the matter, but nonetheless have consciously avoided suggesting that customary cannibalism in some form does not or never has existed' (180). This explicit position has often been misconstrued by others in the process of dismissing their versions of my thesis as absurd. Thus Brown and Tuzin wrote: 'In a study seemingly designed to inspire controversy, Arens (1979b) erroneously asserts that cannibalism as an approved, institutionalized form of behavior has never existed' (1983a: 5). Keesing (1981: 164), Palencia-Roth (1993: 22), and Sanday (1986: xii), among others, offer similar misinterpretations.[3]

My resort to logic in making my case involved more than a

judicious attempt to cover the intellectual rear. The intent was to suggest that even if cannibalism had existed or still did exist, the pervasive anthropological conclusion that it was rampant – and the imagery associated with such a conclusion – was based on something less than a rational evidential process. After all, if it exists, cannibalism should be observable, and ethnography – the presumed hallmark of anthropology – involves the description of custom prior to interpretation.[4] The anthropological fixation has been on the latter with boundless displays of interpretive fancy.[5]

Perhaps I should not be so dismissive of my re-interpreters' intellectual exercises for, despite the difference in focus, I am also not sanguine with the results of my own initial interest in why cannibals abound in Western imagination and anthropology texts. The motivation of both anthropologists and anthropophagists turns out to be equally elusive. I do not disown my initial attempts at explanation, which drew attention to the anthropological repetition of slurs by one ethnic group against the other, or to indigenous myths and legends having been conveyed as facts by a discipline dependent on the exotic other – which has to be created, at least in part, by anthropology itself. To my mind, this accusation of cultural construction is the most sensitive and damaging feature of the overall argument. However, this thrust at the heart and mind of the discipline was generally ignored by critics in favour of a deep concern with proving that cannibals once existed or still do. Thus, in a Distinguished Lecture to the members of the American Anthropological Association, Mary Douglas (1989: 861) remarked: 'William Arens dared to argue that perhaps cannibalism did not exist ... The slur on ethnography was met by a special panel of the AAA on cannibalism, and an important book firmly vindicated the beliefs under attack (Brown and Tuzin 1983b).' In a similar vein Marvin Harris, in his continuously updated textbook that greets each new generation of introductory anthropology students, refers to the work of the sixteenth-century missionary/ethnographer Bernardo de Sahagún as his primary source for fifteenth-century Aztec cannibalism. Giving further support to the idea that the winners write history, Harris adds: 'Many other passages written by Sahagún and historians of the conquest of Mexico tell the same story' (1995: 234).

Although some anthropologists have come to terms with the discipline's need to exoticise its subjects, the community as a whole still feels the urgent need for a collective representation of imagined cannibals in a manner which deserves greater appreciation than I was able to provide initially. Subsequent subtle commentaries on the literature of Western contact (owing much to the pioneering efforts of Baudet (1988) in 1959) have deepened and broadened my own thoughts on the proclivity to recognise the cannibal. In an influential treatise, Greenblatt elegantly summarises the general nature of the problem, arguing that '... Europeans had, for centuries, rehearsed their encounter with the peoples of the New World, acting out, in their response to the legendary Wild Man, their mingled admiration and revulsion, longing and hatred' (1991: 21). In similar fashion others, such as Bucher (1981), Campbell (1988), Hulme (1986), Mason (1990), and Pagden (1993) have also demonstrated that the cannibal was prefigured by the European experience with the internal other of women, witches, and heretics. However, none has examined the performance of the colonial encounter in such damaging detail as Obeyesekere (1992a).

In response to Sahlins' influential, and in many ways admirable, essay on the Hawaiian deification of Captain Cook, also a well-known victim of presumed cannibalism, Obeyesekere counters that rather than historical fact we are confronted with another aspect of Western myth-making characteristic of the colonial encounter. He argues that in the instance of 'the European as god to the natives' (a recurring theme of Sahlins' thinking), we are dealing with a 'myth model', a paradigmatic trope for conceptualising the contact situation (1992a: 10). In passing, Obeyesekere also notes the British fascination with the possibility of Hawaiian cannibalism, especially after the death of Captain Cook. British fixation on the subject led to the native conclusion that their visitors from afar engaged in such behaviour. As Obeyesekere is, in his own words, both the native and the anthropologist – the former now an equally authoritative voice – Sahlins' *ad hominem* response – *How Natives Think* (1995) – has been instructive. Regardless of the outcome, Obeyesekere's conclusion that much of contemporary ethnography rests on embarrassing empirical grounds (1992a: 66) is sure to heat up the debate over the cultural nature of science, and social science in particular.

Such post-modern suspicions, however, were not current at the time of *The Man-Eating Myth*'s publication, so that the eventual anthropological response was often less subtle. After some preliminary positive comments, penned by non-anthropologists in popular fora, the tone changed dramatically. Leach described the argument as 'absurd', given the solid documentation for cannibalism in all parts of the world and for all historical periods (1979: 467). Reflecting on her research in the New Guinea Highlands, Lindenbaum referred to *The Man-Eating Myth* as 'offensive', and the author as having perpetuated 'a devouring attack on members of his own group' (1982: 60). Writing in *Man*, Rivière characterised *The Man-Eating Myth* as 'dangerous' (1980: 205), while Harris deemed it 'mischievous' (1995: 214) and Sahlins decried it as 'a scandal' (1979: 47).[6]

Some years later, in response to an appreciative article in *Science* (Kolata 1986) revisiting the controversy, a colleague responded with a letter to the editor accusing me (as Sahlins had done earlier (1979) and another (Palencia-Roth 1993: 22) would do later), of being in league with those historical revisionists who denied the Holocaust (Riley 1986: 926). I was taken aback by these rejoinders. I thought what I was denying was the common European rationale, that is to say the cannibal nature of the victims, that allowed for these Holocausts – not their occurrence. In another peculiar response, an anthropologist often referred to the former cannibalism among 'his' people in the New Guinea Highlands and then concluded by accusing me of upholding the stereotype of 'savage society' by having examined the topic of cannibalism in the first place (Weiner 1987: 173). It would be unfair, however, to characterise all my critics as making bizarre points since others were more rational and instructive.

A more typical response has been to agree to my argument about the imaginary ubiquity of cannibals but to deny the particulars in some form or another. Thus, to return to Leach, we learn from his overview of social anthropology that by 1982 he had discovered (there were no citations in the passage) that Europeans were fascinated by the possibility of cannibalism among those they encountered, despite little evidence of the fact. He argues, as an example, that none of the people with whom Columbus actually came into contact were cannibals, and that the illustrations in his texts were 'absurd' – a familiar word, since Leach had also used it previously to characterise my argument. However, he goes on to note more 'authentic' accounts of cannibalism among the coastal people of Brazil, presumably the Tupi (Leach 1982: 62–5). In the same vein, Andrew Strathern (1993), who conducted his research in the Highlands of New Guinea, admits that my argument 'scores some very telling hits', but doubts it holds up for his ethnographic area. Others follow along with the addition of other cultures where my otherwise agreeable argument fails to hold: the Fijians,

Hawaiians, Iroquois, Caribs, Anasazi, West Africans, and so on (see Krabacher 1980; Lindenbaum 1982; White 1992). A related response has been to accept my general premise, dismiss existing explanatory accounts of cannibalism for a particular people as vulgar sensationalism, and then offer a more sophisticated and contemporary cultural interpretation of ritual cannibalism in its stead (see Ortiz De Montellano 1983 and Whitehead 1990).

Taken as a whole, the result is in effect the affirmation by contemporary anthropology of cannibal hordes lurking on the border. Thus, there is very little that distinguishes past from present – if not future – anthropology on the subject, except to note that the argument of *The Man-Eating Myth* is at times simultaneously accepted and dismissed. To my mind the demotion of a particular people from the ranks of gustatory to ritual cannibals has very little effect on the popular imagination perpetually stoked by anthropological discourse, which has also become more sophisticated with time. These responses to the argument do, however, lead to the questions of what is a myth and indeed what exactly is cannibalism?

Regarding the first question, I should offer a rejoinder to the common suggestion that *The Man-Eating Myth* accused my own discipline of perpetuating a conspiratorial fraud or hoax on a gullible public. In terms of the anthropological investment in the subject of mythology, I find it odd that some colleagues would equate mythological thought with fraud. Not wishing to disappear among the massive materials on this most anthropological of subjects, I would mention here only that my working definition of myth was that of a belief unsupported by – and more importantly, irrelevant of – facts. Thus the result of the inquiry is precluded rather than concluded.

This suggestion does not imply that anthropologists have been consciously attempting to delude their consumers. Rather they and their public have been equally deluded by a Western meta-myth. Unfortunately, this conclusion is more damning than the accusation of engaging in a hoax, which at least implies some intellectual acuity beyond that of the masses. Sustaining a myth, on the other hand, suggests that those involved, including scholars, are susceptible to the same mundane prejudices and imagery as those they are engaged to instruct. It appears from this misinterpretation of my argument that intellectuals would prefer to be accused of fraud than of myth-making. This is a peculiar state of affairs.

As to the question of what itself is cannibalism, the matter is equally complicated. It was Needham (1980) who in an early and lengthy review pointed out that I did not define cannibalism in the book. This came as an unsettling revelation to me, but it was not followed up by subsequent commentators, who were more interested in proving that cannibalism was a prevalent feature of the Other. In a sense this definitional lacuna is unimportant, since the book clearly implied a general concern primarily with what anthropologists had defined as gustatory and to a lesser extent ritual cannibalism. The first instance implies the consumption of human flesh as a food for the body, and the second as food for the soul. The best known cases – the Caribs, Aztecs, and Fore, at one time or another since intellectual tastes change – were all recognised as gustatory cannibals and viewed as lacking culture in the sense of being unable to distinguish between acceptable and unacceptable foodstuffs. Into the second category fall those presumed cannibals dominated by ritual rather than more concrete concerns. Thus, my interest was with the customary ingestion of human flesh for either purpose. However, the imagery contended with, including the volume's illustrations, was with the grosser gustatory type, so easy to portray and so ingrained in popular imagination.

Although of little relevance to the public perception of the anthropological message about other cultures, the question of what exactly cannibalism is and what form it takes is a legitimate academic concern. In attempting to resolve the matter, Sahlins set himself the exercise of explicating the cultural sense of cannibalism in traditional Fiji by resorting in part to the papers of early missionaries who recorded the reminiscences of 'reformed cannibals' or 'the direct statements of famous cannibals' (1983: 87–8). He concludes his analysis of this documentary evidence with the statement: 'The problem, of course, is that cannibalism is always "symbolic", even when it is "real"' (88). It is difficult to argue with such a conclusion. Any customary practice, including the consumption of food of any kind, is always both symbolic and real. The real question is not whether the presumed cannibalism is symbolic, but whether the behaviour is in fact the deed.

The Man-Eating Myth briefly considered a reported instance of 'bone-ash cannibalism' among a South American group and concluded the evidence was not persuasive enough to support its occurrence. I now believe it was unreasonable to adopt this position. Subsequent reports suggest that the matter of the ingestion of culturally processed human body parts is open to further consideration. In response to the controversy generated by *The Man-Eating Myth*, Gordon-Grube (1988) reported that pulverised body parts were sold by apothecaries for medicinal purposes in Europe and America until the turn of the twentieth century. In our own time there are reports (Janzen 1980) of placentophagic activity as a feature of the organic food craze among some middle-class urban Americans. Those involved believe that the consumption of the human tissue, either raw or cooked (said to taste like liver or kidney), is a healthy procedure since other animals engage in it, as did some Native American groups in former times. (A Native American spokesperson vehemently denied the accusation.) And, admittedly stretching the argument a bit, since injection rather than ingestion is involved, extracts of human cadavers are used in contemporary medicine (see Blakeslee 1991). In both of these examples, the anthropophagic activity is defined as a feature of rational science and medicine despite the fact that many have either died or contracted serious diseases as the result of the treatment. In contrast, similar behaviours engaged in by representatives of other cultures are interpreted as ritualised attempts to show respect, or alternatively disrespect; in either instance there is an effort to incorporate the qualities of the deceased into the living.

I would suggest that none of the instances mentioned above should be deemed anthropophagy. Alternatively one might argue they are all acts of cannibalism. Whichever alternative is adopted, the activities listed above prompt a consideration of the eventual labelling process. To my knowledge no one has ever suggested that Western societies, or for that matter these particular activities or groups, be understood as cannibalistic. (Individuals from other societies have made this association but this conclusion is deemed exemplary of their cultural ignorance (see Turner 1993).) In contrast, the non-Western groups engaged in similar activities always enter the ethnographic record as cannibals (see, for example, Conklin 1995). This selective labelling process does little more than highlight the manner in which we interpret other cultures.

The same selective proclivity holds for sporadic instances of cannibalism on the part of deviants in this society who are judged to be abnormal and are prosecuted for engaging in the activity. (Alternatively they may be celebrated in fiction.) Similar instances encountered for other parts of the world are held as evidence for cannibalism as a custom (see Lindenbaum 1982: 59–60). Indeed, a judge in Papua New Guinea released two individuals hauled before him for improperly interfering with a human body (that is, eating it) since the deeds of the accused were, in His Honour's opinion, neither 'improper' nor 'indecent' in light of 'the strange funerary customs of Papua New Guinea' (Griffin 1971: 79–80).

This amusing incident provides a convenient segue for reconsidering the celebrated case of kuru and alleged cannibalism among the Fore of Highland Papua New Guinea. As the presumed activity took place in the mid-twentieth century, was contextualised by medical research of the most extraordinary kind, and eventually resulted in the award of a Nobel Prize to the principal figure involved, the case provides the best example of the documentation process for cannibalism we can ever hope to consider. Indeed the material is so vast, and continues to accumulate today almost a half century later, that only the salient point can be considered with any justice to the matter.[7] By focusing on the cannibal theme alone it is possible to make continued sense of the matter at issue here, which is: did the research provide requisite documentation for customary cannibalism among these people, or did it provide instead a further instance of the cultural construction of the cannibal?

In 1957, D. Carleton Gajdusek, best described from his published journals as a somewhat romantic[8] and troubled modern itinerant medicine man, found himself in the Highlands of then Australian Papua New Guinea among the Fore, a people visited at the time by a mysterious epidemic of devastating proportions. Although the gravity of the situation was apparent to the authorities on the ground and in Australia, where Gajdusek had just spent a year on a research fellowship, systematic research on the epidemic was delayed due to some unresolved bureaucratic matters. The now published correspondence (Farquhar and Gajdusek 1981) indicates that the Australian assigned to the case was delaying his departure for New Guinea until the matter of his health and life insurance premiums was resolved. He figures little in the subsequent literature on the subject.

Undeterred by such mundane considerations, which rarely culminate in original insights, and much to the dismay of authorities in New Guinea, Australia, and the United States, Gajdusek immediately plunged into the matter with little concern for financial support, bureaucratic niceties, professional courtesy, or for that matter personal health or safety. Individualist he may have been, but he was not a *tabula rasa*. His society's notion of cannibalism on the frontier was already part of his cultural baggage as he entered the contact zone. Almost immediately upon his arrival, the meta-myth kicked in as Gajdusek wrote in his first letter home: 'I am in one of the most remote, recently opened regions of N.G. (in the Eastern Highlands), in the center of tribal groups of cannibals, only contacted in the last ten years and controlled for five years' (1976: 50). Initial responses from his superiors at the National Institute of Health in Washington, DC were less than supportive. However, with time – and as the various implications of Gajdusek's research dawned even on the bureaucrats – encouragement and advice were more forthcoming. A colleague in Australia wrote Gajdusek: 'Get someone to take a shot of you surrounded by the wildest looking natives you can find' (Farquhar and Gajdusek 1981: 300). Another in Washington suggested that Gajdusek return with his data before some cannibal ate his brain (Gajdusek 1976: 177). Despite Gajdusek's (1979: 28) claim that it is 'naive' to ask, as I had done in a letter to him earlier (Arens 1977), about the origin of the idea of an explicit relationship between cannibalism and kuru, with time, and in a manner possible to trace, the linkage became inevitably established in the scientific literature.

Initially, however, Gajdusek began to explore – both literally and figuratively – a vast unknown territory recounted in detail with the publication of his correspondence, diaries, journals, and hundreds of scientific papers and popular accounts. His treks through the area collecting data on the spread and the effects of kuru are now the stuff of legends and a Nobel Prize. Subsequently, he was joined by others, including social anthropologists who lent credence to the notions of cannibalistic savagery among these 'stone age' people (Gajdusek 1970a). The first, Charles Julius, a government anthropologist, spent a few weeks among the Fore conducting some 'veranda' ethnography with native informants. Shortly thereafter he issued a report casually mentioning the (as usual unobserved) custom of cannibalism among the Fore (Julius 1981) reflecting a notion apparent in all the early contact literature for New Guinea. As one observer casually summed up the matter in the 1930s: 'They were dirty, and one could easily picture them eating human flesh; but their simple, childish ways were singularly appealing' (Hides 1936: 14).[9]

In addition to a host of other experts, the expanded team included Robert Glasse and Shirley Lindenbaum, two professional anthropologists whose collaboration with Gajdusek in the early 1960s and on subsequent publications did much to solidify the notion of cannibalism among the Fore. This simultaneous anthropological legitimisation of medical science and scientific legitimisation of anthropology was crucial to the intellectual process. As a result, introductory anthropology texts can now proudly proclaim that it was the detective work of these two anthropologists which established cannibalism as the means of transmission of the disease (Keesing 1981: 164; Mascie-Taylor 1993: 13; and McElroy and Townsend 1989: 47).

These bald statements attempting to demonstrate the practical and scientific nature of anthropology both exoticise and confuse the issue enormously. According to the Nobel Laureate himself – at least at times, depending upon his audience – the ingestion of human flesh was not the actual means of transmission of kuru, but rather contact with infected bodily tissue (Gajdusek 1977b: 956). But this aside also gets us ahead of the story since Glasse and Lindenbaum's fieldwork, as indicated, did not involve observation of the purported custom, despite some detailed accounts of the human butchering procedure (see Glasse and Lindenbaum 1976). What their published accounts tell of instead is the incursion of the cannibalism metaphor into a new era and intellectual context, as Glasse blandly reported that when Europeans entered the 'cannibalism zone' 'the great majority of the women were cannibals', with the mothers'- brothers'- wives of the deceased as the main 'beneficiaries' (1967: 750–2). His explanation for the behaviour was the initial standard gustatory one, that is, human flesh was, according to the natives, 'savory' (752). (Within a decade the Fore were, as usual, converted into symbolic cannibals by Lindenbaum (1979).) Finally, with typical anthropological *sang froid*, Glasse mentioned what a privilege it had been to have lived among them (1967: 754).

It is now difficult to unravel the sequence of all the events. What is clear is that, sometime after the initial field research, laboratory experiments in the United States provided the key to the problem as chimpanzees inoculated with distillations of kuru-infected brain tissue eventually succumbed to the disease (Gibbs and Gajdusek 1965). The discovery of an infectious agent, as opposed to a previously suspected genetic basis, required some backtracking to determine a means of transmission. Now the lingering 'fact' of cannibalism, familiar to Gajdusek from the first day he set foot in the area and subsequently legitimised by anthropologists, took on new and different significance. But the notion had to be inserted into the intellectual process in a convoluted manner, for at the time the disease could not be demonstrated transmissible via the gastrointestinal tract, which presumably also meant not as the consequence of cannibalism. Reflecting on the research process and the role of anthropology, Gajdusek later wrote: 'In the absence of any evidence for infection, it became very difficult to see how cannibalism might be involved' (1979: 29). Re-enter the anthropologists: Gajdusek adds: 'Their major contribution was to reemphasize the concern about cannibalism, which we had largely abandoned' (30).

The eventual outcome of this confusing state of affairs – today, Fore cannibalism is considered to be the means of disease transmission by the general anthropological and medical public – can be understood only in relation to the power of the idea of cannibalism to direct our thinking about other cultures, and the specific way in which the notion infected the researchers' brains. The result is an interesting example of how individuals, in this instance scholars, can maintain contradictory conclusions, even in print, without apparent notice or concern. A few examples from the enormous amount of literature will have to suffice.

Lindenbaum: 'The case of cannibalism as the means of transmitting kuru rests on circumstantial evidence. The hypothesis is simple, predictive, but it remains unproven' (Glasse and Lindenbaum 1976: 51). 'Western scientists now consider kuru to be a slow virus spread by the ingestion of human flesh' (Lindenbaum 1979: 9). A few pages later: 'Our cannibalism hypothesis seemed to fit the epidemiological evidence' (19). Shortly thereafter, in the same volume: 'Gajdusek therefore has suggested that a likely route of infection from contaminated brain was through the skin' (27). 'Eventually, it was hypothesized that victims contracted the kuru virus by cannibalizing the brains of the dead' (Lindenbaum 1990: 12).[10]

As befitting a 'hard' scientist, Gajdusek has been more circumspect but hardly less confusing than his anthropological colleagues. In the captions to some photos (see below, p. 59) from the Fore area to accompany the publication of his Nobel Lecture, the text reads: 'Men, and already initiated boys, *rarely* participated in the mourning rite around the corpse, and *even more rarely* in the dissection and preparation of the kuru victim's flesh for its ritual endo-cannibalistic consumption' (my emphasis). Just below: 'Infection was most probably through the cuts and abrasions of the skin or through nose picking, eye rubbing, or mucosal injury' (1977b: 956). Some years earlier he remarked at a conference that 'Cannibalism ... is more in the nature of an embellishment to our other etiological hypotheses' (Gajdusek in Alpers 1966: 81–2). Later he continued to maintain this circumspect position: 'Even today, we have no evidence that eating the bodies caused the spread' (Gajdusek 1979: 28).

Subsequently, however, and presumably in response to the argument of *The Man-Eating Myth*, the abstract to an article by the kuru team reads: 'Epidemiological surveillance, anamnesis, and missionary reports strongly suggest that all the patients described in this study were exposed to the kuru agent more than two decades ago through ritualistic cannibalism' (Prusiner, Gajdusek, and Alpers 1982: 1). The following text then specifically addresses the sensitive issue of evidence for this claim: 'Considerable debate has surrounded the postulated role of cannibalism; however, one of us (D.C.G.) was present several times just after bodies were dismembered for cannibalistic consumption [2, 8, 19]' (7). The bibliographic citations at the end of the quotation – '[2, 8, 19]', meant to lend scientific authority to the statement – are to two of the authors themselves, and then to Matthews, Glasse, and Lindenbaum. The articles contain no descriptions of dismemberment as opposed to the usual references to cannibalism among the Fore and its possible relationship to the transmission of kuru (see Alpers 1966; Gajdusek 1979; and Matthews, Glasse, and Lindenbaum 1968). In fact, amazingly enough, the Gajdusek piece self-referred to as evidence of cannibalism contains the previous quotation about the lack of evidence for cannibalism and the spread of kuru! Still later, in another of the seemingly endless series of publications, but now with a particular point in mind, the 'Key Words' to identify the subject matter of the article also make an explicit connection: 'Slow virus disease - Viral transmission - Cannibalism' (Klitzman, Alpers, Gajdusek 1984: 3).

In retrospect, with the 'discovery' of the disease, the literary process involved the mention of cannibalism only as a typical textual aside to characterise native culture. Thus, in the first publications (when a genetic mode of transmission was still considered most likely), Gajdusek and Zigas write that prior to government control 'cannibalism, interclan warfare and ritual killings – remnants of all these still survive – were prominent features of Fore culture' (1957a: 977; see also Gajdusek and Zigas 1957b: 745). With the later emergence of the viral transmission hypothesis, this literary procedure was followed by the confused and misleading relationship between cannibalism and kuru in the body of the texts. With time, and with the authors now aware of the evidential problem, the succeeding stage took the form of a conscious discourse strategy as the word 'cannibalism' was employed in the abstract above the text, and eventually in the key words above the abstract to the text, making the connection between the phenomena more authoritative by concision. However, as I have tried to show with a series of admittedly tedious quotations, the matter is far from concise. A few more references to the kuru literature will test the reader's patience.

First, despite his claim to have observed cannibalistic dismemberments (which is not really the same as claiming to have witnessed cannibalism itself), Gajdusek had already written in his 1957 correspondence, but apparently forgot he had done so, that: 'Cannibalism has ceased, did not involve brain as far as we can find, and even if rare cases still occur, many of our youngest patients have certainly not consumed human tissue' (Gajdusek 1976: 311). To be fair, perhaps Gajdusek sighted cannibals later on, though I assume he would have recorded this in his voluminous journals. He has not done so.

A second problem for Gajdusek emerged in 1982 when Stanley Prusiner, the first author of the article with Gajdusek cited above mentioning a sort of cannibal sighting, published another essay in *Science*. In this instance Prusiner wrote: 'Although considerable evidence implicates cannibalism in the spread of kuru, no direct observation of cannibalistic acts in the "endemic" region have been recorded' (1982: 136). Prusiner then further distanced himself from the cannibal theme by noting that the relevant literature indicates it is 'inefficient', and then only sporadically possible, to transmit diseases of this kind orally among experimental animals (136). There was probably more than a breakdown of communication between the two authors, for this publication signalled a profound split between Prusiner and Gajdusek on the whole issue of slow virus causation. The acrimonious and politicised dispute continues to this day (see Kolata 1994).

Despite the preceding mass of contradictions, it is still not surprising that both anthropology and medical students are taught in unambiguous terms that kuru is transmitted by cannibalism. End of story. The cannibal metaphor is too valuable to dispense with merely because of the absence of evidence, presence of contradictory statements, and seeming duplicity by the principal investigators. Thus, in the volume of anthropological essays referred to earlier (Brown and Tuzin 1983b) which, according to Douglas (1989), settled the matter, the editors could write – with reference to the authority of Lindenbaum, who is relying upon the authority of Gajdusek, who is relying upon the authority of Lindenbaum – that: 'the discovery that kuru ... is transmitted through *the eating of human tissue* (Lindenbaum 1979), focused wide-spread scientific attention on cannibal customs and their epidemiological consequences' (Brown and Tuzin 1983: 3; my emphasis). Simultaneously, the authoritative *Cecil Textbook of Medicine* proclaims: 'decreasing incidence has coincided with the suppression of cannibalism is [*sic*] [in] this primitive culture, and there is significant circumstantial evidence indicating that kuru was transmitted during the practice of ritual cannibalism' (Besson, McDermott, and Wyngaarden 1979: 840).

The situation can be reconstructed as follows. The authorities first suggest that kuru is not transmitted by cannibalism *per se*. However, since those afflicted are cannibals, the disease is transmitted during 'ritual' practices associated with the suspected activity. This muddle is then further complicated by subsequent controversy over the evidence for the deed, which results in some rather dubious pronouncements by the principals. Yet despite these twists and turns, there is a single, constant, attending message for others to pick up on: if the Fore were not cannibals, they would have neither contracted nor spread the disease (see Seale 1987, 1989; and Cominas et al. 1989). This morality tale encourages the subsequent direct translation of the cannibal metaphor as objective truth in textbooks for the neophyte.

This interpretation does not suggest that kuru was invented by the investigators. The disease exists and takes the lives of its victims, however they are characterised. Nor am I suggesting that those involved in the scientific research and its cultural interpretation invented the cannibal metaphor. The theme of the 'other' as cannibal had, and has, an existence beyond the control of those employing it at any particular moment. Indeed the cannibal notion has the ability to manipulate those who harbour it rather than the other way around. This is the nature of cultural myths and the fate of their proponents, whether explorer, missionary, scientist, or anthropologist. In a sense the principals deserve some sympathy for their present predicament: having to account objectively for a cultural notion and discourse they merely re-deployed. Nonetheless, the result was that the Fore became double victims of the kuru malady, as they succumbed to both its internal incidence and external interpretation.

Ironically, the perspective suggested here has also been adopted by Lindenbaum when the cultural climate shifted from the Highlands of New Guinea to the West as it contends with the ethical and moral issues surrounding AIDS. In this different context Lindenbaum now remarks that 'some diseases are interpreted through existing cultural categories', and unabashedly refers to the history of 'myth making about disease' and the manner in which interpretation becomes a 'stigmatizing condition'. Agreeing with another commentator, she advises that 'anthropologists might become more sensitive to their own role in the construction of ethnographic facts' (1992: 327).

These present concerns suggest that anthropology has been affected more by cultural space than time in the cultural interpretation of illness. In its own social setting, the discourse takes into account more than hypothesis and data. This mood alteration would count as progress if it were not for the fact that the interpretation applies only to our own rather than to other cultures. They will have to wait their turn.

This particular interpretational shift draws attention to the extent to which anthropology depends upon ethnocentrism in going about its business. Anthropologists, like others before them, are dedicated to the identification of some degree or level of cultural differences. Indeed they are dependent upon them. There is nothing novel, shocking, or necessarily disreputable in this procedure. However, having engaged in the creative activity, anthropology attempts to distinguish itself from its intellectual predecessors with an admonishment to its audience against making any moral judgments on the basis of the cultural differences offered up for consideration. Ethnocentrism thus serves a dual purpose for the discipline as it subsequently engages in a dismissal of the responses to its objective production. In the instance under consideration here anthropology first creates cannibal cultures for the popular imagination and then suggests they not be considered morally inferior by reference to the canon of cultural relativity. Ignoring the implications of this procedure – past and present – smacks of either naivety or duplicity.

The latest campaign in the 'culture wars' exemplifies the intellectual process. D'Souza's (1995) vociferous neo-conservative defence of Western history and cultural superiority relies heavily on the presumed cannibalism of others, most recently popularised by anthropologists such as Marvin Harris's *Cannibals and Kings* (1977), and Robert Edgerton's *Sick Societies* (1992). On the authority of such reports and their psuedo-scientific interpretations, D'Souza takes issue with the principles of cultural relativity and multiculturalism. By implication he also offers up what seems to be a reasonable justification of European imperialism. Thus, in considering Western contact with the New World, D'Souza concludes that in addition to some genuine cultural misunderstandings, 'Europeans also encountered practices that produced an entirely justified revulsion at the native cultures' (1995: 350). The inevitable response will of course be some equally spirited anthropological defence of cannibalism in the name of liberalism. Although this contorted intellectual perspective may be essential to the discipline's continued social relevance, it eventually leads to the excesses and dilemmas reconsidered here.

In rethinking anthropophagy – and to a lesser extent anthropology – I have devoted an inordinate amount of time to the specific issue of kuru and cannibalism. In a consideration of the cannibal image at the turn of the century, it appears that this creature owes its continued existence, beyond literary and cinematic representations, to the efforts of both science and social science, the most important contemporary institutions engaged in the production of knowledge about ourselves and others. This continued re-creation and reinterpretation has always been the fate of the cannibal. Nonetheless, I continue to hope, as I did when first considering the problem, that one day there will be no need for the anthropophagist – but then perhaps there will be no need for anthropologists. The result would be sad, but arguably a well-earned fate.

Appendix

The reproduction of the following illustrations and photographs attempts to convey the text's argument in the proverbial fewer words.

The first set of illustrations, implying photographic authenticity for cannibalism, relates to the kuru research in New Guinea. The first pair (fig. 1) accompanied Gajdusek's Nobel Prize Lecture (Gajdusek 1977a) and its subsequent publication in *Science* (Gajdusek 1977b: 956, figs. 14 and 15). The accompanying text, with an emphasis on ethnographic authority, reads:

> Fig. 14 (top). A Fore mother mourning over the body of her dead daughter, who had just died of kuru ... Men, and already initiated boys, rarely participated in the mourning rite around

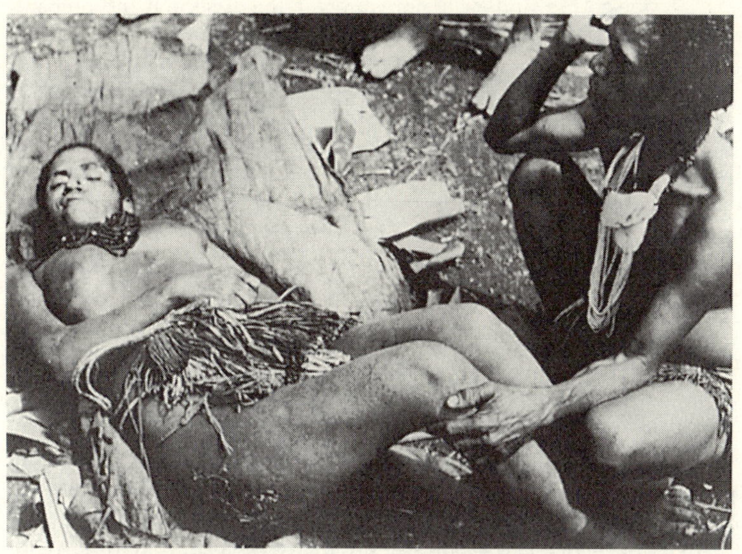

Figures 1a and 1b. From D. Carleton Gajdusek, 'Unconventional Viruses' (1977b).

> the corpse, and even more rarely in the dissection and preparation of the kuru victim's flesh for its ritual endo-cannibalistic consumption. Fig. 15 (bottom). All cooking including that of human flesh from diseased kinsmen was done in pits with steam.

Gajdusek then concludes that infection was 'most probably' through cuts and other similar means, but does not mention consumption.

Having encountered these photographs in the course of researching *The Man-Eating Myth*, I wrote to Gajdusek asking for clarification of the potential relationship between the published images and actual cannibalism. Gajdusek was gracious enough to respond, though in somewhat ambiguous terms on the matter of cannibalism: 'we did not photograph it, except on rare occasions' (Gajdusek 1977c). He also obliquely intimated (as opposed to clearly stating the fact) that the activity shown in his figure 15 actually involved the consumption of pork – not an unusual occurrence. (In light of the now presumed relationship between infected beef and Creutzfeld-Jacob's Disease in Britain, the photograph might actually provide ironic evidence for how kuru was transmitted among the Fore in New Guinea.)[11] However, Gajdusek did explain, with admirable candour, that: 'This paralleled exactly the situation with the children in cannibalistic rituals which we saw in the more remote Fore and Gimi hamlets. I usually make this point with such pictures in lectures, and I fear I made it insufficiently in the caption to figure 15' (Gajdusek 1977c). Thus, the two photographs which were shown at his Nobel Lecture (1977a and 1977b) did not, in fact, provide visual documentation for cannibalism, but were rather illustrations of the deed. In a later attempt to explain the situation Gajdusek is reported to have said that he never publishes actual pictures of cannibalism because they are 'too offensive' (Kolata 1986: 1498).

A further reproduction of the same mourning scene as fig. 1a later appeared in print with the publication of Gajdusek's early letters and field notes on the kuru research. However, the text in this instance reads: 'Kinswomen mourning an adult woman who has just died of kuru. Four women cluster closely around the body while children, whose feet are in the background, look on from nearby. Male kinsmen had assembled for ceremonial distribution of sugar cane and other foods, marking the death' (Farquhar and Gajdusek 1981: figure 29, no page number). Thus, there was no indication cannibalism was involved in mortuary ceremonies when these photographs were first taken; the idea was inserted into the

Figures 2a and 2b. Top 'Men about to roast wild boar'. Bottom 'Men and Children feasting on the freshly roasted meat'. From Vincent Zigas, *Laughing Death* (1990).

discourse later and existing photographs were then used to illustrate the deed.

The next two illustrations (fig. 2) appeared in Vincent Zigas's *Laughing Death*, a subsequent popular account of the kuru research process. The author was the medical officer on the scene when Gajdusek first appeared in the New Guinea Highlands in 1957, and was the co-author of the initial publications on the discovery of the disease. He then drops out of sight and for most part citation. The text for his plate 4 reads: 'Top, Men about to roast wild boar; bottom, Men and children feasting on the freshly roasted meat' (Zigas 1990: viii). Zigas's photograph (fig. 2b) is clearly of the same scene and taken at the same time, and therefore almost identical to the one used by Gajdusek in his Nobel Lecture and publication to imply cannibalism (see fig. 1a).

The next set of images is derived from the work of Robert Glasse and Shirley Lindenbaum, the anthropologists involved in the kuru research. The first (fig. 3) was reproduced in their joint contribution to a medical volume, *Essays on Kuru* (1976). The photograph, captioned 'Preparing an Earth Oven', appeared in the text just below table 5 entitled, 'The Rights of Kin in Cannibal Consumption at Wanitabe' (Glasse and Lindenbaum 1976: 50). By this time it had been established that kuru was a transmittable virus. Although one might reasonably assume a connection between the cannibal table and the smoke swirling up from the earth oven, this is not the case. In an interview (Arens 1995), I asked Lindenbaum if the reader is meant to draw a connection between the cannibal consumption chart and the accompanying photograph. She dismissed the implication that the photograph was meant to illustrate preparation for cannibalism or to allow for that conclusion. She indicated that she did not know how or why the two were put together in this fashion but assumes the decision was made by her co-author Glasse (now deceased) or by the editor of the volume.

The identical photograph appeared a second time in Lindenbaum's *Kuru Sorcery*, with the caption: 'Men prepare for a communal meal before eclipse' (1979: 110). Although cannibalism, particularly among women, is mentioned a number of times in the text of the book as a response to protein deficiency, there is no intimation of a relationship to Fore cannibalism in this instance of the photograph's adaption. (Lindenbaum said she would consider written requests from the editors and myself to reproduce the second use of the

Figure 3. 'South Fore preparing an earth oven'. From Robert Glasse and Shirley Lindenbaum, 'Kuru at Wanitabe' (1976).

photograph only if she were given the opportunity to review this entire essay before making a decision. Since I had earlier indicated to her my intent to discuss the matter of the multiple use of photographs in this essay, I understand her reticence. Nonetheless, I declined to agree to her demand.)

In sum, in contrast to initial impressions, there is no visual documentation for cannibalism in any of these instances. For each example the image was borrowed or adapted from some other source, and even situation, to convey an impression of visual evidence for the deed. Why this impression management inevitably takes place is a complicated and sensitive matter. From our perspective, imagery of this sort may seem excusable for earlier eras when the actors in the cannibal drama were romantic explorers returning from unknown lands, later aided by even more romantic illustrators. It seems less explicable or acceptable in an age of science with, presumably, the more exalted research standards implied. Yet for each time, place, and context everyone – and with good reason – 'knows these people were cannibals'. The existence of advanced technology does not appear to alter the message, merely the medium and the messenger.

Acknowledgements

Thanks are due to Peter Hulme and his colleagues at the University of Essex for hosting the symposium in the summer of 1995, as well as to the other participants for providing a convivial occasion. These remarks were previously delivered at the Humanities Institute and Honors College, SUNY, Stony Brook and the Universities of Uppsala and Göteborg, Sweden. Appreciated comments on this essay and other assistance were offered by Diana Antos Arens, Andreas Beriger, Richard Buchorn, Elov Carlson, Fred Grine, Margaret Gwynne, Anita Jacobson-Widding, E. Anne Kaplan, Adam Kuper, Kaj Arhem, and particularly Donna Sammis of the SUNY, Stony Brook Library. Rodney Needham has been a constant source of inspiration, encouragement, and advice, as well as hospitality, for many years.

3

Cannibal feasts in nineteenth-century Fiji: seamen's yarns and the ethnographic imagination

Gananath Obeyesekere

William Arens was one of the first to demystify the notion of cannibalism and argue persuasively that it was a 'man-eating myth' for savages as well as Europeans, including anthropologists.[1] Arens (1979b) does not deny its practice entirely and is willing to recognise its existence under special conditions; but for the most part cannibalism is a discourse on the Other, defining out-groups in terms of their horrifying man-eating propensities. Peter Hulme (1986) traces one important trajectory of this myth-form, namely, its relation to the colonial enterprise in the Caribbean, the place that produced the very origin of that word. Following Hulme's work I shall define 'cannibalism' as a cultural construction which refers to the inordinate capacity of the Other to consume human flesh as an especially delectable food. In European cannibal narratives this is an almost innate propensity that defines the savage, such that 'cannibal feasts' became the stock in trade of European anthropology and travel writing until very recent times.

In an earlier paper I argued that cannibalism, as it was described in the three voyages of James Cook, was not only a discourse on the Other, but also constituted a complicated series of discourses between native populations and European interlocutors and that it defied simple formulation as an ethnographic category (Obeyesekere 1992b). For example, the mere fact that a native population admitted to their cannibalism was not proof of the existence of that practice because cannibalism became a 'weapon of the weak' to keep European intruders away from native homes and habitations. Native cannibal talk tapped in deadly fashion the European dread of being eaten by savages. In that paper, I do not deny the practice of anthropophagy, either in the context of human sacrifice or, on occasion, as cannibalism itself, particularly in the context of the European intrusion. However, the overwhelming number of cases of imputed cannibalism were products of the European fantasy. Thus, when cannibalism virtually disappeared among those inveterate cannibals, the Maori (after 1840 when the treaty of Waitangi was thrust upon them), it resurged in the Marquesas and Fiji, and the latter became known as the 'Cannibal Islands' in the travel literature of the nineteenth century. One can even make the case, albeit somewhat facetiously, that the decline of Maori cannibalism in the European consciousness was the 'cause' of the rise of the Fijian practice. When 'cannibalism' takes hold of the European imagination, the eating of human flesh (or its mimesis) as a consubstantial act associated with the 'sacrifice' is downplayed or fused with cannibalism itself.

Ethnographers have not been immune to this fantasy in their willingness to uncritically incorporate multiple and disparate accounts of Polynesian cannibalism, native or European, into the ethnography of cannibalism. Even a sophisticated anthropologist, Ross Bowden, subsumes the double features of anthropophagy into the ethnographic category of 'cannibalism'. Thus: 'The victims would be butchered on the spot and cooked in Maori steam ovens ... What was not eaten was packed up and consumed on the way home.' And then to the ritualistic form, also integral to cannibalism:

> Considerable ritual, it seems, was associated with the first victim slain (the so-called 'first fish'). Some accounts state that no part of the body was eaten but was offered up whole as a sacrifice to the deities who presided at the war party; others that only the heart was used sacrificially and the rest eaten ... All writers agree that the bodies of the slain enemies were never used as common food in a village, and that women were rarely, if ever, permitted to eat human flesh. (Bowden 1984: 96)

If one takes the accounts of cannibalism reported by sea captains, missionaries, beachcombers, and traders literally, then Fiji was indeed the haunt of 'cannibals' by the mid-nineteenth century. In this vein Marshall Sahlins, responding to Arens' work, says that the truth of cannibalism is based on 'unimpeacheable testimony' (1979: 47). It is tantamount to denying the Holocaust, he says, thereby casting a dark insensitivity on those who would have the temerity to question the truth of a key ethnographic category. Among such unimpeachable testimonies is 'the narrative of John Jackson, a seaman resident in Fiji from 1840 to 1842 which contains three detailed descriptions of cannibal feasts' (47). Here is a partial quote from Jackson (also known as Cannibal Jack) that Sahlins employs in a much fuller manner:

> The bodies, which were painted with vermillion and soot, were carefully handed out, and placed on the road, or rather square, between the king's house and the bure [temple] ... At last they hauled them up to a place that was used purposely for the dressing, cooking, and eating of human flesh ... The king being very impatient to begin, and not choosing to wait till it was properly prepared, told the butcher just to slice off the end of the noses, and he would roast them while he was getting the other parts ready. The butcher did as he was ordered, and handed the three ends of the noses to his majesty, which he grasped hold of very nimbly, and put on hot stones to warm a little, not wishing to lose any time. The first he hardly let warm through, but while he was eating it, the second got a little better done, which he demolished ... (Jackson 1967: 426–7)

The king greedily eating the noses of the victims comes, I suggest, from the discourse on cannibalism rather than that on sacrifice and is more in tune with European castration fantasies, children's stories, and nursery rhymes like 'Sing a Song of Sixpence' than any Fijian ethnographic reality.[2]

In 1977 Fergus Clunie published his authoritative monograph on *Fiji Weapons and Warfare* containing detailed accounts of Fijian cannibalism, also based uncritically on such sources as John Jackson's. More recently, in her comparative study of cannibalism, Peggy Sanday, relying entirely on the ethnographic information supplied by Sahlins and Clunie can, not unreasonably, describe Fiji as a 'pure culture of the death instinct' (1986: 151). By contrast I want to 'impeach' the conventional cannibal testimonies and suggest that narratives such as Jackson's are based on a genre of seamen's yarns, hence totally unsuitable as an ethnographic resource. I shall present my critique of the ethnographic construction of Fijian cannibalism by examining two authorities that Clunie uses: the first is William Endicott who claimed to have actually witnessed a Fijian cannibal feast; the second is the more complex case of John Jackson.

1 Endicott's narrative: a Fijian cannibal feast

William Endicott, the third mate of the *Glide*, wrote about his experiences during the period 1829–32 in a journal published only in 1923 as *Wrecked Among Cannibals in the Fijis*, with an appendix entitled 'A Cannibal Feast in the Fiji Islands by an Eye-Witness', originally published by Endicott in his home-town newspaper, *The Danvers Courier*, on 16 August 1845. It is the latter narrative that is used by Clunie, Sahlins, and others to further substantiate the accumulating evidence on Fijian cannibalism. To give the reader a feel for the narrative, I shall quote liberally from Endicott's eye-witness account of a cannibal feast in the region of Macuata, in the northern part of the island of Venua Levu sometime during March 1831.

The narrative starts 'on a pleasant afternoon in the month of March, 1831, our ship at anchor off the town of Bona-ra-ra the crew on board employed in making sennet, yard mats, and other ship gear to fill up the chunks of time.' They had worked hard in the forenoon, 'boating oil to the ship, beche-le-mer, weighing, and stowing it away in the hold'. Now they were indulging in telling tales, singing songs, and reflecting on 'better days gone by' (55). At this time women who came on board ship to sell fruit informed Endicott 'that the men had been to a fight with the Andregette tribe ... and had killed and taken three of their enemies, and were now going to have a grand Soleb, or feast'.

'I had heard David Whippy, a man who had long been a resident upon these Islands, tell many a long tale of the manners and customs of the natives, and especially of their cannibalism, and I had a strong desire to see the manner in which they prepared and ate human flesh' (56). Accordingly, Endicott asked Captain Archer's permission; Archer urged him to take care of himself. Because he was friendly with the natives, Endicott felt in no danger and eventually 'landed on the beach just ahead of the savages who were coming in single file to the village'; they were sixty in number, but attended by many others (57).

'The bodies of the three dead savages were carried in front, lashed on long poles in a singular manner. They were bound with wythes by bringing the upper and lower parts of the legs together and binding them to the body, and the arms in a similar manner by bringing the elbows to rest on the knees, and their hands tied upon each side of the neck. Their backs were confined to poles which were about twelve feet long. One was lashed on each pole, with six men, three at each end, to carry it' (58). The carriers had a limping gait and were singing a war song to the rhythm of the gait. Endicott then says that the king sent the smallest of the three bodies to a friendly neighbouring tribe 'from whom he had received similar tokens of friendship'. This was a great day in Bona-ra-ra, because 'more is thought of the savage who kills one man and carries him home, than of the individual who may kill a hundred and let their dead bodies fall into the hand of the enemy. Their chief glory consists not so much in killing, as in eating their enemies' (58).

Now we come to that section of Endicott's narrative which Clunie employs for showing how 'the carcases [*sic*] of someone who had committed a particular wrong against certain members of the community was subject to further insult' (Clunie 1977: 37). Endicott noticed a particular interest being taken in one of the dead savages who apparently had killed a young chief, the son of an old woman present at this scene. This woman went to her hut, got all her son's belongings and came back:

> The angona [kava] bowl was placed near the head of the dead savage; a bamboo of water was brought and laid by his side, when several young men after well rinsing their mouths, were employed in chewing and preparing a bowl of angona. After the drink was made ready this old savage after a short speech from the priest who had continued to make low guttural sounds and shake himself through the whole ceremony, took her small dish full of liquor and presenting it to the lips of the dead savage bade him drink. No sooner was this done than a general yell ran through the tribe – 'Amba cula boy thu-ie', he is a stinking dead man.[3] She then dashed the liquor in his face and broke the dish in pieces upon it. (59–60)

Thereafter she went her way because females could not participate in preparing or eating human flesh. 'The head of the savage on whom this ceremony commenced was first cut off and laid aside, then the furniture that was brought by the old woman was broken up and placed around it, and fire set to it so that the whole was entirely consumed about the head, and rendered thereby in fit state for cleansing; the hair burnt off and the flesh so singed that it was scraped perfectly white' (60; Clunie 1977: 38).

After this there was a dance 'customary on all such occasions' with warriors in a state of complete nudity. 'They were painted in a most frightful manner, as great a diversity of painting, or marking ... each one attempting to outdo the other in the most loathsome obscenity and savage appearance.' There were about a hundred dancers 'who came upon the ground at one and the same time with terrific yells. Their dance was made up of the most violent and distended motion of the limbs, often prostrating themselves on the ground upon their backs, and springing again instantly to their places, without for a moment ceasing to chant their war song in a very low but distinct manner' to the accompaniment of two savages beating upon the end of a hollow log (Endicott 1923: 60–1).

Endicott has a graphic description of the cutting up of the two bodies: the heads were removed, and then the right hand and the left foot and finally 'all the limbs [were] separated from the body'. After which an oblong piece was removed 'commencing about the bottom of the chest and passing downwards about eight inches, and three or four inches wide at the broadest part'. This was for the king and it was laid aside:

> The entrails and vitals were then taken out and cleansed for cooking. But I shall not here particularize. The scene is too revolting. The flesh was then cut through the ribs to the spine of the back which was broken, thus the body was separated into two pieces ... I saw after they had cut through the ribs of the stoutest man, a savage jump upon the back, one end of which rested upon the ground, and the other was held in the hands and rested upon the knees of another savage, three times before he had succeeded in breaking it ...
>
> To show their excessive greediness for human flesh, and their savage thirst for blood, I need only to relate a particular circumstance which took place at the time. The head of the savage which was last taken off, was thrown towards the fire, and being thrown some distance it rolled a few feet from the men who were employed around it; when it was stolen by one of the savages who carried it behind the tree where I was sitting. He took the head in his lap and after combing away the hair from the top of it with his fingers picked out the pieces of the scull which was broken by the war club and commenced eating the brains ... There was no part of these bodies which I did not see cleansed and put in the oven. (62–3)

Realising that the cooking would take some time, Endicott went back to the beche-le-mer shed on the opposite side of the village for a break and then at dawn came back to witness the tail-end of the feast. He was invited by the king to sit with him and eat some of the meat:

> I unwrapped it and found it to be a part of a foot taken off at the ankle and at the joints of the toes. I made an excuse of not eating it, by saying that it had been kept too long after it was killed, before it was cooked, it being about thirty-six hours ...
>
> As the light of day shown into the hut, it revealed a sight seldom witnessed by civilized man. Around the hut sat sixty or seventy cannibals, more frightful than ever if possible; their paint being rubbed together in many instances, gave their

> bodies such an appearance as for a moment to lead one to doubt that they were human beings. Before one savage, would lay a human head, save that part which could be released from it, the lower jaw; which would be in possession of another. The bones of these bodies were well distributed among them, showing conclusively that none had failed to get their share. I had understood by them that the oven was opened about midnight, and that they had now done their feast; what was left was to be given to the boys; the women ... were not allowed to taste of it though they frequently got it by stealth ... (66–7).

Endicott's narrative does seem like a first hand account, especially convincing when he recounts minute details like the part of the victim reserved for the king. It is not surprising that Clunie and other anthropologists have used his, and similar accounts, for their construction of Fijian cannibalism. Some doubts surely should have arisen though: the savage picking the brains seems to contradict the Fijian revulsion for the head. If Captain Archer cautioned Endicott when he gave him permission to witness the cannibal feast, it is odd that he did not recommend him going there with a comrade or two; or that Endicott himself did not think of it. Again the extreme 'accuracy' of the description of the king's portion should have sounded too good to be true.[4]

Now let me present Endicott's own evidence to show that he could not possibly have witnessed this particular cannibal feast. His journal *Wrecked Among Cannibals* describes his voyage to the Fijian islands in the *Glide*, commanded by Captain Archer, to procure beche-le-mer (sea slugs) and tortoise shells in high demand in China. They had to move from place to place owing to conflict with the native population. In one instance, in Ovalau, men engaged in cutting anchor stocks, presumably without permission, were set upon by the natives who killed two sailors. They took their muskets and stripped them of their clothes but, for some strange reason, did not eat them (34). A month later, on 1 January 1831, the crew moved to an island near Bau but here also the natives fired their beche-le-mer sheds and in a skirmish they killed 'a number of them' (36). On 17 February they reached a town in Macuata on the north side of Vanua Levu and the locale of the cannibal feast. Here with the help of the local chief they started 'purchasing and curing beche-le-mer'. 'We continued curing the fish and nothing particular occurred until the 22nd March, 1831, by which time we had procured about 500 piculs of beche-le-mer and 300 pounds of tortoise shell' (37). The

22nd of March was important because a hurricane hit the island and the *Glide* was wrecked. They were befriended by a local chief, but later stripped by a party of mountaineers, until they were taken under the protection of the king of Macuata. On the 28th Captain Archer himself went in search of help from a European ship anchored in another part of the island and did not return till much later. While Archer was away the king invited Endicott and his fellow sailors to witness the payment of tribute to him by local chiefs 'on a beautiful plain where houses were built for the King and the chiefs and their families' (46). This is the same king who plays such a crucial role in the cannibal narrative. Endicott gives a fine description of the festivities associated with this event, the striking feature of which was the absence of the cannibal feast expectable on such occasions.

In his journal Endicott shows a predilection for exact dates; yet his cannibal narrative is vaguely set 'in the month of March, 1831'. The internal evidence of this narrative suggests that he, along with others, was working hard during the forenoon, loading the ship and doing other tasks. It was impossible for him to perform these tasks after 22 March when the ship was wrecked. And look at what he says in his *journal* for the period prior to that date: 'we continued to fish and nothing particular happened until the 22nd March, 1831' (36–7). It is hard to believe that witnessing a cannibal feast was of no particular significance. After 28 March, he could not have witnessed the feast because Archer was not around for him to get permission. This leaves us the period 22 March, the day of the shipwreck, until the 28th, the day of Captain Archer's departure. But this is not likely, since there was no ship for loading beche-le-mer (which is what he claims in his cannibal narrative); and the natives were hostile (contrary to his account). Finally, Endicott kept a log, the likely source for his book, now in the library of the Peabody Essex Museum. Nowhere in the log either is there any reference to his having witnessed a cannibal feast. It is therefore virtually certain that Endicott fabricated his eye-witness account thirteen years later to meet the European demand for savage cannibalism, perhaps provoked by the emerging literature on the subject. What else but cannibalism could one expect to find in the Cannibal Islands?

It seems to me that Endicott is writing two kinds of text. His narrative of the voyage is in the tradition of shipboard journalism and, though Endicott is not a sophisticated journalist, he gives a fairly straightforward account of his experiences. If the first narrative belongs to the genre of shipboard journalism, the second dealing with the cannibal feast belongs to the genre of sailors' yarns. In the South Seas these yarns deal with the purported first hand experiences of the protagonist, generally with his adventures among the natives and witnessing that quintessential attribute of savagery, the cannibal feast.

Endicott himself sketches a plausible context for inventing this account in the beginning of his essay. After working hard in the afternoons, his comrades had time to spare and indulged themselves in 'reveries and yarns' and 'in a sailor's privilege of telling tales, singing songs and reflecting upon "better days gone by"'. While speaking of these he also mentions a raconteur, an American named David Whippy who, we noted earlier, could narrate 'many a long tale of the manners and customs of the natives, and especially of their cannibalism' (56). Whippy reappears in 1840 as one of Captain Wilkes's principal informants in the famous (or infamous) United States Exploring Expedition; Wilkes was so pleased with Whippy that he was later nominated a United States consular agent. About ten years later the Englishman Captain John Elphinstone Erskine also praises Whippy as a 'a man of excellent character' who gave 'a tone of order and true respectability to the community' both white and native (Erskine 1967: 173). No wonder the accounts of Fijian cannibalism that Whippy recounted to people like Wilkes and Erskine carried the stamp of authenticity. In *Typee* Melville's protagonist might have been speaking about settlers like David Whippy and John Jackson: 'Jack, who has long been accustomed to the longbow, and to spin tough yarns on a ship's forecastle, invariably officiates as showman of the island on which he has settled, and having mastered a few dozen words of the language, is supposed to know all about the people who speak it' (Melville 1972: 193). Endicott himself, in true yarnster fashion, has a wonderfully ironic and deliberately give-away line at the end of his essay: 'I am about to the end of my yarn, yet I might lengthen it by knotting on other strands, but my timepiece reminds me that it is past midnight; so I shall take the liberty to belay this and turn in' (Endicott 1923: 70).

The missionary James Hadfield in his 'Introduction' to John Jackson's *Cannibal Jack* mentions another yarnster, a trader named Hayes, 'one of the cleverest raconteurs I have ever met. He had heaps of stories in his repertoire, chiefly of whaling expeditions and cannibal feasts he attended' (1928: xvi). While Hadfield states that 'no one gave credence to any statement he made', he accepts without reservation Hayes's accounts of cannibalism.[5] Even Melville in his preface to *Typee*, published in 1846, the year after Endicott's cannibal tale, identifies himself with this yarnster tradition: 'The incidents recorded in the following pages have often served, when "spun as a yarn", not only to relieve the weariness of many a night-watch at sea, but to excite the warmest sympathies of the author's shipmates' (Melville 1972: 33). There is a critical difference though: Endicott's is an unmitigated yarn; whereas the events in Melville's story *could be spun as a yarn*, implying that *Typee* is based on yarnster material, or could be reconverted into a yarn, without itself being a yarn. It seems that yarnsters like Endicott, Hayes, and the young Melville were a well-known feature of the South Seas land, sea, and beachscapes. Their life ways have been nicely documented by Greg Dening (1980: 129–56).

2 Cannibal narratives of John Jackson alias Cannibal Jack

Fergus Clunie relies heavily on an account known as 'Jackson's Narrative' appended to Captain Erskine's book on his first cruise to the islands of the Western Pacific. On Erskine's request John Jackson wrote this account 'during his leisure hours' when he was employed as an interpreter during Erskine's second voyage to New Caledonia in 1851. Thus Jackson, unlike Endicott, was not a ship's journalist but made into one by Erskine. The talented Jackson met the situation by emulating the style of shipboard journalism.

To properly understand this work it is necessary to consider two other books that Jackson wrote for publication, the first, *Jack, the Cannibal Killer*, now lost, written sometime after 'Jackson's Narrative'; and the second, *Cannibal Jack*, written in 1889 when he was seventy.[6] 'Jackson's Narrative' does not read like a novel, though it records utterly improbable adventures, whereas *Jack, the Cannibal Killer* was explicitly meant to be one; *Cannibal Jack* was labelled an 'autobiography', self-consciously addressed to a European reading public.[7] In 'Jackson's Narrative' the author is John Jackson, which is how he introduced himself to Erskine. In *Cannibal Jack* he has clearly changed his name to William Diapea (he was also called Diaper). I shall refer to him as John Jackson or Cannibal Jack, the popular cognomen by which he was known and one he personally favoured.[8]

'Jackson's Narrative' and the lost novel, *Jack, the Cannibal Killer,* were probably thematically related. The title of the latter suggests that it was a story about Jack who kills cannibals, and these must obviously be Fijian ones. 'Jackson's Narrative' also deals with Jackson's description of wars culminating in cannibal feasts. In this text he is merely a witness of these events; in *Jack, the Cannibal Killer* he must surely have been the hero who, having killed cannibals, saves damsels from the ovens (assuming that he employed the themes of 'Jackson's Narrative' and *Cannibal Jack*). If 'Jackson's Narrative' is not a novel, one can legitimately ask, to what genre does it belong? The clue is provided by Endicott who wrote a similar narrative which I have already identified as a yarnster invention. John Jackson's account was published in 1853 in Erskine's book; it is likely that this event stimulated his alter ego William Diapea alias Cannibal Jack to produce his own books, now more in the style of adventure stories than yarns.

Unlike in Endicott's case, we cannot prove that the accounts of cannibalism in 'Jackson's Narrative' and *Cannibal Jack* are fabrications but one can seriously question their value as ethnography. I will demonstrate this by examining the interconnections between these two narratives and their style and content. Though the events of *Cannibal Jack* take place between 1843–47 and 'Jackson's Narrative' during 1840–43, there is one incident (the Bonaveidogo episode) occurring in both which confounds Jackson's own periodisations.[9]

According to 'Jackson's Narrative', chief Bonaveidogo (Bonavidongo, Bonavidogo) asked the reluctant Jackson at about two in the morning to go with him to a nameless uninhabited island to gather calabashes. They were to go very furtively 'lest we should be seen from the main by the Namuka natives', their enemies. Soon they saw people coming from Namuka in eight or ten canoes. The company trapped their Namuka enemies and killed many of them (and later ate them in the narrative segments utilised by Sahlins and Clunie). One 'fugitive' was seen swimming, following a woman who had just escaped. He was being shot at but when Jackson pleaded with the men not to kill him they scoffed at the idea. 'By this time we were up to the fugitive, when the chief, lifting his tomahawk to dispatch him in the water, I stopped the blow with my hand, and begged him to let the man get on board alive. He threw down his tomahawk, and told me to save him, and I would see the result of being merciful, saying that, instead of being grateful for his life, he would kill and eat me the first opportunity that offered' (Jackson 1967: 437). In fact the 'fugitive' gave some crucial information, namely, that Bonaveidogo's father Tui Mativata (Tui Macuata, chief of Macuata) was now residing at Namuka where he had fled for protection, strangely enough among the very people his son has just killed. Naturally, Bonaveidogo was pleased that Jackson saved the life of this man.

This is followed by a description of the dead being dragged uphill prior to being cooked. John Jackson tries to persuade Bonaveidogo to bury the dead. Bonaveidogo says that he himself was never a cannibal ('daukanatamala') or an adulterer ('dauyalewa'); yet 'he had eaten a little piece now and then just to be in the fashion of the older chiefs' (and yet) 'he took great pleasure in killing his enemies for the old and infirm chiefs to eat' (437–8). The cannibal feast is prefaced by a woman's lewd dance for humiliating the dead, an event crucial to Clunie's conception of Fijian cannibalism. 'I saw their animosity was so great, that they did not consider their enemies being killed and eaten sufficient to gratify their revenge, without deriding and degrading them, as it were, after death, which the young girls were doing in the most lewd kind of dance, touching the bodies in certain nameless parts with sticks as they were lying in a state of nudity, accompanying the action with the words of the song' (Jackson 1967: 438; Clunie 1977: 36).

The other work, *Cannibal Jack*, begins with the same 'Bonaveidogo episode', and one can feel Jackson's physical presence and hear his colloquial voice speaking the winding and long sentences characteristic of his style here:[10]

> Whilst I was enjoying myself as best I could, eating and drinking – drinking the 'yagone' in unlimited quantities and bidding fair to become quite a sot, like the rest of the whites in other parts of Fiji, the principal portion of them being located in a settlement called Levuka situated in the island of Ovalau (Central Fiji or 'Lomai Viti'), – I say, whilst I was doing all these things, alternated by mending muskets and amassing property, and living quite content with my three wives, one morning, or rather perhaps in the middle of the night, as it could not have been much past twelve o'clock, if any, Bonavidogo came along, rousing me up from a long sleep, telling me to buckle on my cartridge box, and which, by the by, contained sixty rounds of cartridges, shoulder my musket, and also not to forget my dirk or sheath knife, and follow him, for the enemy were astir, and 'Bakolas' were to be had just for the killing of them. I followed quite drowsily, not being more than half awake, through the

> effect of the beastly habit I had lately given way to, of imbibing the juice of that very lethargic root, and besides, I followed reluctantly enough, because I was not interested in their murderous kinds of warfare, not caring two pins which side beat as neither party had, at present, injured me, but still I followed in silence, as all the natives maintained the strictest silence, as is their wont when on the war-path. (Diapea 1928: 10)

The group went down to the shore and then sailed in canoes till they sighted a small island (unnamed in this text) where their enemies were collecting coconuts to make sennet from their husks. The 'poor doomed creatures' had not seen the canoes which had 'kept the island between us and the main as well as between their intended victims' canoes and ourselves' (11). Now follows a terrific description of the battle in those same long sentences that involve the reader in the action:

> I had not left Bonavidogo, but remained with him in his canoe, and just as we reached the other side and were right in among the enemies' small canoes, I heard the crash of murder on shore, some of the people being speared and clubbed just as they descended the coco-nut trees, and some as they were in the act of ascending or preparing to do so, and others as they were rushing along towards their canoes, which the one or two which had been left in each one were now fast paddling away, were either speared or shot down with muskets! But there was one man, who had rushed through the spears, clubs, tomahawks, handybillies, and musket balls of our murdering shore party unscathed, and into the water, towards the last of the small canoes, all the rest having got clear of the melee, paddling for their bare lives towards the main. This last and hitherto lingering small canoe now being pulled away by one single paddle, following the rest, all of which were out of all danger now, and this poor fellow, who had already run such a terrible risk, was swimming after it in order to embark with his life. But Bonavidogo's large canoe was being sculled after him and fast coming up to him, but in the meantime some half a dozen muskets had been fired at him. He seemed to have a charmed life. Every shot had missed him. (13)

Bonaveidogo asked Cannibal Jack to fire at him and kill the *bakola* but he didn't. When they came close to the swimming man Bonaveidogo tried to tomahawk him but Cannibal Jack interposed himself between Bonaveidogo and the victim and pleaded with the latter to save the man's life, warding off the blows intended to the victim and telling Bonaveidogo that the man could provide valuable 'news of the movements of the general enemy'. Bonaveidogo responded that this it is not the Fiji custom to spare enemies to which Cannibal Jack replied that 'it was the *humanity* fashion, asking him to place himself, in imagination, in that poor man's predicament' (14). Bonaveidogo continued to be obdurate but when Cannibal Jack swore that he would not be killed while he (Cannibal Jack) was alive, Bonaveidogo yielded. He told Jackson that the man he saved would show his gratitude by murdering his benefactor. Now the prisoner (in Friday fashion) 'clung to my legs with the most frantic terror, kneeling on the deck' (15). Then follows a graphic description of Cannibal Jack saving this man from the rest of the crew, something not found in the earlier version (15–16).

The upshot of all of this is that Cannibal Jack had his way, the prisoner was saved and even Bonaveidogo was pleased because the man provided information on enemy movements, as Cannibal Jack had predicted, but not, as in the previous text, on the fate of Bonaveidogo's father. There follows a description of the dead bodies being 'set up in formal array' though there is no description of the lewd female dance and the cannibal feast. Jackson does say though that the bodies were taken to the temple of Dagei (Degei), 'the god of war', the young girls going through 'the usual degrading obscene rites with their antics over these much-abused bodies ... [which then] were conveyed to the ovens and cooked, and then down the gullets of these determined cannibals' (20).

Let me now compare the same event in the two texts to show how futile it is to treat these accounts as ethnographic verities. In 'Jackson's Narrative' they sail from Udu Point down the coast; in *Cannibal Jack* the group starts off from the island of Ovalau and sails down the coast. In 'Jackson's Narrative' the enemies are the Namuka; in *Cannibal Jack* they are unnamed perhaps because Cannibal Jack realised both the geographical confusion in the former account and the absurdity of Bonaveidogo's father seeking refuge among the very people his son had just butchered. In *Cannibal Jack* Bonaveidogo's group go to the island to kill an unnamed enemy collecting coconut husks; in 'Jackson's Narrative' they go to gather calabashes and are well armed because the island to which they are going is off Namuka, the home of their enemies. In 'Jackson's Narrative' the enemy espies Bonaveidogo's group and tries to ambush them but fails and is surrounded by the latter; in *Cannibal Jack* the enemy is simply trapped and killed. The saving of the prisoner is quite different in the two accounts, *Cannibal Jack* being the more exciting one. In both accounts John Jackson acts in an arrogant manner before chief Bonaveidogo and the latter, in very unchiefly fashion, meekly accedes to his request.

It is time to consider another crucial piece of information, namely, John Jackson's knowledge of local languages. We do know from Hadfield and Erskine that he knew the language of Mare and other islands of New Caledonia, not surprising because this is where he lived longest. Yet 'Jackson's Narrative' starts with his adventures in a Samoan island 'about the beginning of 1840'. As soon as he arrives he speaks fluent Samoan. It is of course possible that he had lived in Samoa before this narrative commenced but, nevertheless, such fluency must be suspect. In *Cannibal Jack* he claims to speak 'the purest Fijian' but the publisher's note says that the sample of two pages of Fijian he employed in the text was 'tedious and inaccurate' and had to be omitted.[11] However, he is more knowledgeable about Fiji and its language than Endicott though the Fijian words that he uses in both texts are perhaps basic beachcomber vocabulary. If so, his rendering of complex Fijian dialogues must be suspect.

Suppose we accept the conventional ethnographic wisdom that Jackson's is an authentic account of Fijian lifeways, then consider what we are up against. In 'Jackson's Narrative', Jackson has several adventures before the Bonaveidogo one, including witnessing the cannibal feast cited by Sahlins; the Bonaveidogo episode is in turn followed by other adventures. *Cannibal Jack* commences with the Bonaveidogo episode and then with the events that followed soon after. Yet, contrary to our expectations, the succeeding events in the two accounts haven't the slightest substantive similarity with each other, again suggesting that we are not dealing with the narration of factual events but with a fictional imagination. Now let me deal with this fictional imagination in *Cannibal Jack* expressed in the events that immediately followed the adventure just recounted.

Following the cannibal feast and the lewd dances of the women there were seven or eight days of sexual abstinence and men slept in different heathen temples. Cannibal Jack slept in the temple dedicated to Degei. There he describes a possessed priest 'smashing old coconuts on his forehead, and reducing those very hard substances to fragments by the mere clutch of his right hand' and uttering prophecies while foaming in the mouth which Cannibal Jack confidently translates. I doubt whether this custom is found in Fiji; it is certainly known in South and Southeast Asia and, if it is the case that Cannibal Jack had travelled to that part of the world as he claims, he might have witnessed it there (or heard about it through shipboard gossip) and grafted it to the present narrative.[12] In any case, the upshot of these prophecies was the god demanding, among other things, the life of 'my poor prisoner'. This time also Cannibal Jack saved his prisoner by paying the priest four whales' teeth (the valued currency in all of Polynesia) 'too good to be refused by the avaricious son of the Fiji Church!' This last event provokes a humourous aside on the local missionary, the Rev. J. Hunt, which I omit.

The next section deals with the impending demise of Bonaveidogo's father, the 'arch-cannibal', Tue Macuaca (Tui Macuata). His wives were ready, and willing, to be strangled 'to accompany him to those regions, where he would have to be waited upon in the same way as he had hitherto been in this, which he was now fast leaving' (Diapea 1928: 25). One of the doomed women, a murdered Englishman's widow known as the 'Rotama [Rotuma] beauty', cast a forlorn glance at Cannibal Jack and said that she wished to run away with him. Cannibal Jack pleaded with his friend Bonaveidogo to let him have her but Bonaveidogo said that, while he was sympathetic to his friend's proposal, he couldn't help him because his half brother, the powerful Vasu Taukei, was a stickler for tradition.[13] Nevertheless Cannibal Jack did manage to elope with the woman. Soon the Vasu Taukei's men constituting 'half a dozen niggers' ambushed them, took Cannibal Jack's belongings, stripped them both naked and, after tying them with large green vines, lashed them back to back, Cannibal Jack's head downward and the Rotuma beauty in the upright position, and hung them on a tree. There was no question that Cannibal Jack would die; if he did not die 'they would revive me by feeding me on my own flesh, cooked or raw, according as their diabolical fancies struck them, and drinking my own blood!' (32). The woman would survive because she would be returned to be sacrificed to the 'manes of the old man-eater'. There follows a description of poor Cannibal Jack's suffering as he awaits death. But this does not happen because he is rescued, in almost miraculous (and improbable) fashion, by the prisoner he had saved from Bonaveidogo's tomahawk. This rescuer is no longer a 'fugitive' or 'my slave' ('kaisi') of the first text: he is now explicitly called my 'protege', 'my faithful "bobula" (prisoner)' and finally, inevitably, 'my man Friday' (36–43). Cannibal Jack now brings his new wife to his home in Natewa on the eastern side of Vanua Levu to join his other three spouses.

At several places in the story, Cannibal Jack says that he has written an autobiography of the first twenty six years of his life in nineteen copy books and that *Cannibal Jack* deals with only three of them, numbers nine, sixteen, and seventeen. In fact the book is in three parts and the episode just mentioned is in the part designated as *No. 9*. The author says that because this copy book has much blank space he now wants to copy numbers sixteen and seventeen into it, so that this composite work can be made available for sale.[14] Interestingly enough he does not tell us why he chose sixteen and seventeen when he could have as easily chosen ten and eleven, which would have provided narrative continuity. It seems to me that the 'autobiography' in nineteen books is also a fictional device. He has to deal with the discontinuity between this part of the text whose locale is the island of Ovalau and parts of Venua Levu and the rest of *Cannibal Jack* (books sixteen and seventeen) located in Taveuni with its well-known capital of Somosomo and in the islands of the Eastern group. The book has no conventional plot of the sort found in later adventure stories; it is held together by the presence of its protagonist and by the improbable adventures and funny vignettes he sketches.[15]

3 Yarning and narrative fiction in John Jackson's Fijian adventures

I hope it is not difficult to persuade the reader that *Cannibal Jack* is neither autobiography nor ethnography but fiction, not the kind of historical novel like Scott's, but a well-written and straightforward adventure story emerging from the European contact with the exotic lands. Polynesia gripped the European imagination in the late eighteenth and nineteenth centuries. The stage had already been set by Melville in *Typee* and it is possible that John Jackson alias Cannibal Jack, who was in his own way a learned man, had read this work.[16] Nevertheless, similar adventures by sailors and beachcombers were being produced elsewhere in the Pacific, as Greg Dening reports for the Marquesas, Melville's islands.[17] Along with work by those with experience in ships and islands were also the beginnings of adventure stories by those who had no first hand knowledge of the South Seas, the most notable case being *The Coral Island* by the prolific and popular writer of adventure stories for boys, R. M. Ballantyne, and published in 1858. The imaginary locale for this story is an idyllic island in the South Seas where the flower of English youth thwart cannibalism and savagery, and exemplify in their own lives both

Evangelical morality and the 'message of empire' (Hannabuss 1989). These kinds of narrative culminated in the proliferation of travel adventures in the late nineteenth and early twentieth centuries, many of which contained the word 'cannibal' (sometimes the related term 'headhunter') in the title, even when cannibalism never appeared in their contents. This was also the fate of Endicott's own journal. Endicott's manuscript was only published in 1923, forty-two years after his death, with the invented title *Wrecked Among Cannibals in the Fijis: A Narrative of Shipwreck and Adventure in the South Seas*, whereas his own read: *Narrative of a Voyage to the South Seas; Shipwreck etc In the year 1829, 1830 and 1831, 2*.

What makes *Cannibal Jack* so interesting is the aura of verisimilitude it conveys. Quite unlike *Robinson Crusoe*, there are very specific and recognizable geographical, political, and cultural details in this new writing. Yet, as Melville has already told us, his own story of the Typee has its antecedents in the yarn. The incorporation of cultural or ethnographic information into a yarn was anticipated in the Pacific by certain personae: by beachcombers, by wanderers turned on by the lure of adventure, by unsettled settlers like David Whippy belonging neither to one culture nor the other, and by sundry 'outcasts of the islands'. Cannibal Jack injects himself into this context and weaves a first person narrative as his precursors did in the Marquesas; which is what Melville also does in *Typee*. The anthropological assumption is that naive sailors writing in the first person must surely be speaking the truth. But, as Salman Rushdie says, 'in autobiography, as in all literature, what actually happened is less important than what the author can manage to persuade his audience to believe' (Rushdie 1992: 325). It is entirely plausible that Jackson alias Cannibal Jack lived in Fiji for at least two years; but this does not render his adventure 'true'. The sense of verisimilitude that *Cannibal Jack* conveys is because he, like a good novelist, can vividly convey the sense of time, history, and place that frames his hero's improbable adventures.

Does our examination of *Cannibal Jack* as fiction mean that his earlier work, 'Jackson's Narrative', is the non-fictional ethnographic account it is made out to be by ethnographers? Endicott's narrative surely should give us pause. Clunie says that 'Jackson's Narrative' is 'far superior and more truthful' than *Cannibal Jack*, even though he does use the latter as a resource for documenting Fijian warfare. Can a particular text be more truthful than another written by the same author and recounting similar events? What has happened is that while one cannot miss the fictional quality of *Cannibal Jack*, one cannot also miss the 'ethnographic feel' of texts like 'Jackson's Narrative' and the Endicott yarn. While Endicott produces sly comments that his is a yarn that parodies ethnographic narratives, there are only veiled hints in 'Jackson's Narrative' and mostly through irony. Reread the text of the cannibal king impatient to eat not-so-fully-cooked-noses and you will appreciate Jackson's comic talent, expressed in sentences like the following: 'The butcher did as he was ordered, and handed the three ends of the noses to his majesty, which he grasped hold of very nimbly, and put on hot stones to warm a little, not wishing to lose any time.' These textual complexities compel us to investigate further the genre of yarns that developed among beachcombers and settlers in the wake of the discovery of Polynesia.

Rev. James Hadfield commenting on *Cannibal Jack* says that he has complete confidence in the veracity of its author because there is 'little or nothing in his book inconsistent with what I have learned during more than 40 years of service in the South Seas' (1928: xviii). Erskine makes the same point about 'Jackson's Narrative': 'there is not one of the savage practices he there describes that I had not been either previously informed of by the missionaries, or of the truth of which I have not since received corroborative testimony' (411). This is true for the most part: the kind of stories that Endicott and Jackson narrate have circulated in this region for some time but that does not in itself endow them with credibility. The term 'narrative' itself occasionally blurs the distinction between seamen's journals and the fictional accounts based on that genre. Thus Poe's 1837 novel is titled *The Narrative of Arthur Gordon Pym of Nantucket*; Poe could 'hoax the general public' (fortunately not all of them) into believing the truth of his account, as John Jackson could gull contemporary ethnographers (Beaver 1986: 8). No wonder, because Poe employs the narrative technique of shipboard journalism and is very specific about dates and times even as he presents his hero's consumption of human flesh (Poe 1986:144–6), his later incredible, sometimes impossible, adventures in a fertile Antarctic island, 'a country differing essentially from any hitherto visited by civilized men' (193) and full of exotic landscapes and creatures.[18]

Seamen's yarns are often characterised by their utterly improbable character, being of a 'marvellous or incredible kind', as the *Oxford English Dictionary* tells us. One technique in spinning a yarn is to make the fantastic seem matter of fact. In our examples yarnsters incorporate well-known ethnographic truths which then are turned inside and out and woven into an episode in a story. Further, as in all oral narratives, we must imagine the setting of their telling. Walter Benjamin tells us that for the storyteller 'boredom is the dream bird that hatches the egg of experience' (1992: 90); and Melville speaks of 'beguiling the weary hours with chat and story' (1972: 70). In tellings and retellings and in their circulation in islands and ships these stories get refashioned in multiple ways. Jackson, like Melville and Endicott, comes from this tradition of story telling; but he is no ordinary yarnster. As a relatively educated person with an enormously creative mind he is reconverting his yarns into two types of written narrative, first in the ethnographic mode of ships' journalism and, second, with greater experience in 'scribbling', in the fictional mode of adventure stories.[19] But in doing so Jackson is giving up yarning for novel writing because, as Walter Benjamin once again tells us, 'the birthplace of the novel is the solitary individual', cut off, imaginatively or in reality, from his comrades in the deck or in the beach (1992: 90). One person who knew Cannibal Jack refers to his 'mania for scribbling', not exactly the talent of conventional yarnsters (Diapea 1928: xxi).

The fictional account that replaced the shipboard journals occurred at an important historical moment. The era of shipboard journalism was coming to an end and Captain Erskine's own narrative was one of the last. The islands of the South Seas were already well charted by the middle of the nineteenth century, and everywhere there were settlements of white missionaries and traders. The kind of ethnographic knowledge that sea captains could bring home was no longer significant; the missionaries and settler whites knew, or ought to know, more about native customs and manners. Erskine, for example, relies very little on information that he himself collects; instead his sources, like Wilkes's before him, were the settlers, among whom were the beachcombers and yarnsters we have talked about. But all these accounts have a theme that must appeal to European readers. They deal with *difference* or, as Endicott (as if echoing Poe) puts it: 'sight[s] seldom witnessed by civilized man'. Difference resonates almost clichetically with the other side of savagery found in European romanticism and which, for Cannibal Jack, means 'a yearning ... for the sweets of that exhilarating, wild, natural life, so distinct from the artificial, craving, envious, selfish, and greedy life of civilization!' (Diapea 1928: 82).

Hence in important ways 'Jackson's Narrative' anticipates the novel, *Cannibal Jack*. It is the counterpart of *Typee* in its relation to *Moby Dick*. It is a fact that Melville lived with the Typee for four weeks (not four months); but *Typee* is no more an account of his stay there than is Jackson's story an account of Fiji. In Melville's own time his publisher wanted 'authentication' of his adventures among the Typee, simply because the genre of travel narratives had to be true. And Melville himself was called the 'man who lived among the cannibals'. And while Melville had little sympathy for colonialism, or the missions, or even the 'scientific' ethnography of that time, he too met the demands of the reading public by evoking in his protagonist the fear that he might be eaten by the Typee. As the story progresses, the fears are dissipated but not fully; they are supplanted by the hero's claustrophobic dread of being held or holed up in the island unable to get out. The dreaded picture of the cannibal Typee that Melville skillfully evokes resurfaces in the rather bathetic reality of their cannibal practice – seen in three skulls, including that of a white man, hanging from a rafter; and then, in more sinister fashion, a prize of victory in war, that of a 'disordered members of a human skeleton, the bones still fresh with moisture, and with particles of flesh clinging to them here and there!' (316).[20] Jackson had much less scruple or talent than Melville, such that his seeming ethnography, 'Jackson's Narrative', contains elements of high adventure that one finds in *Cannibal Jack*. In both Jack has fights with natives; he describes great battles; in both he rescues damsels in distress; both deal with the exotic life worlds demanded by an expanding reading public and seen through the free life of the peripatetic European. Nevertheless, while both narratives contain the same ingredients, the mature novel deliberately employs these themes in a much more creative way. Thus the 'fugitive' rescued from Bonaveidogo's raid is converted into a 'Man Friday' with a crucial role in the denouement of the narrative; the 'Rotama beauty' episode in *Cannibal Jack* is a lot more interesting than his rescue of a beautifully decked virgin in 'Jackson's Narrative' whom he 'was quite certain was to be cooked with the [pile of] yams' on which she was seated (Jackson 1967: 435). Here ethnography is refurbished into story. It is a well-known ethnographic fact, true or otherwise, that when a high Fijian chief dies his wives are strangled and buried with him.[21] This is put to good use by Jackson when, in the Western narrative mode, he saves the Rotuma beauty from strangulation and this in turn provides the dynamo that pushes the narrative forward. In Polynesian ethnography there are several ways in which sacrificial victims are killed but I doubt that they would have to employ Cannibal Jack's stone anchor as 'the site for immolating some yet unborn infants to the bloody gods by dashing their brains out upon it!' (83). The 'ethnographic' text 'Jackson's Narrrative' shares the same propensity. For example: Polynesian ethnography records the 'fact' that human sacrifices are performed at the dedication of newly built canoes, using bodies as 'rollers'. However, consider Jackson's whimsical chief who uses the bodies of forty people under his protection for getting his canoes 'hauled across the isthmus' to the accompaniment of 'the demon-like laugh of their bloodthirsty victors' (Jackson 1967: 472). There is nothing inherently improbable about the corpses of sacrificial victims bound in the manner described by Jackson, but the details of what went on, including eyewitness descriptions of cannibal feasts, are as suspect as Endicott's. What persuaded Polynesian ethnographers probably was Jackson's style of 'data' presentation, though they miss his give-away irony. The enormously talented Jackson imitates the detached and objectivised style of shipboard journalism, the only 'reliable' ethnographic resource available to scholars for early Polynesia.

The relationship between the fiction of ethnography and the ethnography in the fiction can be quite complicated, as it is with the fact of human sacrifice and the fantasy of cannibalism. Take Clunie's example of the 'custom of hanging the enemy sexual organs in the sacred trees' (Clunie 1977: 39). Lieutenant Pollard, visiting Bau in 1850, noted a building to house visitors; behind this was a tree in which were hung 'several scraps of skin like scalps, but from another part of the body' (Erskine 1967: 294). Even if Pollard's is a valid empirical observation and he is correct in coyly hinting that the 'scraps of skin' were from dead men's genitals, very little ethnographic insight could be gleaned from this description. However, Clunie's primary ethnographic source is not Pollard but Jackson's vivid description of what one might call the 'genital tree' of fantasy. If one reads this text alongside descriptions of evisceration and dismemberment during cannibal feasts, it might even mirror the *corps morcelé*, the 'fragmented body', of Jacques Lacan's mirror stage of early childhood fantasy (Lacan 1977: 4): 'Certain nameless parts of the bodies were taken care of to furnish the "akau tabu" (forbidden tree) with a new supply of fruit, which was already artificially prolific in fruit, both of the masculine and feminine gender. The akau-tabu is generally a large ironwood tree, and selected according to the situation it is found in, the most conspicuous being generally preferred' (Jackson 1967: 473; Clunie 1977: 39).

Jackson's 'ethnographic information' originated in beaches and decks where it was possible to enact some of these seemingly real scenarios in humorous fashion. Sailors could enjoy such comically surreal accounts in their multiple retellings, with mimetic enactments alongside vulgar or raucous responses of an audience of comrades. And part of the fun the genital tree provoked was surely this: it boggles the mind how the action in respect of 'female fruit' could be performed in reality. Peter Brooks suggests that what is transmitted from the storyteller to the listener occurs in a special space that seems very much like the space of the Freudian transference (Brooks 1994: 51). This must be the case especially when one is narrating such things as cannibalism and castration. These narrations may have some vague connection with native ethnography but for the most part they are as much invented as Endicott's account of the old woman humiliating a corpse or Fijian girls dancing lewdly and poking at the genitals of corpses waiting to be eaten. All such stories probably receive 'colloborative testimony' in the yarns, chats, reveries (and even ethnographies) about 'savage practices', to use Erskine's phrases, as they operate in the space of the transmission-transference.

Sometimes the 'fantastic' of these accounts anticipates the stuff of later novelists like Rider Haggard. Jackson's sacred 'king eel' is a case in point. Once Jackson was conducted to a temple beside which lay a fresh water-hole wherein he saw 'an immense sized eel'. 'His body at the thickest part was as big as a stout man's thigh, and his head was enormously large and frightful, but his whole length I could not tell; they said it was two fathoms long ... he was a 'kalou' or spirit ... he was of a great age, and that he had eaten several infants which they had given him at different times – children of prisoners taken in war' (Jackson 1967: 434).[22] There is enough of the fantastic in the real life worlds described by ethnographers to seduce one to accept the truth of accounts that tap infantile bogie fears. Nevertheless, when such accounts go into Polynesian ethnography, that genre itself develops what one might call the 'ethnographic fantastic'. Thus a critical theory for this region must entail a rewriting of the Polynesian ethnography invented in the nineteenth century and after. It requires more than a scholarly deconstruction of traditional ethnographic writing. It forces us to explore the deeper question of the relation between the anthropological identity and the reality of cannibalism, at least in the period under review. In present times, however, it looks as if the Other of the nineteenth- and early twentieth-century imagination has shifted to the cannibal and the savage in our midst. Otherness itself shifts ground as the world keeps moving towards increasing globalisation and escalating national and ethnic conflicts. And yet, and yet ... 'cannibal tours' still lure jaded European tourists while ethnography continues to be haunted by older ideas of the West and the Rest and its continuing obsession with *difference* common to popular, philosophical, and anthropological doxa about the Other.

4

Brazilian anthropophagy revisited

Sérgio Luiz Prado Bellei

1 Introduction: the week of modern art and its aftermath

The so-called heroic phase of Brazilian *modernismo* (1920–30) coincides with the last decade of the Old Republic (1894–1930). The nation in this historical period, as literary historian Alfredo Bosi concisely puts it, 'was gradually developing at the cost of a crucial social unbalance' (1979: 341).[1] There was on the one hand the hegemonic domination of the owners of vast rural lands in the States of Minas Gerais and São Paulo, basically used for the production of coffee and cattle raising. Political and economic policies in the country were largely defined as a response to the political power of this dominant class. In the case of a decline in coffee exports, for example, pressure from these landowners would force the state to buy and store surplus production and wait for better times. The relative stability of this dominant force, however, was gradually being challenged by the growth of other social groups in formation: the incipient industrial bourgeoisie of Rio and São Paulo; the liberal professionals; the army; European immigrants settling especially in the central and Southern areas; a growing working class; and marginalised liberated slaves. In the Northeast, the sugar plantations, no longer able to compete with the agrarian economy of São Paulo, and Minas were quickly deteriorating, the Northeast area being as a result increasingly marginalised in social and economic terms. This imbalance of forces between the dominant class (basically rich landowners with the power of political decision) and less powerful social groups in the urban areas (working class, small middle-class, liberal professionals) produced, according to Bosi, conflicting ideologies: on the one hand the agrarian traditionalism with a world view that affirmed stasis and nostalgia rather than process and social change, and on the other a middle-class bourgeois social group resenting its lack of political power and inclined to reform and, to a certain extent, revolution. In cultural affairs, especially in the growing urban centres such as São Paulo and Rio de Janeiro, the representative Brazilian intellectual of *modernismo* responds to this complex and unbalanced political and social situation with a certain resentment and a desire for change in social, political, and cultural affairs. The desire for change was furthermore stimulated by contacts with European and, less significantly, with American culture: intellectuals in the largest urban centres were reading Italian futurists as well as French surrealists and dadaists; listening to the new music of Debussy and Milhaud; watching Chaplin movies and Pirandello's plays. Awareness of Picasso's cubism, Parisian primitivism, and German expressionism was also being intensified, and new areas of knowledge such as Freudian psychoanalysis and Einstein's theory of relativity gradually became accessible to the Brazilian intelligentsia. For Alfredo Bosi, these European developments in arts and sciences were somehow translated in Brazil in the form of a certain 'irrationalism as an existential and aesthetic attitude' that marked many of the *modernistas* (1979: 342). Of course, this response in terms of an emphasis on irrationalism characterised only the cultural elites of the urban centres. Theirs was the task of mediating between European intellectual and social life and their possible relevance to a problematic underdeveloped area in which diverse social groups experienced a profoundly uneven situation of power distribution.

The crucial *modernista* event of the early years of the twenties, The Week of Modern Art of February 1922, was clearly marked by a certain strategic emphasis on irrationalism and primitivism as deconstructive forces that would lead to the aesthetic change commensurate with the political and social changes of modernity. Irrationalism in this first moment of *modernismo* characterised the early poetry of Mário de Andrade and the proposals and manifestos of Oswald de Andrade. The two Andrades were then representative of a new generation of artists and intellectuals that took to themselves the task of defining the meaning of being modern in a peripheral country and proposed several alternative cultural agendas to be followed, among them 'anthropophagy'. The Week itself consisted of three large-scale public performances that took place on 13, 15, and 17 February 1922, in the prestigious municipal theatre in São Paulo ('Teatro Municipal de São Paulo'), featuring lectures and prose and poetry readings by young literary talents (Guilherme de Almeida, Manuel Bandeira, Oswald de Andrade, Mário de Andrade, etc.) determined to shock the public with their radically new literary production. In the evening of the second day, the poet Menotti del Pichia's introductory speech explained to the audience the main ideas shared by the participants in the Week:

> In our art we want light, air, fans, airplanes, employees' demands, idealisms, engines, factory chimneys, blood, speed, dreams. We want the noise of an automobile, in the railways of two verses, to drive away the poetry of the last of the Homeric gods who is still ... dreaming of ... Arcadia and the divine breasts of Helen in the era of jazz-band. [We want] an art typically Brazilian, daughter of earth and heaven, of Man and mystery. (Bosi 1979: 380)

The week also featured exhibits of modern paintings, drawings, engravings, and sculptures by artists such as Anita Malfatti, Di Cavalcanti, Victor Brecheret, and a concert by the composer Villa-Lobos that succeeded in shocking the audience by mixing traditional orchestral instruments with drums and a vibrating metal sheet. Audience response to the performers, both literary and otherwise, varied from qualified approval to imitations of barking dogs, crowing cocks, and hootings that, on some occasions, made it impossible for the performance to continue. The press interpreted the week's events to the public as expressions of the desire to produce a new aesthetics capable of replacing the exhausted art forms of the past with new artistic forms of expression commensurate with the challenges of modernity in the Brazilian context.

The week was followed by the production of a number of literary texts, journals, and manifestos aimed at defining possible cultural trends to be followed in the consolidation of Brazilian *modernismo*. During the heroic phase (1920–30), hardly a year would pass without the publication of at least one major modern classic: *Memórias Sentimentais de João Miramar*, by Oswald de Andrade (1923); Manuel Bandeira's *O Ritmo Dissoluto* (1924); Mário de Andrade's *A Escrava que não é Isaura* (1925); Cassiano Ricardo's *Vamos Caçar Papagaios* (1926); Mário de Andrade's *Clã do Jaboti* and *Amar, Verbo Intransitivo* (1927); Mário de Andrade's *Macunaíma* (1928). As this new literary production (determined both to break with dreams of the 'divine breasts of Helen' and with a certain

Brazilian past, that of the artificial and erudite treatment of Brazilian themes of the Romantics and the Classicists, and to recover popular forms of cultural expression) needed to be explained, the *modernistas* started journals meant to account for the new aesthetics and for their significance in a new political and cultural context. The journal *Klaxon*, founded in May 1922 in São Paulo, lasted until January 1923 and published nine issues. Its main objective was to define, explain, and expand trends only confusedly expressed in the scandalous Week of Modern Art. It is not therefore surprising that the editorial-manifesto of the first issue echoes some of the ideas presented by Menotti del Pichia's introductory speech in the Week: the need to write about the present; the cult of progress; the artist's right to express rather than copy or imitate reality; the need to learn from other contemporary forms of art, such as the cinema. *Klaxon* was followed by other periodicals, some of them published in states of the union other than São Paulo. *Estética*, founded in Rio de Janeiro in 1924, was less successful than *Klaxon* and published only three issues, emphasising the role of the young artists in the effort to modernise Brazil without forgetting either the national cultural production or the European. In *A Revista*, published in 1925 in Belo Horizonte, state of Minas Gerais, and having as one of its essayists the poet Carlos Drummond de Andrade, many of the essays deviate somewhat from the radical affirmation of progress and modernity proposed by *Klaxon* and emphasise the need for a constructive rather than destructive modernist project that would acknowledge the significance of tradition in the production of a modern, national literature. As in *A Revista*, in *Festa*, published for the first time in Rio de Janeiro in 1927, the emphasis on the significance of the Brazilian Symbolist poets indicates an effort to suggest alternatives to the radical break with the past proposed by the Week and *Klaxon*. *Terra Roxa e outras Terras*, published in São Paulo from January through September 1926, defines its difference from other trends deriving from the Week by stressing the need for a typically Brazilian modernism, one that would search for the Brazilian native character as expressed in folklore, accounts of local traditions in the rural areas, and travel writing describing the interior of the country. Finally, from May 1928 through August 1929, the *Revista de Antropofagia* was published in São Paulo, in two distinct 'dentitions' (the word that the directors choose to use, rather than 'editions'), the first running from May through February 1929, the second until the last issue was published in August. Oswald de Andrade's 'Manifesto

Antropófago', published in the first issue of the first dentition, prepares the ground for the main questions to be addressed especially in the second dentition: the question of the need to reaffirm the radical break with the past which marked the Week against all those who had deviated from it in the direction of a pact with the past and a compromise with traditional forms of expression; the question of promoting an aesthetic revolution commensurate with modernity; the question of reconsidering the meaning of primitivism in both the national and international, especially European, contexts. This emphasis on an international and cosmopolitan (rather than on a national and xenophobic) dimension of the *modernista* project as presented in the *Revista de Antropofagia* is particularly important for the comprehension of Brazilian *antropofagia*. As I shall be arguing later, this cosmopolitan bias makes the experience of traveling abroad an essential element in the life and writings of the founding father of Brazilian *antropofagia*.

The first issue of the first dentition of the *Revista de Antropofagia* includes a 'Nota Insistente' (recurrent note) with the following statement: 'The *Revista de Antropofagia* has no general guidelines or thoughts of any kind. It has only stomach' (*Revista de Antropofagia* 1975: 8). In the context of the first dentition, the statement implies primarily the intention to attack and devour those who had deviated from the radical proposals of the Week. In the context of the *Revista* as a whole, however, the stomach without ideas, ready to devour everything, already points to anthropophagy as a metaphor for the cosmopolitan enterprise of absorbing both foreign and native cultures as the means to construe a hybrid and unique Brazilian cultural identity. The enterprise, clearly hegemonic in scope, had not only ambitions of devouring selected cultural texts produced in the past of the native land and in the present and past of Europe. *Antropofagia* in the *Revista* is presented as having, on the one hand, literary but also social and political ambitions of reforming the nation. On the other hand, it is presented as the best cultural strategy to produce national identity and therefore as the one to be preferred to all others. As the *modernista* writer Waldemar Cavalcanti explained in an essay published in 1929, in the *modernista* journal *Leite Criôlo*, 'the anthropophagi with well repaired teeth cavities and dressed in elegant jackets decided to rekindle the fire [of anthropophagy], used more wood, with the purpose to convert [to anthropophagy] all Brazilians that did not want to eat people' (Cavalcanti 1929).

Anthropophagy in this sense is a metaphor for an elitist cultural strategy of identity construction based on a diagnostic of the social evils plaguing an undeveloped, colonised country desperately in need of becoming modern in terms of aesthetics, politics, and social reform. Only by this ambitious programme of reforms would the embarrassing problem of underdevelopment be left behind. The Brazilian *modernista* intellectual of the anthropophagic movement inevitably had then the experience of a split consciousness in which there was, on the one hand, the awareness of a superior Western culture as an object of desire, and on the other the awareness of the distance between this culture and the cultural and material conditions of backwardness of a marginal nation. His function was essentially to travel between these locations with the purpose of, if possible, dissolving the frontiers between them.

I will be arguing in the next pages that the significance of *modernista antropofagia* as a metaphor for identity construction outlasts the *modernista* moment and is redefined in the contemporary scenario as a desirable cultural practice, especially as a result of the influential work of Augusto and Haroldo de Campos. In revisiting the question of Brazilian *antropofagia* today, the main question to be addressed here is that of the split consciousness briefly discussed above, and of the ways in which the anxiety associated with the split is dealt with by means of a reduction of the broader national project of the earlier *modernistas* to a narrower aesthetic dimension.

2 The two meanings of *antropofagia*

Definitions of Brazilian *antropofagia* would do well to acknowledge the literary critic Antonio Candido's warning in an essay published in 1970. While admitting that one can always find in Oswald de Andrade's writings sufficient elements for the comprehension of a few principles, Candido reminds us that 'it is difficult to say what the meaning of *antropofagia* is, since Andrade never defined it systematically' (1977: 84). I will therefore begin with a distinction between two interrelated meanings of the concept, one more specifically associated with the Brazilian *modernista* tradition of 'disruption' (*ruptura*), the other more generally associated with a certain cultural ethos.

Arbitrary as these distinctions may be, the disruptive *modernista* tradition is emphasised, for example, in one of the proposed slogans of the movement: 'Four centuries of beef! How disgusting!'

(Augusto de Campos 1978: 110); or in the 1928 Manifesto's emphatic reference to 'transforming the taboo into a totem' (in Nunes 1990: 48). The dominant idea here is that of a radical break with both the European beef-eaters and the previous soft, idealised treatment of the natives in previous Brazilian cultural practices, such as that of the Romantics and the Classicists. The break is now achieved by means of a peculiar revaluation of primitivism with the help of Freudian theory. Four centuries of European beef-eating refers to the period of civilised, overdressed oppression in which the colonisers used enlightened rationality to repress and destroy the irrational, primitive cultures and peoples that practised anthropophagy. For Andrade, what was being repressed was a form of primitive wisdom that the Brazilian *modernista* revolution should try to recover, redefine, and adapt to the social needs of the industrialised, modern present as a stage in the preparation of the utopian future. Recovering and adapting this wisdom to the present would imply legitimating anthropophagy by transforming the taboo of the primeval father's parricide (the father being in this case the European coloniser) into the acceptable eating (by the colonised) of the totemised animal that symbolically replaced the primeval father. As a symbol of protective power, the totem could not be hurt or killed but was nevertheless ritualistically eaten once every year. Such a legitimisation of anthropophagy, moreover, would mark the originality of Brazilian *modernismo* because Andrade's evil anthropophagus, eater of whites and of their cultural products, was radically different from the Romantics' good, submissive savage to be converted to civilisation by the European coloniser.

Andrade's original *modernista* project as developed in the '20s and especially in the theoretical writings of the '50s (*The March of Utopias* (1953); and *The Crisis of Messianic Philosophy* (1950)) includes a utopian proposal that, although similar in some respects to Gonzalo's commonwealth in *The Tempest*, had nevertheless significant local peculiarities. Andrade's proposed utopia involved a mixture of native cannibalistic wisdom and Western modern technology. The primitive culture that, in his view, had been challenging the hegemony of European rationality since the Age of Discovery and that had been noted by Montaigne's and Rousseau's revaluation of the primitive, presented an alternative to a civilising process marked by religious warfare, inquisition, and patriarchal capitalist exploitation. The primitive native living in a society that knew no form of capital accumulation, Andrade claimed, had been for ages the basis for the construction of European utopias. Time was therefore ripe to actualise these utopias in their proper place, which was of course Brazil. The new utopia would be achieved not by simply returning to primitivism, but by fusing European technology and primitivism or, as stated in the 1924 'Manifesto da Poesia Pau-Brasil', the school and the jungle ('temos a base dupla e presente, a floresta e a escola') (in Nunes 1990: 44). Out of this fusion of European school and Brazilian primitivism, the project for the construction of a better society for all could be started in the present, that is, in the early twentieth century. This society would be matriarchal rather than patriarchal, as Andrade associated patriarchal cultures with messianic myths and economic exploitation, matriarchal cultures with social justice. ('In a society where the image of the father is replaced by society, everything tends to change. Hostility against the individual father marked by the arbitrary will disappears. In matriarchal societies, the feeling of the tribal superego is crucial for the education of the young' (in Nunes 1990: 143).) It was also marked by the primitive, happy idleness of the savage rather than by intense and productive labour ('otium' rather than 'nec-otium', idleness rather than labour), this happy idleness now having been made paradoxically possible by the advances in technology that accelerated production while demanding less human labour ('And today, when technology and social progress have brought us to the time when, as Aristotle wrote, the spinning wheels work independently of human effort, man renounces his slave condition and enters the new Age of pleasant idleness' (in Nunes 1990: 106).

The specific contribution of Andrade to the *modernista* movement as briefly outlined here has been exhaustively discussed by critics interested in emphasising the originality of the modernist revolution. The point is to insist on the uniqueness of a project that, for many, is the crucial achievement of Brazilian *modernismo*. Specialising in what Octavio Paz calls the tradition of disruption ('tradición de ruptura' (Paz 1959: 152)), this critical trend takes for granted those radical and revolutionary aspects of the movement that the *modernistas* themselves had to emphasise in order to present themselves as representatives of a profound break with whatever is out there beyond the truly national boundaries, no matter whether it is the Brazilian past or the European present. It becomes then imperative to either deny or define as irrelevant any stronger connection between Andrade's works and the work of the French avant-gardes of the '20s or of the Brazilian Romantic and Classical writers. Thus, for example, the critic Benedito Nunes goes to great lengths to prove that Andrade had not simply introduced to the Brazilian *modernistas* the Parisian versions of anthropophagy, as Heitor Martins had claimed in a well documented essay published in 1968. Augusto de Campos, while acknowledging that the 'Manifesto Antropófago' had 'a precedent in the *Journal Cannibale* and in the *Manifeste Cannibale Dada* of Francis Picabia, both from 1920', insists that 'neither the Manifesto nor the *Revista de Antropofagia* have significant similarities with its Picabian predecessors, despite the efforts of the referees of our criticism to trap Andrade in some form of impeachement' (Campos 1978: 121; cf. Nunes 1979).

Sympathetic as one may be to these passionate attempts to highlight in Andrade the radical and revolutionary aspects of the movement, the resulting repression of historical continuity makes them excessively reductive. Andrade's *antropofagia* must then be understood in the broader historical context of a certain Brazilian cultural ethos. In such a context, *antropofagia*'s connection with European anthropophagy on the one hand, and with previous Brazilian literary practices on the other, must be brought to the foreground rather than dismissed as irrelevant. It can then be read as a cultural practice aimed at displacing frontiers, analogous in many ways to the practices of the French avant-garde and to nineteenth-century Brazilian writers such as Gonçalves Dias and José de Alencar.

There is in many Brazilian cultural practices an abiding dream of a world in which frontiers should either be abolished or at least made unstable and vulnerable to trespassing. The dream, which of course involves a denial of the tradition of disruption, has as its obvious motivation the feeling of dispossession and helplessness of those who have been forcefully confined to the other side of the frontier by the powerful cartographic dispositions of centralising cultures. It is thus hardly surprising that the dominant discursive strategy used to express the dream involves a denial of the centrality of the centre in metaphors meant either to neutralise difference or to produce decentering. In the nineteenth century, the dominant method for neutralising differences was the exercise in comparative attributes between 'here' and 'there', as in Gonçalves Dias's celebrated lines referring to his voluntary European exile as comparatively deprived of natural beauty when compared to his Brazilian homeland. The frontier between the civilised and the uncivilised was then made less relevant because it could easily be translated as powerful nature versus not so powerful culture, as a nation made more attractive than the land that had produced Goethe because empowered with a sky with more stars, fields with more flowers, woods with more life, and life with more love (in Candido 1977: 312). In the twentieth century, this neutralisation of differences in writers such as Alencar and Dias would be regarded as less believable and indeed insufficient to make frontiers unstable and porous. When, in one of his many visits to Europe, Oswald de Andrade decided to rewrite Dias's poem not as a 'song from exile' but as a 'song of return to the motherland', nature is no longer so significant a contrastive value, as the modern poet wishes to return not to the woods but to the progressive city of São Paulo, and discovers in the motherland not the palm trees ('palmeiras') of Gonçalves Dias but rather the historical violence of whites against runaway negroes ('palmares') (in Candido 1966: I, 82). Alternative mechanisms to deny frontiers and produce decentering were then needed. In the late 1920s, the metaphor of anthropophagy as made fashionable by the Parisian avant-garde movements in their attempt to shock the bourgeoisie was just one such mechanism that could scarcely have been missed by the cosmopolitan modernist Oswald de Andrade.

The idea of *antropofagia* is of course closely associated with the question of boundaries. Anthropophagy is that real or imagined practice that marks the otherness of the barbarian outside the gates. After noting that Jews and Christians as well as Tupinambas and Aztecs were labelled cannibals at one time or another, no matter whether convincing evidence was produced or not, William Arens concludes that

> the assumption by one group about the cannibalist nature of others can be interpreted as an aspect of cultural-boundary construction and maintenance. This intellectual process is part of the attempt by every society to create a conceptual order based on differences in a universe of often-competing neighboring communities. In other words, one group can appreciate its own existence more meaningfully by conjuring up others as categorical opposites. This may be difficult to accomplish when the groups share similar cultural patterns, so the differences must often be invented. What could be more distinctive than creating a boundary between those who do and those who do not eat human flesh? (Arens 1979b: 145)

In the Parisian literary milieu, it is precisely one such exercise in 'conjuring up ... categorial opposites' that marks Francis Picabia's attempt to define the distinctiveness of his own avant-garde group by proclaiming the 'Dada Cannibal Manifesto' (*Manifeste Cannibale*

Dada), which preceded Andrade's *antropofagia* and is one of its probable sources. Whatever the differences between the two manifestos, both are emancipatory performances motivated by a crisis of identity. But it would be misleading to believe that the only function of *antropofagia* in these cases, or at least in the case of Oswald de Andrade, is the production of boundaries between the categorial imperatives of here and there. It would be more accurate to say that cannibalism is being used as a complex strategy to both produce frontiers and deny them. The idea of cannibalism, as Maggie Kilgour has noted, is marked by the radical ambiguity that makes it closely connected with the concept of communion, and therefore both produces and dissolves the apparently fixed boundaries between outside and inside or here and there (Kilgour 1990). This ambiguity pervades Andrade's use of the concept. His redefinition of an anthropophagous Brazilian identity involved a repetition, with a difference, of the Brazilian Romantics' dream to undermine frontiers. Whereas their discursive practice of comparing here and there amounted to a rather unconvincing neutralisation of differences, Andrade's manifesto aggressively challenges the authority of the centre by proposing a reevaluation of the opposition between civilised 'there' and primitive 'here' in which the latter should ultimately become the centre. This of course implied redefining anthropophagic primitivism as a positive value to be adopted rather than rejected by the civilised world. For my present purposes, the emphasis on the continuity rather than on the break with the past is the most interesting part of the *modernista* revolution. This means that I will be more interested in what Antonio Candido has to say about Andrade than in Benedito Nunes's or Augusto de Campos's influential work on *antropofagia*. Candido sees Andrade's manifesto as the reenactment of a characteristic Brazilian cultural practice. I began this section by referring to Candido's warning about the difficulty of defining *antropofagia* except through 'principles' derived from Andrade's fragmentary works. These principles, Candido explains, situate *antropofagia* in the context of a permanent trend in Brazilian literature from colonial times to the present. What are these principles? In two critical essays, one written on the occasion of Andrade's death in 1954, the other in 1970, Candido gives an indication of these principles as associated with the related theme of travelling and of the encounter between cultures (both in Candido 1977). Andrade's life and work, he claims, were profoundly marked by the experience of travelling. Thus *Memórias sentimentais de João*

Miramar and *Serafim Ponte Grande* deal with characters that move 'between the New and the Old World expressing the perspective of the American man'. In Candido's view, travelling was for Oswald 'a means to understand and feel the Brazilian nation, always present and transfigured by distance':

> For this reason, there is [in Andrade] little of the famous North-American exiles who were his contemporaries in France, and much of the Rio de Janeiro students who, in the 1830s, founded in Paris the journal *Niterói* and, from there, achieved a better understanding of what was needed for our [Brazilian] literature. Hence, in his [Andrade's] work, there is a certain reversibility between Brazil and Europe, which points to the significance of travelling as an experience of the spirit and of the national consciousness. (1977: 54)

Candido then proceeds to illustrate this reversibility between two places by referring to a description of travelling taken from *João Miramar*: 'The little steamboat pushed us from Dover on sweeping wheels in the middle of the night. The deck was blanketed in shadows but as we lost the English lights we found the lights of France in the sea'. For Andrade, Candido concludes, 'permanent and redeeming travelling' was 'the magical translation from one place to another, each departure giving rise to the revelation of the arrivals discovered' (54).

Candido's remarkable account of 'Oswald the traveller' defines the founder of Brazilian *antropofagia* as that particular kind of traveller that I would describe as marked by the obsession with frontiers between dominant and subordinated cultures and permanently concerned with cultural self-definition. Endlessly moving 'in shadows' of uncertainty between reversible lights which, in the case of Andrade, were the dim lights of São Paulo as contrasted with the powerful lights of Paris, the Brazilian traveller suffers from a permanent crisis of identity that, as Candido observes, marks certain periods of Brazilian social history. Travelling as an anthropophagus in the early twentieth century, Andrade repeats with a difference the previous travelling of the early nineteenth-century students who 'founded *in Paris* the journal Niterói' (italics mine). Since both journeys are devoted to the anthropophagic practice of devouring and digesting foreign discourses as a previous step for the production of national literature, they can hardly be compared to the Parisian experience of the 'lost generation'. Whatever the reasons that motivated Hemingway or Fitzgerald to go to Paris in the early twentieth century (disillusionment with the materialism of

American culture, preference for a cheaper place to live, the search for an adequate place to cultivate and refine artistic craft), North American exiles did not share with Andrade what I have been calling the frontier experience of the travelling anthropophagus.

The question of travelling and the crisis of identity are thus motifs of major significance in historically defining *antropofagia*. Equally important is the motif of the encounter between cultures and the shock resulting from it. In a later essay (1970), Candido describes the cultural shock experienced by Andrade as 'consistently expressed for the first time in the poems of Basílio da Gama [*Uruguai*, 1769] and Santa Rita Durão [*Caramuru*, 1781]'. Once again, his emphasis is on the centrality of the theme of the frontier. He remarks that 'the subsidiary motif of the immigrant, the modern embodiment of the encounter between cultures', is pervasively present in the modernist movement (1977: 85).

Historically situated, therefore, Oswald's *antropofagia* is a new version of the recurrent motif of the cultural encounter between the powerful and the dispossessed on the frontier. Working along the same lines as Basílio da Gama and José de Alencar in the eighteenth and nineteenth centuries, his proposed strategy of cultural *antropofagia*, however, differs significantly from their previous usage of what might be called the anthropophagus – to be converted to Christianity and European values to the point of losing one's identity. Andrade's anthropophagus always resists being absorbed by the foreign discourse and tries to absorb it instead. For the travelling antropophagus of Brazilian *modernismo* experiencing the encounter on the frontier, the significant move – and here lies perhaps the central significance of modernist cultural *antropofagia* – is the ambivalent strategy of incorporation by means of which the strength of the cultural other is used for the creation of a separate cultural identity. Whether, at the present time, this emancipatory cultural practice that tries aggressively to incorporate the cultural other is an effective social, political, and aesthetic emancipatory strategy is an open question.

3 Andrade and his followers: *antropofagia* as emancipation in the fifties and after

The question must be asked in the attempt to revisit *antropofagia* in the '90s because, in following Andrade's practice of the method, a significant number of Brazilian intellectuals have done their best to affirm *antropofagia* as a fundamental, perhaps as *the* fundamental, practice directed to the production of significant cultural achievements that would redeem Brazilian culture from its peripheral condition and place it side by side with central cultures. Augusto and Haroldo de Campos are today the main representatives of this effort to define the cultural practice of *antropofagia* in quasi-hegemonic terms. Augusto de Campos, in 'Revistas Re-vistas: Os Antropófagos', claims that *antropofagia* not only 'saved the meaning of Brazilian *modernismo*', but is indeed 'the only original Brazilian philosophy and, in some ways, the most radical of our literary movements ... We are anthropophagi' (1978: 124). And Haroldo de Campos suggests that Andrade's cultural *antropofagia* is today a key concept for understanding not only Brazilian literature, but also Western or at least European and Latin American cultural production. 'In Latin America as well as in Europe,' he says, 'writing will increasingly mean rewriting, digesting, masticating' (1992: 255).

The influential critical and literary practice of the Campos brothers can perhaps best be defined by what Haroldo de Campos calls 'transculturation', a practice that, following Andrade's proposals, aims at 'thinking the national in its dialogical relationship with the universal' (234). It consists, in his view, of the activity of devouring foreign discourses. Or, as he expresses it in a striking metaphor, it is the activity of 'crushing the raw matter or tradition with the teeth of a sugar cane machine, transforming sugar cane fibre into rich juice' with the purpose of producing original cultural work in the periphery, following the tradition of the best that has been produced in the Americas. As this tradition has to be invented and canonised, the Campos brothers' efforts are directed to both producing and explaining the mechanism of 'transculturation' and providing it with a tradition. Thus the Concrete poets of the '50s were anthropophagi in the sense that their work involved a mastication and re-invention of the work of, among others, Ezra Pound, e. e. cummings, and Mallarmé. From this mastication resulted literary works in which formal innovation is not only of crucial significance but indeed the very essence of all significant literary production. Haroldo de Campos claims that the emphasis on the formal aspects of language (*materialidade da linguagem*), meaning by that the emphasis on the signifier rather than on the signified, or on meaning as form, characterises not only concrete poetry, but 'the poetry of all times' (254). In his view, practitioners of transculturation in Brazil range from Gregório de Matos through Alencar and Sousândrade in the nineteenth century to Oswald de Andrade and Guimarães Rosa in the twentieth (245). In Latin America, Vallejo, Huidobro, Borges, Octavio Paz, Cortázar, and Lezama Lima are also part of the tradition of transcultural *antropofagia*.

Antropofagia as defined by the Campos brothers is both a continuation and a drastic reduction of Andrade's ambitious efforts. The idea of incorporating foreign discourses remains the basis for an emancipatory project, but now very much restricted to the production of aesthetically valuable cultural artifacts. In Andrade's anthropophagic project of the travelling anthropophagus at the frontier, emancipation is not only aesthetic but also cultural, social, and political. It is *national* in scope and reenacts by different means the similar project of the Classical and Romantic writers. The totalising ambition of this project involving both art and society becomes apparent once writings as distanced in time as the 'Manifesto da poesia Pau-Brasil' (1924), the 'Manifesto Antropófago' (1928), and the writings of the '50s related to the anthropophagic utopia are considered together. In this broader context of a lifetime anthropophagic project, Andrade's writings propose solutions for the nation as a whole in its diverse areas of achievement. Thus while the 'Pau-Brazil' poetry in the 'Manifesto' is presented as 'poetry to be exported' (*poesia de exportação*), in the writings of the '50s Andrade's concern is with an alternative social order that would combine primitive wisdom with technological development. This social order would both modernise Brazil with technology, thus eliminating the gap between developed and underdeveloped nations, and humanise technological nations by a remedial return to certain primitive values. The Campos brothers' proposal of transculturation emphasises the proposals of the 1924 Manifesto and stresses the centrality of poetic production for the global market while minimising the significance of Andrade's proposed utopian program. The social and the aesthetic are therefore now viewed as two separate projects, the latter only remaining as a valid emancipatory practice aimed at producing a world without at least some frontiers.

Andrade's anthropophagic project, in other words, proposed what Roberto Schwarz has accurately described as a 'triumphalist interpretation of Brazilian backwardness' (1987: 37). Andrade saw in the Brazilian social and cultural situation an imbalance between the actual and embarrassing primitive backwardness of a rural and patriarchal society and the social dream of crossing frontiers to become a part of the the bourgeois social order as it exists in Europe. In Brazilian society from the nineteenth century onwards, as

Schwarz reminds us, the modern bourgeois way of life could only be imitated by the dominant classes that had as their source of income not an industrialised economy, but the pre-bourgeois, rural, and patriarchal economic apparatus. Sponsoring bourgeois modernity in Brazil would then mean sponsoring a 'misplaced idea'. Andrade saw Brazilian society as paradoxically divided between two worlds, one primitive and backward, the other bourgeois and modern. But, while to that date in Brazilian history primitivism and backwardness had always been a source of embarrassment, Andrade's *antropofagia* proposes – and in this proposal resides its originality – to treat primitivism and backwardness optimistically as a positive value. Primitivism should no longer be understood as a stage to be overcome, but indeed as a valuable instrument for redeeming modern society from the excesses of capitalism. As Schwarz puts it, 'local primitivism would provide the exhausted European culture with a truly *modern* orientation, that is, free from Christian oppression and capitalist utilitarianism'. In the best of all possible worlds, progressivism would mean a social order in which backwardness would be completed by technology: 'Brazilian innocence (resulting from christianization and a superficial commitment to the bourgeois ethos) plus technology would equal utopia. The idea was to use modern material progress to jump from pre-bourgeois society to paradise' (37). This utopian project of skipping stages in the evolutionary progression towards paradise, Schwarz reminds us, is less awkward than it appears at first sight, as Marx himself had considered an analogous possibility when he suggested, in his letter of 1882 to Vera Sassulitch, that, in Schwarz's paraphrase, 'the Russian rural community might achieve socialism without the capitalist mediation as a result of the means made available by Western progress and technology' (37).

In contrast, transcultural 'mastication' of foreign discourses produces, according to Haroldo de Campos, original work in the form of a 'playful and freely associative multiculturalism, an open, multilinguistic hybridization, a carnivalized transencyclopedia of the new barbarians where everything can coexist with everything else' (1992: 250). National cultures producing these 'multilinguistic hybridizations' can succeed in making a difference in an international context and thus reveal the sociological fallacy of 'underdeveloped literatures'. Concrete poetry is one such example of the achievement of novelty and originality in underdeveloped economies. Concrete poetry was, for Campos:

> the moment of absolute synchronisation of Brazilian literature. It succeeded not only in expressing difference in a universal code [but also] ... in reformulating the code. Difference (the national) became the occasion to actualise a new synthesis of the universal code ... A new process replaced the traditional question of influences, in terms of authors and works; authors of a presumably peripheral literature unexpectedly took possession of the totality of the code, took it as part or their cultural heritage ... to reestablish its operation in terms of a radical, generalised poetics. (246)

The cultural achievement that puts the underdeveloped world side by side with the developed nations is here made possible because 'anthropophagic transculturation' is aestheticised as an autonomous cultural practice that, produced by exceptionally creative minds, transcends local history and economic conditions. Campos openly dismisses what he calls 'epic history', or history of what happens, and proposes to replace it with 'epiphanic history', or story, meaning by that the account of 'how it happens'. Epiphanic history, as he explains it, seems to be an escape from history into aesthetics, as it ultimately reduces the dimension of time to formal patterns in space. The purpose of epiphanic history would be to 'organise factual matter (texts in temporal progression) in a space of coherent constellation' in which literary works are included in terms of their capacity to embody 'textual adventures in the Brazilian literary space' (148). *Iracema*, by José de Alencar, would be included in this spatial rather than temporal history because of its linguistic innovations: it invents a poetic language made original by a process of hybridisation that fused Portuguese and Tupi. Portuguese was thus made strange and new by being contaminated with an indian or pseudo-indian linguistic system. Alencar is thus included in the canon of epiphanic history by his achievement as a master of linguistic invention capable of defamiliarising conventional discourse and not by what Campos sees as his minor achievement in socially oriented novels like *Senhora* (152). It is, moreover, this aesthetic achievement of Alencar in renewing the language that would, in Brazilian epiphanic literary history, grant him a place side by side with Mário de Andrade in *Macunaíma*, Raul Pompeia in *O Ateneu*, and Clarice Lispector in *Perto do Coração Selvagem*. Evidently, there would be no place in epiphanic history for writers committed to realism or social change, such as Lima Barreto. These voices should indeed be excluded from the canon, as all true writers are, for Haroldo, 'makers of language' (284).

What is therefore implied by transculturation is the possibility of redeeming 'national' identity through *antropofagia* as an aesthetic practice. Permanently incapable of competing with the first world politically or economically, third world nations can at least flatter themselves that they are capable of producing first class cultural artefacts. Whether this attempt to use culture as a form of redemption of third world cultures from their backwardness is really effective is a complex question that cannot be systematically discussed here. In any event, anthropophagic transculturation as a separate artistic achievement suggests the irrelevance of the utopic dimension of Andrade's *antropofagia* and marks the break between national and social cultural affairs and the production of cultural commodities. The problem with this separation, of course, is that, while it may or may not expose the sociological fallacy of 'underdeveloped literatures', it certainly reduces the production of artistic goods to the ornamental function of commodities made in Brazil to be sold in the contemporary, late capitalist market. In this context, it seems to me, transcultural *antropofagia* is as distant from Andrade's anthropophagic utopia as it might possibly be. It has not only replaced the traditional connection in Brazilian literature between the national project of modernisation and cultural practices with a contemporary version of art for art's sake, but has also dismissed as irrelevant Andrade's ambitious dream of proposing to dominant civilisations an alternative, non-bourgeois, and more humane way of life. In this sense, contemporary *antropofagia* as transculturation has something to say about the predicament of the Brazilian desire for modernisation in social and cultural affairs. Put simply, the move from *antropofagia* to transculturation might well be a confirmation of the failure of the Brazilian modernising project, at least socially and politically.

According to Roberto Schwarz, this failure to achieve modernisation must be understood as typical of the historical situation of colonies and ex-colonies. In this context, he argues, the idea of modernisation is almost a historical and logical necessity in the sense that the very foundation of colonial societies is based on the dissociation between cultural aspirations (the desire to be a part of European culture and civilisation) and local conditions (patriarchal and rural economic system). To this dissociation the colonies have traditionally responded with the attempt at modernisation in which the population should be brought up as far as possible 'from a semicolonial stage ... to the developed stage marked by decent living and labour conditions under the regime of modern, industrialized economies' (1994: 9). In this modernising process, the primitive components of rural backwardness have always remained a residual force to be either dismissed, reevaluated positively, or used as a form of imperialist protest (in the 1960s). I have suggested that Andrade's originality lies precisely in the attempt to use this backwardness, with its mixture of primitivism and absurdity, but also of attractive simplicity ('before the Portuguese discovered Brazil, Brazil had already discovered happiness' (in Nunes 1990: 51)), as a possible Brazilian contribution for a society less unjust and bourgeois, and more humane than the so called 'developed' societies. By the 1980s, as Schwarz accurately observes, the dream to rescue society by modernisation (the 'developmentist dream') had become 'a shallow concept, or, more precisely, a concept which could not be actualized because there was not enough money in underdeveloped nations'. In the new technological conditions, the necessary changes to complete the process of industrialisation and social integration of the nation had become astronomically unobtainable. The ideals of national development were clearly in an advanced process of deterioration, a process that, for Schwarz, 'marks the end of the century in countries like Brazil' (1994: 6) and constitutes, indeed, 'an aspect of the global industrialization of backward economies, as these are confronted with the growing impossibility of being incorporated, as nations and in a socially coherent way, to the progress of capitalism'. In this context, of course, the idea of nation or national project becomes largely irrelevant. Schwarz concludes his remarks about the Brazilian fin-de-siècle with the following words, that I would like to quote in full:

> In their confrontation with the new structural tendencies of disintegration rather than integration, and with the hard social reality of technological unemployment, it will not be easy for the elites to decide and to understand, even for private consumption, what is the meaning of being a part of a nation or of governing it ... The separation between economy and nation is a trend whose far reaching consequences we are only beginning to see. The question is not rhetoric: what is the meaning of a national culture that can no longer articulate any collective project of material life, and that now exists only floating as a commodity to be advertised in the market, as an attractive but empty shell, as a life style to be consumed among others? This aestheticisation of the desire to belong to the national community is also a mark of the new aesthetic situation. In short, capitalism continues to collect victories. (1994: 6)

Although Schwarz makes no reference to *antropofagia*, the break between the nation and the economy is mirrored by the break that, as I have been suggesting, is operative between the aestheticisation of *antropofagia* and the national project. In this sense, anthropophagic transculturation is an indication of the failure of the project of national development that was still alive in the anthropophagic movement of the '20s and the '50s. This is not to say that Andrade's socially oriented project was not without its problems, the least of which was probably its naivety. Its triumphalism could be a far more serious problem, as it might well be connected to the official triumphalism of the Brazilian dominant class of the Old Republic (Helena 1994: 106). In any event, for Andrade, a social project was still thinkable, while in contemporary anthropophagic practices it seems to have been made impossible. In these contemporary practices, the absence of any 'collective projects of material life' reduces cultural production to aesthetic ornaments circulating as exotic commodities in the cultural marketplace.

4 Post-anthropophagic transculturation and postmodernity

What does the legacy of *antropofagia* as tranculturation in the wake of *modernismo* and the failed dream of modernisation mean? In Haroldo de Campos's enthusiastic evaluation, transcultural mastication of foreign discourses in postmodernity is the effective instrument to produce an aesthetic universe without frontiers in which the cultural production of peripheral nations are emancipated from their 'underdeveloped' condition as a result of pervasive cannibalistic hybridity. In such a world, represented as a vast banquet in which everybody eats everybody else (a 'playful and associative multiculturalism, an open multilinguistic hybridization, a carnivalized transencyclopedia ... where everything can coexist with everything else'), the distinction between who eats and who gets eaten somehow does not apply and thus communion, so to speak, for once prevails upon *antropofagia*. This occlusion of questions of power and violence in the treatment of *antropofagia* deserves closer attention particularly in the context of the present volume, which in many different ways highlights precisely the implications of violent consumption and exploitation in cannibalism as a cultural practice of the civilised West rather than of foreigners and barbarians. Similar implications, by the way, did not fail to surprise some of Andrade's critics as well as Andrade himself. For these critics and for the founder of *antropofagia*, as Benedito Nunes has observed, it seems 'difficult to understand how ... *antropofagia*, potentially open to the glorification of force, to technological barbarism, and to Hitler, led many of its sympathizers in the direction of Marxism'. Andrade himself had been surprized by his own assertion, in an interview to Justino Martins in 1943, that the position taken in 1928 had 'thrust him to the left' (1991a: 52–3).

In a sense, the occlusion of violence in transculturation is a result of the reduction of an originally more complex and ambitious revolutionary project encompassing the social and the cultural in a merely aesthetic context in which it becomes less complicated to define a communitarian banquet. This process of aestheticisation, as Steven Connor reminds us, is typical of the avant-gardes as they progress from the modern to the postmodern:

> Most accounts of modernism stress the progressive narrowing of focus of the avant-garde; beginning as a politically-engaged force, concerned to involve or subsume the products of art to some larger or more inclusive programme (for example in the artists of the Paris commune of 1871, or the Russian avant-garde of the revolutionary period), the avant-garde gradually withdrew to a position of detachment, in a fatal splitting of the aesthetic and political realms, with the result that the political challenges of the early avant-garde could be contained in the controlled explosions of experiment with artistic form alone. (Connor 1989: 237)

Transculturation as a legacy of the Brazilian avant-garde of the '20s is of course no exception to the pattern as described by Connor. But in the Brazilian case, the process must be complemented by Schwarz's suggestion that, in the colonial situation, the retreat into aesthetics was the almost necessary result of the undeniable failure to achieve modernisation because of the specific historical and material condition of poverty. Connor refers to Adorno's concept of the 'negative dialectic' (art as untranslatable form that resists mass culture and bourgeous rationalisation) as a possible but hardly convincing way of justifying formalism in art (238). But in the colonial context, the close association between artistic production and political disillusionment deprives Adorno's concept of the political, revolutionary force of art of any validity whatsoever.

The occlusion of violence by aestheticisation might of course be taken as a pseudo-problem if one takes for granted notions of the postmodern as the condition in which a collapse of frontiers occurs between the traditional realms of the social and the political on the one hand, and of the cultural or of the sign on the other. Haroldo de Campos's definition of transculturation as 'playful and freely associative multiculturalism ... where everything can coexist with everything else' clearly echoes some theoretical descriptions of the postmodern. Thus for Fredric Jameson, as we move from the modern to the postmodern, what we are left with is that 'pure and random play of signifiers which we call postmodernism, and which no longer produces monumental works of the modernist type, but ceaselessly reshuffles the fragments of preexistent texts, the building blocks of older cultural and social production, in some new and heightened bricolage: metabooks which cannibalize other books, metatexts which collate bits of other texts' (1991: 96). As in Campos, cultural production here takes place in a vast cannibal banquet in which the rule is the consumption of all by all of texts deprived of cultural and social depth, as they are simply 'building blocks' that, though once related to a material and social reality, are today pure signifiers to be used in the construction of a 'heightened bricolage'. As in Campos, texts are here only 'multilinguist hybrizations' existing in a pure spatial dimension deprived of any historical depth. Indeed if history exists at all in this context, it is only the 'epiphanic' history that, for Campos, should replace traditional history.

What makes Jameson's account of the postmodern cannibal feast different from Campos's 'carnivalized transencyclopedia of the new barbarians' is Campos's enthusiasm for the barbarians, which in Jameson is replaced by ambivalence or, at best, qualified approval. In Jameson's postmodern cannibal feast, in other words, the question of who eats and who gets eaten becomes a problem which can hardly be ignored. For Jameson, the postmodern cannibal feast is only one of the results of late, multinational capitalism, the other being the fragmented and globalised proletariat serving the interests of the multinationals. As postmodern decentredness, whether cultural or economic, may well be at the service of a form of capitalism that has expanded its reach to an unprecedented degree, celebrations of pluralism of all sorts might be identical with the capitalist system celebrating itself (319–20).

Whatever the reading one applies to transcultural *antropofagia*, whether as an avant-garde purified of social concerns, or as a postmodern proposal for cultural production in a context in which frontiers between the social and the cultural no longer exist, there seems to be scant justification for being enthusiastic about its emancipatory potential, particularly when this potential is contrasted with the the sense of emancipation shared by the modern founder of *antropofagia*. Since national emancipation is in any case limited to the circulation of aesthetic signs, the social project of reform that was crucial for the *modernistas*, and indeed a source of anxiety for the European-oriented Brazilian intelligentsia, exists now only to be dismissed as either irrelevant or as a problem to be taken care of by discursive areas of knowledge or power (such as politics or economics) that must be understood as totally unconnected with the purity of aesthetic discourses. Anthropophagic transculturation thus implies that the anthropophagic project can still be useful so long as one is willing to dismiss its political commitment to reform, which is now viewed either as somebody else's problem or as a problem without any possibility of solution. There is clearly a limitation of scope here that can hardly be a cause for celebration. Oswald de Andrade could still believe that social evils produced by capitalism could be defeated by being devoured by native forces and somehow made more acceptable. Transculturation as the aestheticisation of *antropofagia* for market consumption, on the other hand, seems to indicate not only that the political and social questions of the *modernistas* should be treated separately, but also that, as Roberto Schwarz has put it, 'capitalism continues to collect victories', the victory over Andrade's *antropofagia* included.

5

Lapses in taste: 'cannibal-tropicalist' cinema and the Brazilian aesthetic of underdevelopment

Luís Madureira

> The filmmaker trying to make a popular cinema has ... an impossible, almost mythical task! ... Our cinema is supported by a vehicle for capitalism, a state enterprise. The contradiction is obvious ... But that is precisely the situation of the Brazilian filmmaker who has no other source of capital and tries to justify certain films, allegorical, elitist, and almost masturbatory in their form of expression, in an attempt to reconcile this contradiction. (Ruy Guerra 1988: 102)

> At this point history took such a strange turn that I am surprised no novelist or scenario-writer has as yet made use of it. *What a film it would make!* A handful of Frenchmen ... [who] now found themselves alone on a continent as unfamiliar as a different planet, knowing nothing of the geographical circumstances or the natives, incapable of growing food to keep themselves alive, stricken with sickness and disease and depending for all their needs on an extremely hostile community whose language they could not understand ... were caught in a trap of their own making.
> (Claude Lévi-Strauss 1992: 83; my emphasis)

> There ... they began to mock me, and king [Cunhambebe's] son bound my legs in three places, and I was forced to hop through the huts on both feet, at which they [laughed, and called out]: '*Here comes our food hopping toward us*'.
> (Hans Staden 1929: 80; my emphasis)

One of the grand projects of *antropofagia* which eventually 'came to naught' was the creation of a Little Anthropophagist Library [*Bibliotequinha antropofágica*] in which Mário de Andrade's novel *Macunaíma* (1928) would figure prominently (Bopp 1966: 94, 82). Despite Mário's insistent objections,[1] for Oswald de Andrade, one of the movement's founders, *Macunaíma* remained distinctively *antropofágico*: 'Whatever the outcome of the [anthropophagist] movement [Oswald was to comment years later] it can pride itself for having given *Macunaíma* ....to Brazil' (1991a: 199). Joaquim Pedro de Andrade's 1969 filmic adaptation of *Macunaíma* also amounts to an 'anthropophagist' reading of the novel. The film has been called one of the watershed moments in the 1960s cultural debates around modernity and national culture. As the political and cultural 'crisis' unleashed by the 1964 military coup was pushing the problems of modernity and modernisation violently back to the forefront of national life, *Cinema Novo* cineasts, who had hitherto looked to the social realist or regionalist fiction of the 1930s for their literary sources, began, during this so-called 'cannibal-tropicalist phase' of the movement (1968–71), to return to such 1920s *modernista* currents as *antropofagia* for answers to the 'slippery question' of Brazilian identity (Ramos 1983: 79). Faced with a sharp rise in government censorship and political repression after the 1968 right-wing coup, they resorted increasingly to allegory as their mode of artistic and political expression. And what their cinema allegorised, to paraphrase the title of a recent study of the movement, was underdevelopment itself.

Thus, in Joaquim Pedro de Andrade's *Macunaíma*, modernity, which for so many of the *modernistas* had supposedly loomed like a shining promise just beyond the temporal horizon, lapses into the preterite tense: 'Colonisation, economic expansion, migrations, ore extraction, renewed conflicts between intruders and aborigines, miscegenation; everything has already happened and these processes have left traces in the land where the hero is born as well as in the make-up of his family' (Xavier 1993: 141). The signifiers *primitive* and *modern* are set afloat in the film. They lose their referential moorings. Progress becomes 'an illusion, a bourgeois fabrication' (Xavier 1993: 150). Even *antropofagia*, wrested once and for all from its autochthonous referent, becomes itself the sign of a peripheral modernity: the 'anthropophagic' social relations defining a 'savage' or dependent capitalism (Ramos 1983: 82; Xavier 1993: 150), the 'cannibalistic' accumulation or indiscriminate consumption to which *antropofagia* on a grand scale has been reduced.

Unlike the novel's hero, who is transformed into a constellation (a conversion which one critic reads as 'a hopeful sign' (Ramos 1983: 81)), the film's protagonist is consumed by a *Uiara* (an evil river enchantress) to the accompaniment of a nationalist march by Heitor

Villa-Lobos (*Desfile aos heróis do Brasil*). He is 'devoured by Brazil' itself, to quote the director (1988a: 83), in a scene which either points to the precariousness of the nationalist project (Ramos 1983: 82) or satirises the 'nationalist myths appropriated by the military regime (and summarised in the lyrics of Villa-Lobos' march): the glorification of nature, the cult of heroism, and the tropical paradise and great national destiny myths'. On another level, Macunaíma's death allegorises the dead-end of what has come to be known as the neo-liberal economic model: the assimilation of a logic of capitalist accumulation which Brazil remains incapable of generating on its own (Xavier 1993: 155).

To be 'modern', then, comes to signify the irreflexive reproduction of an imposed socio-economic model, a mimetic – 'Macunaímic' – consumerist impulse shared by every social class which now defines the 'national character'. According to one reading, for instance, Macunaíma's romance with Ci – the novel's traditional 'Jungle Mother' figure converted in the film into an urban guerrilla fighter – signifies exactly this dependency. The film's Ci embodies not just modern technology, but the city itself. She is the imperious machine-mother whose vortical womb – figured by the elevator shaft where she and the hero first engage in violent sex (Xavier 1993: 144–9) – represents a 'gentle uterine prison' (147). She is a metaphor for the contradictoriness and inauthenticity of the condition of underdevelopment itself.

Yet the idea that modernity in the periphery cannot but be a copy already subtends *modernismo* itself. The sign of this simulacrality – or 'referential emptiness' – in Mário de Andrade's novel seems to be the word *rhapsody*, which Andrade proposes, in a 1926 preface, as the definition of *Macunaíma*'s 'style' (Andrade, M. de 1978: 221). In a well-known 1931 rejoinder to Raimundo Moraes' dismissal of prevailing contentions that the book owed more than a substantial debt to a collection of Amerindian oral narratives by the German ethnographer Theodor Koch-Grünberg entitled *Vom Roraima zum Orinoco* (1917), Mário wrote:

> What amazes me and what I regard as sublime goodwill on the part of my detractors is that they forget everything they know, restricting my copying to Koch-Grünberg, when I copied everyone ... I confess that I copied, sometimes verbatim ... Not only did I copy the ethnographers and Amerindian texts, but ... I included entire sentences ... from Portuguese colonial chroniclers ... Finally ... I copied Brazil, at least insofar as I was interested in satirising Brazil through itself. But not even

> the idea of satire is my own ... The only [original] thing left to me then is the accident of the [Pedro Àlvares] Cabrals, who, having by probable chance discovered Brazil for the probable first time, claimed Brazil for Portugal. My name is on the cover of *Macunaíma* and nobody can take that away from me. (322–3)

This open admission of plagiarism obviously undercuts contemporaneous *modernista* calls for the creation of an original national culture. It foregrounds the novel's *literariness*, its iterable and iterated textuality at a moment when oral or 'natural' language was supposedly the privileged mode and referent of literary expression. The originality of that Little Anthropophagist Library thus dissipates before the awesome totality of a Borgean archive comprising 'everything that can be expressed'. The 'primitive' is turned inside out before the 'certainty that everything [about him] has already been written', before an always preexistent Logos which finally nullifies him or makes of him no more than a phantom, a sign (Borges 1993: 61, 65).

So, if this story of a 'hero of our people' (Andrade, M. de 1978: 148) born in 'the depths of the virgin forest' (7) is intended as a narration of the nation, a copy of Brazil proper, then it can only be a blank copy, since Brazil is inevitably at variance with itself. As Mário discovered, Brazil is always already im-proper (*impróprio*), its identity an absent term:

> What undoubtedly interested me in *Macunaíma* [Mário wrote in the 1926 preface] was my ongoing preoccupation with working through and discovering all I can about the national identity of Brazilians ... The Brazilian has no character. And by character I do not simply mean a moral reality ... [but rather] a permanent psychic identity, manifesting itself in everything, in the mores, in outward actions, in emotions, in language, in History ... in good as well as in evil. The Brazilian has no character because he has neither a civilisation of his own [*civilização própria*] nor a traditional consciousness. (218–19)

In the light of this hollowing out of Brazilian-ness, the national symbolism conventionally ascribed to the 'green parrot with a golden beak' which remains to tell Macunaíma's story becomes untenable. Perched upon the national bard's head as it recites the tale out of which will be fashioned the rhapsody of the nation, the macaw appears indeed to figure something like the 'crown' or blazon of narratorial legitimation, to be the light and winged autochthon authorising the singer of tales to recount the narrative of 'our people's hero' in an 'impure language'. But which people is Macunaíma a hero of, one may ask. By posing the question I am not merely suggesting that, since the novel's symbolic structure inheres in an analogical link between two empty places (a characterless hero and a nation without a character), the site of the national in the novel is ultimately a signifying vacuum. What I am asking rather is whether, given Macunaíma's heterogenous and agonistic identifications, he can ever be so unequivocally related to 'the people' (*a gente*), whether 'the people' whose hero he is and in whose name the story is written – the source of narrative authority which the parrot would embody in the last instance – is not in effect the emptiest of the novel's empty places.

'Everything in the last chapters was written in great agitation and sorrow ... The two or three times I reread that finale ... I was convulsed by the same sadness, the same loving desire that it were not so', Mário wrote in a 1942 letter (280), as if insisting that Macunaíma's emergence as a *literary* character was conditioned by what Michel de Certeau has called the 'death of speech' (1986: 78). This is the 'ruin' of the Cannibals which Montaigne supposes 'already well advanced' (Montaigne 1928: I, 228), the dual silencing of an 'original' narrative and of its 'original' narrators. And it is this absent presence exactly that is supplemented by the parrot – the last remnant of a canopy of macaws which, in 'those far-off times when Macunaíma had been the Great Emperor' of the Amazons (148), hovered above the hero's head like an avian crown. In the end, the whole retinue of birds flies off in search of maize to 'the land of the English' (139), and the parrot/narrator itself 'spread[s] its wings bound for Lisbon' (148), just before 'the man' takes up the story. The 'national' bird is thus the residue, the resonating fragment of Macunaíma's ruined (narratorial) authority. Whatever legitimacy derives from its autochthony dissipates in its final flight to Lisbon, for the parrot's body becomes 'literally' metaphoric, a body in transit or trans-lation, in aporetic suspension between 'the depths of the virgin forest' – which for Raul Bopp represent the national substratum indicated by 'the anthropophagic arrow' (Bopp 1966: 71) – and the old colonial metropolis, the very topos of identitarian inauthenticity, the most antipodean of sites in the geography of the nation.

Like Macunaíma himself – who, by the time of his final transformation into Ursa Major, an anthropomorphic constellation 'brooding alone in the vast expanse of the heavens' (145), had of course long been a blond and blue-eyed alien – the parrot is an estranged autochthon for whom the forest has ceased to be the homeland (*país*): 'At that time Macunaíma no longer saw anything worth living for in the land ... At least he would be like all those relatives of his, all the forebearers of earthly beings ... who now live on in the useless brightness of the stars' (144). No longer the privileged place of the national unconscious, the forest arises anew as the pagan outland (the *pagus*, which, as Lyotard points out, is etymologically linked to *país* (country) (1977: 43)). It becomes the periphery, the unknown region, a site of 'non-centrality, non-finality, and untruth' (230) against which the former colonial power appears once again on the verge of reaffirming itself as the centre. Not only is the pagan (the 'native' and the 'natural') overturned as a result into an artifice of writing, but it is effectively made strange, incompatible with the identity of the nation. The 'arrow' described by the parrot's flight is finally that of the novel's language itself: the counter-Mallarméan 'impure speech' (148) into which the human narrator translates the parrot's treacherous, intoxicating, and 'completely new tongue' (147). Thus, at the very moment that it seeks to coincide with its virginal referent ('In the depths of the virgin forest, Macunaíma, the hero of our people, was born' (7)), the novel's writing begins to differ from and defer its object, to curve back – parabolically – toward the 'inauthentic' site whence the authority of the masters' voice originates. The parrot becomes, in this sense, the herald or insignia of *Macunaíma*'s technicity, a phantasmal trace, an echo of the genocidal silence which enables the novel's writing and for which that writing – the proper name 'Macunaíma' – can only be a supplement, a proxy, 'a place assigned in [its] structure by the mark of an emptiness' (Derrida 1976: 145), reverberating mockingly, sorrowfully, in the very last sentence of the novel.

Tem mais não, Andrade's version of the pleonastic, formulaic ending of Tupi oral narratives, is the colloquial (or 'popular') form of the grammatically correct *não tem mais* ('there is no more'). As Mário's own reading of the novel suggests, *Macunaíma*'s last phrase expresses a regret, an impossible desire for presence. The sentence begins as an affirmative (*tem mais*: 'there is more') and closes as a negative. The surplus (*mais*) is ostensibly crossed out by the final particle (*não*) – and yet it remains indelibly inscribed in that negation itself, for *não* is at once the doubling of and a supplement to an omitted particle, that is, [*não*] *tem mais, não*. Replicating the novel's invocation of a cultural presence that is always-already absent, this final word is at once an addition and an erasure: a supplement to a virginal world which never was, or to a world whose virginity is produced by its very dissolution.

In the 1942 letter I quote above, Mário remarked that the *modernistas* of his generation saw *Macunaíma* as '"the lyrical projection of Brazilian feeling, the virginal and unknown soul of Brazil!" Virginal! Unknown! [he protests] Not in the least! My God! A Nazi dog would be a lot more virginal!' (1978: 280). What sets Mário apart from his fellow *modernistas* is precisely this reluctance to retell the West's grand emancipatory narratives, this hesitancy, perhaps even an anxiety, which seems to grip him just before that epistemological threshold where the futural promise offered up by the available teleologies of social and technological progress begins to deploy itself:

> In times of social transition such as the present one, it is hard to make a commitment to what is to come, to what no one knows anything about [he confessed in another unpublished preface (from 1928)] ... I don't wish for the return of the past, and for that reason I can no longer glean from it a normative fable. The Jeremiah mode seems on the other hand just as ineffectual to me. The present is a dense and misty cloud (*O presente é uma neblina vasta*). To hesitate is a sign of weakness, I know. But it's not a matter of hesitation in my case. It is a true inability – the worst one – to know even the name of the unknown. (238–9)

In effect, the novel's last word erases the nativist hyphenations of national identity with the virginity of natural Brazil. *Não* repeats the expunction of the narrative's 'original' referent enacted by the winged cross that is the parrot in flight. A scriptural echo of this cross of feathers, *não* cancels rather than preserves the autochthonous narration, its very signifying structure, plunging it *in an abyss* (*en abyme*: originally a term of heraldry whose approximate meaning is 'placement at the centre' of a coat of arms). The closing phrase is thus an impure translation (a substitution) of the silenced tribal tongue, remitting us back not just to the heraldic parrot in translation, but to a hero translated into a stellar alphabet, to all the dismembered and reconfigured Macunaímas, into 'an infinite chain, ineluctably multiplying the supplementary mediations that produce the sense of the very thing they defer: the image of the thing itself, of immediate presence, of originary perception' (Derrida 1976: 157). In this way, *tem mais não* stages a kind of negative dialectics: a suspension of *modernista* presentations of 'natural man' as a surplus to modernity, to nationality, as a ghostly (*geistige*) positive term to be recuperated, sublated (*aufgehoben*) in *antropofagia*'s dialectic of the Spirit. It places finality itself under erasure.

Macunaíma's ascension to heaven at the end of the novel, his conversion into a starry alphabet ('the beautiful but useless star-shine' (144) that is 'the sorrowful destination of all beings' (252)) is thus precisely not 'a hopeful sign'. It figures not a *telos* but its splintering. It ruptures the dialectic equilibrium between 'the starry heavens above me and the moral law within me' ('the two things [which] fill the mind with ever new and increasing wonder and awe') with which Kant's *Critique of Practical Reason* closes (1993: 169). For Kant, the infinity of the heavens annihilates, in a first moment, the importance of the individual as an animal creature 'which must give back to the planet (a mere speck in the universe) the matter from which it came'. At the same time, the self's faculty to grasp or render comprehensible that

> countless multitude of worlds … infinitely raises my worth as that of an *intelligence* by my personality, in which the moral law reveals a life independent of all animality and even of the whole world of sense – at least so far as it may be inferred from the final destination assigned to my existence by this law, a destination which is not restricted to the conditions and boundaries of this life but reaches into the infinite. (169)

To read Macunaíma's dispersal into an astral alphabet as literature's inward turn is in a sense to transpose into aesthetic terms this consolatory inner infinity. It is also to avert one's gaze from the void, from 'the vast expanse of the heavens' (145) which is a sort of spatialisation of the lingering, genocidal silence repeated (or echoed) in the novel's epilogue. The reading of *Macunaíma*'s star-script toward which I am gesturing here is broached in the following section from Nietzsche's *Beyond Good and Evil*: 'It is to be *inferred* that there exist countless dark bodies close to the sun – such as we shall never see. This is, between ourselves, a parable; and a moral psychologist reads the whole starry script only as a parable and sign-language by means of which many things can be kept secret' (1990: 118). The section's opening or revelatory movement (*Erschließung*), its expression of an epistemological desire to pry into the solar core itself, pierces – dialectically – all the way through the sun of enlightenment and out its other, dark side, bending asymptotically back upon itself, or into an *Abschluß*, a closing down, a cloaking. Unlike Kant's inference of an inner, moral infinity from an outer one, Nietzsche's 'parable' does not allow for an ethically redemptive reading of the 'starry heavens'. It leads chiasmically from an opening (*erschließen*) to an epistemic outer rim, a threshold watched (over) by an exegete (a moral psychologist) whose function, akin to that of a gate-keeper or *Schließer*, is to guard the secret (the silence) of the stars, their parabolic obscurity, rather than to interpret and elucidate.

The sidereal Macunaíma is just as much a sign of occlusion, of the 'other side' of narration and hermeneutics, the topos of the unknowable and the untold, of the parabolic and tropological in the Nietzschean sense. Whatever ethical (national, aesthetic) consciousness lies 'behind' *Macunaíma*'s stellar script is thus either dismembered into 'too many things' or dissolved into 'practically nothing', into 'something provisional ... of the order of astronomy' (63, 64), as provisional and aleatory, in fact, as the legendry of constellations. As with the spatial analysis of the human body hypothesised by Nietzsche (by means of which 'we gain precisely the same image of it as we have of the stellar system'), the hero-constellation collapses 'the distinction between the organic and inorganic' (1968: 357), the corporeal and the spiritual. And the contingent celestial geometry of the Great Bear 'reflects' back upon the written page precisely the annihilation, the fragmentation of a 'paganism' which returns to shake the very ground of a Kantian universal ethics – of the Enlightenment project itself.

One of the effects of the film's allegorical structure is to narrow the terms of the novel's 'critique' of modernity. As Joaquim Pedro de Andrade himself indicates, what motivates the return to *modernismo* is not a *critical* re-examination of the movement's *acritical* acceptance of the ideology of modernism. The lessons of *modernismo* lie elsewhere:

> The *modernistas* of 1922 ... reject[ed] all imported values and techniques not relevant to our reality in favor of authentically Brazilian processes that would be, in principle, communicative and unalienating. The works produced by this movement, according to this rationale, should have had a greater degree of communication than they in fact had. Despite the good intentions of their programme, the movement's complex intellectual processes and intellectual pretension made such communication impossible. We would do well to re-examine the movement of 1922 in terms of the present situation. (1988b: 74)

It is in terms of this disjuncture between the popular artist and the people, in terms of the collapse of the revolutionary politics or the popular-nationalist project of *Cinema Novo* itself, that I think the film needs to be read. In an introduction to the film, written for the 1969 Venice Film Festival, *Macunaíma*'s director, pointing to Oswald de Andrade's 1928 'Manifesto Antropófago' as an important cultural reference point, asserts that the country's situation has not changed since the 1920s, that the same social inequality and brutal exploitation persist (1988a: 82). The cinematic turn to *modernismo* thus becomes itself allegorical. It signals not only the collapse of 'modernisation', but the insertion of the modern into a structure of deferral and repetition in which the 'new' or 'what is to come' comes to mark the 'non-place' (or *u-topos*) of an objectless desire for change. If the horizon of social transformation has been thus effaced, what then remains of the political pedagogics of *Cinema Novo*? Where have the potentially revolutionary classes which would constitute the object of that revolutionary education been relegated to?

For Glauber Rocha, one of the movement's principal theorists, 'popular cinema' seeks to replace an 'alienating' bourgeois aesthetic with an 'aesthetic of hunger'. Its objective is to 'give back to the public a consciousness of its own misery' (quoted in Ramos 1983: 76), to link up filmic production with a popular-revolutionary pedagogics which would ultimately liberate the nation from its dependent or 'neo-colonialist' status: 'The emergence of *auteur* as the name for a filmmaker announces a new artist in our time . . . The *auteur* is the one who is the most responsible for the truth: his aesthetics is an ethics, his *mise-en-scène* a politics. . . . If commercial cinema is tradition, the *auteur*'s cinema is revolution. The politics of a modern *auteur* is a revolutionary politics' (Rocha 1963: 13, 14).

In his influential analysis of the movement, Jean-Claude Bernardet (1978) argues that the aim of the cultural policies put into place by the military regime toward the end of the decade was to sever the *cinema-novistas* from the new public they had begun to interpellate. Until 1975, for example, the military regime imposed no restrictions upon Hollywood distribution chains, virtually ensuring that political or 'art' films would reach only restricted audiences. Paradoxically, it was during its second and most repressive phase that the State initiated a programme of cultural nationalism which coopted and broadly redefined some of the most recognisable components of the 'national culture' project introduced by the Left in the early 1960s. As José Ortiz Ramos argues, the nationalist dream which the 1964 coup cancelled so abruptly resurfaced in the early 1970s as the ideology of the ultraconservative, militarist State (1983: 94–5).

Thus, in 1970, the Minister of Education and Culture (Jarbas Passarinho) made the following pronouncement:

> For me, the ideal culture would not alienate people, in the sense that it would not be dissociated from Brazilian reality, but would serve to validate the country itself in national terms ... I think [this culture] should underpin the belief in a national identity. It cannot be imported, it cannot take the form of the cultural colonialism which we have for so long experienced in this country. (quoted in Ramos 1983: 92)

State intervention in the film industry increased sharply after 1969, the year when a state film enterprise (*Embrafilme*) was founded with an ostensible mandate to promote the distribution of Brazilian films abroad. What *Embrafilme* proceeded to do in effect was to exercise a much tighter control over the content of national(ist) cinema. After the Ministry of Education and Culture issued a series of incentives for their production and distribution, historical films retelling the official story of the nation and geared toward popular consumption became the rage. Cut off from the 'potentially revolutionary' classes, *Cinema Novo* turned inward in a social sense, that is, toward the intellectual élite from which most *cinema-novistas* originated. As Ruy Guerra suggests in the fragment which provides the epigraph for this chapter, the gulf between ethics and aesthetics which the *auteur* was to transcend reemerged with a vengeance.

It is in this context that the intersection between Ci's militancy and the revolutionary pedagogics of *Cinema Novo* acquires a particular relevance. In other words, Ci's presence in the film registers the impossibility of producing a popular cinema. Whether she represents a critique of the 'thoughtlessness' of the armed struggle (Ramos 1983: 82) or a 'utopian reconciliation of opposites ('alienation' and militancy, an archetypally 'feminist' threat to patriarchy and an insertion into consumer culture (Xavier 1993: 148)), Ci, who is killed along with her infant son in a bomb explosion, is also the only oppositional figure in the film, the only character who sacrifices her life for something other than the principle of material acquisition (however ambiguous her political commitment may be). In this sense, the political space she occupies intersects with *Cinema Novo*'s political pedagogics.

The purposelessness of her armed struggle, its removal from an identifiable horizon of revolution or social change, seems to prefigure a radical 'postmodern' politics from which truth, finality or unity have been effectively eliminated. Her struggle includes no programme of mobilisation, no intended public or political pupils, its objective having apparently been reduced to the provisional disorganisation of the enemy, to a retortion or retaliation (*rétorsion*): 'the ruse or machination by means of which the little people, the "weak", become for an instant more powerful than the most powerful' (Lyotard 1977: 154). The radical micrology of Ci's political struggle reproduces the displacement of *Cinema Novo*'s emancipatory aesthetics to the outer rim of national politics, the process at the end of which the 'people' have become as removed from 'popular cinema' – as much an empty place – as they are in Ci's 'autotelic' revolutionary programme.

This metaphorical erasure of the people also subtends Nelson Pereira dos Santos's 1971 cinematic recuperation of the rhetoric of *antropofagia*, *Como era gostoso o meu francês* (*How Tasty Was My Little Frenchman*). Pereira dos Santos has been called the consummate cinematic *auteur* (Rocha 1963: 82). The film, which received funding from *Embrafilme* and became one of the biggest box office hits of 1972, was produced as the Ministry of Education and Culture began its active promotion of historical cinema. The plot of *Como era gostoso* is largely based on one of the classics of *antropofagia*: Hans Staden's 1557 captivity narrative. The ethnographic material derives from Thevet's *Cosmographie* and Léry's *Histoire d'un voyage*. Montaigne's famous essay, on the other hand, informs the film's *ethos*. The historical situation reconstructed is the mid sixteenth-century struggle for the possession of Guanabara bay (present-day Rio de Janeiro) between French and Portuguese colonists. Since the Tupinambá group had allied themselves with the French, and Staden was a German mercenary in the service of the Portuguese, his dilemma upon being captured by the Tupinambá is the same as that of the film's protagonist: to convince his captors of his Gallic ancestry in order to avoid being killed. The film changes the protagonist's nationality (as its title indicates) as well as the historical circumstances surrounding his capture. (As the title also makes explicit, there is no redemptive return to Christian Europe in store for the Frenchman, his journey ending presumably in his captors' digestive tract.) The film's protagonist, then, is a mercenary either executed (thrown in chains into the sea) or banished for allegedly plotting to assassinate the commander of Fort Coligny, a French settlement in the island of Guanabara (Montaigne's *France antarctique*), which prevailed for five years (1555–60) under the ruthless command of its sometimes Catholic, sometimes Huguenot ruler,

Villegagnon. The establishment of this island colony came at the end of a decades-long struggle for control of the coastal trade (pepper and brazil-wood) between the French and the Portuguese.

As the alteration of the redemptive plot of Staden's narrative already appears to intimate, the relationship between the film and its archival sources is not merely documentary but agonistic. At the same time that it anchors itself in this colonial archive, that it elicits from it its ethnographic and historical authenticity, the film seeks, at the level of its thematics, to subvert the epistemological authority of that very textuality. The most commonplace method of undermining the validity of this archive is to oppose it to the images on the screen. The voice-over narration of the accidental drowning of several of Fort Coligny's mutinous mercenaries, taken from a 1557 letter to John Calvin by Villegagnon and read in the mode of a newsreel feature ('the latest news from Terra Firma') in the film's preambular sequence, is belied by a simultaneous scene in which the chained protagonist is hurled into the sea. This juxtaposition of textual obfuscation to cinematic *vérité* would place the film firmly within the anthropophagist revindication of Montaigne's natural man. *Como era gostoso* would thus become the apparent fulfilment of this laconic prophecy from Oswald's 'Manifesto': 'The reaction against clothed man. American cinema will inform us' (Andrade, O. de 1972: 14).[2] The exuberant frontal nudity (male as well as female) which pervades the film would illustrate a similar thematics.

This supposed 'anthropophagic' validation of natural man is epitomised in what could be called the film's epigraph, as the protagonist, now in the service of the Portuguese, captured by the Tupinambá and ordered by the *cacique* to speak, recites the following fragment from a 1558 'Ode sur les singularitez de la France Antarctique d'André Thevet' by Etienne Jodelle: 'Ces Barbares marchent tous nuds: / Et nous, nous marchons incogneus, / Fardés, masquez' (1965: 124) ('These barbarians go around naked, but we walk unknown, made up, masked').[3] By fragmenting its sources into nine intertitles – white script on a black screen – and interspersing them throughout the film, *My Little Frenchman* thus re-enacts in textual space the Tupi ethics of anthropophagy, a sort of revenge of the repressed primitive.[4] The film cannibalises its colonial archive. The latter loses its integrity and is 're-membered' as an assimilated part of a new (cinematic) whole. In this sense, the film would seek to effect the same reversal of historiographic itineraries as *antropofagia*: 'We are against all the histories of men that begin in Cape Finisterre'

(Andrade, O. de 1972: 16). Indeed, its very historical point of departure – a moment of conflict and indecisiveness as to the ultimate (colonial) identity of Brazil – seems to suggest that the Catholic and Portuguese components of the Brazilian 'character' are in fact the result of a historical accident.

Nevertheless, in light of the 'artificiality' of cinematic representation, the film's validation of nudity as truth is evidently ironic. It is the actors, in other words, the 'Indians of Ipanema', to use the director's own expression, who walk around naked.[5] Their elaborately adorned bodies function in this instance as the costumes or masks appropriate to their role as naked savages. There is, in this sense, no difference between nudity and disguise. The film's deployment of the trope of nakedness inserts its presentation of the primitive within the same rhetorical structure which registers his destruction, within a cycle of reproductions and re-presentations which finally divests *Como era gostoso* of its historicity. Other than the writing that retains the trace of the people who hold the cultural secret the film sets out to recover, the film has no referent at all. It is this cultural death which is imprinted in the masked nudity of the 'Indians from Ipanema', and ultimately in the film's historiographic project itself. In effect, the complicity of this project with the violence that it seeks simultaneously to denounce and overturn is inscribed in the very 'interstices' of the filmic space. The return to an 'original' colonial situation thus comes to be performed not under the sign of History but Allegory. Unlike its model, which, as Oswald insists, constitutes a *Weltanschauung*, anthropophagy in the film plays a self-consciously 'prescriptive' role. It outlines a strategy for entering modernity on nationalist or local terms, for an aggressive or 'revengeful' modernisation radically opposed to the conservative or neo-liberal model of development. *Antropofagia* allegorises what Oswald once named the 'third solution' (1991a: 236), in this instance, an alternative model to the unequal exchange defining the economic and cultural relations between centre and periphery, a de-linking from global capitalism which is generally coterminous with the politics of national liberation underpinning Glauber Rocha's call for an 'aesthetics of hunger'.

This is nonetheless a political recipe whose rhetorical conceit is underscored in the scene of the Frenchman's capture by the Tupinambá. The Portuguese soldiers' response to the 'linguistic test' to which the *cacique* Cunhambebe submits them is to recite culinary recipes – a speech act which reaffirms their national identity in folkloric or stereotypical terms (since it evinces the proverbial gluttony of the Portuguese), and simultaneously guarantees and foreshadows (that is 'prescribes') their eventual dismemberment and consumption. The black humour of the sequence is evident enough. At the same time, the juxtaposition of these recipes to the Frenchman's ethical imperative (the fragment from Etienne Jodelle's 'Ode') bares the film's device, as it were. The sequence discloses the prescriptive aim or pedagogics of the film's political allegory, while establishing an ironic distance with that same project. The irony arises not only from the inevitably inauthentic primitive world recreated in the film, but from the assertion of the inauthenticity (or autonomous aestheticism) of its 'popular' aesthetics. In the final instance, then, the anthropophagy of *Como era gostoso* unveils not an ethics but an aesthetics. In a reversal of Glauber Rocha's formula, it returns precisely to the 'alienating' bourgeois aesthetics which, according to Rocha, the cinematic *auteur* should transcend.

What appears to link up the film with *modernismo* is precisely this conventionally modernist inward turn. *Como era gostoso* is thus split between the presentation of a political allegory and an underlying ironic acknowledgment of the latter's technicity, of the irreducible aestheticism of its revolutionary ethics. An example of this irony is the sexual pun in the film's title. (The figurative sense of 'to eat' (*comer*) in Portuguese is 'to copulate'; 'tasty' (*gostoso*) has therefore a clearly erotic connotation.) The phrase expresses both a symbolic anthropophagic vengeance and a female sexual desire. The two meanings are in fact indissoluble, since the phrase is presumably articulated from the perspective of Sebiopepe, the Tupi widow who takes the Frenchman as a consort before devouring him, or, more specifically (if one gives credence to Thevet's 'ethnography'), before eating his 'shameful parts' (1953: 203).

The title's evocation of the *vagina dentata* remits us to the original colonial encounter, to the voracious native woman whose exuberant, overpowering sexuality Vespucci finds at once menacing and fascinating. The Frenchman's native bride is the antithesis both of the 'naked Eves' of Vaz de Caminha's 1500 Letter of Discovery and those of the eugenic narratives of the 1920s. She is the site of a primitive revenge, and the limit of European penetration – the title's *Was* is significant in this respect. She figures a resistant natural world, a native body which refuses to yield to technological transformation, which will (re)produce only on its own terms. The protagonist is thus consistently thwarted in his efforts to present himself either as Sebiopepe's saviour or as a *Caraíba* (a European version of the autochthonous technological hero), and the film's penultimate shot is a close-up of Sebiopepe consuming the Frenchman. At the same time, however, the phrase could be spoken by the implied spectator.

It is either an aesthetic judgment or an expression of desire for a nude actor on the screen. The anthropophagic politics of the film become a self-conscious joke, in other words, and the reconstruction of the primitive world is once again revealed as a masquerade. The luminous writing of the intertitles thus becomes the only space in the film where the primitive lingers: an ironic reference to the star-script which, to paraphrase Mário de Andrade, is the final sorrowful destination of the Tupi being. The last intertitle, which functions as the film's epilogue, is a fragment from Governor Mem de Sá's 1560 letter to the Portuguese Regent describing the amassed bodies of the massacred 'Tupiniquin covering more than five leagues of shoreline'. The quote is both a historical beginning (1560, the year when the French were expelled from Guanabara, also marks the beginning of the process leading up to the consolidation of Portuguese colonial rule), and the last word, the epitaph to a Tupi culture reduced to the 'useless shine' of spectral Anthropophagi upon a silver screen.

6

Ghost stories, bone flutes, cannibal countermemory

Graham Huggan

> The Ghost is the fiction of our relationship to death.
> (Cixous 1976: 542)

> Face to face with the white man, the Negro has a past to legitimate, a vengeance to exact; face to face with the Negro, the contemporary white man feels the need to recall the times of cannibalism.
> (Fanon 1967: 225)

Moving between literature and history, this paper has three objectives. First, it seeks to forge an unholy alliance between the cannibal and the ghost, and to explore their interworkings in the context of revisionist Caribbean history. Second, it examines the cannibal and the ghost as textual mediators, as means by which Caribbean writers reimagine their European literary ancestry. And third, it charts the attempt through the shape-shifting cannibal/ghost alliance to transform the orthodox, largely negative, perception of Caribbean history, and to set up a countermemory to the hegemonic European record. The primary texts are the creolised ghost stories of two modern Guyanese writers: Edgar Mittelholzer's *My Bones and My Flute* (1955) and Wilson Harris's *Palace of the Peacock* (1960). In both of these stories the ghost – the 'uncanny cannibal' – has a dual function, reasserting the presence of a past (or pasts) that had previously been repressed while estranging that past and converting it into forms that sublimate material exploitation.

1 Uncanny cannibals

It is little wonder that Derek Walcott, the Caribbean's best-known poet, begins an essay on the region's past by citing Joyce's familiar epigraph, 'History is the nightmare from which I am trying to awake'. For the Caribbean region is haunted by ghostly presences, reminders of a history seen as loss, distress, defeat. Walcott takes as his artistic task the deliverance from this collective trauma:

> The New World originated in hypocrisy and genocide, so it is not a question for us of returning to an Eden or of creating Utopia; out of the sordid and degraded beginning of the West Indies, we could only go further in indecency and regret. Poets and satirists are afflicted with the superior stupidity which believes that societies can be renewed, and one of the most nourishing sites for such a renewal, however visionary it may seem, is the American archipelago. (Walcott 1974: 13)

Walcott drives out the ghosts that crowd in upon ancestral memory, clearing the space for history to direct its gaze toward the future. Other writers, however, from the Caribbean region – a region defined as much by discursive ties as by history or climate – have found themselves repeatedly, even obsessively, drawn back to the past. Kamau Brathwaite, Edouard Glissant, Alejo Carpentier, Wilson Harris: all of these writers have explored the hidden recesses of Caribbean history, rejecting the Eurocentric claim that the region has no past to speak of, and uncovering instead the 'traces of historical experience [that have been] erased from the collective memory of an oppressed and exploited people' (Webb 1992: 7).

Caribbean literature, in this context, enacts a struggle over origins. Where does the past begin? What might be seen as the region's heritage? And can this heritage – acknowledged as multiple, fluid, and syncretistic – be reinvented to suit the purposes of emancipation and renewal? (Caribbean cultural origins clearly predate the European record, stretching back beyond 'discovery' and the history of slavery to engage with folk mythologies that have survived in adapted forms despite the decimation of both the islands' and the mainland's indigenous peoples.) Modern Caribbean writing participates in a process of perceptual transformation: it submits itself to its own haunting but with a view to overcoming it, and with an aim to convert a spectral past into a speculative future.

It seems appropriate, then, that among the region's most prolific forms is the ghost story, or a hybrid variant of it, at least, derived both from African/Amerindian oral sources and from the repository of Western (Euroamerican) literary fantasy. This paper deals with two novel-length ghost stories set in 'ancestral' Guyana: an area of the Caribbean whose complex racial intermixture owes both to 'mestizo' (Euro/Amerindian) and 'mulatto' (Euro/African) forms of cultural creolisation.[1] Before turning to the works themselves, however, a few prefatory remarks seem necessary, both on the properties of the genre and its ambivalent stance to history.

Ghost stories, according to Gillian Beer, 'elide the distance between the actual and the imagined': they speak, literally and figuratively, of an intrusion into the everyday world. In ghost stories, says Beer, 'the fictional takes place in the everyday: it takes space, and it is this usurpation of space by the immaterial which is one of the deepest terrors released by the ghost story ... [G]host stories are to do with the insurrection, not the resurrection of the dead' (1978: 260).

The return of the undead may act as a trigger for personal memories; for the ghost, as Hélène Cixous reminds us, is 'the direct figure of the uncanny' (1976: 542). Ghosts are uncanny in the Freudian sense that they register the familiar: they belong, as Freud puts it in his essay on 'The "Uncanny"', to 'that class of the terrifying which leads us back to something long known to us' (1959: 369–70). Yet the ghost, and its ambiguous return, also have far-reaching social consequences. History is reintroduced into the arena of the present, but in such a way that it threatens the fixity of existing social structures.[2] Ghosts bring with them a knowledge other than that ratified by social charter: they make a mockery of the institutional respects we pay to satisfy the dead. And to keep ourselves separate from them – for ghosts have contempt for boundaries, for all our cherished social distinctions. They walk through historical walls, co-existing with the present, and literalising the memories we consecrate in metaphor in order to contain them. (Ghosts, after all, are indiscreet: they scorn the blandishments of the tombstone, or the solemn rites that attend the passing of the funeral hearse.) Ghosts bring the past into our midst, that we might recognise it. But they also estrange the past: their relationship to the history that they reinstate is inherently uncertain. What renders the ghost intolerable, according to Cixous, is not so much that it is an announcement of death nor even the proof that death exists, since it 'announces and proves nothing more than [its] return. What is intolerable is that the [g]host erases the limit which exists between the two states, neither alive nor dead; passing through, the dead man returns in the manner of the Repressed. It is his coming back which makes the ghost what he is, just as it is the return of the Repressed that inscribes the repression' (543).

Ghosts are the unwelcome carriers of an occluded history; they show us how we screen, and thus protect ourselves from, the past. They function, to be sure, as agents for the reconstruction of historical memory. But they are double agents: they are working for the 'other' side. They make us recognise another past to the one we might have chosen: they transform, not the past itself but our 'normal', socialised perception of it.

This set of preliminary observations on the disruptive properties of ghosts suggests that ghost stories might be effective as vehicles of historical revisionism, or as means by which repressed histories can be brought back to the surface. It also suggests that ghost stories might help construct a kind of countermemory, in Foucault's sense of the transformation of (linear) history into a different form of time.[3] In the Caribbean context, this need to transform the past becomes an urgent imperative. Denis Williams states the dilemma well:

> We are all shaped by our past; the imperatives of a contemporary culture are predominantly those of a relationship to this past. Yet in the Caribbean and in Guyana we think and behave as though we have no past, no history, no culture. And where we do come to take notice of our history it is often in the light of biases adopted from one [racially] thoroughbred culture or another, of the Old World. We permit ourselves the luxury . . . of racial dialectics in our interpretation of Caribbean and Guyanese history and culture. In the light of what we are this is a destructive thing to do, since at best it perpetuates what we might call a filialistic dependence on the cultures of our several racial origins, while simultaneously inhibiting us from facing up to the facts of what we uniquely are. (quoted in Harris 1970: 13)

Ghost stories in the Caribbean thus often have a dual purpose: they revive in order to dispel the ghosts of a past conceived by Europe, a history couched in the paralysing terms of dispossession and defeat (Huggan 1994). At the same time, they reclaim a past anterior to European conquest, a history whose outlines blend with those of originary myth, and whose ghosts are not horrifying apparitions from another, unwanted era but welcome catalysts for the recovery of a buried ancestral consciousness. Ghost stories, like ghosts themselves, shift the shape of the past(s) that they engage with; they are co-opted, in the Caribbean, into a discourse of conversion, whereby a history of exploitation is estranged even as it is confronted, and a pattern is established for the transformation of individual trauma into the inspiring recollective force that bonds a whole community.

This discourse of conversion goes by many names. It might refer, for instance, to Kamau Brathwaite's project of cultural creolisation, whereby the appeal to ancestors other than the European (such as the African and Amerindian) involves the writer in a 'journey into the past and hinterland which is at the same time a movement of possession into present and future' (1984a: 42). Or then again it might take in Denis Williams's model of catalysis, whereby an interaction between the region's racial groups qualifies each other's self-image, and a history of race-based conflict is turned into a valuable source of artistic creativity. For Wilson Harris, too, adversarial contexts can be productive. Harris's experimental fictions are exercises in what he calls a 'dialectic of alteration': historical antagonisms are converted into a volatile symbiosis (Huggan 1994), with the Old World and the New nurturing each other's creativity; meanwhile, history itself is turned into a set of 'architectural complexes', spatial frameworks offering alternatives to a linear vision of time and to a 'block' perspective on the past that blindly serves self-interest – the obsessive pursuit of material goals that only strengthen social divisions; the obstinate refusal to acknowledge 'visionary' schemes other than one's own (1970: 32). There is an ethical dimension, then, to all of these projects of conversion, which present a challenge to the teleology of imperial conquest, asserting in its place a dialectical or processual view of (cross-)cultural interchange. In proposing what Harris calls 'a treaty of sensibility between alien cultures' (19), each writer recognises the need for continuing self-critique. Caribbean counterdiscourses (in Helen Tiffin's useful gloss on Harris) 'evolve textual strategies which continually "consume their own biases" [Harris's term] at the same time as they expose and erode those of the dominant discourse' (1987: 18). Harris's arresting metaphor of 'consuming one's own biases' is linked throughout his work to the symbolic practice of cannibalism. Cannibals, according to Harris, do not merely feed on the dead; they absorb the dead into themselves, drawing on their enemies' strength but suggesting, at the same time, that the declaration of material hostilities might eventually give way to an uneasy metaphysical truce. Harris explains this process further in his preface to *The Guyana Quartet*. Here he refers the reader to the Carib/cannibal bone flute, an instrument traditionally made from the hollowed-out bones of the Caribs' war-victims and whose music, in releasing the ghosts of victories past, works to sublimate them. The relevant passage is as follows:

> The Carib bone flute was hollowed out from the bone of an enemy in time of war. Flesh was plucked and consumed and in the process secrets were digested. Spectres arose from, or reposed in, the flute. [The anthropologist Michael] Swan identifies this flute of soul with 'transubstantiation in reverse.' In parallel with an obvious violation ran therefore, it seems to me, another subtle force resembling yet differing from terror in that the flute became the home or curiously *mutual* fortress of spirit between enemy and other, an organ of self-knowledge suffused with enemy bias so close to native greed for victory. (Harris 1985: 9–10)

Harris's language is characteristically metaphor-laden and oracular. Peggy Sanday's anthropological analysis helps put it in perspective: 'When projected onto enemies, cannibalism ... becomes the means by which powerful threats to social life are dissipated. By consuming enemy flesh one assimilates the animus of another group's hostile power into one's own' (1986: 6). Harris's description of the bone flute also reflects on Dean MacCannell's more speculative distinction (derived from Montaigne) between economic and symbolic cannibalism: the former motivated by the selfish desire for material gain; the latter, paradoxically, by the mutual need for human kinship.[4]

The flute, which Harris seems to see as an organising metaphor for his work, integrates the cannibal and the ghost – the phobic creatures of a paralysed unconscious – into an alchemical process where they act in tandem as catalysts of transformation. The flute works to sublimate the physical violence it embodies; its spectral music provides both for the rehearsal of cannibal urges and for their translation into an ephemeral form that dematerialises the act of conquest. The flute functions as a mnemonic device whose range is atavistic – to play it is to summon the ghosts of an ancestral past into the present, submitting oneself to one's primal fears and fantasies of the 'other'. It embodies the cannibal act but then converts it into ghostly music; in the process the threat of cannibal destruction is not diminished, but is dispersed in the re-enactments of former cannibal confrontations, dismemberments now re-membered in a disembodied form. The flute transforms the cannibal, the West's irreducible 'other', into a free-floating manifestation of the Freudian uncanny. This cannibal ghost is a blueprint for fantastic liminality: neither alive nor dead, both physical and spiritual, it absorbs the 'other' only to reassert it as a powerful 'absent presence'.[5] By trading on the interplay between containment and dispersal – between the incorporated body and the unassimilable ghost – the bone flute records and regulates the violence of the past while acknowledging that this violence can never be fully controlled.

2 Letting in the demons

In Mittelholzer's *My Bones and My Flute* (1955), the eponymous flute and its ghostly music are associated with the Dutch planter Jan Peter Voorman, victim of a slave revolt in mid eighteenth-century (British) Guyana. Voorman's ghost still roams abroad, it seems, hounded by demonic spirits – spirits whose presence his magic flute had originally summoned, but who now leave him, and all those who associate with him, no rest. A parchment he leaves for posterity draws its readers into a pact: either they must find his bones and flute and give them a Christian burial or they, too, will be lured by the flute's nefarious music to their death. Enter the novel's protagonists, the aristocratic mill-owner and part-time antiquarian Ralph Nevinson, and the narrator Milton Woodsley, an aspiring writer and painter and, like the Nevinsons, from old Coloured – and thus respectable – Guyanese stock. Billed both as a 'good thrilling sort of old-fashioned ghost story, with the mystery solved at the end' and as a 'true record, including nothing that might be attributed to [its narrator's] imagination' (5–6), *My Bones and My Flute* tells the story of Woodsley's and the Nevinsons' quest to lay Voorman to rest. At the same time, the novel reads as an allegory of Guyana's mixed racial ancestry and as an attempt to come to terms with the country's violent colonial past.

From the outset, Mittelholzer's ghost story acquires racial dimensions. 'I curse these black wretches,' Voorman says of the slaves who work for him, 'even as I curse the Blacker Ones', the demons his flute has summoned (29). These demons turn out to be a cross between neanderthals and extra-terrestrials; they shift in shape and form: now ghosts, now beasts, now cannibal vampires. They are, in short, a composite of the white man's racial phobias, phobias linked in Voorman's case to the justified fear of insubordination, and in Woodsley's to the guilt instilled by a puritanical religious education. (The Day of Judgement, says Woodsley's grandmother, might come at any moment, with 'the Righteous lifted as they sleep and transported up to Heaven while the Unrighteous are cast into Eternal Flames with Satan and his *Black Angels*' (57–8, my emphasis).)

The Blacker Ones also have another, literary, ancestry. In recalling the ghostly predators of Poe's and M. R. James's fictions, they remind us of the paranoid racial myths endemic in Western fantasy.[6] James's *Ghost-Stories of an Antiquary* is cited as an intertext, as is, almost inevitably, Poe's *Tales of Mystery and Imagination*. And another text of Poe's appears to lie beneath the surface: *The Narrative of Arthur Gordon Pym*, with its spectral visions of Blackness and its projections of the writer's pathological fears of Southern slave rebellion.[7] *My Bones and My Flute* locates itself squarely within this dubious tradition; but it does so not to reinforce the white man's racial fantasies but to reassess their function within a specific historical context. And the context here is that of British Guyana's colonial history – a record of the drudgery, cruelty, and violence of the plantations, but also of the hybrid cultural forms thrown up by that encounter.

Kamau Brathwaite distinguishes usefully here between two forms of New World creolisation: 'A mestizo-creolization, the interculturation of Amerindian and European (mostly Iberian) and located primarily in Central and South America; and a mulatto-creolization, the interculturation of Negro-African and European (mainly Western European) and located primarily in the West Indies and the slave areas of the North American continent' (1974b: 30). Guyana's history intersects these two different forms of cultural creolisation. In *My Bones and My Flute*, Woodsley and the Nevinsons are the 'olive-coloured' products of racial intermixture: their ancestors, Woodsley tells us, go back to the late eighteenth century, after which time they acquired the 'strain of Negro slave blood that runs in them today' (8). It is significant, though, that each of them downplays this aspect of their cultural ancestry, choosing instead to emulate their (white) European forebears and accepting their 'superior' status within a (post)colonial pigmentocracy.

It is tempting, in this context, to read the novel as an allegory of acculturation and of the 'lactification complex' that afflicts Caribbean societies.[8] Such a reading might account for the Nevinsons' condescension toward their black and/or Indian workers; it might also help explain Mr. Nevinson's and Woodsley's taste for European art. Most importantly, it might rationalise their joint decision to save the planter from perdition: for Voorman's blood is in their veins – theirs is a common history. Woodsley and the Nevinsons stake their claim on a European ancestry; yet as they stave off Voorman's demons, other ghosts come into their midst. These are their 'other' ancestors, the enslaved blacks on the plantations, and their 'absent presence' within the text signals a return of the Repressed. By the end of the novel, Woodsley and the Nevinsons are confronted with a subaltern history; they are made to recognise the past they had disclaimed as being their own.

Voorman ends his diary, which also ends the novel, with a premonition of slave rebellion. Still haunted by demons – the Blacker Ones – Voorman becomes increasingly desperate:

> Last night I heard them speaking in varied languages – languages I know not and yet which I myself spoke. I heard French and German and English and Italian and other tongues I could not identify... They babbled about me in a clamour too deafening to describe. They fumed and wreathed [*sic*] and turned in spirals . . . and the air thundered about me ... A catastrophe threatens. I sense it in the air. I am a thwarted, craven soul, a human tottering on the edge of ultimate darkness. To whom, to what, must I turn for salvation? (174)

Voorman's demons speak in European tongues: they ape the coloniser's language. Yet they also foreshadow an imminent end to white planter autocracy – they usher in, like Poe's Madeline, the downfall of an era, as the white man's fears of violent black revenge are reconfirmed. For Voorman's necromancy converges with the Berbice Slave Rebellion – an uprising that results in his own death and the slaughter of other white families. The white man's spell is broken; the otherworldly Blacker Ones – the emanations of a troubled unconscious – bring with them the ghostly tidings of a decisive break in history. (The date listed for the rebellion – 1763 – is all the more ironic in that it coincides with the year of the post-Seven Years War Caribbean Peace Treaty.[9] Thus, at the very apex of British mercantile achievement comes a revolt that prefigures the fall of their, among other white, fortunes in Guyana.)

Mittelholzer's ghost story, then, seems to clear the space for an emancipatory history. It drives out one kind of demon in order to let in another; but these latter 'demons' are not just the incubi of white colonial history, they are the catalytic agents of revolutionary change.[10] In laying Voorman's bones to rest and relieving themselves of the White Planter's Burden, Woodsley and the Nevinsons are forced to recognise a history they had previously suppressed. Mittelholzer, similarly, delivers himself from his white literary ancestors, acknowledging the influence of Poe and James but taking possession of them, either to turn their ghosts against themselves and render them insubstantial or to redeploy their racial fears as a means of reclaiming black agency.

My Bones and My Flute turns the tables on its literary predecessors. Rather than submitting to a Western (Euroamerican) 'anxiety of influence', Caribbean texts such as Mittelholzer's use the conventions of the ghost story to expose the West to the anxieties of its own imposed authority.[11] The flute – a Prosperan wand – is a generator of illusion; but it is equally deceptive for the person who controls it. Its primary function in the novel seems to be as a conductor for Voorman's evil thoughts and intentions; turning against him, it eventually becomes the instrument of his perdition. The flute also provides the means, however, for Voorman's own salvation and for the reconciliation of his followers to an 'inconceivable' past. Its function is therefore similar to that of the Carib/cannibal bone flute, even though Voorman's flute is made of metal and has no obvious 'tribal' affiliation. (Its closest symbolic connection, perhaps, is to the slave-owner's branding-iron – on more than one occasion, the invisible flute sears its victim's flesh.) The bone flute remains peripheral to Mittelholzer's text: it is a spectral presence hovering around the novel's title credits. Nonetheless, the flute (like Mozart's, to which it more obviously alludes) works a generalised kind of intertextual/cultural alchemy.[12] It releases the collective ghosts of Guyana's ancestral past; not all of these ghosts are a figment of the white imagination. *My Bones and My Flute* is, after all, a creolised form of the Western ghost story: it owes as much to Amerindian as to European sources (see 41–2; 61–2). It is precisely in the syncretism of its forms that Mittelholzer's novel works its magic: in the weaving together of disparate, nominally hostile creative traditions, and in the production of a countermemory to Caribbean material history – one which willingly rehearses the traumas of a brutal past, but then transmutes them into a vision of change that moves beyond catastrophe (174).

3 Transubstantiating hostility

In *My Bones and My Flute,* Woodsley's and the Nevinsons' quest is eventually cathartic: it allows them to confront and accept a hidden aspect of their past by staging the in/resurrection of their ghostly slave ancestors. In Harris's *Palace of the Peacock,* ancestral memory stretches back further, taking in the European myth of the New

World El Dorado and uncovering behind it a rich array of different 'sources'. Ostensibly, Harris's novel recounts the quest for El Dorado within the context of a latter-day journey to (and beyond) an Amerindian Mission. The plot, however, like the journey, is impossibly convoluted, not least because Harris's novel oscillates between past and present. The journey takes place in a dreamtime where history merges with myth and legend, and where the fated expeditions of de Berrio, de Vera, and Raleigh are interlaced with creation myths from both Amerindian and Judaeo-Christian traditions. El Dorado is the meeting-place, the Source of all these sources. But the City of Gold remains, as of course it must, just out of reach; and each successive quest to find it is condemned to re-enact defeat. V. S. Naipaul has captured well the compulsiveness of the delusion, as the 'original' story passed from mouth to mouth, leaving more deaths in its wake:

> There had been a golden man, el dorado, the gilded one, in what is now Colombia: a chief who once a year rolled in turpentine, was covered in gold dust and then dived into a lake. But the tribe of the golden man had been conquered a generation before Columbus came to the New World. It was an Indian memory that the Spaniards pursued; and the memory was confused with the legend, among jungle Indians, of the Peru the Spaniards had already conquered. (1984: 18)

For Naipaul, El Dorado presents a cautionary tale of repeated New World failure. The story outruns, outlasts, and eventually engulfs its actors, revealing the spiritual vacuum behind their dreams of material wealth. Harris's view of El Dorado is, however, somewhat different. He sees an 'instinctive idealism' associated with the adventure, even though he recognises that these ideals usually give way to greed and cruelty.[13] El Dorado represents a chain of contradictory correspondences; in uncovering these correspondences in *Palace of the Peacock*, Harris gestures toward the reversal 'of the "given" conditions of the past, freeing oneself from catastrophic idolatry and blindness to one's own historical and philosophical conceptions and misconceptions which may bind one within a statuesque present or a false future' (1967: 36).

The ghost is a primary instrument of this historical reversal; for the mixed-race crew that sets up-river in search of the Mariella Mission are ghosts returned from the dead to confront, once more, their own mortality. Mariella, the expedition leader Donne's former Amerindian mistress, now pursued by him to the secluded jungle

Mission that bears her name, is herself described as a phantom, a ghostly object of desire. Mariella, at once executioner and victim, pursuer and pursued, becomes a symbol in the novel for the circularity of desire. Her presence, restored in the figure of the ancient Arawak woman, is a reminder to the crew not of what they might gain but of what they have already lost. For as they move beyond the Mission into increasingly dangerous territory, they condemn themselves to a 'second death', as inevitable as the first:

> It was all well and good they reasoned as inspired madmen would to strain themselves to gain that elastic frontier where a spirit might rise from the dead and rule the material past world. All well and good was the resurgence and reconnoitre they reasoned. But it was doomed again from the start to meet endless catastrophe: even the ghost one dreams of and restores must be embalmed and featured in the old lineaments of empty and meaningless desire. (1985: 80)

The ghost is the lack inscribed in their material ambitions; and it is the talisman that presages their own repeated destruction. It reminds them, too, that the past returns to batten on the present; that there is no escape from the phantoms (re)produced by a guilty conscience. (Each of the crew-members is in some way attempting to escape his responsibilities, fleeing a personal history that, just as irresistibly, binds them all together.)

The ghost – that which returns – reinscribes a legacy of shame and fear (69): a legacy associated elsewhere with the involuntary memory of cannibalism. The cannibal act is linked most closely to the expedition leader Donne, whose relentless greed and cruelty amount in the novel to 'an incalculable devouring principle' (79). Yet Donne draws others, too, into a blasphemous communion: the fish the narrator eats becomes 'a morsel of recollection', a 'memory spring[ing] from nowhere into [his] belly and experience' (48); while Donne, the spectre released from a history of cannibal savagery, becomes 'an apparition stoop[ing] before him and cloth[ing] him with the frightful nature of the jungle', striking him dumb with the knowledge that he has swallowed 'a morsel of terror' (52). Donne, here, is the uncanny cannibal, forcing the past into the present, bringing with him unwanted memories and previously ingested secrets. The terror that he induces owes to the yoking of two forces: the all-devouring incorporative principle of the ferocious cannibal and the uncontainable mnemonic power of the surreptitious ghost. Violent assimilation, inexorable repetition: these are the forces that propel the crew toward renewed destruction. And they are also the forces that lock them in an incestuous alliance. For the crew are all related: they are, quite literally, 'one spiritual family' (39) – and cannibalism, as resurrected through the figure of the predatory ghost, is, as Lévi-Strauss reminds us, 'the alimentary form of incest' (1981: 141). Cannibalism, like incest, is a rudimentary form of violation: it transgresses the social boundaries that separate us from kith and kin.[14] And yet, as Harris suggests, it is also born of the need for kinship: cannibalism, again like incest, is a disallowed form of symbiosis. It is this conjunctive aspect to the cannibal infraction that Harris draws upon and absorbs, in turn, into his own 'cannibalistic' text. Thus, whereas in *My Bones and My Flute* the 'cannibal ghost' is a primarily phobic entity, a manifestation of the white man's racial fears and paranoid fantasies, in *Palace of the Peacock* it provides the reminder of a productive violation, displaying the incestuous ties that bond together a Creole (Caribbean) people.[15]

Over and against the Donnean principle of cannibal devoration, Harris asserts a counter-principle of alchemical transformation. The cannibal/ghost alliance – a Donnean conceit if there ever was one – forms the bonding agent that produces an unlikely metamorphosis. This metamorphosis, as Michael Gilkes, among other critics, has suggested, is best seen in alchemical terms as a process of psychic reintegration. Here it is Jung, rather than Freud or Lévi-Strauss, who captures best the nature of Harris's project. Historically, says Jung,

> [Alchemy] was a work of reconciliation between two apparently incompatible opposites which, characteristically, were understood not merely as the natural hostility of the physical elements but at the same time as a moral conflict. Since the object of the endeavour was seen outside as well as inside, as both physical and psychic, the work extended as it were through the whole of nature, and its goal consisted in a symbol which had an empirical and at the same time a transcendental aspect. (1970: 554)

The relevance of Jung's quotation to Harris's novel need hardly be stressed; it might serve, indeed, as an epitaph to the novel's final, epiphanic sequence, where the crew-members, meeting their second deaths, consumed by their own will-to-consumption, realise that 'the wall that had divided [them] from their true otherness' is nothing other than 'a web of dreams' (114). The recognition of 'otherness', and of the 'otherness' in themselves, allows them to cancel the 'forgotten fear of strangeness and catastrophe in a destitute world' (116) and to free themselves from their obsessive desire for material possession. Reborn to themselves, they are reawakened to the world which they see now in its unity; their need for each other fades into the vision of 'one muse and one undying soul' (117). This vision seems to hold as well for the novel's intertextual project: its integration of Western writers working within the Symbolic tradition (the Metaphysicals; Hopkins; Eliot, Yeats, and Conrad) into a unifying pattern of regenerative myth.[16] What is interesting in Harris's case, however, is the attention he pays to context: the violent New World encounters that act as a backdrop to Donne's devotionals; the 'savagery' that Conrad locates at the heart of modern European civilisation. Like Mittelholzer, then, Harris plays on the fears of his European ancestors, 'inhabiting' their texts, preying upon them like a ghost; but also transforming them into actors in a New World spiritual drama, a kind of passion-play which moves beyond the Manichaean categories of Good and Evil. So whereas Mittelholzer releases the racialised spectres that lurk behind the Western ghost story, giving them material form as agents of revolutionary vengeance, Harris invites the cannibal and the ghost to link their other-worldly fingers and to perform together the alchemical work of transubstantiation.

In *Palace of the Peacock*, the cannibal ghost is an inspiring, muse-like figure; it is transformed from a source of terror into a vehicle of reconciliation. This transformation both resubstantiates the immateriality of memory and dematerialises the act of conquest by giving it a spectral form. The cannibal and the ghost are, in this sense, collaborators in paradox: the one breaks down divisions between the eater and the eaten, 'creat[ing] a total identity between [them] while insisting on the unreciprocal and yet ultimately total control – the literal consumption – of the latter by the former' (Kilgour 1990: 7); the other bridges the gap between the actual and the imaginary, producing a hybrid entity that straddles ontological realms. The cannibal ghost, along with the instrument that brings it into being, the Carib bone flute, produces an uneasy harmony from apparently incompatible elements. At the same time, it is a symbol of radical discontinuity (the internalisation of the fragmented body; the defiance of solid form). In this second sense, it features as an agent of countermemory, disrupting a view of history that insists on continuous progress. Countermemory, in Michel Foucault's formulation, consists of three components: 'The first of these is parodic, directed against reality, and opposes the theme of history as reminiscence or recognition; the second is dissociative, directed against identity, and opposes history given as continuity or representative of a tradition; the third is sacrificial, directed against truth, and opposes history as knowledge' (1984: 93).

The cannibal ghost inhabits the interstices of the recognisable past; its discontinuous form eludes attempts at historical identification. The countermemory it instantiates functions on a principle of uncontrollable heterogeneity; the history it perceives 'will not discover a forgotten identity ... but a complex system of ... multiple elements, unable to be mastered by the powers of synthesis' (94). For Harris, cannibal countermemory opposes European history: it fragments the vision of time that underpins an ideology of conquest. The cannibal ghost, however, reinstitutes a form of collective remembrance; it absorbs and synthesises, if in a new substantive form. Here, then, are the two conflicting aspects of Harris's 'dialectic of alteration': on the one hand, a countermemory that challenges reminiscence, and that delivers itself from the 'origins' that Europe has imposed upon it; on the other, an equal and opposite move toward mythic transcendence, restoring collective memory but elevating it to a higher form. This dialectic remains unresolved. The cannibal absorbs the 'other'; the 'other' returns – as a ghost. Yet this cycle of repetition, this pattern of what Harris calls 'infinite rehearsal', need not be seen in terms of alienation or imprisonment; instead, it asserts the principle of creole transmutation, as Caribbean writers, inspired by the bone flute, reinvent their region – and themselves.

I began this essay by invoking the powerful ghost of Frantz Fanon; it seems appropriate, then, to end it by bringing Fanon back out of the shadows. For Fanon, the cannibal – the alibi for a history of race oppression – must be confronted, then surmounted, before being banished into the past. For blacks, meanwhile, the past, restored, ignites the fires of vengeance. But the smoke then clears to yield a glimpse of Fanon's great utopian vision: 'self' and 'other' converge, until there is no self, no 'other'; 'white' and 'black' worlds coalesce, until there are no 'whites', no 'blacks' – there are only people, disabused of the history that once defined them, working together for the creation of a liberated future:

> I am not a prisoner of history. I should not seek there for the meaning of my destiny . . . I should constantly remind myself that the real leap consists in introducing invention into existence . . . In the world through which I travel, I am endlessly creating myself . . . I, the man of color, want only this: That the

tool never possess the man. That the enslavement of man by man cease forever. That is, of one by another ... Why not the quite simple attempt to touch the other, to feel the other, to explain the other to myself? (1967: 229–31)

7

Cronos and the political economy of vampirism: notes on a historical constellation

John Kraniauskas

> Today, however, the past is preserved as the destruction of the past. (Adorno and Horkheimer 1979: xv)

The phantoms of the past – revenants – occupy an important place in the cultural histories of Mexico. The Day of the Dead, in which the deceased return to banquet with their relatives, immediately comes to mind, as does the redemptive invocation of the heroes from Indian pasts in the discourse of the Zapatista rebellion in Chiapas: 'Through our voice the dead will speak, our dead, so alone and forgotten, so dead and yet so alive in our voice and our steps' (Clarke and Ross 1994: 78). Perhaps the most extraordinary Mexican narrative of revenants is Juan Rulfo's short novel *Pedro Páramo* (1955). Written in the context of the refoundation of the nation on the basis of new post-Revolutionary myths ('the Revolution' as the sign of Mexican 'progress'), the novel tells a story of broken families, obsessive unrequited love, a landowner, and a dispossessed peasantry who haunt the text as the living-dead and as its narrators. Rulfo's peasants died of 'fright' (see Escalante 1992). If Benedict Anderson (1991) is right to suggest that the power of national imaginings is that they endow death (and, therefore, life as well) in the modern, secular world with meaning, it is clear that the pact between the state and 'people' that such imagining and meaning would necessarily entail failed to materialise in post-Revolutionary Mexico, whilst the local cultural scripts of peasant communities were shattered under the impact of secular 'developmental' zeal. Rulfo's dead, marginalised by the state, live in a continuous but meaningless present in which their only possible remaining hope for justice and the transcendence community is supposed to provide –

the Church – has been bought by the local landowner: the 'ilusión' (hope) that drives them is an 'ilusión' (illusion). Interpreted from Anderson's anthropological insight into nationalism, Rulfo's novel tells us that these revenants are not the product of a supposed obsession with death in Mexican popular culture, but rather the product of conflicting imaginaries (ways of death) and – here, Rulfo takes us beyond Anderson's formulations – an historical appropriation of existential meaning on the part of the state. Nationhood, from this point of view, is revealed to be the product of a violent overcoding of alternative imaginings.[1]

Phantoms are not the only kind of revenants. Vampires also return from the dead, in search of blood, to exploit; whilst zombies return as forced labour. Horror movies, especially in the Americas, rest on a particularly postcolonial scenario which involves staging the return of the past – usually in the shape of the victims of colonialism and nation-state formation – as a nightmare demanding justice of the present. Guillermo del Toro's recent film *Cronos* (1992), the story of a reluctant vampire, is thus inscribed not only into the European tradition of vampire horror stories, but also into the Mexican tradition of narratives of revenants, and into the American postcolonial tradition of horror. The film graphically reminds us that vampire stories are first and foremost narratives of the social configuration of the body. In doing so, moreover, as well as relocating the experience of colonialism in Mexico into the present as a very special kind of mechanical agency (the 'time-lag' is a strait gate through which a vampire may leap), it also re-establishes the traditional close link between images of vampires and the 'social rule of capital'. And again, in doing so, the film finds echoes in the discourse of the Zapatista rebels: 'They bleed Chiapas a thousand different ways: through oil and gas ducts, electric lines, train cars, bank accounts, trucks and vans, boats and planes ... through wide breaches and little punctures ... and Chiapan blood flows as a result of the thousand fangs sunk into the throat of southeastern Mexico' (Clarke and Ross 1994: 18).[2] Finally and more self-consciously, *Cronos* reveals the melodramatic structure of feeling of a Catholicism founded on symbolic cannibalism (or vampirism). Religion, capital, vampires: such is also the constellation of ideas through which Marx writes of the fetishism of the commodity; and it is with the vampire as the image of a transculturated commodity fetishism that this essay is concerned.

1 The uncanny capitalist

What has the image-fantasy of the vampire, specifically that of Dracula, been associated with in literary and cinematic traditions? A 'decadent' aristocracy obsessed with 'blood' relations (Eagleton 1995); the circulations and flows of monopoly capitalism (Moretti 1982); the threat to national identity and racial degeneration as figured in 'the Jew' (Gelder 1994 and Halberstam 1993); unbridled sexual lust – both hetero and queer: the figure of the female vamp has had quite a long history (Craft 1984); all refocused with the advent of AIDS (see, in particular, Coppola's film version of *Dracula*). In its articulation of a desire for eternal life, the vampire also embodies a form of de-differentiated temporality in which the distinction between the past (dead) and present (living) has been blurred. Similarly, vampires represent the inhuman in the human, the ever-present threat of animalisation that sacrifice is supposed to keep at bay. Whatever the particular symptom, most images construct the vampire as a danger for the ruling bodily regime. Vampirism classically involves the puncturing of the skin-ego (Anzieu 1989), precisely at the juncture of the body and head, such that the established, 'enlightened', hierarchy of the senses is undermined and re-ordered according to an 'other' unconscious logic; but only so as to be immediately re-encoded back again in opposition to particular monstruous forms – such as those mentioned above. In this sense, talking about vampire films, James Donald (1989) is right to suggest that there is a carnivalesque dimension to Dracula, but so is Judith Halberstam, in another, who insists – so that we do not slip into an easy populist celebration of the deterritorialising body – that 'the Gothic novel and Gothic monsters in particular produce monstrosity as never unitary, but always as an aggregate of race, class and gender ... [T]he nineteenth-century discourse of anti-Semitism and the myth of the vampire share a kind of Gothic economy in their ability to condense many monstrous traits into one body' (1993: 334).

American Tabloid (1995) by the self-styled 'demon dog' of US thriller writers, James Ellroy, contains a brief portrait of the well-known capitalist 'vampire' Howard Hughes. It could stand in for the recent ubiquity of images of vampires in both mainstream literature and film, for example, *Mind of My Mind* (Butler 1977), *Almanac of the Dead* (Silko 1991), *The Informers* (Ellis 1994), *Bram Stoker's Dracula* (Coppola 1992), *Interview with the Vampire* (Rice 1976 and Jordan 1994), and *From Dusk Till Dawn* (Rodríguez 1996). It illustrates, moreover, *Cronos*'s contemporary transnational (in this first instance, mainly US) intertextual resonances:

> Littell walked in. The front room was filled with medical freezers and intravenous drip caddies. The air reeked of witch hazel and bug spray.
> He heard children squealing. He identified the noise as a TV kiddie show.
> He followed the squeals down a hallway. A wall clock read 8:09 – 10:09 Dallas time.
> The squeals turned into a dog food commercial. Littell pressed up to the wall and looked through the doorway.
> An IV bag was feeding the man blood. He was feeding himself with a hypodermic needle. He was lying back buck cadaverous naked on a crank-up hospital bed.
> He missed a hip vein. He jabbed his penis and hit the plunger.
> His hair touched his back. His fingernails curled over halfway to his palms.
> The room smelled like urine. Bugs were floating in a bucket filled with piss.
> Hughes pulled the needle out. His bed sagged under the weight of a dozen disassembled slot machines.
> (Ellroy 1995: 583)

In *American Tabloid*, Hughes's nickname is Drac, short for Dracula (417).

Alongside Ellroy's portrait I would like to place another, better known, passage from Marx's *Capital*:

> As a capitalist, he is only capital personified. His soul is the soul of capital. But capital has one sole driving force, the drive to valorize itself, to create surplus value, to make its constant part, the means of production, absorb the greatest possible amount of surplus labour. Capital is dead labour which, vampire-like, lives only by sucking living labour, and lives the more, the more labour it sucks. (Marx 1990: 342)

It is clear that the passage from *American Tabloid* can easily be folded into the passage from *Capital*. Drac, the international capitalist, belongs, 'buck cadaverous naked', to the living-dead and feeds on blood and, moreover, taps into a number of the 'monstrous' associations described above. In this sense, Ellroy's portrait of the notorious paranoid bourgeois and movie-mogul Howard Hughes, as he lies back in a Beverley Hills bungalow after his masturbatory 'hit' to watch the assassination of J. F. Kennedy on TV in November 1963, underlines the well-known association between capitalism, addiction, and vampirism, as well as evoking the thematics of Guillermo del Toro's vampire movie, *Cronos*.

One of the bodies whose story is told in *Cronos* is that of the industrialist De la Guardia. He possesses the manuscript and rule book written by an alchemist who made the Cronos device in colonial New Spain. The device, now in the possession of the antique dealer Jesús Gris, endows its user with eternal life in exchange for blood, and De la Guardia desperately wants it. Like the paranoid capitalist Hughes, the aging and dying industrialist lives in a sealed, sanitised environment (a bunker underneath one of his factories which, we are informed, is 'open all night'!), half of his body preserved in a fishtank. Like Drac, he too tends towards the animal; although not yet an immortal vampire, he already prefigures his desire and walks on four legs, including two metal crutches – which give De la Guardia the appearance, in another of Marx's splendid images of capital, of 'ris[ing] up on [his] hind legs' so as to 'face the worker and confront him' like a voracious insect (1,054). It is his desire to possess the Cronos device, to live forever, thereby becoming a vampire, which sets the narrative going. And it is Jesús's self-sacrifice in preventing this and destroying, first the industrialist, and then the device, that concludes it.

Guillermo del Toro's *Cronos* is a fantasy of the contemporary body, technology, and of time in the accelerated age of late – transnational – capitalism. The Mexican city of the film is, moreover, hardly a 'national' or 'regional' capital in the traditional culturalist sense, but rather, at the level of speech, bilingual (Spanish and English – the latter clearly alluding to US economic power), and at the visual level of writing, multilingual. Both the workplace (De la Guardia's factory) and (Jesús's) home have become globalised sites traversed by several overlaying scripts – displayed in signs and newspapers – which, like a palimpsest (or the alchemist's mysterious notebook), demand to be deciphered for their secrets. Marx's references to capital's vampiric qualities in *Capital* emerge in his discussion of the struggles over the working day (the move from formal to real subsumption of labour to capital, as well as the transition from the extraction of absolute to relative surplus value). This process involves not only the disciplining of capital but also the subjugation of living labour, the body, to the machine ('dead labour') – Fordism or machinofacture – and increasing the rate of exploitation.[3] It can surely be no coincidence that the re-emergence of images and tales of vampires in the 1980s and 1990s has coincided with a massive deregulation of capital that is associated with its transnationalisation and the recent neo-liberal assault on the welfare state, as well as the post-fordist redesigning of the technological relation between capital and labour. Recent developments in the means of production (including information technology) threaten to completely restructure – through 'downsizing' – the social organisation of the world of work and its relation to the private sphere, and thus impinge in a variety of ways on the social experience of the body. Indeed, over the past decade one of the most enduring of social fantasies – evident in film and literature in the figure of the cyborg – has been that of new technologies actually entering the body in such a way that the dividing line between machine and flesh is blurred. The transition to forms of flexible accumulation and associated technologies has only been unevenly felt in Latin America: in the post-dictatorial 1980s, in the form particularly of the debt-crisis; and in the realm of production imposed, more often than not, in the authoritarian guise of 'modernisation'. Interestingly, the 1980s in Latin America are widely known as the decade of 'savage' capitalism.

2 Fetishism and cultural memory: primitive accumulation

'All reification is a forgetting' (Adorno and Horkheimer 1979: 230). Due perhaps to the influence of George Lukács's seminal essay 'Reification and the Consciousness of the Proletariat' (1971), discussion of commodity fetishism has tended to stress the process whereby the commodity form, money and capital itself, mask and naturalise their social content and history as they present themselves to experience: 'It is nothing but the definite social relation between men themselves which assume here, for them, the fantastic form of a relation between things' (Marx 1990: 165). From this point of view – commodity fetishism as reification – the sense of 'things' predominates over 'fantastic form', with the effect that traditional Marxist theories of ideology are founded on a social process of forgetting. Ideology critique thus usually involves the restoration, by the critical critic, of history and sociality to its objects. But could it not be that such a disabling formulation of ideology is itself predicated on a forgetting, of which the image of the vampire is in fact a sign, and thus itself paradoxically ideological? For do not objects and subjects come to critics always already inscribed with history, even if this includes the history of their dissimulation? And, might not capital be one such historical object? Gilles Deleuze and Felix Guattari suggest something of the kind when they talk of the 'miraculating' and 'recording' powers of capital: 'But the essential thing is the establishment of an enchanted recording or inscribing surface that arrogates to itself all the productive forces and all the organs of production, and that acts as a quasi-cause by communicating the apparent movement (the fetish) to them' (1977: 11–12). The capitalist socius thus not only produces but records too, bearing the marks of its history and origins whilst appropriating the history of others. From this point of view, commodification as forgetting becomes, not a wiping away, nor just a re-articulation, but an overcoding. The question might then be: what is the social content of such appropriation and forgetting? Some years ago, Gillian Rose pointed out that the word 'fantastic' in Marx's passage would be better rendered from the German original as 'phantasmagoric', highlighting thus the personification – however dim and ghostly – of commodities, now endowed with a life and power of their own as a 'quasi-cause' (1978: 31). It is for this reason that Marx compares the fetishism of the commodity to religion:

> In order, therefore, to find an analogy we must take flight into the misty realm of religion. There the products of the human brain appear as autonomous figures endowed with a life of their own, which enter into relations both with each other and with the human race. So it is in the world of commodities with the products of men's hands. I call this the fetishism which attaches to the products of labour as soon as they are produced as commodities. (Marx 1990: 165)

Indeed, in *Cronos,* the jewel-encrusted golden device that cathects itself to the body and exchanges eternal life for blood comes to Jesús, the antique dealer, inside a statuette of an angel, as if from heaven. Such fetishistic miraculation is similarly apparent in the voracious appetite ascribed to capital (dead labour) for living labour in the passages from Marx quoted above. It is only that now, so as to 'enter into relations ... with the human race', the fantastic form of a vampire has taken the place of the fantastic form of Christ (Jesús). Etienne Balibar has recently explicitly opposed fetishism to ideology (and forgetting) and suggested that the former would be better thought of as a 'mode of subjection', that is, as the main process involved in the making of economico-juridical subjects 'subordinated to the reproduction of exchange value' (1995: 77); crucially, the dispossession and disciplining of the peasantry and the creation of 'abstract labour'. My own hypothesis is that, at least in one of its primary guises, the figure of the vampire represents, not just a forgetting, nor a mere Gothic literary figure with which Marx has endowed capital with 'character', but the phantasmagoric trace of its origins; in other words, the cultural memory of the violent 'subjection' of bodies and lives to the laws of the market and the nation-state: so-called primitive accumulation.

In a chapter of her novel *Almanac of the Dead* called 'Vampiric Capitalists', Leslie Marmon Silko writes that one of her native Indian characters, Angelita La Escapía, 'imagined Marx as a story-teller who worked feverishly to gather together a magical assembly of stories to cure the suffering and evils of the world by the retelling of stories' (1991: 316). Such an interpretation articulates, it seems to me, something like a subalternist approach to *Capital*, one that reads into the theory of value traced there the cultural experiences and memories of those subjected to the rule of capital. Might it not be the case that Marx's image of the vampire emerged from such collection? Here, Marx the intellectual and critic almost takes the shape of a shaman or medicine man – an anti-vampire – who in *Capital* rearticulates the stories of those who have experienced 'subjection' to capital (not, however, in the form of an ethnological collection of popular folklore, but as political critique).[4] What Balibar calls 'subjection', Marx calls 'primitive accumulation'. The obverse side of creating new economico-political subjects is their dispossession: 'As a matter of fact, the methods of primitive accumulation are anything but idyllic ... The expropriation of the agricultural producer, of the peasant, from the soil is the basis of the whole process ... And this history, the history of their expropriation, is written in the annals of mankind in letters of blood and fire' (Marx 1990: 874, 876, 875).

In Marx's account, the historical process of primitive accumulation produces the conditions of existence for capitalist exploitation, and involves not only the dispossession of the peasantry, but also new legal means of coercion, the creation of new state forms and national markets (nation-states). European nations also benefitted from colonial plunder, for example, Aztec and Inca gold – the same that made the Cronos device. I would like to suggest, however, that there is also such a thing as on-going contemporary primitive accumulation (which, in the historicist sense, would mean that it was not so 'primitive') that feeds contemporary fetishism and accompanies the 'social rule of capital', ever-extending commodification on a transnational scale (see the later chapters by Phillips and Bartolovich). In other words, processes of dispossession continue – apparent, for example, in the well-known phenomenon of mass migration – 'freeing' labour for capital, de-differentiating it through real abstraction, and which are experienced now as 'modernisation', 'social mobility' or 'national integration'. In Latin America these processes have generated a series of fantasies of the violently broken body, of vampirism, cannibalism, and the collection and trafficking of body organs and fluids. Apart from providing *Cronos* with Latin American cultural resonances, such stories, coming mainly from Peru and Bolivia, also offer clues to the historical emergence of popular images of vampires in Europe.

3 Latin American vampires

'And gradually as he speaks, I myself am filled with horror' (Wachtel 1994: 57). According to the anthropologist Nathan Wachtel in his *Gods and Vampires: Return to Chipaya*, 'the intrusion of modernity into the heart of Bolivian Andean communities threatens the very roots of their identities' (89), and it is from the ensuing process of social and cultural restructuring that a popular image of a vampire emerges. The anthropologist's horror comes as he listens to a former Uru informant tell of his ordeal after being accused of being a *kharisiri* (known in Peru as *nakaq* or *pishtakos*):

> one of the greatest dreads of the Andean world ... more or less mythical characters who accost their victims on deserted roads or break into their houses at night, sending them into a deep sleep by use of various powders, and taking advantage of their unconscious state to extract their fat (or their blood according to other, more recent versions). Several days later the victims feel weak, suffer from a kind of apathy, or anemia, then die. In the ethnographic literature ... the *kharisiri* generally appears with the features of a gringo, the diabolical incarnation of the outside world. (52–3)

What made this case so interesting to Wachtel was that the victim was from the community itself, though occupying a marginalised position within it. In 1978 a number of people of the community had been, it was said, 'stricken with a strange illness, characterised by sudden fatigue, a state of prostration from which many died. Suspicious-looking spots were found on the bodies of the sick (on their arms and chests), little dots that seemed to have been caused by the pricks of a needle: these traces clearly demonstrated that they had been victims of *kharisiri*' (54). The Uru narrator was accused of having taken their blood with a 'little machine'. He was beaten, tortured and even bled, and only saved by a detachment of soldiers who imprisoned him and then let him go. Wachtel was horrified because friends and other former informants had been involved in the persecution. According to local records, moreover, the number of deaths in 1978 proved in fact to be below average.

These events occurred at a moment of local crisis, when the victim was identified with outside forces: he had always been a marginalised member of the community, an orphan, extremely poor. But then he became relatively wealthy. He acquired a shop in the village with his savings and was involved in local community officialdom in positions – the peasant union and education – that administered local processes of national integration and modernisation. Crucially, according to Wachtel, he had also traded with an outsider who was similarly accused in his own community, and whose grandfather had also been accused and killed for being a *kharisiri* in the 1950s. The biography of the victim of this popular fantasy cuts across intrafamilial and inter-moiety conflict in the community which is focused on land ownership and associated with the emergence there of new anti-syncretic ('pagan': Uru and Catholic) religious practices. Wachtel suggests that these events in some sense produced a moment of cross-religious unity in the community, the victim functioning, perhaps rather too classically, as something like a scapegoat. Interestingly, one of Wachtel's conclusions is that the victim had come to speak to him of his experience because of the anthropologist's own marginal position in the community, and that he too, in his codification of local Andean religious and magical traditions, was, in this context, something of a vampire.

A similar cultural fantasy emerged approximately ten years later in Peru, now in an urban environment, underlining the continuity, through re-articulation, of 'magical' beliefs there. Over two or three weeks in November and December 1988, women in the shanty towns of Lima protested in their hundreds, demanding that the local authorities protect their children from 'sacaojos' (eye-snatchers) who were kidnapping them so as to sell their eyes abroad. Other versions included the selling of body parts or blood and fat to the metropoli as fuel for factory machinery and computers (traditionally – that is, during the colonial period – human fat was supposedly extracted for the manufacture of bells), or to provide food for special restaurants frequented by members of the armed forces (Portocarrero Maisch et al. 1991). The 'sacaojos' are modern and urbanised versions of the rural, pre-hispanic, and subsequently colonial, *pishtako* or *kharisiri*): white doctors, sometimes with black assistants, carrying identity cards given to them by the then President of the Republic, Alan García (see Ansión 1989). Indeed, a group of medics was almost lynched in December during this mass popular fantasy. One version refers, again, to a *machine*, 'a transparent box ... two wires stuck on to the head by the nose and ears, and a button which, when pressed, popped the eyes out into a round receptacle' (Portocarrero Maisch et al. 1991: 38). According to Portocarrero Maisch and his colleagues this fantasy – which I would want to call 'postcolonial' – emerged *in the place of* violent protest or strikes against austerity measures introduced by the government in the midst of a severe economic and political crisis associated with massive external debt, on the one hand, and the activities of Sendero Luminoso, on the other. The effects included a more than 50 percent cut in popular purchasing power, scarcity of basic foodstuffs, unemployment, and uncertainty. The context is, therefore, one of generalised fear displaced onto the health service in particular, and condensed into the racialised (both black and white, rather than the Indian or 'mestizo' *pishtako*) 'sacaojos' (doctor). This overtly political fantasy, it is agreed, also functions as a critique of the traditional political sphere, projecting new political subjects into the streets (housewives and mothers). The writers on these recent events in Lima suggest, furthermore – and this assists our contextualisation of *Cronos* – that they were the culmination of a region-wide rumour 'that seems to have circulated throughout Latin America. In Mexico in 1986 and in Brazil in 1988 where, it was said, bands of criminals kidnapped babies for their vital organs, which were sold in Europe and the US for huge profits' (35).

Such popular fantasies of *kharisiri*, *pishtakos*, and eye-snatchers are clearly postcolonial and transcultural signs of contemporary social processes, evoking as they do the cultural memory of changes in the social experience of the body and its perceived invasion and colonisation by new institutions (medical) and regimes (technologies), modern doctors having taken the place of colonial priests in an ongoing history of dispossession. From this subalternist point of view, the vampire becomes a kind of 'anti-shaman', capital's wicked medicine-man, the equivalent of the colonial church's priest: 'converting' subjects and bodies in the name of a new order.[5]

4 Jesus the vampire

'It seems to me that what I have said is enough to horrify you, indeed, to make your hair stand on end': so says Jean de Léry in his celebrated account of cannibalism in Brazil (1990: 131). His words reveal the rhetorical intentionality of his text. For, having desisted from relating further 'acts of cruelty', he turns to his readers so as to remind them of similar ones – including cannibalism – in Europe itself. In this way, horror at cannibals in Brazil is channelled into European affairs (Léry wants his words to be written into the very body of his readers) and the chronicle's political logic revealed.

On the one hand, Léry mobilises his account of the 'savage' practice of cannibalism to identify and mark 'our big usurers ... sucking blood and marrow, and eating everyone alive – widows, orphans, and other poor people, whose throats it would be better to cut once and for all, than to make them linger in misery' (132) (linking cannibalism in America to images of vampirism) whilst, on the other – by way of a number of references to religious wars throughout the continent and to contemporary Christian practices, including the symbolic cannibalism of Catholic liturgy – the Huguenot writer attacks the 'savagery' of an institutionalised Catholicism apparently in retreat (linking cannibalism to Catholic liturgy). In sum, 'real' and 'symbolic' cannibalism, along with an evocation of vampirism, emerge as an imaginary constellation in a region racked by religious wars, hunger, and fear (see Lestringant 1994 and Delumeau 1989). Colonialism constitutes the background to these processes, and the drinking or 'sucking' of blood is what unifies this fantastic constellation of images, as a crisis in social imaginaries associated with the emergence of absolutist states begins to configure new ways of living and dying, and of relating bodies to environments. In this regard, it may be well to remember that, years later, Bram Stoker's 1897 classic *Dracula* springs from an imaginary meeting of Europe's cultural frontiers that brings together its Far West (beyond lies America) and its Far East (once the border of Christendom, now the border of the Enlightenment): that is, Ireland and Transylvania. The colonial circuit from which *Dracula* comes, in other words, is as follows: Bram Stoker, the author, migrates to London from Ireland, whilst the travels of his character Jonathan Harker take him (and his readers) the rest of the way to Transylvania. In so doing, moreover, the novel also unites the memory of hunger and dispossession with a 'decaying gentry' in the context of a rising industrial capitalism (Eagleton 1995: 214–16). And beyond the contours of this imaginary map of European 'civilization' exist the real 'uncivilised' cannibals, who rather than just sip at their victims' necks, barbecue or boil them up in pots and devour them.

William Pietz has shown how the idea of fetishism emerged from a complex process of colonial transculturation and primitive accumulation (1985). I have attempted to show that this may be the case for postcolonial images of vampirism too; and, furthermore, that images of the violent appropriation of body fluids and body parts constitute a decisive cultural component of the popular experience of on-going primitive accumulation. The 'fetishism' of Catholic liturgy in Protestant discourse was a key moment of its history as an idea, as it is a key transcultural component of images of vampires (and *pishtakos*) as well. Guillermo del Toro has insisted on the importance of Catholicism in his film, and if we translate the names of two of its main protagonists this is made very clear: Grey Jesus and Guardian Angel. *Cronos* banalises and melodramatises Christ's self-sacrifice by making of it an everday family romance.

There are two aspects of *Cronos* which must be underlined as we examine the story of another of its bodies, and of the device itself. Firstly, that with the emergence of a popular-mass genre of vampire novels and films (horror), the historical and cultural significance of each work does not lie merely in its relation to its contexts. This relation has become mediated by the logic of production of the genre itself which, of course, has its own socio-cultural content, but whose effect may be to *abstract away from* particular contexts. *Cronos* is, in other words, a genre movie. The inventiveness of any particular work belonging to such a genre would then relate to the ways in which it reflected back upon such a cultural dynamic. This fairly obvious point brings me to my second one: in *Cronos*, it is not the usurer/capitalist (aristocrat or bourgeois) who is the 'real' vampire, nor is it simply a member of the general public participating in the cannibalistic and sacrificial symbolic structure of Christianity (although this may be Aurora's story in the film), but Jesús himself, *now banalised* and *become* a member of the general public. In *Cronos* there is no 'living labour', so to speak, the machinery of De la Guardia's factory lying, for the most part, dormant. Nor is there a 'queering' of sexual desire, rather a narcissistic obsession with youth which modestly rekindles and, eventually, reconfirms the family through sacrifice. Del Toro's film, therefore, operates a kind of *double abstraction* away from both social context and generic convention, and in doing so, displaces the cultural experiences of capitalism and 'real' and 'symbolic' cannibalism into the *everyday* reluctant vampirism of Jesús (whose only real victim is De la Guardia, the capitalist who wants to be a vampire). No wonder that Jesús's body is literally ruined by the weight of such massive cultural and historical condensation. From this point of view, it may be possible to read the film as a horrific dismantling of a myth.

'I am Jesús Gris' (Grey Jesus). The story of Jesús's body is inseparable from that of the Cronos device – made from (presumably Aztec) gold by an alchemist in colonial New Spain, and shot, David Lynch-style, as a 'mini-factory' – and the insect-like organism that inhabits it and lives on blood (the 'real' industrial vampire). The continuity between De la Guardia's factory and the Cronos device is made clear in such shots, identifying the capitalist and the insect-organism inside the device. In this sense, the identification, through addiction, of Jesús and the machine, is really a lethal *mis*-identification. Whilst the camera probes at the transformations in Jesús's body as he becomes first animal and then mineral, the film tells of how Jesús, through death and resurrection, comes to embody his name. It also tells how, through addiction, he becomes uncannily identified with the device and unable to calm ('civilise') his appetite. Two extraordinary scenes foreground the banality of Jesús's hunger. In one we see him slowly licking a spot of blood off the floor of a public toilet during a New Year's Eve party; whilst in the other we watch as he is driven to the verge of autophagy by an itch he cannot control. One scene, of course, encourages identification with Jesús's need, whilst the other acts to repel. He is eventually brutally killed by De la Guardia's nephew Angel in search of the device. Hilariously dressed and sown together by a mortuary attendant, Jesús begins to look like one of his granddaughter's scruffy dolls. Indeed, in a parody of the class connotations of the classical film Dracula as played by Christopher Lee in aristocratic style, he makes his way back home with his black and white suit on back-to-front, as if Aurora had twisted his head around 180 degrees. There, hidden away, he spends the night in her chest of toys (substituting for the coffin), now a character in her world. With her assistance he eventually disposes of both De la Guardia and his nephew in the factory. Jesús's body is now crumbling, studded with shards of glass; he is shedding his dying grey skin and revealing his white flesh beneath – which must be fed. He has become Grey Jesus and, like the alchemist before him, he needs human blood. Without it he and the device will die. Jesús has also become animal-like, tending towards the inhumanity of the organism. Finally, realising that Aurora is next on the menu, he destroys the device and sacrifices himself to the light. Jesús, antique dealer, scruffy doll, and eventually ruined statue, dies so that she may live.

At a time dominated by fantasies of a technologically redesigned 'post-human' subject, this representation of a vampire seems to rather evoke a sort of melancholy neo-animalisation, even the ruin of a body without subjectivity. Indeed, the simultaneous appearance of the modern vampire and Frankenstein had already displayed such opposing experiences – a body invaded and a body made – of capitalist transformation. Jesús, as we have seen, is the victim of a pre-industrial colonial cyborg experiment gone horribly wrong. Not only has he become a doll, but even mineral and animal. In *Cronos*, the gap – so often occupied by 'real' or 'symbolic' cannibalism (sacrifice) – that supposedly separates the human from the animal (and nature) has broken down through the banal animalisation of the very figure that is to maintain it, the figure of Jesús (as De la Guardia notes, blood-sucking insects, such as the mosquito, walk on water too). The vampire is half-spectre, half-animal. Like Derrida's spectres, it is a revenant; a species of the living-dead, it returns from the grave to prey on the living. Unlike Derrida's spectres, however, the vampire is not entirely 'of spirit' – a ghost – for it rather tends towards the animal (see Derrida 1994). It is blood that keeps Jesús (and Drac) in this in-between state, this gap structuring the symbolic order, neither dead nor alive, animal *and* human.[6]

Finally, one more short-story. As I have mentioned above, Jesús eventually does die so that Aurora (Dawn), his granddaughter, may live. By giving himself up to the light (and spirit), he shores up the shaken sacrificial structure of the human and the family. In doing so he redeems himself, and reveals, moreover, the melodramatic dimension of the story of Christ on which his own is based. Which brings us to Aurora. What does she do in the film? Well, she behaves like the fascinated spectator, in thrall to the iconic illusion of the moving image. Aurora bears witness, and looks on as Jesús gives himself over to the Cronos device, to addiction, hunger, momentary youth, and death. By turn visibly angry, jealous, dumbfounded, and afraid, she watches over him, silently fascinated by the bloody drama (film) played out before her eyes (cf. Marina Warner's chapter, below). She takes care of her grandfather, makes him one of her toys, and then, of course, as Jesús stares hungrily at the blood pouring from her hand, she speaks for the first time. And she utters his name. Classically, she recognises and confirms the mythical foundations of a shaken symbolic order, whose sacrificial logic, from having been threatened, is now, once more, in place.

8

Fee fie fo fum: the child in the jaws of the story

Marina Warner

1

The fairy tales of Charles Perrault, *Contes du temps passé*, published in 1697 (Perrault 1967) contain 'Puss in Boots', 'Cinderella, or the Little Glass Slipper', 'The Sleeping Beauty in the Wood', and other favourites and classics of the nursery. They have been told to children, and almost exclusively to children, for nearly three hundred years. In the frontispiece to the first edition, the traditional storyteller, the crone or old wife of the old wife's tale, is shown sitting in front of the fire with the children of the household – they may be portraits of Perrault's own family – gathered around her. Yet three of these cosy fireside tales feature the eating of young human flesh; and when the cannibal monsters fail to gobble their intended victims, they are themselves boiled alive or otherwise savagely despatched.

In 'Hop o'My Thumb' (Le petit Poucet), the hero finds himself lost in the forest with his brothers and sisters and takes shelter in the house of a giant: 'an ogre who eats babies', warns his grieving wife. But Hop o'My Thumb is undaunted; he notices that the baby ogres sleep with gold crowns on their heads, and so he switches them for the caps of his own six brothers. The ogre comes fumbling in their bed for a night-time snack: 'Why, what a nasty trick I have almost played on myself!' he says, when he finds the crowns. He changes direction, looking for the caps, and 'With that, he slit the throats of his seven daughters.' In the morning, when his wife goes to the children's room, she finds her 'seven daughters, with their throats cut, swimming in blood'. 'She responded with a fainting fit,' writes Perrault: 'Most women faint in similar circumstances' (Perrault

Figure 4. The ogre comes looking for a night-time snack and is tricked by Tom Thumb into murdering his own children. Gustave Doré's illustration to Perrault's classic tale.

1977: 124–5). (This is typical Perrault, of course, dry, mocking, world-weary – and manipulative with his sophisticated ironical clichés.)

In 'Little Red Riding Hood', the wolf is not an ogre, strictly speaking, but he devours the little girl and, in his granny disguise, combines both female malevolence and male cruelty and violence; this classic fairy tale has no fairies in it, and no happy ending either. Gustave Doré's little girl, from the 1862 illustrated edition of the *Contes*, placed in bed with Granny, epitomises the wide-eyed innocence laced with perverse curiosity that the nursery version has emphasised in Red Riding Hood's character, which leads to penalties – as it almost does but not quite with Goldilocks. The harsh ending, in which the wolf eats both, was however considered too grim, and a new happy ending, introduced by the Grimm Brothers, introduced a gallant huntsman to cut Granny and little girl from the wolf's belly; in yet later variants, her father, kind but severe, comes to the rescue.

In 'The Sleeping Beauty', the theme of cannibalism inspires a spectacular ogress: the wicked mother-in-law, who is so jealous of her son's lovely wife and children that she orders her cook to serve them one by one with 'une sauce Robert'. He is worried however that the Beauty might be tough, because after all, 'The Queen was twenty, now, if you did not count the hundred years she had been asleep' (Perrault 1967: 79). (This kind of cannibal joke survives unmarked by age.) An English chapbook translation of around 1750 gives the recipe for the sauce in question: 'This is a French sauce', a gloss informs the children, 'made up with onions, shredded and boiled tender in butter; to which is added vinegar, mustard, salt, pepper and a little wine' (Perrault c. 1750: 18). The cook, like the huntsman in Snow White, can't bear to kill the lovely children or their mother and hides them one after the other. Eventually, the wicked ogress is thrown to stew in her own pot: 'The Prince could not but help feeling a little sad; she was his mother. But he soon consoled himself with his lovely wife and children.'

Only four stories by Perrault do not feature cannibalism as such ('Cinderella', 'Donkeyskin', 'The Fairies', 'Bluebeard'). In the Grimm Brothers' later, seminal anthology, the tally can't be made, as stories of ogres and flesh-eating witches are so numerous, and many of them overlap. Yet these collections are the foundation stones of nursery literature in the West.

The word 'ogre' was introduced into English from French, via Italian, and the current in which it swam, from the late seventeenth century onwards, was fairy tales, both the Arabian Nights and the ornate, ironical French variety. Translations of Marie-Catherine d'Aulnoy's effervescent stories as well as of Perrault's more succinct *contes* introduced the word; in 'L'Abeille et l'Oranger' (The Bee and the Orange Tree), the author eavesdrops on the conversation of Ravagio and Tourmentine, who are 'tall as giants and their skin was pistol-proof', as they discuss a foundling human baby, Aimée (d'Aulnoy 1956: 145). She has fun with the wordplay: 'See, Ravagio, here is some fresh meat, nice and fat, nice and tender, but, by my head, you shan't even nibble a morsel of her. It's a pretty little girl, and I am going to nurse her. We'll marry her to our little ogrelet, and they'll make ogrelings together, of remarkable appearance, to rejoice us in our old age.'[1]

Such a scene is highly comic: there is pleasure in imagining ogres, in entertaining the outrageous scope of their desires, in watching the spectacle of their ultimate defeat. But what else besides does the ogre motif mean, why does it continue to endure, to bring pleasure? What relation does it bear to young women and children, the specific chosen audience of such material after the seventeenth century? I am going to pick out some distinctive aspects of male appetite for babies in the kind of fairy tales sometimes termed 'swallow tales' because of the amount of devouring that takes place in them (Opie and Opie 1974: 55).

2

The word's Italian predecessor, 'ogro', meaning monster, derives from the Latin Orcus for Hades, the God of the Underworld, or Hell. Hades in turn bequeaths his character to Christian eschatology, to the Christian Lord of Tartarus or Hell, the kingdom of the shades, where dwell the dead: Lucifer, or Satan. The Devil bridges the transformation of Hades, Greek Death, into the ogre, the legendary and nursery variety. And the dominant activity which they share, which represents their terror, is cannibalism, the sign of their evil, to be defeated and undone.

Dante's vision of Satan in the grip of the terrible ice of Tartary, the lowest circle of Hell, draws on earlier traditions, and then dominates imagery in fresco and manuscript illumination throughout the medieval period. Satan is all orifice, and each one stuffed with another victim:

> Con sei occhi piangea, e per tre menti
> gocciava 'l pianto e sanguinosa bava.
> Da ogni bocca dirompea co' denti
> un peccatore, a guisa di maciulla,
> sí che ne facea cosí dolenti.
> A quel dinanzi il mordere era nulla
> verso 'l graffiar, che tal volta al schiena
> rimanea della pelle tutta brulla

('With six eyes he was weeping and over three chins dripped tears and bloody foam. In each mouth he crushed a sinner with his teeth as with a heckle and thus he kept three of them in pain; to him in front the biting was nothing to the clawing, for sometimes the back was left all stripped of skin' (Dante 1958: xxxiii: lines 52–60)).

The principal victims of this carnivorous mangling are named in Dante: the traitors Judas, Cassius, and Brutus. But artists relished the opportunity to feed Satan's ravenous appetite in ever more terrifying envisionings of the Dante Inferno: Fra Angelico in

Figure 5. Dante's vision of the Inferno profoundly influenced visual eschatology, including the image of Satan sunk in the deepest pit of hell, with traitors stuffed in his several mouths as he gorges on the damned. Fra Angelico, Hell, from 'The Last Judgment'.

Florence, Taddeo di Bartolo in San Gimignano, in his fresco painted in 1396, and Giovanni da Modena, around 1410, in the Basilica of San Petronio in Bologna depicted in detail the cycle of ingestion, digestion, and regurgitation that conveyed eternal suffering in the Christian underworld (see Kilgour 1990: 65ff.).

So the gnashing of teeth does not so much describe the activity of the damned, as they wail and weep and bemoan their fate, but rather the response of the devils as they seize their prey. Hell is frequently imagined as a profane banquet, and the devil demands sacrifices of babies at his Sabbaths: Goya, in the *Caprichos* and other works, returns to one of the most persistent fantasies of the witchhunters, and shows women bringing infants to sacrifice to the goatish beast, another guise of the Devil.

Diabolical predators are not however always cannibals who eat their victims raw; sometimes they like their meat cooked, and the fires of hell then become culinary; hell's kitchen, in an apocalyptic vision from *The Hours of Catherine of Cleves*, painted in Utrecht around 1440, sees to sinners on barbecues, cauldrons, kettles, griddles, spits, with pitchforks and brazing irons; in other images, sinners are cast on the ground, to be eternally gnawed like bones by curs or wild cats strewn on a kitchen floor. The need to encompass both the aspects of the cannibal penalty – raw and cooked – sometimes inspires artists to depict a cauldron *inside* Hell's Mouth, as in the Last Judgement carved in bas relief on the facade of Ferrara cathedral.

So with that literal-mindedness that is a feature of much fantasy material, death is the most obvious meaning that the ogre conveys. But the nature and status of that death – material or spiritual – changes, and fairy tale cannibals refract different motives in the story, as and when it is told and as it is received; the plots carry different warnings depending on the sex of the protagonist, which often itself reflects the target audience. The cannibal is a subject in a gendered plot, and on the whole, the boy's own variety has eclipsed the girl's.

3

Ogres' key characteristics in giant-killer nursery stories have been inherited from the epics of the classical corpus, starring heroes. In the *Odyssey*, the cannibal giant Polyphemus, the Cyclops, captures Odysseus and his men and holds them prisoner in his cave, and begins feasting on them; but he is destined to be duped, as are his nursery epigones: Odysseus tells him his name is Nobody, and so when the giant howls that his captive has put out his eyes, and his fellow Cyclops ask who has blinded him, he can only cry out that Nobody has done the deed. And so the giants settle back and do nothing. In early modern fairy tales, ogres are similarly large, rich, strong, and very stupid; though Tourmentine, the ogress, is cleverer than Ravagio, Madame d'Aulnoy informs us. In the Grimm Brothers' 'Hansel and Gretel', however, the witch who wants to eat Hansel has short-sighted red eyes, and is consequently as easily bamboozled as her male counterparts, mistaking a twig for Hansel's finger when she is testing him for plumpness.

In 'Jack and the Beanstalk', the traditional English pantomime variant on this tale of giant-killing, Jack kills one giant: 'And in the next room were Hearts and Livers ... the choicest of his diet, for he commonly ate them with Salt and Pepper.' But no sooner has Jack dealt with this ogre than his brother, Blunderboar, comes sniffing for him. Jack swaddles his own tummy, stuffs it with animal lights and other grotesque foodstuffs, and then slits it open, proclaiming loudly that in this way he can feast on his dinner over and over again. The giant is delighted at this economy, and greedily imitates Jack, slitting open his own belly in emulation: 'and out dropt his Tripes and Trolly-bubs' (Opie and Opie 1974: 55).

A heroine at the heart of the plot generates a different antagonist; whereas the boy giant-killer confronts the dumb giant and fells him, she frequently faces a mysterious, terrifying, monster bridegroom. A story like 'Bluebeard' can be read from the point of view of young women, catching common fears from their angle of view; when the ogre eats his own, or threatens to, his devouring may represent another, metaphorical form of incorporation: conception and pregnancy, experiences also fraught with widespread, common fears of extinction.

The template of the story type, 'Cupid and Psyche', first appears as an interpolated fairy tale romance in *The Golden Ass*, written by Apuleius. The beautiful Psyche is warned by her sisters:

> The husband who comes secretly gliding into your bed at night is an enormous snake, with widely gaping jaws, a body that could coil around you a dozen times and a neck swollen with deadly poison. Remember what Apollo's oracle said: that you were destined to marry a savage wild beast ... [H]e won't pamper you much longer ... [W]hen your nine months are nearly up he will eat you alive; apparently his favourite food is a woman far gone in pregnancy. (Apuleius 1988: 110–11)

In myth and fairy tale, the metaphor of devouring often frequently stands in for sex from the point of view of the inexperienced, nubile young woman, often a bride. 'Bearskin', for example, attributed to the seventeenth-century French writer Henriette-Julie de Murat, opens with an ogre called Rhinoceros, who simply threatens to eat the king and queen and everyone in the kingdom if the princess is not handed over to him to be his wife (in Warner 1994c: 99–100). Sometimes these ogres are originally members of the same species as humans, but not always. But the multiple significances of consumption cannot be drained by this account of fear of the sexual act. The woman's fears do not focus on the act itself, but on its consequences, which are also often spoken of in images of eating: the woman's body, especially pregnant, is especially delicious to beasts, it seems. The greedy villains of fairytale particularly relish babies: their appetite first aims at women, but with an ulterior motive of devouring their offspring.

This cannibal motif conveys a threefold incorporation: sexual union, by which a form of reciprocal devouring takes place, pregnancy, by which the womb encloses the growing child, and paternity, which takes over the infant after birth in one way or another. The metaphors are enchained, one to another – sex, obliteration, food – as language strains to convey the tension between union and separation, individuality and connection, autonomy and possession. Ogres, be they gods or fairy story giants, threaten the weak with an enduring metaphor of annihilation and loss of self – being eaten alive. The boundaries of the body are breached as that body is gnashed and ground and digested.

The cannibal ogre takes his victims prisoner, and shuts them up: before being engulfed by his body, they are sealed into an enclosure which he means to control; his castle is usually a forbidding place of gloom and hierarchy, for all its domestic uses. The dozens of fairy tale princesses enclosed in towers are themselves metonymically swallowed up. In a story popular in English variants, 'The Discreet Princess', which was sometimes attributed to Perrault and to D'Aulnoy, though it was in fact written by Marie-Jeanne L'Héritier, the heroine, Finette, dupes the villainous seducer: using one of Jack's and Tom Thumb's well-tried tricks, she places a dummy in her bed. Her stratagem succeeds in defending herself against his advances – and it's significant that both her sisters, who have foolishly believed in his false love, are pregnant by him. Another of Marie-Jeanne L'Héritier's tales, *La Princesse Olymphe, ou L'Ariane de*

Hollande (1718: 96–176), describes how Olymphe is abandoned on an island where a monster roams who devours young women; later, it turns out he is an ordinary man in disguise who keeps his victims alive, but captive underground. Again, the threat of being eaten stands for the dread of being immured, confined. Some of the sources for Perrault's 'Bluebeard', in hagiography and ballad, focus on the figure of Sainte Triphine, who tried to run away from her husband, Cunmar the Accursed, after she was warned by her several predecessors that he would kill her if she was pregnant. The legend – about an historical ogre, a Breton war lord – vividly conveys the former close connection between death in childbirth and marriage (see Warner 1994b: 259–65).

Fear of death of mother and child may represent one of the Bluebeard story's latent meanings, but it does not figure among its patent messages, and it does not survive into the Victorian nursery, however much multiple pregnancies remained a danger for future wives and mothers. But while tales of dragon-slayers and giant-killers still flourish in popular narratives for boys – from video games to comics – ogres who consume female victims have rather become popular figures in adult, secular mythology. Bluebeard's story exhibits a characteristic with particular affinity to the present day bestsellers and crowd-pleasers: seriality. The ogre has reentered current narrative as a mass murderer, a kidnapper, a serial killer: a collector, as in John Fowles's novel; a monster of gluttony and rage and lust, as in Peter Greenaway's *The Cook, the Thief, his Wife and her Lover*; an obsessive, like Hannibal Lecter in *The Silence of the Lambs* (Cannibal Lecher) or the terrifying, righteous villain of the horror thriller *Seven*. Real-life examples carry out the gruesome horrors of fairy tale cabinets, of their bloody chambers. But there is a contrast here: cruel women, human or fairy, still dominate children's stories with their powers. But these Bluebeard figures now feature in material requiring restricted ratings as well. More surprisingly, perhaps, the story appeals to women writers like Margaret Atwood (1987) and Angela Carter (1975), both of whom have produced contemporary treatments for adults, and to artists like Cindy Sherman, who recently illustrated the Grimms' version of Bluebeard, 'Fitcher's Bird' (1992). These female interpreters are maybe expressing the fear of the bogeyman in order to contain it. Sherman has specialised in an atmosphere of menace in her work and frequently picked out sex crimes as a particular area of interest.

The two strands in the character of fairy tale ogres – the dumb and terrifying giant, and the sexual predator – interestingly twist together in the film *King Kong* (1933), which was devised and produced by a double act of male buddy adventurers Merian C. Cooper and Ernest Schoedsack, and co-written by Schoedsack's wife Ruth Rose, who made the two American heroes into portraits of her husband and his partner (see Mayne 1987, Snead 1991, Warner 1995). *King Kong* openly dramatises both Cooper and Schoedsack's fantasies about their experiences in Africa and other distant parts. In doing this, the film draws deeply on the tradition of fairytale ogre and cannibal representation: it introduces Kong at the beginning as a giant of hugely exaggerated size, the ravenous monarch of a terrifying, distant, enclosed kingdom (Skull Island), who requires a tribute of young bodies, preferably female. He's a monster, intermediate between human and animal, man and ape, and he eats human flesh. The famous scene when he snatches Fay Wray and stands her on the palm of his hand and inspects her, enthralled, modulates his appetite from animal hunger to erotic desire in a manner that reflects earlier fairy tale monster bridegrooms. The relation is made explicit in the celebrated epitaph with which the film closes: 'No, it wasn't the aeroplanes. It was Beauty killed the Beast.'

But what is not often noticed about the film is that *King Kong* opens with a rip-roaring, boy's own adventure story, featuring a type of intrepid photographer-explorer, armed with gun and camera, familiar from popular empire fiction. When Carl Denham captures 'Kong – the Eighth Wonder of the World' and brings him back to New York, Kong goes on his famous rampage in pursuit of Fay Wray, tearing up the City, symbol of progress and civilisation, until he falls from the pinnacle of the Empire State Building, brought down by her protectors. Cannibal indulgence and loss of control over women go together, and both spell catastrophe to civilisation. Kong's spectacular sacrifice reinvents the Victorian myth, that at the foundation of human society, cannibalism must be instituted, represented again and again as overcome, as finished (see Kilgour, below). With *King Kong*, 'Beauty and the Beast' meets *King Solomon's Mines*, and the fairy tale ogre's tyrannical bloodsucking and flesh-eating are converted into the lurid evidence of the imperial, ethnographic masquerade.

The mytheme of the ogre as black savage, preying on women, has left a deep trace in post-imperial historical memory. The Trinidadian calypso singer Mighty Sparrow plays with it with intent to scandalise in his song, 'Congo Man' (1988):

Two white women travelling through Africa
Find themselves in the hands of a cannibal headhunter
He cook one up an' he eat one raw
But dey so good he wanted more.

With much lip-smacking, throat-gurgling, slurping, and trilling, Sparrow conjures up his 'big brother' exulting in the complete primal cannibal scene, dancing round a 'big, big pot'. This outrageous piece of carnival bawdy seizes hold of the cannibal trope, making fun of white fears of blacks – though it must be admitted that in the typical calypso manner, women's fears in particular are to be played upon, mocked, and exploited. The *double entendres* in the chorus attack the convention in carnivalesque fashion by striking at the core of the fear: not of being eaten, but of being raped. Here again, in Sparrow's gleeful transgressive calypso, food stands in for sex, and the ogre's appetite threatens his victims with rather more than gastronomic consumption:

Oh, I envy de Congo Man
I wish it was me, I wanna shake he hand
He eat until he stomach upset
And I – I never eat white meat yet.
What about you? I never eat a white meat yet.

4

Though it is useful, for the purposes of criticism, to distinguish monster bridegrooms who prey on maidens from giants through whom heroes define themselves as heroes, the motif of cannibalism, in its earliest mythological expression, enfolds a threat to children, above all, and appears to dramatise the struggle for survival of the family – mother, father, and infant. The unholy combination of infanticide and cannibalism is a divine patriarchal prerogative, it could be said, part of the founding myth of the Greek divine pantheon itself, as told by Hesiod in the *Theogony*. Cronus, chief of the Greek gods in the first generation, as supplied in the genealogies of Hesiod's *Theogony*, is told that one of his children will supplant him, so he devours them one by one. But Zeus survives as a baby only because his mother Rhea foils his father's plan when it comes to his turn to be eaten, as all his elder brothers and sisters have been before him. Rhea wraps up a giant stone in swaddling bands and Cronus, the precursor of many duped ogres, swallows it down unsuspectingly (1982: 38–9, lines 453–93).

Images of Cronus devouring his children are rare before the fifteenth century – the Warburg handbook of Renaissance sources gives no classical models (Bober and Rubinstein 1986; see also Klibansky, Saxl, and Panofsky 1964). But in later visual renderings, a discrepancy exists between image and story: the logic of the narrative implies that, if Cronus could be tricked by a stone wrapped in swaddling bands, which he swallows as if it were simply a large pill of some kind, then he is not likely to have torn his other children naked limb from limb, piece by piece, gnawing and biting and chewing their undraped and vulnerable flesh as depicted with such appalled fascination by artists like Rubens, in his famous painting 'Saturn Devouring his Children' of 1523 in the Prado, or Goya, in his even more ferocious fresco of the same subject painted on the walls of the Quinta del Sordo of 1821–3.

Such representations of Cronus were perhaps influenced by the more famous cannibal ogre, Polyphemus the Cyclops. Renaissance artists did know classical interpretations of this scene, showing the Cyclops dragging one of Odysseus' men by the arm to the pot, and they strongly borrowed elements of the iconography to depict Cronus (Bober and Rubinstein 1986: 157, plates 124, 143a). But the deeper reasons for the myth's reappearance in this savage mood, in materials as wide ranging as fairy tales and Goya's Black Paintings, have to be looked for elsewhere.

The famous Olympians, male and female – Hera, Demeter, Hades, Hestia, Poseidon – are devoured every one in this way at birth in the Hesiod foundation myth. Later, when Zeus grows up, he tricks his father into taking a purgative which makes him vomit: and one by one the gods are reborn whole from their father's belly. Again, this later segment of the myth contradicts the graphic depiction in Goya of Cronus' crazed gorging. But practical intelligence does not govern the incidents in stories of this kind, only symbolic desire: the sleep of reason produces monsters. Cronus devours his children alive. This magical, implausible reprieve casts Cronus as a surrogate mother, giving birth to the gods and goddesses as the issue of his body, of his mouth. In this way, they reenter the world, twice born of their father, begotten and brought forth. The devouring here acts as a prelude to birth; being eaten equals incorporation and this in turn stands for a surrogate though unwitting pregnancy – of the male.

The myth, as it grapples with the question about children's origin, passes through two phases before it interestingly suggests an answer: at first Rhea recognises Cronus' paternity by allowing him

Figures 6 and 7. Saturn, a figure of Father Time, was assimilated in the Renaissance to Cronus, who devours his own offspring to prevent their supplanting him; nevertheless, they are reborn to become the Olympian gods and goddesses who do indeed depose their unnatural father. Rubens painted the episode from Greek myth, a work Goya knew; he reinterpreted it in one of the ferocious Black Paintings of his last years.

to eat his children, and make them part of his flesh; and secondly, Cronus reaffirms his biological paternity when he vomits them out of his mouth. But this anomalous behaviour implies the difficulty of male identity in the ordinary course of nature when it comes to parturition – later Zeus, his son, will give birth to Athena from his head in order to claim her as his true daughter. But Cronus' story – and indeed Athena's outlandish birth – both admit that the riddle cannot be solved except by prodigious, anomalous procedures, and this leads to an unspoken admission of the limits of paternal authority. The ogre, in the midst of asserting his absolute rights to incorporate, to make the child one with him, take it into his body as if it were his own, has to accept defeat. The motif of the trangressive cannibal parent, as excess, as outrage, may serve to define limits: on the father's power.

Cronus' devouring of his children follows his own act of parricide against his abusive father Ouranos, or Heaven. Cronus' mother – Gaia or Earth – hid her offspring from Ouranos's jealousy, and then conspired with Cronus to castrate his father (Hesiod 1982: 28–9, lines 155–82). Hesiod gives the celebrated episode in *Theogony*, with its fantastic consequence: Aphrodite, goddess of love and beauty is born from the foam on the sea where Cronus has scattered his father's seed (lines 159–206).

Interestingly, later readers had the same difficulty as today's in keeping the generations of filicides and parricides distinct. An edition of the *Ovide moralisé* of 1493, published in Paris, compresses the story into one vividly dramatic woodcut: Cronus devours a child, while bleeding from the wound between his legs, and his daughter simultaneously rises on her shell beside him. Cronus here appears holding the scythe of the planet Saturn, with whom he was identified in the middle ages, and on the helve of the scythe, a dragon devours its own tail – another image of cyclical time, another expression of the desire for eternal return. The smiles on the faces of the onlookers seem to approve this divine refusal of the laws of nature.[2]

The vigorous woodcut dramatises the themes as well as the story with entertaining clarity. The issues at stake among ogres and cannibals of myth and fairy tale are, first, the onward march of time. But secondly, and more particularly, their stories engage with the fundamental enigmas of kinship with which myths struggle. What relation exists between identity and origin? To whom do babies belong? Mothers or fathers? How can they belong to both? In what

Figure 8. The fifteenth-century woodcut compresses three major episodes of originary mythology: Saturn with his scythe is castrated by his son, as was Uranus, and gives birth to Aphrodite from the sea; meanwhile, he is also shown eating one of his children, as does Cronus in Hesiod's *Theogony*. Frontispiece to *Ovide moralisé* (Paris, 1507).

form can this doubledness of origin be expressed? How does the natural – biological origin – convert into social relation? Who has control of the identity of children?

In the woodcut from *Ovide moralisé*, we see Cronus as a kind of unnatural mother, a man operated as it were to acquire a woman's bodily functions, a kind of sex-change: a man who gives birth twice over, through his mouth after he has eaten his children, and through the semen frothing on the sea from his severed phallus. The medieval text's collapse of diachrony into synchrony opens a door onto one meaning of the death that the ogre and his food supply might signify: the jealousy of women's bodies as birthgivers. Such stories recognise the aggression felt towards this female capacity, because control of fertility is crucial, as we know, to the establishment of family and kinship boundaries.

In the middle ages and Renaissance, the name Cronus (beginning with Greek Kappa) became assimilated to the word for time Chronos (spelt by contrast with a Chi). Hence in traditional Zodiac imagery, and numerous astronomy and astrology treatises, the complex figure of Saturn, presiding genius of Melancholy, holds a scythe and hourglass as he rides in his chariot round the wheel of the heavens; sometimes he is shown devouring his children, who are allegorised as the Hours. He comes to represent the unrelenting passage of Father Time, who devours all, as in a characteristically grotesque portrayal, in Marteen van Heesmkerck's engraving, from the end of the fifteenth century.

But the problem with this is that the myth of Cronus and Zeus tells of time's eternal victory from the point of view of the vanquishing children who take over, not the triumph of the hoary old patriarch. The medieval and Renaissance allegory reassigns the laurel – to the old, to Father Time, because in terms of chronology, the metaphor of the hours being inexorably swallowed up as Time rolls on works in a familiar way. But it misses the human point: it's an inadequate metaphor to capture all that is happening in the original mytheme of Cronus devouring his children. Cronus is attempting to halt time: the children represent the future generation and announce his redundancy, immortal or no: time will roll on *for him*.

The Grimm Brothers' extraordinary tale, 'The Juniper Tree', could almost be read as a macabre recasting of this foundation myth for the modern nursery, in which mortals take the place of immortals, and the ogre's attempt to destroy a member of the future generation is frustrated. But in that story, the father is portrayed as innocent, as ignorant of his act of cannibal incest – or has he been shielded by the story from complicity in the dark events, as other fathers are in other tales of the Grimms? However it may be, in 'The Juniper Tree', incorporation into the father – when the little boy is unwittingly eaten for dinner by him – does not spell absolute death any more than it does to the Olympians whom Cronus devours. Paternity, in this fairy tale as well as in the Greek myth of divine origin, can bring forth the whole child again. And it also narrates, by the by, the salvation and healing of a tragic family as it regroups around the figure of the good father and expells the wicked, controlling, murderous false mother – in a conclusion which mirrors the end of 'Hansel and Gretel', as well. The consequences of these widespread family romances have not really been sufficiently examined.

The Grimms' famous, extraordinary fairy tale, written down in the stark affectless tone of psychological macabre, revolves around the themes of child murder and fingers again many of the sore lesions in the ancient myth of Cronus. Although the wicked ogre figure here is a woman, the father exhibits various ogreish standby traits – he's easily deceived, and he eats human flesh.

A child is born to a woman whose blood falls on the snow – and he's as red as blood and as white as snow; during her pregnancy she eats the fruit of the juniper tree, which makes her sick, and so, even though she is so 'delighted' when she sees him born, she dies, asking to be buried under the juniper tree. The father, of course marries again – and the wicked stepmother has a daughter and hates the child red as blood and as white as snow she has inherited from her husband's first marriage. She maltreats him and when he asks for an apple, she kills him, by dropping the lid of a trunk where the apples are stored and cutting his head off so that it rolls in among the red fruit. She then takes the head, and adjusts it back on the child's body with a handkerchief at the neck to hide the wound – the gap – and props him up at the table, leaving his fatal injury for her own daughter Marlinchen to discover when she offers her stepbrother an apple and knocks his head off. Marlinchen is terrified, but the mother hushes her worries: she's a veteran cannibal persona, for she tells her 'be quiet and let no one know it; it cannot be helped now, we will make him into black puddings'. She chops him up and serves him to her husband; he sups with relish on his son, not knowing of course what or whom he is eating. Meanwhile, the sister weeps, unable to share the gory supper of black puddings. Later, however, she gathers up the bones he has tossed under the table and buries them under the juniper tree, and lies down under it and feels strangely quietened, happy. Then a beautiful bird rises out of a mysterious fire that appears in the tree like a mist, and sings:

> My mother she killed me,
> My father he ate me,
> My sister she gathered my bones.

The magic bird flies around, singing and drawing the marvelling pleasure of its listeners, who give him in return precious and fatal objects, including a millstone, which twenty millers are needed to lift. He takes it, and sings outside the juniper tree house, and the wicked stepmother feels as if she is on fire. She runs out of the house, and the bird throws down the millstone on her head. Fire explodes around them, and when the flames have died down, the little boy who was devoured is standing there: 'And he took his father and Marlinchen by the hand, and all three were right glad, and they went into the house to dinner, and ate' (Grimm 1975: 229).

Both the Greek myth and the German Romantic fairy tale about the filiphagous father encode resignation to the passing of time, the overtaking of age by youth, and the necessarily stepped character of the genealogical ladder through time. The Grimms' 'Juniper Tree', a story which exists in numerous versions in different countries, was passed on to the Brothers by the German Romantic artist Philipp Otto Runge, who collected it in a Pomeranian dialect version. In his own paintings Runge insists on the almost preternatural vitality of children, who burst with life as their elders seem to fade away. In Runge's portrait of his parents and his children painted in 1806, the old couple in their dark clothes, shaded and withered, are withdrawing into the shadows, but the two children are fingering lilies of the field, divinely granted life and beauty and splendour, and they glow with colour and energy and *élan vital* while the little girl eyes her grandparents, almost sceptical of their continuing existence.[3] Runge may have responded to 'The Juniper Tree', and to fairy tales in general, because he was living at a historical moment when the child emerges as a subject – and a hero (as we saw with Hansel and Gretel); they are child-centred narratives, proclaiming the resilience and the eventual emergence of the small as supreme. This frame of mind will eventually lead to Darwin's insight into natural selection and the survival of the most adaptable – the tricksters who dominate through intelligence and bravery.

Running counter to this interpretation, however, is another, rising from the other master plot of the Victorian symbolic imagination: the hunger of the son to depose and supplant his father. The myths of Ouranos and Cronus were frequently muddled, as in the *Ovide moralisé* frontispiece, but it is interesting that no less a figure than Freud also conflated them, making Zeus a father castrator in his own father's image. The passage targets paternal authority in his own time, using the Greek gods as examples: 'Kronos devoured his children, just as the wild boar devours the sow's litter; while Zeus emasculated his father and made himself ruler in his place.' Freud goes on to comment, 'The obscure information which is brought to us by mythology and legend from the primaeval ages of human society gives an unpleasing picture of the father's despotic power and of the ruthlessness with which he made use of it' (1983: 357).

Later, Freud, to whom the mistake had been pointed out, cited it when he examined the truthtelling value of such errors in *The Psychopathology of Everyday Life*, and revealingly linked his conflation of Cronus and Ouranos to a remark his much older half-brother had made to him, when he told him: 'One thing you must not forget is that as far as the conduct of your life is concerned, you really belong not to the second, but to the third generation in relation to your father' (1975: 279). Freud implies that his repression of the myth's sequence represents his own refusal to be considered so junior as to be his half-brother's son rather than his father's. Again, the myth of the murderous father repeats a lesson about genealogical time. Freud's insistence on the sons' parricidal intentions effaces paternal animus – the foundation myth of Abraham and Isaac, of God the Father and Christ, of Oedipus exposed by his own father Laertes – in the interests of emphasising the father's vulnerability at the mercy of the Primal Horde. The ogre as a generic father, whom sons murderously oppose and defeat, meets some of the cases told in myth and fairy tale; but it is significantly emphasised in the nineteenth century; when the domestic and psychological meanings of such material come to dominate the social and political. As Jerry Phillips pointed out in the Symposium discussion, Freud's Oedipal plot has itself become a dominant tale of our time.

5

When potential victims are given images of their own victories over tyrants, when children are promised deliverance from giants and ogres, is the table-turning absolutely cathartic? Or do the threats continue to hang in tension, between enemy and victim? Does the power of the ogre, evident in the tales, leave a trace in memory and fantasy? Could it be that the ogres, however defeated, are there to remind the audience of the existence of such violence, of obstacles and danger which might not be so summarily dealt with?

In the late eighteenth and nineteenth centuries, the ogre and the monster bridegroom undergo a metamorphosis: no longer a simple menace to the central, sympathetic characters in the story, like Bluebeard's latest wife, he or, sometimes she, takes on a disciplinary role, as a bogeyman. The Devil in medieval hells such as Dante's does the creator's work, punishing the guilty, and the ravenous ogre, his epigone, metes out death as penalty for sin. The double outrage of child-murder and cannibalism flouts all shared norms of human society; such behaviour comes to characterise the underworld of sin. This is one unfortunate reason for the transgressive motif's survival in fairy tales: it is linked to possible future punishment in hellfire, and this punitive aspect of the sadistic pleasures they bring lends them to nursery adaptation later. The tale Bluebeard, for example, acquires a subtitle: 'Or the Effects of Curiosity'; the wife's disobedience is reproved, the emphasis falls on her reprehensible curiosity, so typical of womankind, and illustrators like Walter Crane in his picture books make open hints at her kinship with Eve, and Pandora, both fatal foremothers. The murders of the husband recede into insignificance, a trifling exercise of *droit de seigneur*, beside the wickedness of unwifely independence. The ogre becomes comic, too, not as a dumb giant, but as a wicked and lovable old duffer.

This instrumental use of the tale, to train and whip audiences into line – 'to house train the id', in Angela Carter's characteristically caustic phrase – conferred on giants and monsters a pedagogical character too. The Erl King bogeyman makes an early appearance in the margin of a medieval manuscript, with his basket full of children he has already stolen away; and in Berne, Switzerland, there is a fountain called the 'Child-Guzzler' (Kindlifresserbrunnen) where the sixteenth-century polychrome ogre stands, children slung about him from his belt, in his pouches, on his back and under his arm. These are the ancestors of the Sandman, Wee Willie Winkie, and all the other wandering and hungry spirits nurses – and mothers and fathers – have used to scare, cajole, bully children into obedience and quiet. In an English chapbook translation of Perrault's 'Sleeping Beauty' in 1750, the author adds a helpful footnote to explain the feminine of the word ogre: 'An Ogree [*sic*] is a Giant with long teeth and claws, with a raw head and bloody bones, who runs away with naughty Boys and Girls and eats them all up'. Here we have the metamorphosis of the cannibal giant into a nursery bogey, a relative of the fearsome Croquemitaine of French tradition, with his undertaker's name, who sweeps up bad boys and girls, of Father Flog and Madam Flog, reproduced in a nineteenth-century edifying US cartoon. The ogre in the stories can therefore act as a point of identity for the teller: the child-minder, parent or carer, places centre stage a horrible possibility. In French, the expression 'faire barbo' refers to just this device of terrifying children by playing ogres.

But the interpretation of the material can't come to a rest here either, with the manipulation of children's terror by adults: some of the oldest child's play in the world, as represented on Greek pots and Roman sarcophagi, consists of frightening the wits out of your playmates by pretending to be an ogre: putting on a monster mask with a big enough mouth to push your fist through and make-believe to grab your friends. The trope recurs, in the Renaissance, under classical influence, as in a drawing of the school of Mantegna.

This theatrical defiance exemplifies a defensive response: internalising the aggressor in order to stave off fear, as children like to playact the monstrous part and feel the pleasure of imagined power. The ogre and his imitators presents what is possibly one of those rare universal metaphors, for children are still making up cannibal stories and passing them on: an anthropologist, working recently in France, collected several hilarious and hair-raising examples. These are not fairy tales but anecdotes which claim to be true – they're even presented sometimes as autobiographical. One group rings variations on the theme of paternal cannibalism and castration in a contemporary setting:

> Suddenly there was Jack, he goes into a butcher's, then there was an attic, so he goes into the attic and he sees a hole, he says 'Shit, what is that?' So he takes his willy and he pushes it into the hole. Then suddenly there's a woman and then she says: 'So there's no more sausages', then he [the butcher] says, 'No'. And she says, 'Yes, yes there is one'. Then, 'Perhaps it's the last one', then he takes it and he cuts it off, Snip! Then he gives it to the woman. The woman eats it and the next day, she comes back and she says, 'It was really good your sausage, haven't you got another' and Jack says through the hole, 'When it grows back.'[4]

Claude Gaignebet's collection includes a variant of the story, in

Figure 9. 'The Child-Guzzler', a sixteenth-century polychrome sculpture standing in the streets of Berne, Switzerland, portrays a cradle-snatching bogeyman, such as used by exasperated nurses, mothers, or other carers to bully children into going to sleep or good behaviour: he has several victims slung about him, and is just crunching down on the head of another.

which it is the *father's* willy that is cut off – he too concludes with the line, 'When it grows back.'

Gaignebet himself does not think the ending of the tale is savagely ironical, about a poor dumbling protagonist who is such a fool he doesn't know that penises don't grow back. Gaignebet heard the children telling the story without cynicism, and he praises their spirit of comic optimism, the rude health of their humour. It is the first variant, in which the child's penis is eaten instead of a sausage, that seizes on the message of the myth of Cronus: that the young suffer the aggression of their elders but can comfort themselves that they will inevitably gain ground on the old. The second variant however contains the threat of repetition: the struggle will go on. Gaignebet does also point out that these are boys' stories – told by boys and starring them as victims in the first place, then as heroes.

6

The ogre who eats babies figures forth in myth a monstrous and anomalous paternal response to the anxiety their offspring will supplant them; he can also reveal the social and human imperative that the young must be allowed to thrive and grow. Child murder is the most heinous of crimes, and this is imputed to the devil, and to the particular cyclical stasis of eternal pain in Hell. But the nursery ogre's baby-eating also reflects, in the medieval and early modern narratives, the spectre of death caused by child-bearing, both of mothers and babies. This has developed in women's contemporary work into an explicit exploration of sexual fear.

In the Victorian nursery and the modern playground, the ogre has returned in the guise of a bogeyman, a character he already enjoyed in classical and medieval times. He persists as a threat consciously flourished by child-carers bent on discipline, and unconsciously invoked in the many scary stories which children are told or read.

In fairy tales the commingling of bodies in the cannibal act threatens to wipe out the smaller, younger characters, as we have seen, in the same way as Cronus' impious devouring of his children almost succeeds in exterminating any successors who might rival his rule. Baby-eating returns in such narratives to affirm in topsy turvy the social imperatives of procreation. The new generation must be allowed to survive: forces which attempt to engulf it, to halt age and time appear as brutal, stupid, and ultimately powerless. In this sense, fairy tales do offer allegories of time and resignation: the future belongs to the young giant-killer, to the young prince and princess, and the stories press their claims to autonomy and happiness, and warn the old, the big bosses, the authorities that their time is up. Fairy tales have transformed cruel, classical myths into narratives of family disfunction and social disorder, but recast the ogres and ogress, as figures of fun, bogeys to delight an audience with shivers and thrills and neutralise the very real threat they incorporate and make present. Children have not been passive in their reception of such material, and they have found their own ways to reinvent the ogre, to turn the tables on him themselves and frustrate his appetite for power.

9

Cannibalism qua capitalism: the metaphorics of accumulation in Marx, Conrad, Shakespeare, and Marlowe

Jerry Phillips

> ([T]hey have a manner of phrase whereby they call men but a moytie one of another.) *They had perceived, there were men amongst us full gorged with all sortes of commodities, and others which hunger-starved, and bare with need and povertie, begged at their gates; and found it strange, these moyties so needy could endure such an injustice, and that they tooke not the others by the throte, or set fire on their houses.*
>
> (Michel de Montaigne, 'On Cannibals' (1928: I, 229))

> [R]iches gotten by good means and just labor pace slowly... When riches come from the devil (as by fraud and oppression and unjust means), they come upon speed. The ways to enrich are many, and most of them foul.
>
> (Francis Bacon, 'Of Riches' (1942: 147))

The accumulation of wealth – by the few at the expense of the many – has perenially given rise to metaphors of moral protest. A prime example of the moral-metaphorical vision of accumulation is afforded by the trope of cannibalism. This essay explores the complex relationship between the trope of cannibalism, the economics of capitalism, and the poetics of the literary text. The accumulation of wealth under capitalism involves both rampant commodity fetishism and the ideological debasement of the many whose interests conflict with the few. In my reflections on cannibalism as literary trope, I shall address commodity fetishism through the Marxian concept of 'primitive accumulation', and ideological debasement through the psychoanalytic concept of 'overdetermination'.

The metaphorics of accumulation illuminate the centrality of racism and anti-semitism in the capitalist moral universe; how 'white', christian supremacism, in the words of Oscar Handlin, passes from 'a body of ideas' to 'a deeply felt need' (Handlin 1957: 126). In this writing racism is viewed as an integral aspect of imperialism, accumulation beyond national borders; while anti-semitism is viewed as key to the moral critique of mercantile and finance capital as beings in a fallen world. The motif of cannibalism imprisons the Jew or the colonised native in an exotic mythology of the dangers proffered to the 'universal' subject – dismemberment, ingestion, castration, the measures of bestial appetite. The metaphorics of capital accumulation turn, then, on a perceived difference between the moral and the amoral, the civil and the savage, the human and the subhuman. Indeed, as dramatised in texts, the charge of 'man-eating' functions as an 'ideologeme', which singularly reveals capital's dependence upon the philosophy, psychology, and politics of achieved social distance, what might be called the territorialisation of *ressentiment*.[1] I delve into the metaphorics of accumulation with two broad goals in mind: to elucidate the moral controversies of the colonial imaginary; and to foreground the political implications of a certain anti-capitalist discourse. The tropics of cannibalism in the colonial world will be addressed through analyses of texts by Karl Marx and Joseph Conrad. The tropics of cannibalism as an anti-semitic, anti-capitalist politics, wherein the Jew becomes the moral scapegoat for the debasement of 'community' wrought by unfettered accumulation, will be addressed through analyses of the literary poetics employed by Christopher Marlowe and William Shakespeare in the medium of drama. We begin with Marx and Conrad.

The notion of modernity as a project of transcending the limitations of nature, with a view to the attainment of the ultimate civil polity, has long provided the context for deciding the morality (and reality) of cannibalism. For instance, Marx concluded his analysis of British rule in India with a striking image of class struggle giving way to communism, or History negated by utopia: 'When a great social revolution shall have mastered the results of the bourgeois epoch, the market of the world and the modern powers of production, and subjected them to the common control of the most advanced peoples, then only,' Marx contended, 'will human progress cease to resemble that hideous pagan idol, who would not drink the nectar but from the skulls of the slain' (Marx 1977: 336). The human adventure ('progress') is here imagined as a savage god, whose power derives from ritual sacrifice, a theology of murder. For Marx, 'the bourgeois epoch' bears witness to the most advanced form of exploitation, whose proper moral analogue is a cannibalistic 'pagan' idolatry. In short, capitalism is the ultimate statement of the 'savagery' of history – the violence of class struggle.

Marx's vision of capital bestowed on radical thought the burden of a moral paradox, which still troubles the theorising of radical politics: on the one hand, capitalism is regarded as an agent of 'progress' because it starkly reveals the necessity of the historical voyage toward utopia; but on the other hand, capitalism is also viewed as a bloody and barbarous system, which gives succour to all that is base in the human animal, greediness, selfishness, ruthlessness, the predatory virtues of the jungle, of all-out war. The conception of capitalism as the 'hell' that illuminates 'heaven', as the savage state that casts into relief the last civil polity, leads to an oxymoronic model of history which I shall call the primitivism of progress. Marx imagined capitalism as cannibalism with two ends in mind: to emphasise the sheer brutality of the profit-motive as a measure of human affairs, and to emphasise the profound irrationality of a system that must perforce devour itself. According to Marx, capitalism will produce revolution (effectively, cannibalise its own body) because the human being is condemned by his or her nature to struggle for freedom. Thus the historical voyage toward utopia, where the last shall be the first.

If men and women are by nature freedom-loving creatures, then capitalism, as a systemic negation of freedom, will always do violence to flesh and blood individuals by offering them no authentic alternative to commodified, alienating work. Capitalism can never abolish its propensity to dehumanise the quotidian human world. Marx repeatedly advances this point through lurid or gothic images of man-eating. For example, as regards the commodification of human time, he defined capital as 'dead labour, that vampire-like, only lives by sucking living labour, and lives the more, the more labour it sucks' (Marx 1990: 342). In its 'blind and measureless, its insatiable appetite for surplus-labour, capital oversteps not only the moral, but even the merely physical limits of the working-day' (375). Then again, Marx characterised the bourgeois rationalisation of the peasant small-holding (a significant background factor in the 1848 French revolution) in the following terms: 'The bourgeois order, which at the beginning of the century set the state to guard over the newly arisen small-holding and manured it with laurels, has become a vampire that sucks out its blood and brains and throws them into the cauldron of capital' (1977: 320). Note the merest hint of the cannibal cooking pot (a trope which looms large in the colonial imagination) in the image of 'blood and brains' thrown into a 'cauldron'. (We shall see below that the vampire is a near relation of the cannibal in the political demonology of anti-capitalism. As an ideologeme in the fascist protonarrative of the desirable community, the trope of the vampire helped to create genocidal social distance between Christians and Jews.) For Marx, the vampire is nothing less than the truth of capital; as an abstract metaphorical value, the notion of the dead as thriving on the blood of the living provides the answer to the rhetorical question that he had posed in his critique of British imperialism: 'Has [the bourgeoisie] ever effected a progress without dragging individuals and peoples through blood and dirt, through misery and degradation?' (Marx 1977: 335). The answer, of course, is no. Capitalism has never known bloodless or peaceful progress.

The primitivism of progress refers, then, to the bloody, vampiric, or cannibalistic character of capitalism. If one wants to be certain that modernity is, in fact, a species of 'barbarism,' then one should not look to 'home', where 'bourgeois civilization' assumes 'respectable forms'; one should look to 'the colonies where it goes naked' (335), like the typical 'savage' of colonial lore. In the colonial world, capitalism, as the negation of human freedom, comes into its own. Marx noted that the 'treasures captured outside Europe by undisguised looting, enslavement and murder flowed back to the mother country and were turned into capital there' (Marx 1990: 918). This is the process he termed 'primitive accumulation', the anarchic plunder of the earth and the gross exploitation of foreign peoples, wholly careless of moral law.[2] It seemed that colonial capitalists – imperialists made gold out of nothing. Great fortunes sprung up like mushrooms, 'as with the stroke of an enchanter's wand' (919). The colonial capitalist was the 'vampire' who gave life to the 'cannibal' elite that ruled at 'home', with the aid of 'respectable forms'. As Marx put it, 'the veiled slavery of the wage-labourers in Europe needed the unqualified slavery of the New World as its pedestal ... If money ... "comes into the world with a congenital blood-stain on one cheek," capital comes dripping from head to toe, from every pore, with blood and dirt' (925–6). This stunning image of capital as a bloody ghoul, or an utterly savage beast, is meant to obtain, I think, the unnatural, even demonic, aspect of riches that 'come upon speed', almost without labour, certainly without ethics as a real abiding concern. If capitalism is the apotheosis of the savagery of history, then primitive accumulation can be interpreted as capitalism's basic instinct, capitalism's soul. In classical Marxist theory, primitive accumulation is associated with primary capital formation; but, in my view, it should be regarded as the permanent destination of capitalism, in its aggressive imperialist mode. The conception of the colony as merely a 'pedestal' for the consolidation of wage labour in the metropole has long complemented the notion of 'advanced industrial production' as the authentic terrain of class struggle, the engine of History. The metropolitan bias built into this model of passive objects and purposive subjects is not readily distinguishable from the eurocentric claims of colonial discourse, which held that 'real history' happens only in the West. If we would keep class struggle as the preeminent theme of fallen human history then it behooves us to recognise the point made by J. M. Blaut, that 'production on a slave plantation is just as much production as is production in a Birmingham needle factory' (1993: 205). Thus, in this writing, the adjective 'primitive' is not employed as a stadial or evolutionist measure of the accumulation process; rather, it refers to the purely brutal extraction of surplus value from the colonial labour force.

Few authors have depicted primitive accumulation with the imaginative power of Joseph Conrad, in his classic novella *Heart of Darkness*, published in 1901. In *Past and Present*, Thomas Carlyle noted that the nineteenth century was increasingly investing itself in 'a new theology, with a Hell which means "failing to make money"' (quoted in Sandison 1967: 3). The theology of business that Marx understood as a theology of murder; the hellishness of money-making which inevitably entertains (as an alluring ideal) the 'devil' of 'riches come upon speed'; the deepening alienation of the human world and the baseness of bloody 'progress' (for which cannibalism is a synecdoche) – these are the major themes of Conrad's tale.

At one level *Heart of Darkness* is a parable about the anthropological being of *homo economicus*, specifically, its verging on the absurd. According to Adam Smith, 'the [human] propensity to truck, barter, and exchange one thing for another' is as natural as breathing (1986: 117). Smith contends that in 'the general business of society' (109), people exchange commodities on the basis of a rational calculus concerning egoism. As Smith writes, 'It is not from the benevolence of the butcher, the brewer, or the baker that we expect our dinner, but from regard to their interest. We address ourselves, not to their humanity but to their self-love and never talk to them of our necessities but of their advantages' (119). However, notwithstanding the elevation of egoism, the market achieves the common good and rescues the value of 'humanity' by dividing labour and appropriately rewarding (by leave of the 'invisible hand') discrete expertise. Thus the essential economic transaction is always eloquent of interdependence: 'Give me that which I want, and you shall have this which you want' (118). *Homo economicus*, the hero of classical political economy, is imagined, then, as a composite of egoism and rationalism, allegedly the authentic nature of 'Man'. As Alexander Pope opined in *An Essay on Man*: 'Two principles in human nature reign; / Self-love to urge, and reason to restrain'. The struggle between 'self-love' and self abnegation, between senseless appetite and reasoned restraint, is central to the narrative action of *Heart of Darkness*. Conrad's incisive vision of primitive accumulation allows for a discourse of cynical reason that goes 'beyond good and evil', as conventionally defined. In *Heart of Darkness*, capitalist anthropology (the promotion of *homo economicus*) is shown as necessarily tied to the obscenity of capitalist anthropophagy (men and women devoured as expendable commodities). The 'jolly pioneers of progress' (Conrad 1967: 218) (the men who 'run overseas empire', who seek 'to make no end of coin by trade') become cannibals incarnate, slaves to gross appetites, symbolic of the egotistic pleasures of the market gone wildly astray.

Conrad shows that, with regard to capitalism's attempt to reduce the world to the terms of *homo economicus*, exchange value is the ideal stage on which the drama of capitalist expansionism (read: colonialism) is played out. Marlow tells us that in exchange for ivory, trading companies make available to African nations 'trade goods' such as 'ghastly glazed calico that made you shudder only to look at it, glass beads, value about a penny a quart, confounded spotted cotton handkerchiefs' (238). This grossly unequal exchange – the plundering of valuable resources 'compensated' by a steady trickle of 'trade goods' – remains fundamental to colonial capitalism, and nowhere more so than in the transactions that pit the rich countries of the North against the poor countries of the South. Conrad, like Marx, sees the supposed 'market relationship' between the capitalist and his 'other' as little more than a cruel farce, which essentially disguises the reality of robbery, the profoundly criminal character of riches come upon speed. Marlow observes of the entrepreneurial adventurers and company traders: 'To tear treasure out of the bowels of the land was their desire, with no more moral purpose at the back of it than there is in burglars breaking into a safe' (240). Here capital (in the form of the adventurers and the traders) is imagined as a bloody savage who dismembers the body of the earth. Note that the 'treasure' is located in 'the bowels of the land'; thus, in psychoanalytic terms, money-lust and man-eating are linked to an infantile scenario, eloquent of *homo economicus* in a market universe: the hoarding of excrement, the pleasure of 'banking' faeces. This is the sense in which primitive accumulation is linked to the overdetermination of capitalist desire: on the one hand, the pursuit of 'treasure' through trade is the engine of 'progress', the spur of the human adventure; but, on the other hand, the fetish that is money encourages real regression, insofar as it socially valorises the anal, and egocentric, fantasy of retention, the seductiveness of the hoard.

Conrad explores this problematic through the figure of Mr Kurtz, the ivory trader who 'sends in as much ivory as all the others put together' (228). Kurtz enters the Congo as an 'emissary of pity, science, and progress' (235), as the living embodiment of the 'unselfish idea [of empire]' (215) – the 'civilizing mission', the work of 'uplifting' the 'dark', 'backward races' whom Kipling described in 'The White Man's Burden' as 'half-devil, half-child'. But the 'wilderness' finds Kurtz out, and he fanatically embraces the theology of trade as it plays into infantile fantasty. Marlow relates how Kurtz had presided over 'certain midnight dances ending with unspeakable rites' (262). 'Savage' cannibalism thus becomes the measure of degeneration, the temporal and moral inversion of 'progress'. In the philosophical context of classical political economy, Kurtz becomes *homo economicus*, with all his egotism, his propensity to 'self-love', but with none of his 'reason', his sense of communal obligation. Kurtz had 'collected, bartered, swindled or stolen more ivory than all the other agents put together' (259). In plain terms, 'he raided the country' (268), and 'ruined the district' (270) for other traders. Marlow comes to see Kurtz as the irrational, 'cannibalistic' principle of colonial expansionism, the corporeal symbol of an utterly amoral desire to incorporate all within the province of exploitation: 'I saw him open his mouth wide – it gave him a weirdly voracious aspect, as though he wanted to swallow all the air, all the earth, all the men before him' (272). The sheer insanity of capitalist desire is pointedly expressed in the totalitarian fantasy that marks Kurtz's discourse: 'You should have heard him say, "My ivory,"' implores Marlow,

'"My Intended, my ivory, my station, my river, my –" everything belonged to him' (260). The fantasy of total incorporation is wedded to the fantasy of absolute possession; thus, 'oral' and 'anal' values meet on the plane of capitalist utopia.

'Mr Kurtz lacked restraint in the gratification of his various lusts' (270). Kurtz loses his 'humanity' (in Adam Smith's terms, his capacity for 'benevolence') as he wholly identifies with the inhuman object of his outrageous desire: a 'fascinated' Marlow notes Kurtz's 'ivory face' (283). In this respect (on the terms of a psychoanalytic model of the desiring subject, in which hoarding money is a substitute for hoarding faeces), Kurtz becomes money becomes capital becomes excrement – 'the horror, the horror' of degeneration into total narcissim, well beyond ethical imperatives.

That Conrad intends for us to read Kurtz's downfall as a parable about the primitivism of progress is made clear by the emphasis placed on the fundamental amorality of colonial space, the way it is easily lent to barbarous trading practices. Marlow is told that 'there was nothing on earth to prevent [Kurtz] killing whom he jolly well pleased' (269), that 'anything can be done in this country' (243). Colonial capitalism not only demoralised the land and its native populace, it also de-moralised the accumulation of wealth, by placing undue emphasis on the ends of capital (power and profit) at the expense of the ends of the commune (human welfare and the fate of the earth). Kurtz's fantasy of incorporating the entire world within the confines of his desire naturally entails the apocalyptic dimensions of the theology of murder: 'Exterminate all the brutes', writes Kurtz, exterminate all the 'backward' peoples who stand in the way of the hoard. In one respect, genocide is the logical destination of totalising infantile egoism. Kurtz's deadly imperative asserts that the world is merely a foil for the realisation of the imperial self.

Heart of Darkness deconstructs from within the cardinal myth of colonialism: 'the white man's burden'. Under the sway of a racist evolutionary model of human development, colonial agents were wont to represent themselves as doing God's work on earth. Marlow, the philosopher of cynical reason, parodies the pretentiousness of the civilising mission by describing himself as 'something like an emissary of light, something like a lower sort of apostle' (221). However, the colonial subject could only elevate himself by denigrating other human beings, who then become simply 'other'. As demonstrated by Kipling's claim that the dark native is 'half-devil, half-child,' denigration most often followed the routes of infantilisation, demonisation, and animalisation. Patrick Hogan points out that 'understanding someone through an infantile stereotype implies a certain way of treating him or her, a way which is different from the behavior entailed by a bestial stereotype' (n.d.: 6); but, significantly, all three routes to denigration – the route to 'the child of nature', the route to 'the imp of the devil', and the route to 'the savage beast' – can be extended to arrive at the racist stereotype of the unthinking cannibal. In an ethnographic commentary on people deemed as 'other', the colonial subject might travel on all three routes at the same time.

Thus Captain John Moresby, a nineteenth-century Pacific trader, wrote enthusiastically of 'our duty' towards the people of New Guinea, who are outcasts from 'the human family', insofar as they practice the 'customs' of 'infanticide, self-mutilation, human sacrifices, cannibalism' (1876: 300). Moresby demands of his reader: 'Are these men to rise so far, and no farther, above the level of the brute?' (300). (The recourse to the bestial stereotype). He argues that God and Natural Law decree that we make 'ourselves tutors of the childhood of those races that lie directly within our influence, and [that we shall lead] them up to moral and intellectual manhood' (301). (The recourse to the infantile stereotype.) Then again, Moresby can also write of 'dark, treacherous Melanesian [types]' (82), people who seem evil by nature. (The recourse to the demonic stereotype.) One should note that Moresby's primary motive for publishing his book was not to advance the humanitarian cause of the moral uplift of 'the heathen', but rather to instruct his readers 'as to the value of the commodities that await us in New Guinea and some of the islands, and the capabilities of the soil for growing various crops' (304). The proposal to tutor the savage must be seen, then, in the light of a worldly desire for manual labour, to harvest profits as yet only imagined.

For Captain Moresby, Melanesians, in their uncolonised state, are exiles from 'the human family'. Moresby's equation illuminates the pretentious patriarchal ideal that formed the 'moral' ground for colonial authoritarianism: the fatherly colonist dispensing the message of human value to infantile natives. The pedagogy of 'humanisation' (in this writing: the pedagogy of the oppressor) involves notions of work, restraint, obedience, and responsibility.[3] In the classroom of colonialism, the subaltern must not speak of his or her own desires. The Colonial Father knows what is best for all.

Conrad shows that the infantilisation of the native rests ultimately on the edifice of racism, the denial of existential unity (between the European and the African) in the name of 'white' supremacy. As Hogan argues, racism 'operates to undermine inter-group understanding and empathy, and thereby to perpetuate or extend an oppressive economic and political structure' (1). In *Heart of Darkness*, Marlow repeatedly ponders the ethics of racist sensibility. For instance, as the steamboat passes a festive African village, he notes that 'what thrilled you was just the thought of your remote kinship with this wild and passionate uproar' (246). Conrad understood that racism is 'a strange conmingling of desire and hate' (285), and in this respect it has a firm foothold in psychopathology. Colonial capitalism made racism palatable, even necessary, to the colonising subject by providing a definite 'moral' measure of preindustrial cultural forms, which failed to complement the subject's dream of treasure, housed in the body of the earth. What David Roediger has said of 'race' in relation to the making of the American working class, is directly relevant to the understanding of the colonial (racial) imaginary:

> [R]acism grew so strongly among the Anglo-American bourgeoisie during the years America was colonized because blackness came to symbolize that which the accumulating capitalist had given up, but still longed for. Increasingly adopting an ethos that attacked holidays, spurned contact with nature, saved time, bridled sexuality, separated work from the rest of life and postponed gratification, profit-minded Englishmen and Americans cast blacks as their former selves. Racism ... served to justify slavery but also did more than that. Racists still pined for older ways, and even still practiced old styles of life guiltily. All the old habits so recently discarded by whites adopting capitalist values came to be fastened onto blacks ... Blackness and whiteness were thus created together. (Roediger 1991: 95)

As indices of the psychopathology that is racism (the 'strange conmingling of desire and hate'), the concepts of blackness and whiteness entered the world together, like siamese twins. Similarly, civility and cannibalism were born together in the colonial imaginary, insofar as the former made of the latter its absolute moral antithesis. For example, in Columbus' second voyage to the Indies (really an invasion), cannibalism looms large in the invention of Carib 'savagery' – to be sure, a politics of displacing the truly savage intention of the invading forces: 'to tear treasure out of the bowels of the land' by enslaving or exterminating the indigenous populace.[4] In his memoir of what he calls the conquest of New Spain, Bernal Diaz tells us that Hernando Cortés, the leader of the expeditionary force, was wont to inform the indigenous peoples that he (Cortés) had been sent by God 'to warn and command them not to worship idols, or sacrifice human beings and eat their flesh, or commit sodomy or other bestialities' (Diaz 1963: 190). The other side of this early coinage of 'the white man's burden' is Cortés's habitual ultimatum to resistant groups: that he 'would kill all their people if they did not now come to terms' (150). Colonial discourse was heavily invested in the spectacle of savage cannibalism because, as Marx pointed out, 'civility', as a cultural ethics of negotiating stark human differences, was obliged 'to go naked' in the colonies – revealing itself as a 'morality' of plunder and murder. To the extent that it encouraged a certain moral violence against the unity of humankind, that is, the hierarchical division of peoples into races, states, and types, the discourse of civility gave leave to barbarous trading practices. Once 'Man' discovered 'the beasts', primitive accumulation could proceed without shame – and indeed it did. We know that the white man's burden made of the subaltern a beast of burden, who laboured, from 'sunup to sundown', on plantations, down mines.

In the passages quoted earlier, Roediger contends that racism 'served to justify slavery but also did more than that'. In his view, it ministered to the longing and disdain for the preindustrial universe (if only imagined) of festivity, natural communion, unbridled sexuality, and unalienated work. The disciplinary apparatus of capital drove these ideals into the moral underground, by conflating them with 'infantile pleasures', best despised. Here lies the social utility of racism, the sense in which 'blacks' came 'to symbolize that which the accumulating capitalist had given up'. The alleged profligacy, immorality, childishness, and laziness of 'blacks' (standard racist tropes) asserted to the 'white' proletarian subject that those renunciations he had made – in the realms of desire, communality, and play – were truly worthwhile, morally correct. In short, proletarian white supremacism is a (false) idol formed out of the raw materials of desire and hate, envy and enmity, nostalgia and estrangement, which combine in the ideological crucible of industrial discipline.

Drawing on Roediger's argument, I submit that cannibalism appears in the moral theatre of the colonial capitalist world as the ultimate polymorphous perverse, or infantile, pleasure. The spectacle of the cannibal feast makes the subject's longing for the preindustrial universe (of festivity and communality, of pleasure before business) an ethical impossibility, since 'nature' is wholly identified with inhuman savagery or 'beastliness'. The state of nature, as a bestial condition of existence, is typically what political economy – as a project of modernity – claims to negate. In this respect, beastliness is the 'primitive' truth of capitalist discipline as 'moral progress'; or to put it differently, it is the truth of 'Man labouring to transcend nature.'

Note that in secular, materialist terms capital sees in nature not an 'other' to be transcended for the good of all on earth, but a quotidian utopia of commodities, latent and manifest, which might be exploited for profit. Indeed, on a purely ethical level, spectacular accounts of the beastliness of cannibalism (Bernal Diaz claimed that the Tlascalans kept 'men and women' imprisoned in wooden cages 'until they were fat enough to be sacrificed and eaten' (183)) often served to disguise the banality of evil that marks primitive accumulation. In other words, man-eating in the visceral sense of ingesting human flesh could be made to obscure man-eating as a morally instructive trope, whose real world referent is the colonialist extermination of peoples envisaged as 'brutes.'

Writers like Conrad and Marx develop a critique of primitive accumulation that attempts to liberate the trope of cannibalism from its racist envelope.[5] Both Marx and Conrad show how visceral man-eating is not to be compared with its political/metaphorical counterpart: the latter far outstrips the former in its ferocious commitment to barbarism, values that are anti-human. I must now turn to cannibalism as a trope of anti-capitalism which yet admits a profound barbarism of its own.

According to Marx, 'world trade and the world market date from the sixteenth century, and from then on, the modern history of capital starts to unfold' (Marx 1990: 247). He contends that 'the Middle Ages had handed down [to the early modern period] two distinct forms of capital ... usurer's capital and merchant's capital' (914). Prior to the sixteenth century, the social influence of the former was checked by cultural customs and moral statutes derived from what Adam Smith termed a 'religious zeal [that] prohibited all interest' (191); the latter was checked by the political reality of limited trading opportunities, that is, the inaccessibility of key regions of the globe to European merchants, most notably the fabled

East. 1492 put paid to the real (historical) limits on amassing capital. In the new golden land of the Americas (with its fantastic array of resources and its wealth of potential slaves), 'the heirs of Columbus' could not resist the temptation of reimagining Paradise in the terms of Mammon. Thus primitive accumulation facilitated the ideological triumph of capital over values supportive of the commune (that is, notions of solidarity, spirituality, and recreation). As beings in the world – as forces deeply implicated in colonial expansionism (consider the resonance of the term 'venture') – finance and mercantile capital made communitarian ideals 'residual' rather than 'dominant' or 'emergent'.[6]

A key measure of the triumph of capital over the commune is the individual's sense of herself, as either a private agent (a subject committed to egoism) or a social being (a subject committed to others). The former ultimately bespeaks the moral universe of bourgeois political economy; the latter the ideal universe of anti-materialist or anti-elitist systems (for example, Christianity or Communism). The divide between the ego and the community (which capitalism insists upon) makes possible the existential distinction between the morally inauthentic and the morally authentic life. The distinction plays a fundamental role in the critique of capitalism as a political economy of 'man-eating'.

For Marx, the existential predicament of the subject under capital (that is, the individual's authentic relation to the lived experience of the inauthentic life) is nowhere so plain as in the dramatic tension between political community and the economy. Marx wrote in 'On the Jewish Question':

> When the political state has achieved its true completion, man leads a double life ... He has a life both in the political community, where he is valued as a communal being, and in civil society, where he is active as a private individual, treats other men as means, degrades himself to a means, and becomes the plaything of alien powers. The political state has just as spiritual an attitude to civil society as heaven has to earth. (Marx 1977: 46)

Interestingly, political community preserves the letter of communitarian law, even as the spirit is daily destroyed by the dystopian forces of capital – individualism, greed, aggression. Marx wrote 'On the Jewish Question' in response to Bruno Bauer, who argued that in order to live together peaceably, both Jews and Christians had to renounce their religious identity. Better to accept the secular identity promised by civil rights (the 'citizen') and work for the emancipation of all within the framework of the state, contended Bauer. Marx used the particulars of Bauer's argument to advance a general critique of what he took to be the ethical shortcomings of bourgeois liberalism, particularly its faith in statist social reform. The bourgeois state is formally based on the ideology of 'the rights of man'; but, for all that they articulate the abstract value of political community, these rights are the wards of 'alien powers' (commodification, fetishism, surplus value, and alienation), which determine the concrete experiences of men and women in (class divided) civil society. As Marx put it, 'none of the so-called rights of man goes beyond egotistic man, man as he is in civil society, namely an individual withdrawn behind his private interests and whims separated from the community. Far from the rights of man conceiving of man as a species being, species life itself, society appears as a framework exterior to individuals, a limitation of their original self-suffiency' (54). In short, 'the rights of man' can never bring about the ideal political community, because they are properly speaking the rights of capitalism's *homo economicus* – 'man' as an egotistical, property-holding, money-hoarding being.

The dialectical tension between inauthentic life in the political community and authentic life in the economy, turns men and women inside-out, forces them to pursue their desire for the commune as if it were naught but a fantastic dream, impossible to realise on earth. Thus the communitarian subject (in bourgeois parlance: the citizen) becomes an 'abstract fictional man'; 'man as he actually is', 'the egotistic individual', turns history into the negation of utopia. It is in this context that Marx asserts: 'The actual individual man must take the abstract citizen back into himself and, as an individual man in his empirical life, in his individual work and individual relationships become a species being ... Only when this has been achieved will human emancipation be completed' (57). Contrary to Bauer, who contends that German Jews can only be liberated by trusting in the abstract justice of the state, Marx argues that Jews cannot be free until all men and women are liberated from the state itself – the death of the citizen makes possible the historical rebirth of 'Man' as a communal being.

Significantly, in Marx's critique of Bauer, Jews become paradigmatic of the moral corruption brought into the world by the emergence of unfettered capital. Marx suggests that the 'infantile' values of the bourgeois marketplace – their appeal to the oral pleasure of reducing the objective world to a property of the self and to the anal pleasure of establishing a hoard – are perfectly realised in the secular reality of Judaism ('commerce'). Thus: 'From its own bowels civil society constantly begets Judaism' (60). As one reads 'On the Jewish Question' one is cunningly drawn deeper into the country of Marx's irony. It soon becomes clear that Marx means by 'the Jew', not a figure of human qualities, but an abstract (popular) figure of capitalist dehumanisation.[7] Anti-semitic discourse declares that 'Money is the jealous God of Israel before whom no other God may stand' (60). Marx collapses the house of anti-semitic motifs by showing how Judaism is made to bear the moral anxieties brought on by the supreme rule of capital.[8] In capitalist society 'the god of practical need and selfishness is money' (60); thus within the terms of the complex irony that Marx employs, those men and women who wholly identify with capitalism's *homo economicus*, who look for the 'god' of money in the bowels of the earth, might well be described as 'Jews'. Note that Marx is not concerned to address Judaism or Christianity as such; indeed, Marx views them less as religious systems than sociological categories, less theologies than metaphors. His real target is the 'human basis' of 'practical need' as determined by capital. Those who think of themselves as living in the commune (that is, 'Christians'), must recognise their real existence in capitalist civil society (that is, as 'Jews'). As Marx comments, under the rule of capital, 'the Christian egoism concerning the soul necessarily changes into the Jewish egoism concerning the body; heavenly need becomes earthly, and the subjectivism becomes selfishness' (62). In making the Jew the living symbol of finance and mercantile capital, Marx's intention was not to speak of Judaism, but rather to attack the alienating (cannibalistic) force of abstract economic values. The historical connection between anti-semitism, capitalism, and cannibalism (a triptych which Marx seeks to critique even as he theoretically exploits it) is cast into sharp relief by the literary stereotype of the Jewish merchant, made famous by Christopher Marlowe's *The Jew of Malta* (1966: written c.1591–2 (*JM*)) and William Shakespeare's *The Merchant of Venice* (1970: written 1600 (*MV*)).

In both Marlowe and Shakespeare the tension between the commune and capital, between spiritual community and the profit motive, between sociality and individualism, is dramatically figured in the ethical (and existential) distance between Christian righteousness and so-called Jewish 'avariciousness'. The dramatic action of *The Jew of Malta* and *The Merchant of Venice* culminates in a singular moral claim: 'Excess of wealth is cause of covetuousness; / And covetuousness, O, 'tis a monstrous sin' (*JM*, I.ii.125–6). In *The Jew of Malta*, Barabas the Machiavel dismisses pious 'Christian poverty' with the cynical boast that Jews, although 'a scattered nation', have 'scrambled up / More wealth by far than those that brag of faith' (*JM*, I.i.123–5). In Shakespeare's play, Shylock, the usurer become 'bloody creditor', despises Antonio (his debtor), partly because Antonio 'lends out money gratis and brings down / The rate of usance here with us in Venice' (*MV*, I.iii.40–1). What Antonio, the good Christian, calls 'interest', Shylock, the 'faithless Jew', calls 'my well-won thrift' (I.iii.46–7). Marc Shell has noted that early modern drama is often 'informed by a conflict between a supposedly unnatural (chrematistic) merchantry and a supposedly natural (economic) mercy' (1978: 111). In this respect the dramatic sterotypes of the Jewish merchant and the Jewish 'money'd man' (*JM*, I.ii.54) appear as the historical anticipation of the anti-capitalist version of capitalism's *homo economicus*: a sensual, infantile, and cunning being, a violent traducer of communality, a cannibal, a vampire, in short, as Shakespeare's Salerio would have it, 'a creature that ... bears the shape of man', and yet 'so keen and greedy' in its devotion to man-eating.[9]

In *The Jew of Malta* and *The Merchant of Venice*, the political logic of the Jew as anti-citizen, as a subhuman being beyond the moral boundaries of political community, is caught up in the labyrinth of attitudes peculiar to animalisation and demonisation as oppressive tropes. As regards dehumanisation through a discourse of animality, Barabas is made to say: 'We Jews can fawn like spaniels when we please; / And when we grin we bite; yet are our looks / As innocent and harmless as a lamb's' (II.iii.20–2). He promises to show that, within the self, he has 'more of the serpent than the dove' (II.iii.36–7). The linguistic denigration of Shylock is still greater. Shylock is a 'cutthroat dog', a 'wolf', an 'impenetrable cur'; utterly infantile in his resentment of Antonio, he is an 'unfeeling man', who desires, instead of money, a 'weight of carrion flesh' to 'feed [his] revenge' (*MV*, III.i.47). Shylock asks, hath not a Jew the same human nature as a Christian? Now, even if the answer is in the affirmative, the play itself shows little interest in the existential kinship between Jews and Christians. Instead, the 'currish spirit' of Shylock, which puts Gratiano in mind of 'a wolf ... hanged for human slaughter' (IV.i.133–4), is repeatedly interpreted in the context of Shylock's

'Jewish heart' (IV.i.80), the very heart of a savage. Shylock 'will have the heart of [Antonio] if he forfeit' (III.i.111–12). The parasitic usurer of lore ('such a one is to be hated of God and Man' (*Ecclesiasticus* 20:15)) becomes the predatory financier of tomorrow, the man whose being is realised in the perennial pursuit of 'fair advantage', whose desires are 'wolvish, bloody, starved and ravenous' (*MV*, IV.i.137–8). In short, the barbarism of usury (the harvest of human flesh) looks foward to the full-blown cannibalistic savagery of capital accumulation (the historical process that broods over the action of both plays in the form of merchant 'ventures'). Significantly, Barabas' defence of Jews as merchant traders leans heavily on the rhetoric of empire, the theology of business brought on by the expansion of the known world, and its greater accessibility:

> Thus trolls our fortune in land and sea,
> And thus we are on every side enrich'd:
> These are the blessings promised to the Jews,
> And herein was old Abraham's happiness:
> What more may heaven do for earthly Man
> Than thus to pour out plenty in their laps,
> Ripping the bowels of the earth for them,
> Making the sea[s] their servants, and the winds
> To drive their substance with successful blasts? (I.i.105–13)

One recognises here the enobling rhetoric of empire so pointedly critiqued in *Heart of Darkness*.

Viewed from an ethical perspective, both Barabas and Shylock are outcasts from normative human society. What the Duke says of Shylock applies equally well to Barabas: 'Thou art … / an inhuman wretch, / Uncapable of pity, void and empty / From any dram of mercy' (*MV*, III.v.3–6). Both Marlowe and Shakespeare toy with the idea that the devil walks the earth 'in the likeness of a Jew' (III.i.19); this idea is both asserted and undermined by the dramatic action of their respective plays. Nonetheless, the demonisation of the Jewish merchant/usurer provides a grammar of images – eloquent of disease, malign intelligence, disguise, temptation, and conspiracy – which (even in our time) overtly and covertly informs the rhetoric of anti-capitalism. In his discourse of revenge, Barabas calls into being (that is to say, plants into the minds of the audience) the historical memory of the Jew as a ritual murderer of Christian children (this popular medieval motif – known as the blood libel – thus offers some measure of the play's moral action): 'I'll be reveng'd on this accursed town; … / I'll help to slay their children and their wives' (v.i.62–4). Note also that in response to a report of Barabas' wrongdoing, Friar Jacomo is quick to inquire: 'What has he crucified a child?' (III.vi.49). This explicit reference to the myth of the blood libel is not without significance for the stereotype of the Jew as a fiendish cannibal.

For instance, in the Trent ritual murder trial in 1475, a number of Jews were tortured and executed for the alleged murder of a Christian child. The official sentence was death to 'a thief, eater and drinker of Christian blood, poisoner, blasphemer, traitor, and an enemy of Christ and Godly majesty' (quoted in Po-Chia-Hsia 1992: 104). Po-Chia-Hsia points out, in his analysis of the trial documents, that 'drinking human blood was a practice the Church most frequently attributed to heretics and witches ... For the magistrates, cannibalism was surely a demonic inspiration, characteristic of Jews and witches' (89). Not unlike the charge of anthropophagy visited on colonised people all the world over, the blood libel pronounced that the 'Jewish heart' was mired in an amoral polymorphous perversity.[10] Heinrich von Langenstein, a fourteenth-century theologian, held that Jews 'cannot be persuaded by the path of reason ... because they are stubborn' (quoted in Po-Chia-Hsia, 1992: 12). This conception of the Jew as a wholly irrational barbarian is suggestive of what Hogan has termed 'the adolescent model [of anti-social otherness] which counsels unbending discipline, stringency, authoritarianism' (n.d.: 9). The reestablishment of the appropriate political order is, of course, the *telos* that informs the plot structure of both *The Jew of Malta* and *The Merchant of Venice*. Indeed, neither play does anything – by way of dramatic irony – to undermine the paranoid ideal of anti-semitism: to expose to the light of day the conspiratorial activities of the 'all-powerful', 'grasping' Jew. Both plays are heavily invested in a politics of policing social identities, which entertains as an absolute subject: the complete unmasking of Jewish villainy. Thus the cathartic effect of the drama is identical with the triumph of the Christian commune over 'Jewish capital'.[11] This (utopian) scenario has exercised not a little seductive force in the twentieth century.

In the context of the Trent ritual murder trial, Giovanni Mattia Tiberino, a physician who examined the corpse of the child allegedly slaughtered by Jews, wrote in an open letter to his fellow Christians that 'Jesus Christ Our Lord, as much out of pity for the human species as the horrible crime that has to be stomached', intends to strengthen 'our Catholic faith' in order that we might 'create a tower of fortitude, and that the ancient infestation of the Jews may be wiped out from the Christian orbit and the living memory of them may completely disappear from the earth' (quoted in Po Chia-Hsia, 1992: 53). The genocidal longing of the committed anti-semite is no doubt the corollary of that subject's investment in the paranoid fantasy of Jews as an all-devouring, conspiratorial force.[12] In other words, the anti-semite desires the total disappearance of the Jews in direct proportion to the extent that he or she imagines them to be in total control. In common with colonial ideology, anti-semitic discourse never strays far from the concern of useful intelligence, a political anthropology of the hated or feared 'other'.

In the modern era, the classic statement of the anthropological dimension of anti-semitism is Adolf Hitler's *Mein Kampf*. In *Mein Kampf* the anti-semitic underpinnings of a certain metaphorics of accumulation are made abundantly clear. The Jew 'comes as a merchant' (Hitler 1943: 308). 'Finance and commerce have become his complete monopoly' (309); 'with his deftness, or rather unscrupulousness, in all money matters he is able to squeeze, yes to grind, more money out of his plundered subjects' (311). The Jew is 'the eternal bloodsucker', a 'vampire', a 'parasite on the body of other peoples' (310, 327, 304). Through his subtle control of the banks and the stock exchange, the Jew 'organizes the capitalistic methods of exploitation to their ultimate consequence' (318). Hitler's contempt for the Jew harbours a critique of capitalist accumulation, with its elevation of that anal ideal – the great hoard. 'If Jews were alone in this world they would stifle in filth and offal' (302), argues Hitler. As money is to excrement, so Judaism is to capitalism – one and the same. Hitler draws on a well-stocked historical archive of anti-semitic motifs, none being more important that the stereotype of the Jew as an anti-citizen, an outcast from moral community. The swindling merchant and the greedy usurer of the medieval and Renaissance political imaginary, becomes, in the modern era, the rapacious financier, the profit-hungry banker – in brief, the capitalist as savage cannibal.

In the strange moral universe of anti-semitic discourse, Jews exist to do business; that is to say, Jews live in order to make money, they do not make money in order to live. Viewed from a communitarian perspective, this reversal of economic logic is both irrational and immoral, because it elevates the pursuit of an abstract object – namely, money – above concrete human relationships. That this is true of capitalism in general, that the profit-motive has no necessary connection to human welfare, cannot be admitted by the followers of Hitler, who typically target despised groups rather than oppressive structures. In making the Jew the lord of 'unproductive wealth', who unjustly degrades 'honest producers' to misery and want, the anti-semite speaks of the annihilation of the Jews but does not speak so loudly of the abolition of banks – thus indicating that the bank is really a pretext and not a reason for his commitment to hatred. George Mosse notes that, in the nineteenth century, the myth of world-wide Jewish conspiracy to undermine the spiritual integrity of Christendom 'fed into the uncertainties and fears' associated with modernity generally and capitalism specifically; it also bridged 'the gap between ancient anti-semitic lore and modern Jews in a world of dramatic change' (1978: 118). To this day, the uncertainties and instabilities generated by capital accumulation and the forces of modernity incite people to find security and meaning in anti-semitism.

German National Socialism was in one respect the attempt to apply the racist imperialist model of culture and power (long advanced by countries such as England and France) within, rather than without, Europe's borders. In *Heart of Darkness*, Mr Kurtz, the first of the colonial pillagers, is described as 'a universal genius ... He would have been a splendid leader of an extremist party' (Conrad 1967: 286–7). Kurtz imagined the extermination of 'the brutes'; Hitler presided over the Final Solution to the so-called 'Jewish problem'. The unethical ethics of genocide were formulated on the basis of a communitarian or 'civilized' critique of cannibalism as an inhuman process. In the colonial imaginary, the cannibal negatively symbolised a state of existence that had to be morally degraded, in order to deflect attention from the utter barbarity of primitive accumulation. In the overdetermined political imaginary of anti-capitalist discourse, the cannibal (that is, the financier or the banker) draws the populist contempt for unproductive wealth – a contempt that, all too easily, becomes anti-semitism. In both imaginaries – the colonial and the anti-capitalist – cannibalism is inseparable from the ideological work of transferring and displacing social aggression, stoked-up by zero-sum competition (for resources, respect, and rights). In our time, the infantile force of the human personality is ever finding more room for its operations. This is a natural consequence of a world given over to racism. Mosse notes that 'The Holocaust has passed ... But racism itself has survived ... As many people as ever before think in racial categories' (235). Yet racism has always involved the substitution of myth for reality. As Mosse puts it, racism makes 'the sun stand still and it [abolishes] change' (xiii) – truly infantile scenarios.

'At the end of capitalism,' wrote Aimé Césaire, 'there is Hitler' (Césaire 1972: 15). If we are to avoid the eternal end of capitalism that is Hitler, then we must attend to the end of history that is utopia – a state of unadulterated communality.

Consumerism, or the cultural logic of late cannibalism

Crystal Bartolovich

> The new world facing us . . . [is] a wonderful world of discovery.
>
> (George Bush, 'The Possibility of a New World Order' (1991: 452))

> To articulate the past historically does not mean to recognize it 'the way it really was' (Ranke). It means to seize hold of a memory as it flashes up at a moment of danger.
>
> (Walter Benjamin, 'Theses on the Philosophy of History' (1992: 247))

1 Conspicuous cannibalism

The final scene of Peter Greenaway's 1989 film, *The Cook, the Thief, his Wife and her Lover,* is remarkable not only in its content but also in its implication of the viewer. A low-life extortionist with pretensions to high-life cuisine and trappings, the eponymous 'thief' spends most of his time making everyone around him miserable in ways that depend upon the alimentary canal. In the film's main setting, a posh French restaurant called 'Le Hollandais', he consumes fancy food while seeing to it that others are compelled to swallow – for example – dog shit, shirt buttons or rotten meat. Fittingly, then, in the last scene, he is invited by a number of his former victims to a special meal at 'Le Hollandais' and placed before the roasted remains of his wife's lover, over whose grisly death (by a forced-feeding of book pages) he had presided. 'You vowed you would eat him,' his wife observes, 'now eat him.' The camera slowly pans across the steaming body (glazed with an orange sauce) surrounded by vegetables, a mocking allusion to still life painting. His wife then repeats her order, and points a gun at him to give it emphasis. At that moment, however, the camera shifts to an extreme close up of the wife, placing *the viewer* at the end of the barrel, taking the full force of her contempt and rage. Briefly, the camera returns to the thief as he first throws up and then takes a nibble of his former rival. As he chews, the gun discharges, throwing him to the floor, dead. The next shot returns us to an extreme close-up of the wife; 'cannibal', she observes. Once again, however, the intended recipient of this charge is equivocal because she seems to look straight at the viewer as she makes it. In a film preoccupied with appetite, even the viewer's 'consumption' *of the film* apparently comes into question – in terms which suggestively conflate cannibalism and consumerism.

First, it should be noted that *The Cook* is not the only recent film to deal with consumerism (or capitalism more generally) allegorically via cannibalism: *Eat the Rich* (1987), *Consuming Passions* (1988), and *Parents* (1988) – among many others – also toyed with this theme.[1] In these films, 'cannibalism' is a very complex sign, sometimes signifying resistance to capitalism (as in *Eat the Rich*) and other times conflating capitalism itself with cannibalism. In all cases, the films rely on generating disgust for their impact. None are as successful in this respect, it seems to me, as *The Cook*. Nor are any of the others nearly so contemptuous of their audience. Greenaway's own comments on the film stress the importance of the cannibal scene (and suggest why the wife seems to include the audience along with her husband in her accusation):

> the film's preposterous notion is cannibalism in a sophisticated Western restaurant. We come across cannibalism when a small plane goes down in what's left of the Amazonian forest, and the pilot eats the passengers or vice versa. But we're not used to seeing cannibalism portrayed as it exists in our own sophisticated lives ... [T]hese are the kinds of taboo areas Jacobean drama investigated so thoroughly. I wanted to use cannibalism not only as a literal event but in the metaphorical sense, that in the consumer society, once we've stuffed the whole world into our mouths, ultimately we'll end up eating ourselves. The film is intended as an allegorical consideration of what cannibalism means, as well as being a literal event. (Indiana 1990: 120)

The film's intended target is 'consumer society', Greenaway claims here, by which he seems to mean (if his film is any indication) a culture driven to consume for its own sake, without thought, discretion or taste. I shall return to this point – and to the way it subverts the film's potential critique of capitalism – at the end of this paper. For the moment, I want to pursue Greenaway's 'historical' reference, which traces *The Cook*'s preoccupation with transgression and excess to a specifically 'Jacobean' sensibility.

Of course most viewers likely to choose to see this film (which, for the most part, was distributed in the art-house circuit in the USA) would not need Greenaway's assistance to appreciate its vaguely 'early modern' resonances. The diners in 'Le Hollandais' (the film's main setting) eat their meals beneath a wall-sized reproduction of Frans Hals' 'Banquet of the Officers' (1616). As is typical of Greenaway's films, many of the shots in *The Cook* echo this painting – among many others.[2] Even to a viewer without an encyclopedic knowledge of art history, the stylised costumes, and tableaux of meats and fruits, would declare their anachronism and Renaissance aesthetic values. Aside from its direct citations of early modern portrait and theme paintings, *The Cook* also makes general and repeated reference to still life as a genre. In the kitchen and dining room of 'Le Hollandais', huge piles of fruits, vegetables, and meats cover tables, racks, shelves: every available surface. These tableaux bespeak abundance, but an abundance which is vaguely sinister, echoing as it does the huge truck full of rotting meat from which the thief makes food-poison-inducing deliveries to the owners of restaurants who are behind in their 'protection' money payments. Accumulation and rot are in this way made to seem strikingly contiguous. Even in 'Le Hollandais' the piles of game with feathers still intact look more like dead birds than food; the fruits look too perfect to eat; the piles are bewilderingly, overwhelmingly excessive.

A similar suspicion of excess is evoked in *The Cook* through its plot, which takes up elements of early modern revenge tragedy (as Greenaway signals in his somewhat overly precise reference to its 'Jacobean' elements) – although not in a systematic way. Shakespeare's *Titus Andronicus*, for example, offers us a special invitation feast of human flesh, prepared by Titus ('I'll play the cook' (v.ii.204)) himself, as an aperitif to a revenge killing but, for the most part, Greenaway's fascination with excess and transgression – rather than specific details of plot – seem to be what attracts him to early modern revenge drama.[3] The lists cataloguing the content of these plays in the early modern period give some indication of their 'excessive' quality, and how well they construct a world in which Greenaway's thief – who extorts, bullies, and steals his way to wealth – would feel at home: 'The matter of *Tragedies* is haughtinesse, arrogancy, ambition, pride, iniury, anger, wrath, envy, hatred, contention, warre, murther, cruelty, rapine, incest, rovings, depredations, piracyes, spoyles, roberies, rebellions, treasons, killing, villany &c. and all kinds of heroyck evils whatsoever' (Greene 1615: 55–6). Lists such as these are the linguistic equivalent of still-life's represented accumulation of objects (which, in turn, is the visual arts equivalent of dramatic excess in revenge tragedy): copia ('abundance'), collections, and multiple murders are all figures of accumulation which preoccupy the Elizabethans and Jacobeans who interest Greenaway.[4] We might pursue the implications of this elaborate network of historical citations.

The Cook's linkage of a particular past (the 'Jacobean'/early modern) and present (contemporary 'consumer society') invites us to follow Benjamin's injunction to 'seize hold of a memory as it flashes up at a moment of danger' (1992: 247). In the context of a generalised faux 'early modern' aura, the shocking memory invoked by *The Cook* is of 'cannibals' – a figure of terror in the incipiently colonial European imaginary from which Greenaway draws *them* as well as the generic conventions of revenge tragedy and Renaissance oil painting. Two things about this particular 'memory' are especially worth noting. First of all, cannibals as such *emerge* at this historical juncture when Europeans encounter the 'New World' and give this name to a group of (ostensibly) man-eating 'savages' in the Caribbean. This name then becomes (for Europeans) the universal signifier of anthropophagy, as the work of Peter Hulme has shown (1986: 1–87). There had, of course, been stories generated about man-eaters of various kinds earlier, but *cannibals* mark a very particular figuration of them, inscribed with colonialism and incipient capitalism. Secondly, 'New World' imagery proliferates in the modern West in many ways, which inflect and are in turn inflected by Greenaway's conjuring up of cannibals. The quotation at the beginning of this essay, culled from a speech by George Bush, which I paired with the passage from Benjamin, reminds us how emphatically a certain 'memory' of the New World engages the contemporary world. Such 'discovery' images can in part, of course, be attributed to the near occasion of the Columbus quinticentennial (1992) – but not solely.

How are we to read such a convergence 'dialectically'? Cannibals, as we shall see, are doubly charged to those who are preoccupied with them. They evoke both repulsion and desire, rejection and wonder. Benjamin points us to another dialectic, however: early modern collides with contemporary cannibals in a flash; in this forced encounter, 'awakening', a collective redemptive recognition, is possible. Margaret Cohen has observed of Benjamin's historical practice that (for him) 'if images from the past spring legibly to the present it is because they speak to its concerns' (1993: 11). Interrogating the image of the cannibal, then, gives us another chance historically – which is to say, in lived practice. At the early modern moment of appearance, cannibals provided a rationale for destruction, exploitation, and enslavement. Their reappearance argues for rememoration – and alternatives.

The task of understanding the cultural work performed by recent evocations of a New World and its cannibals seems all the more pressing and pertinent because a fascination with cannibals manifests itself not only in the cultural sphere at the current conjuncture, but in the economic as well. One of the most prevalent terms deployed to describe competition within saturated markets in contemporary business journalism is 'cannibalisation'.[5] The term 'cannibal' takes on a number of meanings in business publications, but its general sense seems to be the 'eating up' of one's own, or a competitor's, market share (and, thus, profits), either by bringing out a product which steals sales from another (instead of producing a 'new need') or by oversupplying a given area with a certain outlet – fast-food restaurants, for example, or supermarkets. In a 1993 article about US supermarket chain expansion in Tijuana, a spokesman for one of the chains acknowledged that such outlets are particularly vulnerable to 'cannibalisation', a term which the article takes to be so obvious in its meaning that it does not even bother to gloss it. Often, however, the analogy is made more explicit: 'the fast-food thing has turned into a cannibal circus', remarks a franchise operator in Ohio. 'They are eating their own young right now.' The reporter explains: 'instead of developing products that have expanded the market, the major fast-food chains have taken to stealing sales from one another'. In each case, the articles invoke 'cannibals' when a *limit* is approached, beyond which further expansion of consumer appetite is deemed impossible. Cannibalism, then, is the mark of absolute saturation – and stasis. This contrasts rather markedly with the deployment of cannibalism in films such as *The Cook* to mark a voraciousness of appetite (for food, cruelty, domination, etc.) that seems to have no limits whatsoever.

In contrast to the limitlessness depicted in the film, the business accounts are likely to describe cannibalization in zero-sum terms: 'companies are spending millions of dollars, trying to cannibalize the membership rolls of competing health care organizations'. Small businesses complain about the ogre-like consuming capacities of larger ones: 'They strangle competitors and cannibalize markets.' The threat is so potent, apparently, that it can drive corporations inward, to feed on their own markets before another corporation can get to them: 'Even though there may be some [self-]cannibalization, if we [Subway] don't go in there [an available location], then Blimpies or Thundercloud will go in there.' This practice is often referred to as 'planned cannibalization'. Planned or not, however, this sudden emergence of cannibals is generally seen as a crisis: 'it's not the way Costco [wholesale warehouse] would prefer to grow. But, with the industry becoming saturated, analysts ... believe cannibalization will be a way of life for Costco for some time to come'. Reinforcing the sense of crisis, several reports, with headlines such as 'Economy Kills Appetite for Restaurant Stocks', stress that the stock market reacts unfavourably to such cannibal activities.

When we bring the cannibals from films such as *The Cook* and business journalism together, we might well ask how it happens that the same term has come to be deployed in cultural texts criticising 'consumer society' and in business journals lamenting the limits of consumer appetite. However we answer this question ultimately, we can begin with the observation that 'cannibal' seems to be a site of conflict in which different groups meet in their quite different uses and accentuation of the term, and struggle over its meaning.[6] Both Greenaway and the business journalists tend to attach a negative charge to it, but this is virtually their only point of agreement. At least two conflicting fears inhabit 'cannibal' as a contemporary sign: one (Greenaway's) concerning a dispersion and attendant excess of consumption, and another (entrepreneurial) obsessed with a failure of consumption.

Greenaway alternately gratifies and mortifies the cannibal (that is, extreme) appetites of his viewers who are, on the one hand, elaborately feasted on elegant sets, sumptuous costumes, a gallery catalogue of art citations, and a Nyman score, while, on the other hand, they are assaulted with repulsive spectacles involving bodily emissions and violence. If Greenaway were less elitist, one might suspect a sort of 'surprised by sin' logic to his film, which would encourage all viewers to acknowledge the 'thing of darkness' within themselves – and pledge to keep it under control as best they can; however, for Greenaway, consumption *only* seems to be a problem in a (mass) consumer society where the 'wrong' people have access to the means of consumption. Greenaway's cannibal thief and his crew, though spectacularly rich, are marked by accent, manners, and habits as stereotypically 'low' – they are slovenly, crude in speech, belch, and chew with their mouths open. To indicate that they desecrate any space they enter, Greenaway relies on citations of church architecture and accoutrements. The thief and his followers are walking advertisements for the vulnerability of high culture to debasement if offered up for general consumption. The wife, the cook, and her lover, on the other hand, are *tasteful*. They appreciate subtle flavours and unusual dishes; they are quiet, polite – genteel. Proper appreciation of the film, then, *may* be a sign of refined (anti-cannibalistic) taste. But by the arrangement of the closing shots, the viewer is left wondering whether he is a cannibal or not. There is a predestinarian undercurrent to the film which renders it undecidable whether one really belongs to the aesthetic elect. To buy or not to buy – that is, whether one is worthy to buy – remains a troubling question.

This is hardly a consummation devoutly to be wished from the perspective of the business commentators who use cannibalism quite differently. For an entrepreneur worried about moving merchandise, the thief and his crew would be a dream come true: a pool of consumers with endless appetites, and the money to support them. The 'thief' is not a cannibal from this perspective; to the contrary, cannibals emerge for entrepreneurs where consumer appetites have failed, and thus competition among cannibal competitors (providers of goods and services) arises for the limited appetites of consumers. While for Greenaway the cannibal is the mark of limitless (and unlimited) consumption, for contemporary capitalists, the cannibal is the competitor who threatens a static (limited) market share.

But why *cannibals*? To answer this question, we need to take a historical excursus from the current moment of late capitalism back to the very moment Greenaway's film calls to our attention: the moment of primitive accumulation, when not only the wealth that would become capital was being amassed, but also its subjects – and its appetites.[7] Stories about cannibals played a crucial ideological role in the primitive accumulation of – the establishment of the conditions of possibility for – capital. Many discussions of cannibalism have suggested that European cannibal narratives have been important in justifying colonial violence and theft,[8] but they also operated in a rather different, though related, way in the early modern European imaginary: by providing both an example of – and a limit text for – European proto-capitalist 'appetite', which was tending in its mercantile and colonial forms toward limitlessness, as the logic of capital – ambivalently – requires. These two positions on contemporary cannibalism outlined above each focus only on part of its early modern matrix of meaning, as we shall see. Greenaway sees a *transgression* of limit, voraciousness, when he calls up an image of cannibals, while entrepreneurs see stasis and limit. Cannibals have been, and are, obliged to be a site of negotiation of specifically capitalist crises in appetite (even prior to the dominance of the capitalist mode of production). In the early modern period, the contradiction in capitalist-to-be appetite figured in the cannibal/capital binary is the simultaneous drive to endless consumption of labour power by the capitalist, and the necessity of observing limits to preserve production (that is, fuel reproduction). Contemporary capital figures different problems in the cannibal, placing an emphasis on mass commodity consumption. In each of these moments, however, a crisis in appetite conjures up cannibals.

This is not to suggest that a capitalist economic 'base' was already exerting pressure on political and cultural life in the early modern period. To the contrary, capital later was able to reclaim cultural and political forces that it did not itself generate, elements of the social formation, in fact, which preceded its own dominance. To borrow Gramsci's lexicon, merely 'conjunctural' phenomena, may, in the long run, take on an 'organic' function, but in a given moment, many things are possible.[9] The places in the pre-capitalist social order where 'appetite' as unrequitable desire was produced were providing training for the appetite necessary to subjects of capital. These appetites need not in any way have already been articulated with economic (much less specifically 'capitalist') forces. Rather, cultural, political, and economic forces inflect each other at a moment of crisis, resulting in a particular combination of forces rather than others. Thus, it is crucial to note the ways in which the appearance of cannibals on the scene plays historically specific roles in particular moments. The next section argues that cannibal appetite helps illustrate the problems with (and potential of) 'voracious hunger' and thereby 'in-forms' emergent subjects of capital-to-be. Then, the third section discusses how this appetite contributes to and conflicts with early modern forms of 'supplementary logic' which render endless productive accumulation – necessary to capitalist accumulation – imaginable. Finally, the paper returns to the current moment to suggest how cannibals today are like and unlike their early modern namesakes.

2 'Primitive' consumption and the problem of 'preposterous desire'

Let me begin by offering three typical descriptions of cannibal appetite from early modern English travel narrative (drawn out of Hakluyt's collections):

> The Tabaco of this place [St. Vincent] is good: but the Indians being Canibals, promising us store, and delaying us from day to day, sought onely oportunitie to betray, take, and eate us, as lately they had devoured the whole companie of a French shippe. (1965: x, 478)
>
> There remaine some among the wild people, that unto this day [1572] eate one another. I have seene the bones of a Spaniard that have bene as cleane burnished, as though it had bene done by men that had no other occupation. (IX, 397)
>
> Over and beside the knowledge how to till and dresse their grounds, they shal be reduced from unseemely customes to honest maners, from disordered riotous routs and companyes to a well goverened common wealth, and withall, shalbe taught mechanicall occupations, arts and liberall sciences: and which standeth them most upon, they shalbe defended from the cruelty of their tyrannicall and blood sucking neighbors the Canibals, whereby infinite number of their lives shalbe preserved. (VIII, 120)

Let us now add three descriptions of capitalist appetite from *Capital*:

> The prolongation of the working day, into the night, only acts as a palliative. It only slightly quenches the vampire thirst for the living blood of labor. Capitalist production therefore drives, by its inherent nature, towards the appropriation of labor throughout the whole of the 24 hours in the day. But since it is physically impossible to exploit the same individual labor-power constantly... capital has to overcome this physical obstacle. (Marx 1990: 367)
>
> We have observed the drive towards the extension of the working day, and the werewolf-like hunger for surplus labor, in an area where capital's monstrous outrages, unsurpassed, according to an English bourgeois economist, by the cruelties of the Spaniards to the American red-skins, caused it at last to be bound by the chains of legal regulations. (353)
>
> Alongside the independent producers, who carry on their handicrafts or their agriculture in the inherited, traditional

> way, there steps the usurer or merchant with his usurer's capital or merchant's capital, which feeds on them like a parasite. (645)

From these passages emerges a certain thematic of appetite. In the first set of quotations cannibal consumption is depicted as absolute, unlimited – cannibals suck blood until the life is utterly departed from the body; they 'clean burnish' bones until no flesh is left; they devour 'whole companies'. And, by this absolute consumption, they divert local populations from proper trade and 'occupations'. The English habit of devouring mere land and labour-power – stopping short, as it must, of absolute consumption – is offered as desirable (infinitely desirable) in comparison, since by it 'infinite number of ... lives shalbe preserved'.

The second set of passages suggests, however, that capital's own 'hunger' and 'thirst' for the 'living blood' of labour is only reluctantly abandoned, and only then to preserve a minimal existence in which labour-power can reproduce. Indeed, its most fervent desire is cannibalistic in the sense the first set of quotations indicates (tending toward absolute consumption) – but it cannot go so far and preserve the system as a whole. It continuously comes up against the 'physical obstacle' to its own consumption, which it then must meet with ingenious methods to consume more labour power without killing off its agent. Thus, capital must be less absolute in its consumption: a vampire, werewolf, or parasite, who continuously feeds off a living worker. There is no exaggeration in the translation; the words Marx uses to describe the appetite of the capitalist are cognate with English, and unmistakable: 'vampyrdurst', 'werwolfsheißhunger', 'parasitenmaßig'. And (if we accept this critique) these analogies suggest that the capitalist is a cannibal-manqué. Rather than concurring with the capitalist's protestations of a moral basis for this 'restraint', we might well observe with Montaigne on this score: 'I thinke there is more barbarisme in eating men alive, than to feed upon them being dead' (1928: 1, 223).

The worlds of Montaigne and Marx are not the same to be sure, but the former lives in the time in which the conditions of possibility for the industrial capitalism which Marx decries in *Capital* are emerging. In their struggle to emerge, these conditions effect massive disruptions in the early modern social order, calling for massive ideological restructuring. The process of primitive accumulation establishes both the relations of capital and its start-up wealth. Cannibals were useful in the latter task by justifying the old world theft of New World wealth, and providing Europe with its self-consolidating other. Cannibals, however, played a role in the first aspect of primitive accumulation as well: they help to establish certain (not quite cannibalistic) appetite relations between capital and labour by way of a simultaneously positive/negative example. The cannibal appetite is the self-consolidating other of capitalist appetite as well as European civility. After their appearance on the scene, they can be called up whenever a crisis of appetite or civility is encountered.

To criticise capitalism by declaring it a form of cannibalism might seem tempting in certain ways, but to do so is to miss the point. It *must* be parasitic rather than cannibalistic, and, indeed, Marx was not alone in seeing capitalists as the parasites of his day. With a quite different set of preoccupations and investments, Henry Mayhew was drawn to the same metaphor, as were other reformers of various stripes. 'In all civilized countries,' Mayhew muses, 'there will necessarily be a greater or less number of human parasites living on the sustenance of their fellows' (1967: I, 3). He includes in this category a broad range of people from 'those who will not work' (beggars, criminals, and the assorted other outcasts belonging to what Marx called the lumpen-proletariat) to 'those who need not work' (landlords – and capitalists). In his latter category, by including capitalists, he deviates from the attempts by figures such as John Stuart Mill to place capitalists among 'Enrichers' or productive workers. Mayhew scoffs, 'nothing could be more idle, for surely they [the capitalists] do not add, *directly* [i.e. by their labour], one brass farthing, to the national stock of wealth' (IV, 28, emphasis Mayhew's). He finds these parasites, it should also be noted, while undertaking an exploration of the 'undiscovered country of the poor' about whom 'the public had less knowledge then of the most distant tribes' (I, preface). Among the 'distant tribes' there are cannibals; at home, there are parasites. This cannibal/parasite distinction is a crucial one, distinguishing not only the civilised from the barbarous, but the capitalist from the primitive. Parasitism, 'eating men alive' (as Montaigne put it, even though the proto-capitalists did not) – is justified by a prior demonisation of (and preoccupation with) 'eating them dead' in early (and, indeed, later) colonial practice. On the side of civility is placed consumption of human labour power; on the side of savagery consumption of human flesh. A virtue is produced out of a capitalist necessity. To track the production of this virtue, we need to turn to the early modern figurations of appetite and consider the multiple ways they worked to distinguish 'European' from 'Savage' peoples.

The distinction between cannibalism/capitalism in their emergent forms renders any easy equation of the two problematic.[10] The absolute consumption of the cannibal (whether a European fantasy or an actually existing practice)[11] is at odds with capitalist accumulation; indeed, it bears more resemblance to aristocratic surplus consumption – to which emergent capital was forming itself in opposition. Resources previously directed to consumption of luxuries needed to be redirected into investment (ultimately, consuming of labour power) if capital were ever to emerge and reproduce itself. It is, thus, precisely in the domain of eating that early modern landowners were often taken to task by mercantile, colonial, and incipient agrarian capitalist interests.

Peckham, for example, urges his readers: 'I most humbly pray all such as are no nigards of their purses in buying of costly and rich apparel, and liberal contributors in setting forth of games, pastimes, feastings and banquets (wherof the charge being past, there is no hope of publique profite or commoditee) that henceforth they will bestowe and empty their liberality (hertofore that way expended) to furthere of these so commendable purposed proceedings [voyages of 'discovery', trade, and colonization]' (Hakluyt 1965: 96). Private consumption is to be foregone in the interest of 'publique profit'. Or, in other words, cannibalism – exhaustive consumption (at 'feastings and banquets'!) – is to be foregone in the interest of proto-capitalist accumulation (joint-stock company investment). Hakluyt's word choice makes the contrast between capitalism and cannibalism even more explicit; the gentry need, he claims, to invest or engage in colonial activities instead of 'those soft unprofitable pleasures wherein they now too much *consume* their time and patrimony' (Hakluyt 1907: 40–1, emphasis mine). From right and left alike, unproductive consumption came under attack in the early modern period. Hence Thomas More, in *Utopia* (1517), complains: 'one greedy, insatiable glutton ... may enclose many thousand acres of land within a simple hedge' (1992: 12). This is despicable, according to More, because primary producers are thrown off the land and replaced by sheep, so that a few people might be 'given over to ostentatious extravagance of dress and too much wasteful indulgence in eating' (15). More's charges collapse a critique of ostentatious late feudal consumption alongside a prescient attack on the enclosures which were helping to establish agrarian capitalist relations in the countryside – declaring a pox on both the old and new economic houses.

Although it would be misleading to claim that only recalcitrant 'feudal' agents tended toward exhaustive consumption and that there was no drive to absolute consumption among incipient capitalists, cannibalistic incorporation and the 'supplementary logic' (to be elaborated in the next section) of capital are nonetheless incommensurate. To the extent that proto-capitalists did feel driven toward exhaustive consumption, they were working against their own long-term interests which it took them some time to learn. The training of appetite, then, unsurprisingly, becomes a preoccupation of period commentators on trade, discovery, and production. In the *Divers Voyages* (1582), for example, accumulation is depicted as potentially unlimited, but Hakluyt is also at pains to differentiate the English from their competitors (which include, of course, the so-called cannibals) with an ostensibly specifically English recognition that limits must be preserved in a proper colonial project. Indeed, he draws attention to the difference between the behaviour of foreigners, as established in their accounts, and proper English behaviour. What had been badly done in the past would be set to right by England. For early modern English readers, what was 'divers' (several/different) could also be – according to the *OED* – 'perverse'. Although there is no indication that Hakluyt considered calling his first collection the 'Perverse Voyages', there are certainly indications that he saw perversities among the travellers and colonisers he discusses.

In the *Divers Voyages*, at least two kinds of evil are described: those encountered by travellers in the course of their journeys (cannibalism, violence, sexual depravity) and those that the travellers brought with them (greed, slavery, theft, violence, sexual depravity). Given their status as 'other', as the product of labour of 'strangers', the narratives Hakluyt collects in the *Divers Voyages* (made up almost entirely of accounts of travels made by, or recorded by, foreigners) could have been kept separate to demonstrate differences among the travellers, and indicate a place for the English to insert their own labours as 'good' men. As the elder Hakluyt explains, both 'the Savages' and 'civill Princes' could 'anoy us in our purposed trade' (1966: H[1]^{r}). Therefore careful distinctions needed to be made, and the English had to fortify their own positions, militarily and rhetorically. Such distinctions were frequently made in the realm of 'desire', especially between what Hakluyt called (in his 'Epistle Dedicatorie' to the *Divers Voyages*) 'preposterous desire', or 'seeking ... gaine', and 'desire of seeking ... Gods glorie'. The tension between these two 'desires' marks the struggle to justify and rationalise the violence necessary to make both 'England' and her colonies, and also to inspire the proper appetite for the development of capital.

The first page of Hakluyt's dedication in the *Divers Voyages* argues that the English voyages should be undertaken to undermine the evils perpetrated by travellers from other nations:

> but when I consider thate there is a time for all men, and see the Portingales time to be out of date, & that the *nakedness* of the Spaniards, and their long hidden secrets are nowe at length espied, whereby they went about to delude the worlde, I conceive great hope, the time approacheth and nowe is, that we of England may share and part stakes (if wee will our selves) both with the Spaniarde and the Portingale in part of America, and other regions as yet undiscovered.

'Nakedness' used to describe the Spaniards, in the context of a collection of travel narratives which often use this word to describe the 'savages', banishes the European nation into the benighted category of the uncivil. In his *Discourse of the Western Planting*, Hakluyt decries the moral culpability of the Spanish even more emphatically: 'The Spaniards,' he writes, 'have executed most outrageous and more than Turkish cruelties in all the West Indies' (Taylor 1935: 212). Hence, while the Spaniards bring devastation to their colonies, Hakluyt claims that the English will bring salvation, 'the advancement of the kingdom of Christ, and the enlargement of his glorious Gospell'. This distinction is coded in terms of observing limits – that is, not being 'outrageous' (*OED*: 'exceeding proper limits'). The cannibals are described in the passage from Peckham I quoted at the beginning of this section as guilty of 'cruelty', an attribute that they share with the Spanish, who are similarly depicted as engaging in 'more than Turkish cruelties'. Both groups are accused of exceeding proper limits, and thus are produced as other to proper English desire.

The 'nakedness' of the savages was alternately seen as a sign of their barbarity, and an indication of an attractive market opportunity. 'Nakedness', interestingly, works similarly in Hakluyt's passage (cited above) about the 'nakedness' of the Spaniards. For Hakluyt, this nakedness opens the competitors to be viewed as both 'outrageous' and exemplary, so that the English can *take their place* –

yet be more worthy of keeping it. Thus, a reader of the volume is encouraged to have his desire provoked – and then partially inhibited (or set in a different direction) – by the example of the Spanish. A similar dynamic was imagined in dealing with trade issues and savages, whose tastes and appetites must be encouraged – but only in certain directions.

Hence Hakluyt understood well that 'a more godly course' was not necessarily an attractive course for the merchants and other wealthy subscribers who made English exploratory expeditions possible.[12] He knew more fully than his public protestations suggest that the desire of potential investors was closer to the 'preposterous' than 'God's glorie'. Thus, while his public stance regularly gave precedence to converting native peoples, Hakluyt's private correspondence reveals other priorities. In a report to Walsingham in 1584, Hakluyt describes the money to be made in fur trading in Northern America as he had heard it extolled by a French merchant. He then notes with some urgency that 'the present [English Colonial] experience is like soone to waxe colde and fall to the ground unlesse ... al diligence in searching out *everie* hope of gayne be used' (Taylor 1935: 206, emphasis mine). In dire times, spiritual profit must take a backseat to material. Like the discourses of the Spaniards he decries, Hakluyt's own public 'glorious words' do some 'pretending'.

His dilemma, of course, is that he simultaneously had to disparage the competition *and* offer them as models of emulation since the Spaniards and Portuguese were indeed 'successful' colonisers. Hakluyt needed to evoke competitive desire through his book because if he cannot convince investors to underwrite the cost of fitting ships for exploration, the expeditions could not take place at all. The great travel narrative collections did not emerge in Spain or Portugal, Jonathan Haynes (1986) claims, because in these countries the Crown suppressed information on the voyages it sponsored itself, and attempted to keep knowledge about their colonies as secret as possible. In England, on the contrary, advertisement for voyages was necessary to encourage private investment since the Crown was not the main investor in exploration schemes. Although in other matters censorship was common in the period, the dissemination of information about travel and exploration was actually encouraged by the government. Hakluyt worked with the knowledge and support of not only merchants, but also government officials. Hence, page after page of narrative by first person narrators is used to urge individual participation and speculation in what Hakluyt referred to as 'like enterprise'. Lists of commodities to be found at the ends of journeys, hints of the presence of gold, exhortations to spread Christianity and serve England: all these are offered as possible rewards for investing in exploration.

The collections needed to elicit an excitement about 'enterprise' which they by no means could presuppose.[13] One tactic was simply to declare it a 'naturall inclination' as does Robert Thorne, the 'merchant of London', who argues that 'Experience proveth that naturally all Princes bee desirous to extend and enlarge their dominions and kingdomes' (Hakluyt 1966, B[1]^{r}). However, in spite of claims that expansion was 'naturall', Thorne's text depicts the very waking of desire that it hopes to elicit, rather than taking desire for travel for granted. The Thorne letters, which are exercises in persuasion, suggest that even kings need to be induced to this 'naturall' enterprise. He writes to the English Ambassador Ley: 'I knowe it is my bounde dutie to manifest this secrete unto your Grace which hitherto as I suppose hath beene hid: which is that with a small number of shippes there may bee discovered divers newe landes and kingdoms' (Hakluyt 1966: B2^{r}). He refers to the colonial enterprise, thus, not only as 'natural' but also as an *inherited* disease: 'I reason, that as some sicknesses are hereditarious, and come from the father to the sonne, so this inclination or desire of this discoverie I inherited of my father' (D2^{v}). Similarly, the travel narrative writers help produce desire by attempting to pass it along to their readers.

Thorne continues his discussion by comparing the wealth of the old world with that of the new: 'For as with us and other, that are aparted from the sayde equinoctiall, our mettailles be lead, tynne, and yron, so thers be golde, silver and copper' (B4^{r}). This observation leads him to consider the relative availability of products as influencing 'appetite unto', rather than making the usual assumptions that the peoples of the world new to Europe were fools for not properly valuing commodities which the Europeans value: 'And I see that the preciousness of these things is measured after the distance that is between us, and the things that we have appetite unto. For in this navigation of the spicerie was discovered, that these ilandes nothing set by golde, but set more by a knife and a nyle of yron, than by this quantitie of Golde; and with reason as the thing more necessarie for mans service' (B4^{r}). Thinking with the rational relativism of a businessman, Thorne uses a market model of scarcity and surplus to explain the existence of different desires, which he recognises as necessary for trade and therefore not a mark of inferiority. If all people desire the same things equally then there could be no trade at all. The travel narratives make a particular point of hoping to generate the most trade-beneficial 'appetites' in the natives, while stimulating Europe's own appetite for conquest, trade, accretion, investment. The need to retrain the appetites of New World inhabitants (as well as Europeans) is a preoccupation of these texts – and as the most extreme threat to European purposes (as the passages quoted at the beginning of this section indicate), the cannibals are most in need of retraining. It is important to recall that the production of certain appetites (and not others) was crucial to the development of capitalist and colonial enterprise.

'Wants', 'desire', and 'appetite' are, therefore, one of the most prevalent themes of the narratives and other exploration documents. Included in the essay 'Notes in writing besides more privie by mouth that were given', written by Hakluyt's cousin, a lawyer of the Inner Temple, is a section entitled, 'Which ways the Savage may be made able to purchase our cloth and other their wares', which describes how to incite good market behaviour among the Indians. It begins: 'If you finde any Iland or mayne lande populous, and the same people hath need of cloth [because they are naked]; Then are you to devise what commodities they have to purchase the same withall' (Hakluyt 1966: H2^{v}). The discussion continues with directions to show the Indians how to produce a commodity which the English 'want', so that they will be able to trade for the items that the Indians 'want'.

Often there is a fantasy assumption that the market for English cloth is 'natural' among the 'naked' savages. According to Peckham: 'it is well knowen that all Savages, aswell those that dwell in the South, as those that dwell in the North, so soone as they shall begin but a little to taste of civility, will take marvelous delight in any garment, be it never so simple; as a shirt, a blew, yellow, read or greene cotten cassocke, a cap, or such like, and will take incredible paines for such a trifle' (Hakluyt 1965: VIII, 111). Once their 'taste' is set in the right direction, savages can be counted on to consume the proper commodities. Peckham further assures his readers that 'people in those parts are easily reduced to civility both in manners and garments'. The benefit of such turn in 'taste' is not only to the 'savage' (who gains 'civility'), or to the merchant (who takes a profit), but also to the unemployed at home in England, who will, by means of the savage's consumption of cloth (rather than the merchant), be 'reinstated to their pristinate wealth and estate'. Peckham (or, perhaps, an editor), includes a long list of ostensible beneficiaries of the trade which includes: 'clothiers, woolmen, corders, spinners, weavers, fullers, sheermen, diers, drapers, cappers, hatters, &c, and many decayed towns repayered'. What matters here is not the accuracy of Peckham's report with respect to the 'savages'; what interests me is the metaphoric system on which he draws to describe them and their relationship to Europeans. The consumption of labour at home (setting men to work) is linked repeatedly in the travel literature to the retraining of appetite abroad. Proto-capitalists imagined their success in the reduction of cannibal (improper) consumption abroad in order to further the aims of facilitating the consumption of labour power at home.

However, in spite of the elder Hakluyt's assumption that the peoples of the new world 'want' cloth (which England was eager to unload on them), the travellers who encountered them often discovered an indifference to cloth. An account of a journey into 'Morumbega' by John Verrazanus is quite emphatic on this point. Describing the preferences of the natives when confronted with European goods, he remarks that 'they did not desire cloth of silke or of golde, muche lesse of any other sorte' (Hakluyt 1966: B[1]^{v}). The elder Hakluyt's essays stress the importance of attempting to arouse an appetite for English goods in the natives when it is absent: 'If the people be content to live naked, and to content themselves with few things of meere necessity, then traffick is not. For then in vaine seemeth our voyages, unless this nature be altered as by conquest and other means it may be, but not of a sudden' (Taylor 1935: 332). Hakluyt's cousin is ominously silent about just what those 'other means' might be, but whatever he had in mind, his assumption is that desire must be produced.

Resistance from indigenous peoples to the 'alteration' of 'nature' encouraged by the elder Hakluyt is illustrated by the narratives in which natives are sometimes depicted as more likely to devour the Europeans themselves than their wares. The mythical voyage of the Zeno brothers which Hakluyt includes in his collection reports that a group of mariners of their acquaintance 'were taken in the countrey and the most parte of them eaten by the Savage people, which feede upon mans fleshe, as the sweetest meate in their judgementes that is' (Hakluyt 1966: D[1]^{v}). Having read accounts such as these, later voyagers were easily made suspicious of natives, especially uncooperative ones. Verrazanus describes this suspicion and how it could give rise to a misreading of signs. Coming into a populated area of northern North America, he sent a man to present the indigenous peoples with some 'trifles'. Battered by waves, the man arrives on shore rather faint and is surrounded by the 'Indians', who 'ranne to catch him, and drawing him out [of the water] they carried him a little way of from the sea ... and putting off his clothes they made him warme at a great fire, not without our great feare which remained in the boate, that they would have roasted him at that fire and have eaten him' (Hakluyt 1966: A3[r]). However, the people prove friendly, and release the courier after he revives, to the surprise of the mariners. The natives were apparently satisfied with the 'sheetes of paper, glasses, belles, and such like trifles' which the Europeans left behind.

It becomes the hope of the English that they can retrain the appetites of the natives by careful control of trade so that they would always prefer 'trifles' to human flesh. The elder Hakluyt's essay of advice argues

> for that the people to the which wee purpose in this voyage to goe, be no Christians, it were good that the masse of our commodities were always in our owne disposition, and not at the will of others. Therefore it were good that we did seeke out some finall Iland in the Scithian Sea where we might plant, Fortifie and Staple safely, from whence (as time shoulde serve) wee might feede those heathen nations with our commodities without cloying them, or without venturing our whol masse in the bowels of their country. (Hakluyt 1966: H[1][r])

'Feede,' 'cloying,' and 'bowels': the imagery subtext indicates a fear that unless 'the people' are induced to proper consumption, the English merchants might find their 'whol masse' – themselves included – consumed by them instead. Indeed, in another set of instructions, the elder Hakluyt makes this threat even more explicit. Once again, he argues the importance of establishing a permanent trading post, but adds: 'The people there to plant and to continue are eyther to live without trafficke, or by trafficke and by trade of marchandize. If they shall live without sea trafficke, at the first they become naked by want of linen and wollen, and very miserable by infinite wantes that will otherwise ensue, and so will they be forced of them selves to depart, or els easely they will bee consumed by the Sps. by the Fr. or by the naturall inhabithants (sic) of the countrey' (Taylor 1935: 117). Again and again in the narratives, we come up against this problem of proper versus dangerous appetites – and the difficulty of managing the dividing line between them successfully.

This 'appetite' dilemma confronts Europeans both at home and abroad. Not only does a taste for investment need to be developed among the propertied, but also, at a time when the Hakluyts note that those starving in England for want of work were 'redie to eate upp one another' (Taylor 1935: 234), eating imagery not only links cannibals and the proto-proletariat, but suggests that the two groups were paired in the minds of proto-capitalists as equivalent threats, both requiring careful regulation of appetite. The proto-capitalists need to maintain and draw upon a labour pool to satisfy their own appetite for labour, manage markets for the fruits of that labour by encouraging the proper consumption behaviours in the new world inhabitants, and see that all inhibiting appetites are squelched.

Hence, although 'unnatural' appetites – a desire for human flesh and a lack of interest in European commodities – coupled with heathenism, rendered the inhabitants of the New World eminently worthy of expropriation from a European perspective, this was not the only ideological role performed by cannibals in the early modern European imaginary. Cannibals also embodied an appetite both instructive to emergent capital – and interdicted by it. If the cannibal represents consumption without reserve, then capital must meet in cannibalism not only its own limit – that which it must renounce – but also the figure of its own desire. Peter Stallybrass and Allon White have argued in their study of transgression that 'the bourgeois subject continuously defined and redefined itself through the exclusion of what it marked out as "low" – as dirty, repulsive, noisy, contaminating. Yet that very act of exclusion was constitutive of its identity. The low was internalized under the sign of negation and disgust ... But disgust always bears the imprint of desire' (1986: 191). In the case of the early modern European encounter with cannibals, the disgust/desire nexus indicated a conflictual space in capitalism as well as in the capitalist subject, whose appetite must continuously be fueled – and controlled. The next section discusses the 'supplementary logic' which helps spur that subject on – and then requires an imposition of limits.

3 Primitive accumulation, or 'hee gathered many notable things'

In the discussion of the cannibals above, their early modern form of appearance is brought into an encounter with a system of metaphors deployed by Marx in his discussion of nineteenth-century capitalism. This section explains the reason for this intrusion of a third historical moment in my theorisation of a late modern echo of the early modern. Cannibals find their way into *Capital* at a crucial moment. Scoffing at the claims of the political economists that exploitation is 'natural', Marx writes: 'we may say that surplus-value rests in a natural basis, but only in the very general sense that there is no natural obstacle absolutely preventing one man from lifting from himself the burden of labor necessary to maintain his own existence, and imposing it on another, just as there is no unconquerable natural obstacle to the consumption of the flesh of one man by another' (1990: 647). He adds in a footnote that 'according to a recent calculation [no source provided] there are still at least 4,000,000 cannibals in those parts of the earth which have so far been explored'. Marx, it seems, needs the cannibals to be there to make a certain point. That point, however, is *not* (as other critics of capital have on occasion suggested) that capitalists and cannibals are metaphorically equivalent; instead Marx by-passes the opportunity to make such a comparison. His point is rather to unsettle the conviction of naturalness attributed to the production of surplus-value by comparing it to an activity that was often and vehemently proclaimed unnatural in the West. To the extent that consuming human flesh and consuming human labour are equivalent, they are equivalent only as horrors. Leaving aside the interesting question of why Marx was so willing to believe that so large a number of the earth's population are indeed cannibals, I will turn instead to the reason why Marx would *not* equate capitalism with cannibalism.

Specifically, 'capitalist accumulation', for Marx, is necessarily investment in productive activity, or the extraction of surplus-value, which is, simply put, labour for which the worker is not paid under conditions of capitalised commodity production. In other words, capitalist accumulation is not hoarding, or the profit the capitalist directs to his own consumption. Rather it requires a constant extraction *and redeployment* in production of surplus-value. Thus, the capitalist's 'voracious appetite' ('Heißhunger' as Marx put it) for surplus-value (and hence, surplus labour) is characteristic of capital as a mode of production, although such appetites can be aroused as soon as production for exchange rather than use arises (1990: 739). What distinguishes capitalised production from any prior (extra-ordinary) appearance of 'Heißhunger', is that for capital, surplus extraction is necessary to production itself (not just to the maintenance of the non-labouring elites): 'the development of capitalist production makes it necessary constantly to increase the amount of capital laid out in a given industrial undertaking, and competition subordinates every individual capitalist to the immanent laws of capitalist production as external and coercive laws. It compels him to keep extending his capital, so as to preserve it, and he can only extend it by means of progressive accumulation' (348). This extension, however, reaches limits at various points, one being the level of subsistence for the workers, which is necessary to ensure the continued provision of labour.

In spite of this limit, early capital, spurred by competition into a boundless hunger for surplus-value extraction, had to be disciplined by State regulation into foregoing absolute consumption of labour-power in its drive for profit: 'the limiting of factory labour was dictated by the same necessity as forced the manuring of English fields with guano. The same blind desire for profit that in the one case exhausted the soil had in the other case seized hold of the vital force of the nation at its roots' (348). Emergent industrial capital had apparently learned the lessons of increasing its appetite for labour without learning so well the necessary limits to this appetite. In this early stage, it can be seen as tending towards a (self-destructive) cannibalism, understood as total incorporation of its necessary other, labour-power, embodied in the labourer – thus threatening not only the reproduction of the labour pool, but of capital itself. Cannibalism understood in this way represents the necessary – but impossible – *Heißhunger* of capitalism.

That capitalism is, on the one hand, driven to consume labour power utterly, and, on the other hand, absolutely prevented from doing so if accumulation is to continue, marks one of its principal contradictions. It is not so very surprising, then, that cannibals arrive on the scene with capital's primitive accumulation. Cannibal appetite is essential to capitalist/colonial forces which reinforce proto-*Heißhunger* as a general acquisitive energy even as they undertake a repression of its 'savage' (that is, unlimited) form. I want to consider in this section some of the ways in which this 'boundless' and 'voracious' appetite was encouraged in early modern England (prior to its extensive application in early industrial capital), and why limits might have been harder to teach than what I will be calling 'supplementary logic,' an assumption that further extension of, or addition to, some already constituted 'whole' is always possible, without in any way undermining the integrity of the whole.[14]

To explain the significance of supplementary logic to capital, it may help to contrast it with more 'feudal' ways of seeing the world. Perry Anderson helpfully distinguishes between feudal and capitalist understandings of competition in this way:

> The normal medium of inter-capitalist competition is economic, and its structure is typically additive: rival parties may both expand and prosper – although unequally – through single confrontation, because the production of manufactured commodities is inherently unlimited. The typical medium of inter-feudal rivalry, by contrast, was military and its structure was always potentially the zero-sum conflict of the battlefield, by which fixed quantities of ground were won or lost. For land is a natural monopoly: it cannot be indefinitely extended, only redivided. (1974: 31)[15]

What Alexandre Koyre (1957) has described as the movement from a 'closed world to infinite universe' has its corollary in parts of the social formation other than astronomy in the early modern period. One shift required as a condition of possibility for properly capitalist accumulation was a conceptualisation – and celebration – of amassing for its own sake, toward infinity. This accumulation could then later be directed toward capitalist enterprise which operates according to an expansive ('additive') logic, directing accumulation toward particular (endless) ends.

Primitive – or originary – accumulation is one of the great cruxes of capitalist production for Marx. Capitalist accumulation, as I noted above, requires surplus-*value* (not mere surplus-labour) extraction, which assumes capitalist relations of production. Where, then, did the originary capital come from? Marx outlines what he describes as the pre-history of capital in answer to this question. In Europe (England is his case study), primitive accumulation involved the separation of the primary producers from the means of production – in other words, the driving of peasants from the land in what was still principally an agrarian economy in early modern England. By this concentration of all land in a few hands, the conditions of possibility for capitalist *relations* of production were established. The start-up 'capital' for investment in capitalist enterprise-to-be, however, was supplied largely in the non-domestic sphere, according to Marx: 'the discovery of gold and silver in America, the extirpation, enslavement and entombment in mines of the indigenous population of that continent, the beginning of the conquest and plunder of India, the conversion of Africa into a preserve for the commercial hunting of blackskins, are all things which characterize the dawn of the era of capitalist production. These idyllic proceedings are the chief moments of primitive accumulation' (1990: 915).[16] In this dual process (the displacement of primary producers in Europe from the means of production, and the theft of New World wealth) the European proto-proletariat and cannibals (among other 'savages') in the New World are brought into relation by the mediation of the 'voracious appetites' of the proto-capitalists. This appetite, along with the relations and means of capitalist production, needed to be accumulated.

To better understand the cultural logic which helps make thinkable the conjuncture of appetite, capital and cannibals, we should recall that for Europe, the New World was ex-orbitant, as Montaigne put it: an 'other world' (1928: 1, 216). It exceeded the limits of what was suddenly transformed into the 'known world,' by the discovery that there were parts unknown by Europeans. In disturbing and disorienting ways, the New World opened up the possibility that the previously coherent and 'whole' world might be subject to (perhaps limitless) supplementation: 'I wot not whether I can warrant my selfe, that some other [world] be not discovered hereafter, sithence so many worthy men, and better learned than we are, have so many ages beene deceived in this,' observes Montaigne (216). Echoing a similar, although colonially inflected, sentiment, the English collector of travel narratives, Richard Hakluyt, writes that 'I conceive great hope that the time approacheth and now is, that we of England may share and part stakes ... both with the Spaniard and the Portingal in parts of America, and other regions as yet undiscovered' (1966: [1][r]). The shock of the New World encouraged a supplementary logic to displace previous assumptions of static totality: where there had been simply 'a' world, now there was accumulation, the promise of supplementation induced by the sense of 'regions as yet undiscovered'. A potential terror was negotiated by the turn to an accretive view of the world, which assimilated the new by *adding* it to the 'known world'.

The collecting of narratives of these 'adventures' into volumes for sale not only turned a profit for printers and booksellers, but also helped reinforce the process of topographical (and commodity/subject/appetite) accretion which they described. Hakluyt's practices suggest that he understands geography to be the setting end to end of the narrative and descriptive accounts of individual travellers, letters patent, essays of advice, tidbits of information, maps, and exhortations to explore, trade and colonise. As the preceding description of his collections suggests, perhaps the most obvious work performed by Hakluyt's texts is *accumulation*. On the list of geographers Hakluyt includes in the *Divers Voyages*, the descriptive phrase following the name of Hakluyt's model, John Baptista Ramusius, the Italian editor of travel narratives, reads 'hee gathered many notable things.' Hakluyt's volume certainly gathers 'many' things, as well; this accumulation is not in itself capitalist, but helps produce reading subjects who anticipate further installments, accretion rather than synthesis (the medieval model of geographic writing which Hakluyt specifically rejects).[17] It helps, in other words, turn a 'zero-sum' culture into an 'additive' one, to use Anderson's distinction between the feudal and capitalist views of competition quoted above.

'Divers' is an appropriate adjective to describe a volume encouraging the production of an additive ideology, since the word implied an indefiniteness, an uncertainty, about the number of items included. There are good reasons why a collection of traveller's tales published in England during the late sixteenth century would be described in indefinite terms. In 1582, the collecting of colonies and tales about them, was still in the future for the English. A letter from an English merchant, Robert Thorne, to Henry VIII, which Hakluyt includes in the *Divers Voyages* is encouraging: 'with a small number of shippes *there may be discovered* divers newe lands' (1966: B2^{r}, emphasis mine), but in the early 1580s when Hakluyt published the letter, English expeditions were still few, especially when compared with those made by the Spanish and the Portuguese to their vast imperial holdings. 'Divers', an indefinite number word, could camouflage an inferior performance on England's part. In addition, since the potential number of colonies was indeterminate, the number of voyages and accounts was also indeterminate. 'Divers' allowed for expansion, for future collecting of both land and travel accounts.

For so large a claim, the *Divers Voyages* may seem, at first glance, to be too slight a volume, consisting as it does of only 141 pages in the modern edition, and even fewer in the sixteenth century.[18] However, the *Divers Voyages* does not stand alone, but opens out into the vast and growing collection of narratives which Hakluyt and his successors continue to amass. The first edition of the *Principal Navigations* dwarfs the *Divers Voyages*; much new material was added to the second edition of the *Principal Navigations* (1598–1600), and Hakluyt continued to solicit, collect, translate, edit, organise, and publish supplementary narratives until his death.

Samuel Purchas later published the massive collection of manuscripts Hakluyt left behind in the *Hakluytus Posthumus* (1625) volumes, which contain over four and a half million words and fill twenty volumes in the modern edition. Richard Eden's *Decades* (1555) had been extended by Richard Willes in 1577, just as even earlier, new volumes of the *Viaggi* (1550–9) had continued to appear after Ramusio's death. This common publication practice for the collections suggests that early modern geography was operating according to a logic of supplementation.

Travel narratives were not the only object of early modern collecting. While gathering material for the *Principal Navigations*, Hakluyt examined at least two 'Wonder Cabinets', or curiosity collections. Attempting to describe the relationship between the collections of objects he had viewed in the cabinets and the collections of texts he was in the process of assembling, he generates a list: 'in the course of this history often mention is made of many beastes, birds, fishes, serpents, plants, fruits, hearbes, rootes, apparell, armour, boates, and such other rare and strange curiosities, which wise men take great pleasure to reade of' (Hakluyt 1907: 12). The reader is confronted with a string of words, as if describing the wealth of the new world demanded a certain verbal excess. But the sight of the objects themselves impoverishes the words, according to Hakluyt, in spite of the 'pleasure' words give to 'wise men'. The objects listed in the text provide 'much more contentment to see', Hakluyt insists, and offers his own experience as evidence of this contentment: 'herein I my selfe to my singuler delight have bene as it were ravished in beholding all the premisses gathered together with no small cost, and preserved with no litle diligence, in the excellent Cabinets of ... Richard Garthe ... and William Cope'. The 'ravishing' pleasure of entering the cabinet and exploring its wonders seems to be due, however, as much to the evidence of the 'cost' and 'diligence' expended in compiling the collection as to the objects themselves. It is the objects *as a collection*, as a massing of wealth and as evidence of effort required to amass it, which delights. Hakluyt is not only 'rehearsing culture' here, it seems to me, but also celebrating the primitive accumulation of the desire to accumulate.[19]

It is easy to imagine how Hakluyt's collections might participate in primitive accumulation as well if we think of it in broadly cultural terms. Richard Halpern has argued in *The Poetics of Primitive Accumulation* for just such a broad view: 'What we have here [in

Renaissance England] is a genealogy of elements – political, legal, economic, cultural – which all later combine into or contribute to a capitalist social formation' (1991: 13). Halpern is interested in seeing primitive accumulation not so much as a set of historical events, but as a means of theorising transition. What he finds particularly compelling in Marx's discussion of the prehistory of capital is the means it gives a theorist to discuss what are 'not yet' but 'will be' elements of a social formation in which capitalism is dominant. Along these lines, Hakluyt's various collections would not themselves be determined in form by a dominant capitalist logic; rather, since Hakluyt was responding to local, conjunctural concerns, the political and propagandistic demands of his moment, we should focus instead on the ways in which his texts had the effect of promoting a supplementary logic with more general implications for capital only later.

This supplementary logic is particularly evident in the final document included in the *Divers Voyages*, a list of commodities available in the New World compiled by Hakluyt from reports given by travellers. It follows immediately after the final words of the elder Hakluyt's exhortation to potential explorers and colonists, 'you ought greedily to hunt after thinges that yeelde present reliefe' (1966: K3^{v}). For a greedy gatherer, Hakluyt's list might well appear enticing. It includes sustenance categories (fish, fruit) as well as luxury items, such as precious stones. The names of commodities are culled out of the various narratives Hakluyt has read, including several not presented in the *Divers Voyages*. Since he has no first hand knowledge of the commodities mentioned, he is careful to emphasise their textual status; he is repeating the '*names* of commodities' that he has found in written sources, not recording the items he sees as he surveys a landscape (emphasis mine). His collection of signifiers is all the more conspicuous because it contributes to the text's lack of closure.

The list is explicitly open-ended (to entice potential 'greedy gatherers'). Its title announces *partialness* (and therefore promises supplementation); in it, Hakluyt claims that his travellers 'have seene these things amongst many others' (1966: K4^{r}). Then, again, at the end of the list, in its 'final' category, inexhaustiveness is stressed: 'So as the commodities already knowen, besides many yet unknowen are these, and that in great quantitie' (K4^{v}). There is, in addition, no 'finis' at the 'end' of the list, even though it comes at the very 'end' of the book. Whereas two other sections of the book close with 'Finis', seeming to mark the end of the text, in each case the ending turns out to be false. Precisely in the place a 'finis' would be expected, however, at the supposed 'end' of the book, following the list, it fails to appear. The list refuses closure and leaves the book open to more collecting, more annexation, which Hakluyt provides in subsequent volumes, and which other editors continue after his death. The *Divers Voyages* both begins and ends with lists and these lists encourage the reader to imagine their continuation, and see the book, as well as the world outside of England, as in process.

The lists themselves are not, of course, (economic) 'investment', but rather a sort of linguistic excess, operating textually to figure an abundance that will encourage investment on the part of readers – investments, as it were, of *desire*. Enticed by the verbal copia, the reader may learn to accumulate and invest in order to acquire what is textually promised: an endless supply of the listed commodities, along with much else besides. A portion of this accumulation, in turn, can be directed toward yet more multiplication. The lists, by emphasising the agglomeration of signifiers to figure the agglomeration of things, are helping to forge a crucial linkage between accumulation-investment-accumulation-investment, etc., as an ongoing process in excess of use-value.

Lists of commodities are a commonplace of the literature of travel and colonisation; sometimes they are printed separately from the body of the text, as in Hariot's description of Virginia, but usually they are integrated into the narrative itself. The merchant Robert Thorne, for example, sees a landscape filled with potential for profit whenever he gazes toward the New World: 'the islandes are fertile of cloves, nutmegs, mace, and cinnamon; with gold, rubies, diamonds, Balasses, Granates, Jacincts and other stones (and pearles, as al other lands, that are under and nere the equinoctial. For we see, where nature giveth any thing, she is no nigarde' (1966: B3^{v}). As nature in the New World is represented as setting no limits to its resources, its European exploiters need set no limit on their accumulation. The limits to the potential commodities and colonies had not yet been reached, encouraging an orientation toward limitless accumulation rather than zero-sum rivalry.

The limitless accumulation urged by supplementary logic could not continue. In the real world of a non-infinitely consumable labour-pool and resistant natives, supplementary logic met its limits. To deal with these limits required an eschewing of absolute (cannibal) consumption. The cannibal, then, emerges into a crisis of appetite to figure desire for infinite (capitalist) consumption and its impossibility. Even if he never did exist, he would need to be (in some fashion) invented (as William Arens, among others, claims that he was). The *Divers Voyages* and *Principal Navigations* as collections of separate narratives which share the function of in-form-ing England, fragmented the world to allow England to emerge from those fragments as whole. This supplementary logic renders possible a sense of infinite extension while preserving the comfort of a distinctive 'whole' from which to imagine it. That whole, however, was precarious, threatened all around. One name given to this threat – past and present – is cannibal.

4 Consumption and the New World Order

One of the persistent observations made by critics of the contemporary global scene is that the world in which we live operates as a system to an unprecedented extent and in previously unknown ways. Many theorists have attempted to describe and explain this 'new' system: is it a new stage of capitalism? (Jameson 1991); a new regime of accumulation? (Harvey 1990); a 'borderless world'? (Miyoshi 1993). At the conclusion of my essay on cannibals as a historically and spatially inflected sign which marks a struggle over appetite and its expression, we should consider what is 'new' (in relation to the early modern world) about the contemporary world in which this sign is now deployed.

One particularly striking restructuration of capital over the course of the twentieth century has been the development in the West of a mass market – with a wage structure and consumer ideology to support it. 'What ultimately separates Fordism from Taylorism,' David Harvey explains, was Ford's 'explicit recognition that mass production meant mass consumption, a new system of the reproduction of labour power, a new politics of labour control and management, a new aesthetics and psychology, in short, a new kind of rationalized modernist, and populist democratic society' (1990: 126). Consumerism is the ideology which helped transform the subsistence worker of the pre-Fordist period into a mass consumer. Marxism has tended to view this shift with suspicion, sceptical of both the power and pleasures of consumption in any capitalist order. The residue of this asceticism adheres to Stanley Aronowitz's observation that: 'buying and eating [have] become the wages of alienated labour, the means by which the hunger for recognition, satisfying work and play, and decent human relationships, are spuriously satisfied' (1990: 247). Consumerism, in this view, not only prevents the revolution but feeds only 'spurious' foods. Where substantial social sustenance should be, consumer capitalism offers only the metaphysical equivalents of Cheetos.

Seeing shoppers merely as dupes of advertising has, however, recently become more difficult, as has assuming that workers are simply bearers of false consciousness imposed on them by a ruling class. With Gramsci now the theorist of choice on much of the left, it is far less acceptable to refuse to take the 'consent' of people to consumerism seriously and to fail to try to understand it complexly.[20] One reason to pay especially careful attention to the politics of consumption today is that both globally and within individual countries the gaps between the richest and poorest segments of the population are widening. Most of the planet still struggles to obtain basic subsistence; for them, consumption of mass consumer goods is not the issue. Even in wealthy nations, the consumption capacity is eroding for large numbers of the population. Richard Barnet marshals the following statistics to emphasise this point:

> [T]he world's 358 billionaires have a combined net worth of $760 billion, equal to that of the bottom 45% of the world population ... The average C.E.O. in the United States now brings home about 145 times the average factory worker's pay ... In recent years an estimated 18% of American workers with full-time jobs earned poverty-level wages ... Every other black baby in America is born into a family living below the poverty line ... Since 1973, the number of American children living in poverty has increased 50%, so that 22% now grow up poor, and the number keeps increasing. (1994: 754)

Barnet's point is that we should no longer assume that corporations have the best interests of the US at heart when they plan their global strategies. Fordist paternalism is over. However, we need not adopt Barnet's position on the need for a rekindling of corporate responsibility for citizens in order to see that consumption has become a political, cultural, and economic issue of enormous consequence in the modern world.

This brings us back to cannibals. At the beginning of this paper I pointed out that cannibalism has emerged as a persistent motif in contemporary film, and that it has often been deployed quite specifically as a critique of consumerism; I also noted that cannibalism has emerged simultaneously as a preoccupation of contemporary entrepreneurs and franchisers battling over market shares, hurtling accusations of cannibal at each other (and, occasionally, themselves). The ensuing pages indicated, in their detour through early modern England's confrontation with cannibals, that 'cannibal' in its moment of emergence, served the ideological purpose of helping early modern proto-capitalists negotiate a crisis in 'appetite' production, as they developed the necessary hungers for (and began to encounter limits to) capitalist primitive accumulation. The most recent appearance of cannibals also marks a crisis in appetite, but not the same crisis.

'Crisis,' Gramsci tells us, occurs when 'the old ways are dying and the new cannot yet be born' (1971: 276). In the moment of transition, he observes, 'morbid symptoms' appear. Preoccupation with cannibals, I have suggested, is one of the morbid symptoms of capitalist appetite in crisis. To understand why early modern cannibals have reappeared on the scene of late capitalist enterprise, let us consider one of the most striking differences in the deployment of the signifier cannibals in the two moments. Early modern 'cannibals' were emphatically represented as the West's others; they were the farthest extreme of savagery, to which the civility of Europe was made to stand as (superior) contrast. Conversely, contemporary cannibals are sited by Western subjects *among themselves* rather than in a distant 'other' world.[21] Not only is cannibalism no longer an attribute of the other, it is differently demonised. Indeed, the cannibal theme in contemporary business discourse ranges from alarm and excoriation through resignation to teeth-gritting determination (of the 'it's a tough job, but somebody has to do it' variety). In spite of the falling away of the charge of 'otherness', however, both early modern and contemporary cannibals are capital's competition and limit. Contemporary capital (mis)-recognises (what originary capital could not): that cannibal appetite is its own impossible desire.

Greenaway's film, *The Cook, the Thief, his Wife and her Lover,* on the other hand, takes on the task of urging the limits to consumption for which the early modern cannibal was an advertisement/warning. The anxiety manifested in both film and business discourse perhaps suggests a transition underway in the organisation of global consumption which rivals in magnitude the early modern transition in production. In the late sixteenth century, England was still in the throes of the difficult transition to capitalised social and economic relations. Capital was not only not dominant; it was barely emergent. Today, on the other hand, capital is not only hegemonic, it has saturated virtually every inch of the planet (although not everywhere in the same way). In the late sixteenth century, the conditions of possibility for capitalised relations were being established in England as the peasantry was thrust from the land (a process which took several centuries to complete), and the first proto-capitalist workers were being disciplined to sell their labour power (although there were not yet enough buyers). In this moment, the cannibals that emerge are depicted as threats to production; they inhibit trade, the establishing of colonies, the proper occupation of men.

Relations between capital and labour have been renegotiated numerous times since the sixteenth century, but one of the biggest changes is marked in the emergence of consumerism. The most recent business and cultural discourses on cannibals displace the emphasis from capitalist production to mass consumption, viewing people primarily as purchasers of fast food burgers and toiletries rather than producers of these items, although they also flip the burgers and supervise the machines that fill the shampoo bottles and toothpaste tubes. Shifts of greater proportions of Western populations into work in the 'service' sector, and the increased mechanisation of production, have assisted in this change in focus. Whether seeing the world in terms of production or consumption, however, industry spokesmen seem to discover cannibals where appetite encounters a limit. It is on this field of competition between the inducement to appetite and its 'limits' that early modern and contemporary cannibals meet: European dismay in the face of 'clean burnished' bones is the precursor of saturated markets of which entrepreneurs shrug and declare 'if you don't eat your own lunch, someone else will', as one manager put the predicament as he saw it for a newspaper reporter. In this fixation on 'limit', we can discover the real horror of the cannibal to the capitalist.

Capital's most serious propensity for crisis is an effect of 'overaccumulation': too many commodities in relation to buyers, or too much capital in relation to potential for investment. In the early modern period, as we have already seen, one of England's concerns in colonial expansion was to boost the cloth trade, or find alternatives to it. Geographical expansion, however, provides only a temporary fix: 'if continuous geographical expansion of capitalism were a real possibility, there could be a relatively permanent solution to the overaccumulation problem. But to the degree that the progressive implantation of capitalism across the face of the earth extends the space within which the overaccumulation problem can arise, so geographic expansion can at best be a short-run solution to the overaccumulation problem' (Harvey 1990: 183). Hence, we can see how cannibals, who in the early modern period were the symbols of resistance to expansion by European colonial forces, could later re-emerge in the established territories of capital itself after it succeeds in saturating the globe. In their first emergence, however, cannibals were primarily figures deployed to work out a properly capitalist relation to labour power by illustrating overconsumption. Contemporary cannibals, on the other hand, are more likely to be figures deployed to work out a new and uncertain relation of men to commodities.

In such a symbolic universe, what kind of intervention can a film such as *The Cook* make when it critiques consumer society by equating it with cannibalism? If the thief is to be seen as the hyperbolic representative of this society, clearly it has no redeeming qualities in Greenaway's filmic universe. He is loud, greedy, cruel, gauche – and marked by his accent as distinctly lower class. His wife, her lover, and the cook, on the other hand, the most sympathetically treated characters in the film, are quiet and refined (but not ascetic) in their tastes, and attracted to high European (especially French) culture. Indeed, the film takes pains to reinforce the very distinctions between high and low which it has been the work of cultural studies to call into question. For Greenaway, the alternative to consumer society seems to be elitist cultural refinement and aesthetic sophistication. Hence, the wife can direct her charge of cannibalism at both husband and audience, since some (most?) of those viewers may not be worthy to sit at Greenaway's 'high table'. This is not a film which concerns itself with the problem of unequal distribution, either local or global. Rather, Greenaway seems to be haunted by the spectre of mass consumption, and finds his cannibals there.

What can we learn by constellating twentieth-century cannibals with their early modern counterparts? I have argued that the work performed by the citation of early modern cannibals in the New World Order is a recognition of, and attempt to contain, a crisis in appetite. Contemporary capital evokes more appetite than it can satisfy, both on the side of entrepreneurs and consumers, both globally and in the 'developed' world, which we can see as a problem. But equally important are all the voicings of desire that are not heard, that never have a chance to enter this debate in which the production and circulation of meanings is multiple, but unequal. The 'danger' at this juncture in which the cannibals have been hustled in, is that, as in the past, its 'resolution' will perpetuate and reinforce a symbolic system in which the production and satisfaction of appetite will continue to be negotiated in grotesquely uneven fields. Recognising the work of cannibals, in a Benjaminian flash, directs us otherwise.

11

The function of cannibalism at the present time

Maggie Kilgour

> We are perhaps more distracted by incest than by cannibalism, but only because cannibalism has not yet found its Freud and been promoted to the status of a major contemporary myth.
> (Girard 1977: 276–7)

1

While my title might seem a simply presumptuous and perverse parody of Matthew Arnold's 'The Function of Criticism at the Present Time', there may be something deliciously appropriate in my originally frivolous crossing out of 'criticism' and inscription of my own master metaphor. Arnold's essay is a plea to the British public of his time to take criticism seriously as a high and autonomous form of intellectual activity rather than a mere parasite on the body of artistic creation. While he himself does not explicitly use this metaphor he easily could have. Critics have often been denounced as cannibals, parasites, vampires, and predatory ghouls who, unable to create themselves, feed on the work of others. So in Arnold's time, Gautier claimed that critics 'have never produced a work, and can do nothing but bespatter and spoil the works of others like veritable stymphalian vampires' (n.d.: xxxvii). In a similarly splenetic vein, in *The Battel of the Books* Swift personified Criticism as a 'malignant Deity', a monstrous self-consuming artifact, (constructed out of leftover bits of Spenser's Envy and Milton's Sin), whose:

> Eyes turned inward, as if she lookt only upon herself: Her Diet was the overflowing of her own Gall: Her Spleen was so large, as to stand prominent like a Dug of the first Rate, nor wanted Excrescences in form of Teats, at which a Crew of ugly

> Monsters were greedily sucking; and, what is wonderful to conceive, the bulk of Spleen encreased faster than the Sucking could diminish it. (1973: 386–7)

Books are for her only things to be literally consumed as she is surrounded by 'numberless Volumes half devoured' (386). Criticism is a sinful and destructive force that invidiously preys upon artistic creativity, and perhaps also upon itself – as Malcolm Bradbury also suggested in his satire of academic life, *Eating People is Wrong* (1959).

Of course critics are not alone in being represented in this unsavoury fashion. Cannibalism is a conventional satirical topos, which has been traditionally used for political purposes to demonise and attack forces seen as threatening social order. This is partly because food in general is both the most basic human need and a highly complex symbolic system used to define personal, national, and even sexual differences. As 'you are what you eat', cultural identity is constructed by dietary taboos that prescribe what is and is not edible. Foreigners are frequently defined in terms of how and, especially, what they eat, and denounced on the grounds that they either have bad table manners or eat disgusting things – as the French are defined as 'frogs' for eating the frogs' legs no dainty Brit (nourished on nice blood pudding and other assorted organs) would deign to touch. Eating thus becomes a means of creating cultural differences. As an even more charged kind of consumption, one that is generally considered an 'unnatural' form of feeding, cannibalism provides an image for the construction of clear boundaries between groups: 'we' are civilised and eat nicely, 'they' are barbaric and eat savagely; 'we' eat normally, 'they', perversely. Cannibalism can be used to justify attacks against groups seen as different from and thus threatening to a body politic, which therefore deserve to be, if not literally subsumed, at least incorporated through assimilation.

The obvious utility of cannibalism as an ideological device for justifying racism and imperialism has caused William Arens to argue in his controversial *The Man-Eating Myth* (1979b) that it may never have existed as a ritualised practice, but is rather a myth used by races to assert their superiority over others. In response to Arens, other anthropologists have presented convincing documentation to substantiate reports of cannibalistic activity (Sahlins 1979, Abler 1980, Brady 1982, Forsyth 1985). For Arens, such reactions are a product of anthropology's anxiety about its own identity. In Arens's reading, cannibalism itself becomes the tool by which anthropology cannibalises the primitive: *anthropology* constructs itself as a discipline through the opposite image of *anthropophagy* (and obviously the pun is used to suggest the structural interdependence of the two). Arens's chief interest lies in a critique of his own discipline, which, emerging as a science in the nineteenth century (both the height of the British empire and the beginning of its decline), he implies is a prime example of what is now called 'colonial discourse': the strategies through which imperialism justifies its own desire to absorb others by projecting that desire onto a demonised 'other'. Cannibalism is the tool of empire, be it the British empire or the empire of anthropology.

As Arens shows, cannibalism is traditionally used to establish difference and construct racial boundaries dividing the civilised from the savage. This seems somewhat paradoxical as the act itself involves the complete and utter loss of difference. This unsettling of discrete categories is part of its horror: it is the place where desire and dread, love and aggression meet, and where the body is made symbolic, the literal the figurative, the human reduced to mere matter. In fact, cannibalism involves both the *establishing* of absolute difference, the opposites of eater and eaten, and the *dissolution* of that difference, through the act of incorporation which identifies them, and makes the two one (Kilgour 1990: 7). Partly because of this association with the confusion of opposites, and also because I simply don't feel qualified to evaluate the evidence, I don't want to enter into the 'did they or didn't they?' debate – though I should probably confess my completely unscientific, unrigorous, and utterly subjective certainty that cannibalism has been practised, which I can only attribute to my own ghoulish nature, nourished no doubt by my mother's cannibal jokes and the fact that my sister's ex-roommate was eaten. My interest here, however, is in the role that cannibalism is playing in our imaginations today. At the time in which cannibalism is disappearing, or at least shrinking, as a reality, it seems to be gaining force as a symbol, both in criticism where it is associated with the tools of oppression used by a guilty imperial past, and in popular culture, where it seems to suggest fears about the present. While in 1972 René Girard (see epigraph to this paper) lamented that cannibalism had not yet received the kind of attention Freud gave to his other taboo subject, incest, since the 1960s the cannibal has become a modern mythical figure – appearing in films ranging from Romero's cult *Living Dead* series, through other fringe hits such as *Soylent Green*, *The Texas Chain Saw Massacre*, *Eating*

Raoul, Parents, Eat the Rich, Big Meat Eater, CHUD, and more recently breaking into art films: Greenaway's *The Cook, the Thief, his Wife and her Lover, Delicatessan, Cronos*. Even more tellingly perhaps, it has moved into the Hollywood mainstream, through *Fried Green Tomatoes*, and *The Silence of the Lambs*, which sent a cannibal to the academy awards.

I will return in the second half of this chapter to this most famous of contemporary cannibals, Hannibal Lecter, in whom cannibalism finds the Freud needed to make it a contemporary myth. Here I want to begin by positioning him in relation to a larger cultural obsession which might seem suspicious: is our interest in this lurid subject a sign of the complete degeneration of modern taste, and our progressive acceptance of all atrocity? Or, contrarily, is confronting cannibalism a sign of society's courageous voyage into its own heart of darkness, to break down the barrier of the final taboo, in the belief that by exposing and confronting our demons we can exorcise them? In many of these works, cannibalism clearly provides a perfect, if rather simplistic, image for the nightmare of a consumer society, uneasy about its own appetites, including its own increasing hunger for such lurid tales. So, for example, in Romero's *Dawn of the Dead*, the refugees from the cannibal zombies hide in a shopping mall, whose walls separate two mirror forms of conspicuous consumption. While cannibalism has been traditionally used to satirise members within a society who are seen as parasitical – lawyers (Rabelais' voracious Grippeminault or Dickens' vampiristic Mr Vholes), aristocrats (the classical fable of the belly), women ('vamps'), as well as critics – in a capitalist society revolving around the poles of production and consumption, it takes on new resonances, as a means of attacking those who are seen as consuming without producing.

Cannibalism is thus again a means of satire, a trope with which we parody more idealised myths about ourselves. At present, there is some concern with our cannibal past – not our savage prehistory, but the history of imperialism and its subsumption of 'cannibal' societies – as well as our cannibal present – the modern world of isolated consumers driven by rapacious egos. As the Symposium out of which this collection of papers emerged suggests, cannibalism is an important topic in criticism today, thanks to anthropological, New Historicist, postcolonial, and feminist analyses of literature and society, concerned with undoing the myths through which the modern world has built itself on the blood and bones of others.

While this fascination might seem to confirm that critics are always themselves cannibals, eager to sink their teeth into fresh kill, I think that the function of cannibalism in culture and criticism today lies in its utility as a form of cultural criticism. Where in the past the figure of the cannibal has been used to construct differences that uphold racism, it now appears in projects to deconstruct them. But, inspired by Arens's critique of his discipline's dependence on the cannibal for its own self-fashioning, I want also to suggest how the figure of the cannibal reveals some of the contradictions within our own reimagining of this function of criticism.

As Arens suggests, the category of the cannibal has always played a part in the construction of cultural or national difference: it is the archetypal 'other', the bogeyman who represents all that a civilisation as it defines itself wants to insist it is not. Until recently, cannibals have tended to be remote figures, distant either in time or space. In the ancient classical world, there were always rumours of others who lived on the fringes of civilisation, and whose half-human status was signified by the fact that they were said to eat each other. The anthropophage provides an image for the forces hostile to the civilising process, a wild untamed nature that threatens the advances made by culture. That force can be projected also onto the culture's own past, as a state of savagery out of which it has just emerged and back into which it fears it may fall; the figure of the man-eater can thus support narratives of evolution and development, showing how superior the civilised is to the natural (Arens 1979b: 14–16).

These symbolic resonances of anthropophagy become increasingly important with the discovery of the New World, which some New Historicists have argued was central to the formation of modern European culture and psyche. The general myth of the anthropophage took on a new life and more specific function when it became, dangerously, projected onto the figure of the New World cannibal. Peter Hulme especially has analysed the role of the cannibal as a means of boundary definition in the construction of modern Western identity. Hulme shows how the newly defined cannibal (itself a misrecognition of the 'other' created through a misappropriation of an alien language) served both as a foil for the emerging modern subject, and, conveniently, as a legitimisation of cultural appropriation (1986: 15–87). The modern Cartesian subject depends for its self-definition as an independent entity, clearly differentiated from others, on the image of an 'other' who destroys such boundaries (Garber 1985: vii–viii). As the modern Western ego is founded upon faith in production, progress, and individual autonomy, the cannibal inversely represents consumption, regress, and the annihilation of discrete identity. While serving thus as a mirror to the European subject, the cannibal threatened to swallow it, both literally, and also through representing the danger of 'going native', which would cause the civilised man to return to an original state of barbarism (Kilgour 1990: 25–8; Greenblatt 1980: 174–92). Conquest was thus justified by the law of the jungle: eat or be eaten.

As critics have shown, however, many early modern writers and scholars were ambivalent about the project of and necessity for imperialism.[1] The figure of the cannibal has always been an object of desire as well as dread: it seems significant that the inhabitants of the classical Golden Age, the cyclops and their ruler Saturn, were portrayed as anthropophages. For Montaigne the cannibal is the pure direct self, uncontaminated by society – a proto-romantic reading of the 'natural'. As Montaigne knew too, if the cannibal represents the forces that threaten the cherished values of a society, it can also be used satirically to attack despised values and expose hypocrisy. For Montaigne, the natives' cannibalism is not an adequate excuse for their extermination, as civilised man is far more savage. As he notes wryly:

> I am not sorie we note the barbarous horror of such an action, but grieved, that prying so narrowly into their faults we are so blinded in ours. I thinke there is more barbarisme in eating men alive, than to feed upon them being dead; to mangle by tortures torment a body full of lively sense, to roast him in pieces, to make dogges and swine to gnaw and teare him in mammockes ... than to roast and eat him after he is dead. (1928: I, 223–4)

Therefore, 'we may then well call them barbarious, in regard of reasons rules, but not in respect of us that exceed them in all kinde of barbarisme' (224). While Montaigne still sees an absolute difference between 'us' and 'them', in a move anticipatory of some recent critiques, he turns the (dinner) tables to argue that the natural is superior to the artificial, the savage to the civilised.[2] It is the natural man whose life has nobility and meaning: acts of real cannibalism are symbolic and therefore have a purpose and function, in contrast to European acts of violence which make no sense at all. Montaigne thus upholds the difference between 'us' and 'them', but in so doing still turns 'them' into an inverted image of 'us': the cannibal is now the *idealised* rather than *demonised* opposite of the European, whose natural life exposes the hypocrisy and artificiality of modern society.

Regardless then of its existence in reality, the cannibal, that great figure of rapacious introjection, became appropriated as a projection of modern dreams and fears. As an object to be feared, the cannibal is a perfect demon for a culture based on geographic and scientific expansion and progress, which yet fears its own imperialist appetites. It is a fitting double too for the modern insular ego produced by such a cultural dream, which both depends on a clear sense of its separation and detachment from others, and yet, perhaps imperialistically, wants to set sail and expand its own boundaries. The internal tension produced by these antithetical drives – the desire for autonomy and for transcendence of selfhood – is made clear later by Freud who makes cannibalism a threat to the progress of the self, not because it lurks at the fringes of society, but because it constitutes its very centre. For Freud, cannibalism is the basis of civilisation, which, in the grim myth of *Totem and Taboo*, originates in the murder and eating of the father by his sons. Moreover, individual development internalises and recapitulates this historical act of cannibalism. In Freud's quest-romance of sexual development, the individual begins life in a state of oneness with the world, in the oral phase of sexual development which Freud characterises as a cannibalistic existence. In this phase, the infant at first has no sense of its own separation from the world: it is aware only of the mother's breast, which it does not see as a separate object but, as it can be taken inside itself, as part of itself. The individual's original existence, the Golden Age of the infant, is thus described as a cannibalistic experience of fluid boundaries between self and world, who are joined in a symbiotic oneness.

For Freud, however, the attainment of a sense of separate self is absolutely necessary for normal individual development. The oral cannibal stage must be left behind; for Freud, all pathology stems from either fixation in or regression to an earlier stage (1961c: 77, 101). However, development never involves a total break with the past; rather it is incremental: 'one phase does not succeed the other so suddenly but gradually, so that parts of the earlier organization always persist side by side with the later, and ... even in normal development the transformation is never complete, the final structure often containing vestiges of earlier fixations' (1963: 247). This is especially true of the oral phase, as the act of corporeal ingestion becomes the model for later (and therefore new and improved) acts of psychic introjection, identification, and internalisation, through which individual identity is formed (1965a, 56; Kilgour 1990: 229). Individual progress is thus marked by a kind of sublimation through substitution, in which actual incorporation is succeeded by a higher form of psychic subsumption. The individual responds to the realisation of the fact that he cannot physically consume the world by learning to symbolically appropriate it. Individual development thus again recapitulates Freud's narrative of historical evolution from a state of nature to culture, from the literal to the figurative.[3]

Progress is thus an incremental process, which involves internalising and sublimating desires from previous stages. But it also creates a longing for the past. As adults we sense that our present relation to the world around is merely 'a shrunken residue of a much more inclusive – indeed all-embracing – feeling which corresponded to a more intimate bond between the ego and the world around it' (Freud: 1961b, 15). The price of individual identity is the awareness of the loss of a greater corporate identification, the original symbiosis with the mother. The primal state of total satisfaction of desire, of an utter coincidence between inside and outside, influences our later models of contentment. So Freud says that 'No one who has seen a baby sinking back satiated from the breast and falling asleep with flushed cheeks and a blissful smile can escape the reflection that this picture persists as a prototype of the expression of sexual satisfaction in later life' (1961c: 48). Genital sexuality (our mission) retains traces of its oral roots, as 'the child sucking at his mother's breasts has become the prototype of every relation of love' (88). The language of love is stuffed with metaphors of eating, devouring a loved one – a sweetie – which identify eating and sexual intercourse. For Freud, we are thus torn between a desire for autonomy that moves us forward, and a desire for identification that moves us backward. The march of the ego towards independence produces a simultaneous desire to return to our original experience (which for Freud becomes identified with the death drive): to relinquish the discontents of civilisation for an original state of unity and oneness with the world, signified by the act of cannibalism. Our original desires are not easily abandoned or suppressed: 'The repressed instinct never ceases to strive for complete satisfaction, which would consist in the repetition of a primary state of satisfaction. No substitutive or reactive formations and no sublimations will suffice to remove the repressed instinct's persisting tension'; it is only because the path backward is obstructed that we move forward at all, 'though with no prospect of bringing the process to a conclusion or of being able to reach the goal' (36). Desire craves its original form of satisfaction, and only accepts later symbolic substitutes reluctantly.

A tension emerges, therefore, as regression is feared as pathological, destructive of the separate identity that is valued in an individualist culture, which yet suspects that individualism itself stands in the way of the Golden Age of perfect happiness. Thus while the ego struggles to assert its detachment from the world, love, like pathological states, aims to break through that isolation and return to the first oral state of union with the world: it 'strives to make the ego and the loved object one, to abolish all spatial boundaries between them', so that: 'At the height of being in love the boundary between ego and object threatens to melt away. Against all the evidence of his senses, a man who is in love declares that 'I' and 'you' are one, and is prepared to behave as if it were a fact' (15). Erotic desire is a consuming passion, as Lucretius knew when he described lovers kissing 'with ravenous teeth':

> They greedily imbrace, joyne mothes, inspire
> Their soules, and bite through ardour of desire:
> In vaine; since nothing they can thence translate,
> Nor wholy enter and incorporate. (quoted in Sandys 1970: 207)

Lucretius suggests, as Freud will later, that love is ultimately unsatisfying for the reason that it craves but fails to recreate the absolute intimacy between subject and object which we experienced in infancy. Moreover, in the intensity of its thwarted desire, love begins to blur with aggression, the desire to completely consume the other in order to achieve such a union. Cannibalism itself has been seen as a confusion of desire and hatred (Sagan 1974: 81); in Voltaire's *Philosophical Dictionary,* the entry for 'antropofages' follows immediately after 'amour', and so Voltaire coyly opens by saying, 'I have spoken of love. It is hard to move from people who kiss each other, to people who eat one other' (1962: 86) – knowing full well that it is not hard at all.

From this perspective, cannibalism can become an image for an intense and ambivalent hunger for liberation from a discrete individual identity through reabsorption into a greater corporate identity. The cost of modern autonomy is solitary confinement, isolation in the prison-house of the self, in contrast to which cannibalism becomes an ideal of a Golden Age of a larger corporate social identity (see also Bahktin 1968: 281). Cannibalism is thus associated with the desire to return to an original state of unity. This symbolic function of cannibalism informs the Christian ritual of communion, in which the eating of God's body becomes a means of identifying the human and the divine; it appears in classical myths, and in Neoplatonic readings of the myth of Saturn devouring his children as a symbol of the soul's return to its source (Plotinus 1964: 99). Cannibalism becomes a ritual of reunion; what anthropologists call 'endo-cannibalism', eating of one's kin, is a way of absorbing the individual into the community, restoring the social wholeness that has been violated by death.

Cannibalism might thus also be seen as a form of nostalgia; it seems appropriate that the cannibalistic Saturn is both ruler of the Golden Age and also god of melancholy. Our interest in the topic today seems to correspond to other forms of nostalgia: our longings for lost decades, worlds, species, even barely buried fashions, as well as a deeper, if ambivalent, desire to recover a time before the emergence of modern individuated subjectivity. Perhaps the focus on cannibalism today is also partly a sign of our culture's refusal to let go of the idea of the natural, the wild, the savage, at the very time in which it is disappearing in the external world, and, through constructionist arguments, also as a philosophical or psychological category. But cannibalism in culture today is used less to invoke a lost Montaignesque ideal, and more often to attack our own rapacious egos, and express our rage at the isolation to which the modern world has condemned us. While with the discovery of the New World, the figure of the cannibal is used to reinforce the need for progress, individualism, capitalism, and imperialism, today it appears to denounce them. No longer the enemy of progress, the cannibal is now seen as its creation, the product of the European mind.[4] The figure of the cannibal is used to expose the fact that the construction of the modern subject against an 'other' demonised as a cannibal, ironically produces a 'cannibal ego' more insidious than any hottentot (McCannell 1992: 25, 266, 68). The man-eating myth is still with us, but now explicitly revealed to be a story about *ourselves*, not others, as the cannibal has moved from the fringes of our world to its very centre. If the New World cannibal was a mirror opposite of the Renaissance ego, with its sense of a universe opening up endless potential for fashioning a new world and self, the contemporary cannibal tells us of the modern consumer society ego, as hungry as ever, but also frightened as it witnesses the effects of its own appetites seeking more devious and sophisticated forms of satisfaction. In *The Silence of the Lambs*, the cannibal Hannibal Lecter, becomes an image for the modern self as epitomised in the consuming reader and critic.

2

Hypocrite *lecter*, – mon semblable, – mon frère!
(Baudelaire–mildly mutilated)

The Silence of the Lambs is an extremely allusive work, which, as one critic has said, cannibalises past horror stories (Halberstam 1991: 38, 51). Hannibal Lecter is a version of the gothic novel's mad scientist, who contains elements of his ancestors – Frankenstein, Dr Jekyll, Dr Moreau, transgressive experimenters who tamper with nature. In its play too on the identification of analysis and detection, and their mutual relation to unnatural forms of feeding, *Silence* also looks back to *Dracula*, where, with its use of the madhouse as a backdrop, the relation between Van Helsing and Dracula is also indirectly that of doctor and patient. Lecter's crime is both more subtle and more gross than those of his ancestors. He is an evil genius, a true individual who is isolated from others by his brilliance. His attempt to be superhuman, to distance himself from the natural world through detachment and objectivity, turns him into a subhuman monster, whose unnatural barbaric behaviour is worse than that of any savage beast. His crime, cannibalism, is significant in a number of ways. It seems overdetermined by rhyming logic, which would force *anyone* named Hannibal to become a cannibal. The unusual name also gives him a classic heroic precedent, which distances him from the modern world, identifying him with a past, and specifically an, albeit failed, imperialist project. If, as Freud said, all pathology is a return to our own past stages of development, Lecter is the oral phase writ large, and thus a reversion to our most primitive state. As a literally cannibal ego, however, Lecter is also the most exaggerated version of the modern Hobbesian individual, governed only by will and appetite, detached from the world and other humans, whom he sees only as objects for his own consumption. Progress and regress merge: Lecter is a man of great culture and refinement, a well-mannered gentleman (who never eats ladies), who quotes (if misquotes) Donne, a man of both cultivated aesthetic as well as crude savage taste, who exposes the affinity between barbarism and civilisation.

As the modern cannibal ego, Lecter has even more delicious resonances. Lecter reminds us that, while as Girard complained, psychoanalysis has focused generally on the taboo of incest, Freud was equally interested in cannibalism, which, in *Totem and Taboo*, is posited as the dark secret behind the origins of civilisation. With Lecter, however, cannibalism becomes the terrifying truth *psychoanalysis* conceals. For Freud, the analyst is, amongst other things, an explorer of the dark continent of the unconscious and the repressed (1965a: 51, 64; Day 1985: 177–90). The id also is 'the dark inaccessible part of our personality', a chaotic and confused territory in which 'contrary impulses exist side by side' (Freud 1965a: 65), and which threatens the ego with annihilation (1960: 47). Part of the analyst's goal is to help make the unconscious conscious, to free us from our own desires, and to colonise the territory of the barbaric id, so that, as Freud formulated his dream of internal imperialism, 'Where id was, there the ego shall be. It is a work of culture – not unlike the draining of the Zuider Zee' (1965a: 71). In *The Interpretation of Dreams*, Freud confessed that his childhood hero had been Hannibal, whose war against the Roman Empire he had read as an analogue of the Jews' struggle against the church of Rome. Hannibal had helped him understand 'what it meant to belong to an alien race' (Freud, 1965b: 229). As an analyst, Freud turns Hannibal's defeat into a triumph, as the alien outsider becomes the imperialist conqueror. In Hannibal the Cannibal, Freud's dream is further literalised. While analysis could be seen as the most benevolent and civilised form of imperialism, as it conquers the mind rather than the body, in Harris's work the pretence of refinement masks a secret and increased appetite for flesh. The text thus swallows also Conrad's *Heart of Darkness*, in which the colonising impulse to civilise the cannibals becomes real, and not just symbolic, cannibalism. In *Silence*, the psychological imperialist turns out to be a real cannibal.[5] Cannibalism is Lecter's way of effecting a complete cure, or at least of putting an end to analysis interminable; he kills and eats one patient when 'Therapy wasn't going anywhere' (Harris 1988: 54). By making the head shrinker a cannibal, the story suggests that, as one critic has argued, 'stripping the mind is no less a violation than stripping the body' (Halberstam 1991: 48; see also Young 1991: 5–35). Analysis and cannibalism thus form a continuum, differentiated only by degree, not kind, as to see into the minds of others is an act of aggression, a psychic imperialist invasion, which leads to a physical consumption.

Like many other gothic works, the novel depends upon a pattern of doubling, which establishes similarities between apparently different activities and figures.[6] The logic of such doubling has itself a kind of cannibalistic quality, as it suggests opposites will turn out to be the same, even as one destroys the other. In Harris' earlier novel, *Red Dragon*, Lecter and the other orally obsessed psychopath, the 'Tooth Fairy', are pitted against a male scientist-detective, Will Graham. The novel raises the classic gothic problem, given the underlying similarity, of distinguishing pursuer and pursued, detective and criminal; Lecter tells his antagonist, 'we're just alike' (Harris 1982: 67), and part of Graham's goal is to reassure both himself and others that they're not – that there is a way of telling the two apart. In *Silence*, Lecter's counterpart is Clarice Starling, whose bond with him is apparent from their first meeting when she notes that 'he was small and sleek; in his hands and arms she saw wiry strength like her own' (16). The two opposites are working together, exchanging knowledge, *quid pro quo*, analysing each other, and exchanging secrets so that it's difficult to tell who's who. Both are detective (as Freud also imagined himself; see Day 1985: 177) and analyst, and also patient under analysis. Both are interpreters, each reading the other for clues to the secret knowledge they desire.

Starling's motive for meeting Lecter is to harness psychic surveillance, which threatens to consume society, for social surveillance; to turn, ideally sublimate, literal cannibalism into a more socially acceptable form of containment. To lure him into helping her against another criminal, Buffalo Bill, she offers herself as bait, gradually revealing to him her own secrets. Motives then provide one means of differentiating between the two doubles: Clarice serves society, while Lecter serves society to himself. In the classic gothic dualism, altruism is pitted against selfishness, the community against the ravenous individual ego. Moreover, Lecter alone is the criminal. Clarice's secret, the clue to the meaning of the title, is not one of real guilt. Nor is it of a sexual nature (a family romance), as orthodox Freudianism would lead us to expect. In general, the secrets of the story are not explained in terms of sexuality, even in the case of Buffalo Bill (Tharp 1991: 109–13). Clarice's uncanny past consists of some traumatic experiences – the brutal death of her father, her subsequent exile to first relatives and then an orphanage, and, especially, her terrifying experiences at her aunt's slaughterhouse –

which explain the title of the story, but which also link her to Lecter, as, growing up around an abattoir, she 'from early life had known more than she wished to know about meat processing' (27).

The titular lambs reinforce patterns of religious imagery in the text, which introduce the central themes of change, renewal and rebirth. Most of the patterns are parodic: the image of the 'floaters', which suggest a demonic baptism; the burial and resurrection of the girls on the third day as part of Bill's gruesomely literal conversion, in which he will put off the old man to put on the new girl. Cannibalism (like Dracula's vampirism) itself appears as a perversion of the sacrament of communion, and Lecter is surrounded with twisted icons – his own drawings, of Golgotha and the Christ on his crucifixion watch (onto whose body he has superimposed Clarice's head), as well as his crazy neighbour Sammie (descendant of both Dracula's Renfield, and gothic tales of religious enthusiasts). Clarice's story, in contrast, suggests a potential norm of change and development, as the novel charts her growth and liberation from her traumatic past.

In this plot, Clarice's role is that of the patient, whom Lecter helps to cure. Her narrative is a version of Freudian analysis, which depends upon a complete and usually gendered difference between doctor and subject.[7] The male scientist cures the female patient by exposing a previously buried past which, because it was hidden, had haunted her. The last paragraph of the novel focuses on this break from her past, suggesting that even her subconscious has been purged of its demons, as she falls asleep and 'sleeps deeply, sweetly, in the silence of the lambs' (367).

The film also foregrounds Clarice's metamorphosis, but to bring out a slightly different narrative model: the gothic scenario, which itself lurks beneath the analytic relation. In the traditional gothic too, the heroine has to be freed from a haunting past, in order to grow up and attain adult female identity. The film opens with a scene in which Starling is running through the woods. We first might interpret this as a gothic scene of pursuit, but soon realise that she is on an FBI training course. The opening scene indicates self-consciously how Clarice plays the role of gothic heroine, whose experiences enable her to confront and come to terms with a past that haunts her, associated with her father's murder, but also, beyond that, with her ancestors, invoked at several points as a primitive race.[8] As a modern woman, she tries to separate herself from these barbaric origins, wanting to change, as Lecter recognises when he mocks her for being, like all gothic heroines, 'Desperate not to be like your mother' (22). As a woman too, she is identified with the murder victims, who are images of a self she might have been if she hadn't 'evolved' out of the swamp of archaic femaleness. She detaches herself from this identity through forensic analysis. In so doing, she disassociates herself also from the traditional figure of the gothic heroine, who is usually passive, and incapable of separating herself physically and emotionally from her family. Clarice Starling, whose first name evokes the sentimental Richardsonian model of femininity which influenced the gothic, is a new type of woman, and part of a current vogue for female detectives, quite different also from Christie's Miss Marple. In the course of the film and book we see her evolve into this type before our eyes, battling not only against the killer of women, but against the feudal sexism that still haunts the system.

In *Silence*, Clarice's sexual identity might offer one obvious difference between the two central characters. At the same time, however, as critics have noted, all the characters are sexually ambiguous. Becoming an agent, Clarice enters the male world of the FBI, so that she appears an androgynous figure (whose sexuality is unclear in the movie, though not in the book), while Lecter is given some feminine traits. His homosexuality is suggested, though never made explicit; in this world, cannibalism is certain and direct, while sexuality, and the difference between male and female, is murky and hard to determine. At the same time, the story draws indirectly on the traditional association of homosexuality with cannibalism, both conventionally feared as involving a loss of differences (Crain 1994: 25–53). The slipperiness of gender as a mark of difference is literalised in the figure of Buffalo Bill, who further intensifies the identification between Clarice and Lecter. Bill plays Renfield to Lecter's Dracula – serving as a kind of perverted double of an original perversion. To Lecter's Dr Jekyll, he is 'Mr Hide' (a name which takes on a whole new meaning in this context, as it's his alias). If Lecter is a descendent of Victor Frankenstein, Bill 'combines both Frankenstein and the monster; he is the scientist, the creator, and he is the body being formed, sculpted, stitched and fitted' (Halberstam 1991: 46). Lecter and Bill have complementary methods of incorporation which break down the opposition between self and other, inside and outside: where Lecter takes others inside himself, Bill puts himself inside others.[9] As skin is the border between the self and the world, his appropriation of others' surfaces is a further parodic version of more traditional ways of encountering others. By merging his own body with women's, Bill blurs the boundaries between male and female in a literalisation of the marriage ritual in which man and woman become symbolically one flesh.[10] Like cannibalism, Bill's crime is also a weird parody of a consumer mentality which, like colonial discourse, enables him to objectify his sexual 'other' in order to 'suit' himself and subsume her. But Bill's real goal is to be a complete constructionist, who can 'fashion' for himself a new female self, turning male into female and thus transcending gender differences. By seeking to transform himself, he thus becomes a distorted version of Clarice. As she flees the limits of traditional femininity, he seeks, through more direct means, a way out of orthodox masculinity. He understands the symbolic nature of his attempt at self-transcendence, as the presence of a moth in the mouths of his victims indicates. It suggests Buffalo Bill's motives are renewal and change; like Clarice, he is trying to free himself from a past self limited by conventional ideas of sexual difference.

Both Bill's and Clarice's stories of development and self-transformation, of attempts to transcend the confining boundaries of their natural gendered identities, relate back to the story of Lecter. Lecter's role in the plot is a neat example of the kinds of cannibalistic inversion the story demonstrates: while logically a peripheral figure, brought in ostensibly simply to help the good guys against the bad, the chilling Lecter becomes the central figure – as Anthony Hopkins well knew. As European explorers had feared, the marginal cannibal outsider colonises and takes over the centre. We never learn anything about Lecter's past – what caused this monster – which makes him all the more unsettling. If Bill is the evil that can be reduced, as it is later by reporters, to an 'unhappy childhood' (357), Lecter is a larger evil that contemporary society both creates and denies. When Clarice asks her superior, Jack Crawford, what Lecter is, Crawford replies, 'I know he's a monster. Beyond that, nobody can say for sure' (6) – suggesting that he is the uncanny thing that normal language cannot define. His intelligence is 'not measurable by any means known to man' (199). He has a nice sense of poetic justice; as he tells her: 'A census taker tried to quantify me once. I ate his liver with some fava beans and a big Amarone' (24). Instead of being contained by the system he swallows it – a truly subversive element. The analyst resists analysis, reduction in terms of his own theories, which cannot contain him any more than the prison system (whether that be the prison-house of language or a jail), or census taker can. Even his motives are never clearly defined: part revenge, part perverse pleasure and an aesthetic appreciation of murder as one of the fine arts. We can't analyse him scientifically to say, reassuringly, what the cause of his evil is. He mocks Clarice when she comes with her questionnaire: 'You'd like to quantify me' (22), 'do you think you can dissect me with this blunt little tool? ... You can't reduce me to set of influences. You've given up good and evil for behaviorism, Officer Starling. You've got everybody in moral dignity pants – nothing is ever anybody's fault. Look at me, Officer Starling, Can you stand to say I'm evil? Am I evil, Officer Starling?' (21). Lecter suggests that he is a deeper moral evil unleashed by a relativistic world which reads good and evil only in terms of social conditioning. He is the monster that is created by and feeds upon a society which no longer believes in stable absolute differences.

Like Clarice, Lecter is free in the end. For him, identity can be simply remade as he first literally takes a new face in order to escape, then uses plastic surgery as a method for conversion, which affords him also the Frankensteinian power to reconstruct himself as a new man. In the novel, the exposing of Clarice's demons seems an exorcism that enables her to sleep 'silently', in the arms of her lover. The happy romantic ending, which suggests that the banishing of a demonic past leads to the attainment of heterosexual love, is disturbed by the resonances of the last lines, which echo the title. Moreover, if the demons have been exorcised that may mean less that they have been successfully contained, and simply that they, in the form of the cannibal, are now free and uncontrolled. The film ends with the figure of Lecter whose break and reconstruction of identity also becomes a parodic version of Clarice's, in which, furthermore, the parody usurps the place of the norm. In the film, the last scene is of Lecter pursuing his real nemesis, the odious and lecherous Dr Chilton, who was guilty of harassing Clarice. Reasserting his bond with her against a common foe, Lecter calls her to say: 'I'm having an old friend for dinner.' The movie thus ends with a cute pun. Poetic justice triumphs, as one bad doctor eats another. While in one sense the ending is left open (conveniently allowing for a lucrative sequel that fleshes out the further madcap adventures of Hannibal the Cannibal), in another, it is resolutely shut, through the projected union of the two opposites. Cannibalism itself becomes a tidy image for closure – a quick, if cheap, resolution of differences which both seems provocatively witty and subversive, and yet also satisfies the reader's desire for a neat and, in some sense, happy ending.

The end of the film suggests further the possible dissolution of the difference between Clarice and Lecter, not only by focusing on their common enemy, but by juxtaposing scenes of their respective liberty.[11] The penultimate scene focuses on Starling's graduation, which marks the climax of her quest as the attainment of autonomy and independence, when she becomes literally an 'agent'. Elizabeth Young argues that the relation between the final scenes reveals that while Clarice's development may distance her from her former self, it identifies her further with Lecter; it suggests that while she becomes an agent, it is of the state, and she is 'now fully trained to enforce the power of the state through modes of invasion, surveillance, entrapment, discipline, and punishment that not only parallel but literalize, as Freud's work helps to remind us, the operative modes of psychoanalysis itself' (25). The psychic scrutiny of the analyst feeds into and makes possible the social scrutiny of the FBI. The movie thus could be read as showing the transformation of the detective into the criminal she was pursuing, eradicating the difference between good and evil. The bourgeois myth of progress (here personal development and evolution) turns into a story of regress, in which all change is merely parody and distortion.

In its final identification of detective and criminal the film picks up the theme of Harris's earlier novel. At the end of *Red Dragon*, the good guy is left wondering if he is indeed any different from the criminal, as he faces his own destructive nature, musing 'that he contained all the elements to make murder' (Harris 1982: 354). Harris thus suggests that the dark truth of civilisation is that what is most highly civilised is most savagely cannibalistic – a message with which Montaigne would agree and that Conrad also conveyed, though with somewhat more style and subtlety. This is a favourite theme of contemporary gothic and horror films, which appear to make us confront our own insatiable appetites – at the same time, of course, as they gleefully (and profitably) feed them. The scene of Clarice's final pursuit by Buffalo Bill, which repeats and literalises the opening episode, gives us a real image of gothic pursuit, shot from the perspective of the pursuer, with whom the viewer therefore becomes identified. The film also leaves us siding with Lecter, rooting for him as he sets out for dinner, and so suggests our own identification with the cannibal, who becomes our gothic double.

This replicates, more graphically, the way in which in the novel the readers' reading is slyly mirrored back to them. Reading is a form of consumption too; Lecter's ambiguous analysis within the text is analogous to the activity of interpreting the text itself. The text's moral might then be 'caveat Lectorem' – not reader beware, but beware of the reader. Critics, readers, interpreters, those who consume what others have produced, are cannibals after all (see also Young 1991: 27–8).

This may be a useful moral for an author who, like Swift with whom I began, gets to demonise and so perhaps subtly subsume the reception of his work. Harris sets a cunning trap for us, which lures us into a reading that appears to reproduce the crimes represented within the text, which originate in the confusion of differences. But while the text thus seems to reaffirm conservatively the need for stable boundaries, it implies they are no longer possible, and that there is no alternative means for discrimination. Like the act of cannibalism, the narrative sets up absolute oppositions, only to suggest that they are the same, that there are no differences after all. The serial killer and psychiatrist are at heart both barbaric head shrinkers.

However, it seems rather puritanically severe to identify Lecter and Chilton, the mass murderer and the jerk. The neat elision which both book and film perform prevents us from thinking about the real if less extreme differences between the cannibal and the male chauvinist, the dismemberer and the reader. Such cannibalistic logic seems often too prevalent today, where arguments over differences tend to become polarised. In criticism, cannibalism is playing a significant role in thinking about the concept of 'difference', and its relation to definitions of identity, either individual, textual, sexual, national, or social. By analysing the political uses of the figure of the cannibal, some critics have argued that there are no natural differences between 'us' and 'them', the natural and the cultural,[12] barbaric and civilised – that such boundaries are exclusionary, racist, sexist,[13] motivated by pernicious ideology. This dismantling of oppositions is occurring, however, at a time also of new territorialism, when differences are frequently celebrated, and we are warned against the danger of appropriating others' property – including their voices and identities. If breaking down boundaries appears to some an attack against an old imperialist ideology, to others, it simply reproduces it. As part of current projects too, the modern subject, the autonomous individual of bourgeois capitalism, is currently being deconstructed, reconstructed, dismembered, and sometimes rather Frankensteinly stitched back together. The poor insular ego, once the brave New World of Descartes and Freud, is now under attack on all its shores. Post-structuralist and Marxist arguments show that the self's construction *of* others conceals the self's true construction *by* others and, generally, external forces, while feminists oppose the ideal of a detached subject with 'relational' models for identity. The purpose of many such critiques is to break down the myths that wall in the isolated individual and establish more permeable, fluid relations between selves and others, beyond the rigid opposition of eater and eaten. This is a time (like most times, of course) of both boundary formation and dissolution. This is true even in the realm of criticism itself which has recently been marching imperialistically into territories previously not its own (including anthropology) and colonising other disciplines to help it redefine its own identity and relation to the outside world. It is always possible that criticism is projecting its own hunger for territory and for the power to construct, as well as deconstruct, people, onto an imperial past, from which it can claim to have evolved. Yet our distrust of other narratives of evolution and enlightenment might remind us of the fragility of our difference from that past and the dangers in our own narrative.

It may seem a rather perverse form of self-consumption for me to use cannibalism as a dark double of our critical predicament: our simultaneous desires for autonomy and for identification, for the subversion of boundaries and their reinforcement. Though it's tempting to follow Arens and bite the hand that feeds me, I don't want to fuel any glib denunciation of the critic as cannibal – quite the contrary. There is obviously a real difference between the critic and the cannibal, as there is between all acts of figurative cannibalism and literal (if it existed) cannibalism. The problem is that the subject itself is a murky realm in which differences, partially because they seem so extreme, disappear. Let me end, though, by reading the true story of Jeffrey Dahmer, the most famous example today of real cannibalism, as an almost Dantesque parody of our own critical appetites. To me, Dahmer's story suggests how cannibalism both signifies the destruction of community through the alienation of modern life and the desire to recreate it. Cannibalism both marks Dahmer's difference from us, and his attempt to transcend that difference. The autonomous subject of modern capitalist economy becomes the complete loner, alienated from others (a fact which was emphasised by media accounts of how neighbours ignored the strange smells and noises coming from his apartment, and the police refused to intervene in what they were told was a gay domestic dispute), who, in the privacy of the home that is his castle, creates an alternative and completely infernal community. While on the one hand, Dahmer stands as the epitome of the modern individual, defined through his independence and detachment from others, on the other, his gruesome ritual is a grotesque attempt to heal that alienation through his own literalised form of communion. Cannibalism becomes an image of the forces generated by society that are tearing it apart, especially an ideology of individualism which defines us as isolated consumers and so dismembers the body politic as well as the individual bodies of its members. At the same time, however, cannibalism is also a (obviously literal and horrible) response to that fragmentation and isolation. It was Dahmer's grotesquely pathetic way of trying to transcend the isolation of his private subjectivity, to reestablish identification with others, by deconstructing, literally dismembering, differences. In a materialistic world based on a market mentality, which reduces us all to insatiable consumers, it is a perverse attempt to turn the material into the symbolic – which seems a rather gruesome reminder of the need to discriminate between them.

This may seem a rather tasteless digression – a manifestation of this critic's need to impose meaning on the most meaningless and frightening of acts. Interpretation is always driven by a desire to make sense of what otherwise might appear threateningly senseless. By analysing, dissecting, interpreting our terrors, whether they appear on the screen or in the world around us, we create some element of stability and safety for ourselves, asserting our control over a world which increasingly appears to lack meaning and coherence. Like all insatiable appetites, the hunger for significance can go too far, but it is a real hunger. I don't mean to trivialise the horror of what Dahmer did to real human beings, by reducing this terror to a mere figure for modern life. Yet I also need to find in it a symbolic meaning, albeit a personal and provisional one in which I identify it with our more theoretical attempts to take apart the western subject. Dahmer is both product and response to a modern consumer society, in which the isolated ego is alienated from others. While our critical responses to this world take a more refined and intellectual form, they may be hampered by similar factors. In this period of self-scrutiny, in which we, following Freud, hope to reveal and so conquer our dark secrets, it is too easy to be suspicious of all our own motives. In a materialist time, we tend to see all drives as material, appetitive ones, appropriate to our consumer world.[14] For Freud himself, of course, all basic drives were ultimately sexual; in Harris's revision of Freud, the sexual urge itself turns out to be only a cover for even more primal cannibalistic urges. *The Silence of the Lambs* suggests that, far from being sublimated into symbolic forms or even sexual desire, our original appetites still move us, so that we remain trapped in a new oral phase of consumption. The work implies that man-eating is a reality – it is civilisation that is the myth. Perhaps its popularity stems from a widespread scepticism towards ideals of transcendence. We are dubious of a difference between a model of *sublimation*, in which a lower desire is successfully transformed into something higher, and the mere *repression* of desire, which, as Freud has taught us, leads to the destructive return of our ferocious buried hungers. While therefore for the anthropologist Peggy Reeves Sanday, ritual cannibalism is a form of sublimation, as it is an attempt to transform the merely physical into the symbolic, for us cannibalism is inversely a means of demystification, a satiric weapon which literalises in order to expose the dark truth under our ideals. Perhaps the danger of this function is that it makes it hard to maintain any ideals at all, if all of our desires, dreams, hungers for transcendence, can be reduced to the same cannibalistic act.

Notes

1 Introduction: the cannibal scene

1 For examples of recent work on Montaigne's essay, see Lestringant 1994: 163–89; Quint 1995.

2 'I talked a good while with one of them, but I had so bad an interpreter, and who did so ill apprehend my meaning, and who through his foolishness was so troubled to conceive my imaginations, that I could draw no great matter from him' (Montaigne 1928: I, 229).

3 Another observable practice among the categorisers which tends to throw doubt on the validity of their categories is the persistence with which – at different moments and in different parts of the world – the indigenous population is divided into the good and the bad, the friendly and the hostile, the noble savage and the cannibal. From Arawak and Carib in the Caribbean to Polynesian and Melanesian in the Pacific, the practices of the describers make identical moves, inevitably casting doubt on the objectivity of the descriptions offered. That categorical imperative operates some fine discriminations. In Brazil, where the French found cannibals wherever they looked, distinctions were necessary between good cannibals and bad cannibals, Tupinambá and Ouetaca, where the former killed and ate for vengeance (honourable cannibals), while the latter killed for food, were reputed to be vampires, and ate their flesh raw (Léry 1990; cf. Lestringant 1994: 125–6). Even within the honourable Tupinambá there were divisions to be made since the old women tended to have a real taste for human flesh.

4 See Arens's chapter below. Needham (1980) is the most thoughtful of the immediate reviews; Brady (1982) one of the longest and most considered.

5 See also Claude Rawson's important work in this area: 1978–9, 1984, 1992.

6 Sahlins 1979: 47. This paragraph of Sahlins is referred to and quoted from by Deborah Lipstadt as an example of how 'respectability for

outrageous and absolutely false ideas' – such as Holocaust denial – can be gained in the academic arena (Lipstadt 1993: 27). Sahlins's reference to the Holocaust may have been prompted by the recent declaration ('La politique hitlérienne d'extermination. Une déclaration d'historiens' in *Le Monde*, 21 February 1979) of France's leading historians (organised by Pierre Vidal-Naquet and Léon Poliakov) protesting the attempts by Robert Faurisson to deny the Holocaust.

7 Collected with other essays on the same topic in his *Les assassins de la mémoire* (1987), from which I quote here. (There is an English translation: Vidal-Naquet 1992.)

8 Others have adopted the analogy: 'Where, asks Arens in a tactic reminiscent of those used by revisionist Holocaust historians, are the survivors of cannibal feasts?' (Palencia-Roth 1993: 22); and Lestringant refers to Arens's 'parenté indéniable avec les historiens négationnistes de l'Holocauste' (1994: 31 n.15). Cf. Arens, below, p. 44.

9 As Noam Chomsky once observed: 'if you take any two historical events and ask whether there are similarities and differences, the answer is always going to be both yes and no. At some sufficiently fine level of detail, there will be differences, and at some sufficiently abstract level, there will be similarities.' The key question 'is whether the level at which there are similarities is, in fact, a significant one' ('Intervention in Vietnam and and Central America: Parallels and Differences', in James Peck, ed., *The Chomsky Reader*, New York: Pantheon Books, 1987, p. 315; quoted from Stannard 1992: 153).

10 For Tim White, Arens's refusal of 'the hard scientific evidence' is 'like the flat-earthers denying the roundness of the earth' (Osborne 1997: 38).

11 On the vexed question of the comparability of the Jewish Holocaust and the genocide of American Indian populations, see Stannard 1992: 149–54. On wider questions of the limits of representation, see Friedlander 1992.

12 For a fuller analysis, Hulme 1993; and for supporting arguments from this area, Hulme 1986: 46–87; Wey-Gómez 1992; Felix Bolaños 1994. The difficulty of distinguishing bones marked by cannibal practice from bones marked by funerary practices continues to dog the current archaeological debates about the existence of prehistoric cannibalism (for a summary, see Osborne 1997).

13 Originally in Peter Martyr (D'Anghera 1587). I refer here to the Spanish translation: 'Encontraron también la cabeza de un niño recién muerto colgada de una viga y todavía empapada en sangre' (Gil and Varela 1984: 52). Martyr's description probably owes much to the classical accounts of cannibal meals in Ovid's *Metamorphoses* and Seneca's *Thyestes* (see Gillies 1994: 208 n.14).

14 On Vespucci and Pseudo-Vespucci, see Formisano 1992, who actually suggests the term 'para-Vespuccian' to describe the *Mundus Novus*.

15 Pratt 1992: 1–11; see also Pratt 1994: 24–46. Other relevant works in this general area are Ferguson and Whitehead 1992 and Hill 1996.

16 The *Adventure*, companion ship to Cook's *Resolution*, had its own 'cannibal' experience when ten sailors were killed by Maoris on the South Island of New Zealand. James Burney found the remains and took these to be 'most horrid & undeniable proofs' that they'd been cooked and eaten. Burney wrote that what he had seen could 'never be mentioned or thought of, but with horror', and his father observed that after his return to London he 'always spoke of it in a whisper, as if it was treason' (quoted from Guest 1992: 120; with interesting analysis).

17 See Morgan 1975: 73; 'The Sea Voyage' (Fletcher 1995) and 'The Tempest or The Enchanted Island' (Dryden 1970).

18 The most powerful fictional evocation of the cannibal feast is in José Juan Saer's novel, *El entenado* (translated as *The Witness* (1990)): cf. González n.d.

19 The religious concern for the wholeness of the body had become a major issue during the Crusades, when many European noblemen who died far from home were boiled to their bones for easier transportation back to their family vaults. On 27th September 1299, Boniface VIII issued the bull Detestande feritatis in which he forbad such practices, declaring that 'the minds of the faithful would no longer be horrified and the human body no longer be torn to pieces' (quoted in Brown 1981: 221).

20 Piersen 1993: 11–12; and cf. Forbes 1992 and Root 1996. For images of cannibalism in the nineteenth century, see the fine study by H. L. Malchow (1996: 41–123).

21 Although the novel does draw on the traditional association of cannibalism with homosexuality (cf. Crain 1994 and Bergman 1991).

2 Rethinking anthropophagy

1 The extent to which anthropologists commend colonial and missionary authorities in print for pacifying the natives and eradicating cannibalism among them is embarrassing. Reliance upon these accounts is equally disconcerting, and at times points to an unfortunate relationship among the three institutions and their perspectives.

2 See Leroux's (1982) newspaper interview with Marshall Sahlins, 'The Professor Who Was Consumed by Cannibalism'.

3 Sanday's (1986) latter-day review of the literature – via a tour of the Human Relations Area Files, which relies heavily on explorer, colonial, and missionary accounts – uncovers a veritable horde of cannibals, now including the 'pygmies'.

4 Brown and Tuzin's (1983b) edited volume attempted to resolve this dilemma in response to the publication of *The Man-Eating Myth*. Most of the essays are based upon reconstructions of events since, as is typically the case, the presumed anthropophagy had ceased sometime prior to the arrival of the anthropologist. A notable exception is provided by Porter Poole who wrote: 'All *observed* instances of Bimin-Kukusmin anthropophagy however, are *customary* aspects of mortuary rites' (1983: 15, author's emphasis). To my knowledge this

detailed description is the only published eye-witness account of cannibalism in the anthropological literature. In a subsequent informal discussion of the matter, Poole indicated to me that although the participants were told the substance was human flesh, he had no idea if this was indeed the case and it 'could have been anything'. (The author failed to respond to two letters from me requesting written confirmation of this conversation.) The ritual also involved the sacrifice and consumption of parts of cassowaries and wild boars (Poole 1983: 24). See also Baal's (1984) dismissal of cannibal 'stories' told to initiates and outside observers during rituals. Porter Poole also mentions that he is not interested in the debate about whether or not cannibalism actually occurs and 'is concerned with a cultural interpretation of *ideas* and *perceptions* of cannibalism' (1983: 6–7, my emphasis). In sum, this ethnographic account of the deed is not necessarily what it seems to be.

5 In attempting to 'illustrate the logic of cannibalism,' Sanday psychobabbles: 'I suggest that ritual cannibalism is part of a system of symbols that predicates social and individual consciousness by transforming inchoate psychological energy into social channels through the mechanism of identification' (1986: xi). She later clarifies the matter by suggesting that: 'rituals of cannibalism summarize and express an ontology, provide a model for individuation, and control violent emotions' (xii).

6 In the only instance of a response to a negative review by a colleague, I wrote to the Honorary Editor of *Man* inquiring of the reviewer exactly what there was about *The Man-Eating Myth*, or for that matter any book, to conclude by condemning it as 'dangerous' (Rivière 1980: 205). She declined to print my reply with the explanation that it was not clear what would be gained by asking such a question in this form (Strathern 1980).

7 For an early attempt to draw attention to the issue of BSE transmission and to de-sensationalise the related kuru references, see Taylor (1989). The alarm over Bovine Spongiform Encephalopathy, or 'Mad Cow Disease', in Britain and the resulting Creutzfeld-Jacob's Disease – a variant of kuru – in humans has recently added to the literature and references to this and related diseases. No one has yet to suggest CJD and similar viral diseases among European populations are transmitted by cannibalism (see Arens 1990). However, Gajdusek's latter day emphasis on cannibalism *per se* as the means of transmitting kuru has directly affected the interpretation of the European variant. In 1994, an article by two clinical microbiologists (Lacey and Dealler 1994), warned of the potential transfer of BSE to humans from infected meat and then the transfer of the disease by other means to members of the same species, including among humans. The argument was immediately denounced by other commentators. Paul Brown of the National Institutes of Health (Gajdusek's research unit) called it 'mischief'. His reason: Gajdusek has shown that the New Guinea variant of the disease was transmitted by cannibalism. Thus the fear of contracting it from beef was 'misinformation'

(Brown 1994: 1,797). Two other research scientists responded to the Lacey and Dealler suggestion, which they opined could cause 'serious distress' among the beef-eating public, with the same strategy. They lectured their misinformed colleagues that 'a wealth of published information on kuru over thirty years (Gajdusek 1990) shows it was due to cannibalistic rituals' and the facts 'could not be more plain' (Will and Wilesmith 1994: 1,799). Brown also noted at the time that, due to the slow nature of the disease in expressing itself, it would be years before he or his opponents could gloat over who was correct on this issue. However, 1995 showed him to be wrong as the consumption of infected beef was accepted as the cause of CJD in humans. Shortly thereafter, it was also determined that cows could pass the infection on to their offspring. There is no word yet if the same possibility holds for humans but a similar scenario cannot be dismissed.

8 In Port Morseby just two days after leaving the Highlands, Gajdusek wrote in his journal that he already missed 'my kukukukus, ... I do love these kuks, ... They are my people' (1968: 153). In addition to the professional literature on the topic, I also refer to a number, but not all, of Gajdusek's candid journals on his research and travels. These include Gajdusek 1963, 1968, 1970b, 1971, 1976, and 1981. The availability of those documents eventually led to the investigation of Gajdusek for child pornography and his eventual plea of guilty to the sexual abuse of one of the fifty-six boys he had brought from New Guinea to his home in Maryland. The newspaper article on the topic concluded as usual that Gajdusek traced the spread of kuru to the local custom of eating the brains of the deceased as a sign of respect (Molotsky 1997).

9 In addition to the usual unsubstantiated asides to cannibalism among the natives, the literature reeks of racism. It is difficult to imagine how contemporary scholarship could rely upon it for any purpose.

10 In an interview (Arens 1995) on the kuru research, literature, and relevant photographs, Lindenbaum informed me that this sentence was inserted by the editor of the *New York Times* review of Zigas's *Laughing Death* (1990). She admitted that it was in error and misleading, but failed to object to its inclusion in the published text.

11 In considering this topic I do not deem it necessary to provide an alternate medical hypothesis for the transmission of the disease in opposition to the faulted one (see Steadman and Merbs (1982) on Fore mortuary ceremonies for an alternative possibility). However, it is now becoming apparent from the concern over BSE disease that the consumption of infected animal, as opposed to human, flesh is a reasonable alternative to consider. Gajdusek was struck by this vector possibility almost immediately since the pig meat 'is notoriously undercooked'. He also noted that children were often given raw meat to eat, presumably by their mothers (Gajdusek 1976: 312). Moreover, at the time, women who lived with and cared for the animals suckled both piglets and children. Mothers also deloused

both and reportedly ate the parasites. These observable and photographed practices (see Sorenson 1976: 55–6), ceased at the time of the research, along with the alleged cannibalism. The continued incidence of the disease on a lesser scale some forty years later also suggests a more mundane explanation for its transmission. The recognition of this fact even twenty years ago led to the assumption that kuru has a longer dormancy period among 'admitted cannibal' patients than previously imagined (Prusiner, Gajdusek, and Alpers 1982). Nor, to my knowledge, was the potential role of institutionalised homosexuality or homoeroticism in the area (see Gajdusek 1963: 79–80 and Herdt 1984) explored as a means of transmission of the virus.

3 Cannibal feasts in nineteenth-century Fiji

1 I am grateful to the Harry Frank Guggenheim Foundation for a grant to hire a research assistant to collect data on cannibalism in Polynesia and Melanesia during the calendar year 1991; and to Sasanka Perera who carried out the research. I am deeply indebted to the following colleagues and friends for the help they have given me: John Koza, Steven Phillips, Librarian of the Peabody Essex Museum, who sent me photocopies of the relevant portions of Endicott's logs and provided me the original cover page of Endicott's narrative; Albert Schutz of the Department of Linguistics, University of Hawaii, who helped straighten out the partially garbled Fijian terms in the narratives that I use; Deborah M. Cordonnier of the Firestone Library at Princeton who helped with last-minute references, and Joan Dayan, Jeanette Mageo, Tom Johnston O'Neill, Geoff White, David Hanlon, Paul Lyons, James Boon, Ranjini Obeyesekere, Ernestine McHugh, and Peter Hulme who read earlier versions of this article and made important suggestions.

2 In a later scholarly article Sahlins (1983) has important insights into Fijian human sacrifice but, like Ross Bowden's, his discussion is oriented towards the inordinate consumption of human flesh, namely cannibalism, owing to his reliance on cannibal narratives of dubious value by such authorities as Jackson (and William Diapea and William Endicott whose work I will examine later).

3 According to Albert J. Schutz, this phrase is probably a corruption of 'a bokola boi ca' which means 'stinking corpse to be eaten'.

4 Endicott was seated on 'the large roots of a coconut tree in front of the whole ceremony' (1923: 59) and it is doubtful that he could have had a close-up and uninterrupted view of the details of the 'butchering' from his vantage point.

5 This includes Hayes's own practice of cannibalism, in spite of the fact that Hayes himself denied it. So was it with Cannibal Jack. Figures like Hayes and Cannibal Jack were, on one level, quite as 'savage' as the natives in their midst, as far as missionaries were concerned.

6 The title of the book as conceived by its author reads as follows: 'A

Few Extracts From The Autobiography of William Diapea Alias "Cannibal Jack". These Extracts Embrace The Long Gone-by Years of 1843 Up To 1847 – The Last Inclusive.' In the very first sentence Cannibal Jack says how he earned the 'disgraceful-sounding sobriquet' of Cannibal Jack. He had written a first book entitled *Jack, the Cannibal Killer* hoping that a title like that would enhance its circulation. Unfortunately, he himself got stuck with that name. Jack adds that when people heard that he had lived for such a long time among cannibals they concluded that he was one himself. After this brief preface he tells us that this book contains extracts taken 'almost at random' from the autobiography of William Diapea, *alias* Cannibal Jack. Page ninety-one makes it clear that he himself is attached to the 'disgraceful-sounding sobriquet'. Julian Thomas, an early travel writer on the Western Pacific, says that he met a white man in 1880 in Levuka 'who rejoiced in the name of "Cannibal Jack"' (1886: 8).

Jackson flamboyantly claims to have been a truant and wanderer for fifty years and visited every place in the vast expanse of ocean, bounded on the north by California, Japan, China, and India; and on the south by Tasmania, New Zealand, and Australia; and in such places as Peru and Chile in South America, and Papua, adding up to a thousand islands and residing in nearly a hundred (6).

7 Cannibal Jack refers to the 'reader' several times, pointing clearly to a literate audience given to reading books. 'The reader may be tempted to think' (1928: 79); 'the difficulty with the reader of these extracts' (90).

8 Cannibal Jack was wanted by the French in New Caledonia on charges of running guns to native rebels and of murder, which, I suspect is the reason for changing his name. Moreover, in spite of the name change, part of his earlier name was retained in the latter two volumes as 'Jack', suggesting strongly that John Jackson was the original name. A further point: in *Cannibal Jack* he tells us that he was called 'Cannibal Jack' because that was the title of his first novel (1928: 3). If this is true, then it is likely that the lost novel *Jack, the Cannibal Killer* was written after 'Jackson's Narrative' because that text has no reference whatever to his nickname.

9 'Jackson's Narrative' has clear reference to dates: the adventures start in Samoa in 1840, and continue into 1841 and 1842, both dates being mentioned. The adventures in *Cannibal Jack* start in 1843 with the Bonaveidogo episode which, according to the previous text, started in 1841. It seems that John Jackson is treating *Cannibal Jack* as quite distinct from the other work, even though the crucial Bonaveidogo adventure overlaps both. If one is to pick actual dates, 'Jackson's Narrative' sounds more plausible to me as the period when Cannibal Jack was in Fiji (whether he was ever there during this period we will never know for sure). He was probably in and out of the Fijian islands right through his life. Julian Thomas saw him in Ovalau 'loafing about the beach at Levuka' in 1880 (1886: 8), and referred to him disparagingly as a 'drunken loafer and an outcast' (16).

10 About this style H. De Vere Stacpoole, a modern writer of South Sea romances, says in his foreword to *Cannibal Jack*: 'Cannibal Jack does not write, he talks: he button holes you, he belches in your face; when he is done, it is not the end of a book, but the stopping of a voice; the end of a bottle of whisky; with a plate full of cigarette ashes on the table and the tropic dawn standing at the door' (Diapea 1928: x).

11 This is one of two excerpts that the publisher omitted.

12 Basil Thompson (1908: 159–62) has a good description of a Fijian priest possessed by a deity and uttering prophecies very much like Cannibal Jack's priest. However, there is no reference to head bashing. Though I have not heard of Fijian head bashing, coconuts are used for purposes of divination in Fiji. See for example, A. M. Hocart (1929: 203); and Thomas Williams (1870: 193). For an account of a possessed priest from South Asia smashing coconuts on his head, see Gananath Obeyesekere (1981: 142–59).

13 The author translates 'vasu' as someone dependant on a powerful lord, whereas it generally refers to the relationship between a man and his sister's son. 'Vasu i taukei', according to Capell's Dictionary, means 'when he is born in his mother's village'. The missionary Thomas Williams writes: 'The word means a nephew or niece, but becomes the title of office in the case of the male, who, in some localities, has the extraordinary privilege of appropriating whatever he chooses belonging to his uncle, or those under his uncle's power' (1870: 16).

14 Cannibal Jack says that his 'book is a mere specimen of the whole, and which will be for sale, providing this is accepted and paid for, but if rejected as no use to other people, I fully depend on the honour of the peruser in having it returned'. Unfortunately, Hadfield did not read the manuscript till much later and Cannibal Jack never got his payment.

15 I refer the reader to his romantic adventures with the lovely Litia, starting at the end of book sixteen and spilling over to seventeen, and containing the following ingredients: a shipwreck and Jack's miraculous escape; his conversion experiences; his rescue by Litia on the island of Komo; his marriage to Litia; the conflict between the 'cannibal party' and the Christian 'religious party' in Komo; Litia in Pocahontas style protecting Jack from the leader of the cannibal party; the killing of all members of the cannibal party and the voluntary self-immolation of their wives; the ultimate triumph of the religious party and the inauguration of an indigenous Christian civilisation in Komo; and finally the death of Litia at childbirth which releases the protagonist once again to perform more adventures and write more books.

16 In his book Cannibal Jack makes much of the fact that he collected books from ships and had a small library (233). This might well have been the case: he also refers to Byron's poetry (199), to Locke (173), to phrases like the 'yellow and sere', and to Bligh's account of the mutiny.

17 Greg Dening writes: 'John Coulter, a supernumerary on board the *Stratford* ... stayed some months at Fatuiva and Hiva Oa in 1833 and wrote of his experience in *Adventures in the Pacific* [1845]. William Torrey, sparked no doubt by the success of Melville, published in 1848 the *Life and Adventures of William Torrey Who for a Space of Twenty-five Months within the Years 1835, 1836, 1837 Was Held a Captive by the Cannibals of the Marquesas*.' Dening adds that Torrey's capture was 'more in his mind, or perhaps in the mind of his publisher, than in reality' (Dening 1980: 132).

18 Whether Poe's account of Arthur Gordon Pym's adventures should be taken as a hoax, a spoof, a straightforward romantic novel, or a complexly intervowen symbolic narrative has been the subject of considerable recent debate. See David Ketterer (1992: 233–74).

19 Sailors may not be good scribblers but they used to read quite a lot. Thus Nathaniel Ames writing in *Nautical Reminiscences* says: 'No class of people are more fond of reading than sailors' (1832: 46).

20 Paul Lyons points out that, irrespective of Melville's anti-imperialism, he might have been guilty of inventing Typee cannibalism. His wife Elizabeth Melville wrote in response to a 1901 article by Mary Ferris: 'Mr. Melville would not have been willing to call his old Typee entertainers "man-devouring", as he has stated that whatever might have been his suspicions, he never had evidence that it was the custom of the tribe' (Leyda 1969: 137; Lyons 1996: 72). For a more benign view of Melville's cannibalism as a fictional device, see Herbert (1980: 160ff).

21 I am not arguing that forms of widow immolation did not exist in Fiji (and elsewhere) but we will never learn about these practices from texts like Cannibal Jack's.

22 The god Degei has a serpent form in Fijian mythology and it is likely that Jackson incorporated some of this mythology into his text though the infant-eating eel is, I suspect, Jackson's own invention.

4 Brazilian anthropophagy revisited

1 Unless otherwise indicated, translations throughout are my own.

5 Lapses in taste

1 In a well-known letter to Alceu de Amoroso Lima (May 1928), written as the galleys of *Macunaíma* were being set, he 'regrets' the unhappy coincidence between the publication of his text and the appearance of 'Osvaldo's [*sic*] manifesto', and the fact that, although written during six days in December 1926, and 'corrected and amended in January of 1927', the book will still 'appear entirely anthrophagic' (Andrade, M. de 1978: 256–7). All quotations from *Macunaíma* are to this edition and are included parenthetically in the body of the text. Unless otherwise noted, all translations are my own.

2 It is perhaps relevant in this context that the film which is said to

have launched the movement in 1963, *Os Cafajestes* ('The Hustlers') by Ruy Guerra, counts among its most 'scandalous' innovations the first representation of full frontal nudity in Brazilian cinema. As a result, the film was banned ten days after its screening. The police commissioner who issued the decree branded the film as 'immoral, filthy, and repugnant', and an apology for rape, kidnapping, licentiousness, the use of narcotics, and other crimes against Christian morals and behaviour (Johnson 1984: 94).

3 Since the historical events upon which the film is based take place around 1557, this represents undoubtedly an intentional anachronism.

4 The texts cited include the royal cosmographer André Thevet's *Cosmographie universelle* (1575), his Huguenot rival Jean de Léry's *Histoire d'un voyage faict en Brésil* (1578), Hans Staden's narrative, the letters of the Jesuit missionaries José de Anchieta and António Nóbrega (two of Brazil's mythic founding fathers), the *História* of Brazil (1576) by Magalhães Gândavo, a 1587 treatise by the plantation owner Gabriel Soares de Sousa, and finally a 1560 letter to the king by Mem de Sá, the third governor of Brazil.

5 In private conversation with the author.

6 Ghost stories, bone flutes, cannibal countermemory

1 On creolisation in a Caribbean context, see Brathwaite 1974b; also Glissant 1989, especially Book Three. In a specifically Guyanese context, see Harris's essay 'History, Fable and Myth' (1970).

2 See Jackson's discussion of the social implications of the fantastic in the opening chapters of her study *Fantasy: The Literature of Subversion* (1981).

3 Countermemory, says Foucault, loosely following Nietzsche's *Untimely Meditations*, presents an alternative to the 'traditional' historical view of a continuous past. Countermemory opposes the holistic pursuit of historical retrieval; instead, it traces a genealogy of breaks, fissures, disruptions. The purpose of countermemory – a genealogically guided history – is not to recover the origins of personal/cultural identity; it is to chart the faultlines that cross-hatch the remembered past, and to register the discontinuities that traverse the (social) body. Countermemory is disruptive, but it has creative uses - as in the Caribbean, where the compulsion to rehearse a history of deprivation is a spell that must be broken, revealing in the break a different future.

4 See the introduction to Sanday's *Divine Hunger* (1986); also the first essay in MacCannell's *Empty Meeting Grounds* (1992: 17–73). MacCannell's distinction between economic and symbolic cannibal registers is discussed in my forthcoming essay in *Eating Dis-orders* (Huggan n.d.).

5 On the ghost as a liminal figure and a looming 'absent presence', see Freud's essay on 'The "Uncanny"' (1959); also the discussions of Freud in Todorov (1975) and Jackson (1981), and the psychoanaly-

tical debates surrounding the figure of the (Freudian) phantom in Abraham (1987) and Cixous (1976). Phantoms, says Abraham (following Freud), are not representations of the dead but collective metaphors for the 'gaps left within us by the secrets of others' (287).

6 Surprisingly, neither Todorov nor Jackson, in the standard introductions to fantasy, has very much to say on the subject of race. Fantasy, as a privileged site for race-based traumas and delusions, would clearly benefit from a more sustained (Fanonian?) cultural analysis.

7 On racial paranoia in Poe, see Rowe 1992.

8 In *Black Skin, White Masks*, Fanon's classic study of interracial neurosis based on his research in the Caribbean, he speaks of the 'lactification' or 'whitification' complex as being among the foremost of an 'arsenal of complexes that has been developed by the colonial environment' (1967: 30). For Fanon, the lactification complex – the desire of blacks to wear white masks – is emphatically *not* the projection of a collective psyche predisposed toward dependency; instead, it is the product of colonial brainwashing: of a systematic attempt to lower blacks' self-expectations, and to force them to see themselves in the distorting mirror of the white (wo)man's world (34).

9 See Williams' account of eighteenth-century Caribbean history (1984: chapters 10–14). Here, Williams outlines both the conflicts of the European imperial powers over Caribbean trade and the growing resistance of Caribbean plantation workers to their European 'masters'. This culminated in the mid eighteenth century in a sequence of slave revolts – including one in Surinam in 1763.

10 The slave revolts of the mid eighteenth century arguably culminated in the revolution in San Domingo in 1791, which eventually led in 1804 to the establishment of the world's first black republic (see Williams 1984: chapter 15; also C. L. R. James' magisterial study of the Haitian Revolution (1963)).

11 See Huggan 1994. Here I argue that one reason for the plethora of revisionist texts in the Caribbean is the writers' collective attempt to turn the tables on their European precursors: 'Far from submitting to a Bloomian anxiety of influence toward the Great Tradition of European literature, [these texts] subject that tradition to its own anxiety: first, by charting the contradictions and inconsistencies within a European colonialist discourse which has co-opted the "otherness" of "non-European" cultures in order to consolidate Europe's own sense of self; and second, by taking up that "otherness" and using it as "the sign of systematic opposition to the [European] metropoles and of affirmation of an independent identity"' (658). The embedded quotation comes from Wasserman (1984: 132).

12 For a reading of *The Magic Flute* informed, via Jung, by alchemical symbols, see Koenigsberger 1975. Koenigsberger sees Mozart's opera as tracing 'the search for self-perfection': its main characters are alchemically fused in 'one being, one psyche, one soul' (231). *The Magic Flute*, of course, is known for attracting contradictory readings: the flute itself, like Voorman's (and, before it, the bone flute of

the Caribs), can be seen both as a fatal lure and a medium of reconciliation.

13 For a comparison of Naipaul's and Harris's views on El Dorado, see the opening chapter of the former's *The Loss of El Dorado* (1984) and the latter's *Tradition, the Writer, and Society* (1967: especially 35–6). For a comparative critical treatment, see also McWatt 1985.

14 See Freud, *Totem and Taboo* (1983), especially the final chapter; also Girard 1977: 192–222, 274–80. Although the Oedipal dimensions of *Totem and Taboo*, as Girard points out, are understated, Freud nonetheless links cannibalism to the patricide prohibition and to its incarnation in the surrogate sacrifice of the totem feast.

15 For a celebration of the Caribbean's mixed cultural heritage, see Harris 1970; also, in a broader context, the 'miscegenated' aesthetic theory of his *The Womb of Space* (1983).

16 See the early critical essay by Howard 1970; also the later studies of Gilkes 1975 and, particularly, Drake 1986.

7 *Cronos* and the political economy of vampirism

I would like to thank Carol Watts, Roger Luckhurst, and Peter Hulme for their help in writing this chapter.

1 Indeed, from the point of view of the literature that has reflected upon the Mexican Revolution – beginning in 1915 with Mariano Azuela's *Los de abajo* (1974) through to 1963 with Carlos Fuentes's *The Death of Artemio Cruz* (1973) – such a pact between the new ruling class and the 'people' was never anything more than cynical rhetoric. Insofar as Rulfo's novel implies that, in the words of Walter Benjamin, 'even the dead will not be safe from the enemy if he wins', that is, that the ruling class makes history in its image, appropriating lives and deaths, it may also suggest that Anderson's preference of 'style' over 'adequacy' of national imaginings may have to be rethought from the point of view of their social content (Benjamin 1992: 257; Anderson 1991).

2 The idea of commodity fetishism as the 'social rule of capital' comes from William Pietz (1993: 119–51); for the 'time-lag', see Bhabha 1994: 243. The image of Latin America as a body that has been plundered and 'bled' was systematically set out by Eduardo Galeano in his important book *The Open Veins of Latin America* (1973). Michael Taussig's pathbreaking *The Devil and Commodity Fetishism in South America* (1980) has influenced my own reflections here.

3 In this regard, Marx makes an interesting historical and geographical comparison: 'So far, we have observed the drive towards the extension of the working day, and the werewolf-like hunger for surplus labour, in an area where capital's monstrous outrages, unsurpassed ... by the cruelties of the Spanish to the American red-skins, caused it at last to be bound by the chains of legal regulations' (1990: 353). As always, Marx insists that transformations in the economic structure are accompanied by new legal forms of subjection.

4 'Marx was the first white man La Escapía had ever heard call his own people vampires and monsters. But Marx had not stopped with accusations. Marx had caught the capitalists of the British empire with bloody hands. Marx backed every assertion with evidence; coroners' reports with gruesome stories about giant spinning machines that consumed the limbs and the lives of the small children in factories. On and on Marx went, describing the tiny corpses of children who had been worked to death – their deformed bodies shaped to fit inside factory machinery and other cramped spaces' (Silko 1991: 312).

5 For the idea of vampirism as a kind of bad shamanism, see Augé 1972.

6 Derrida has recently become interested in such issues as the sacrificial structure that has historically defined the 'human', a structure that specifically involves the eating of flesh, human or animal (1991). Cf. this related passage: 'As I have tried to show elsewhere, carnivorous sacrifice is essential to the structure of subjectivity, which is also to say the founding of the intentional subject and to the founding, if not of the law, at least of law (droit), the difference between the law and law (droit), justice and law (droit), justice and law here remaining open over an abyss. I will leave these problems aside for the moment, along with the affinity between carnivorous sacrifice, as the basis of our culture and our law, and all the cannibalisms, symbolic or not, that structure intersubjectivity in nursing, love, mourning, and, in truth, in all symbolic and linguistic appropriations ... If we wish to speak of injustice, of violence or of a lack of respect toward what we still so confusedly call animals – the question is more topical than ever, and so I include in it, in the name of deconstruction, a set of questions on carno-phallogocentrism – we must reconsider in its totality the metaphysico-anthropocentric axiomatic that dominates, in the West, the thought of just and unjust ... From this very first step we can already glimpse the first of its consequences, namely, that a deconstructionist approach to the boundaries that institute the human subject (preferably and paradigmatically the adult male, rather than the woman, child or animal) as the measure of the just and the unjust, does not lead to injustice, nor to the effacement of an opposition between just and unjust but may, in the name of a demand more insatiable than justice, lead to a reinterpretation of the whole apparatus of boundaries within which a history and culture have been able to confine their criteriology' (1992: 18–19).

8 Fee fie fo fum: the child in the jaws of the story

1 'Tiens, Ravagio, voici de la chair fraîche, bien grassette, bien douillette, mais par mon chef tu n'en croquera que d'une dent; c'est une belle petite fille; je veux la nourrir, nous la marierons avec notre ogrelet, ils feront des ogrichons d'une figure extraordinaire; cela nous réjouira dans notre veillesse' (d'Aulnoy 1956: I, 145).

2 See *La Bible des poètes* (1485), frontispiece, handcoloured; different edition, with woodcut frontispiece (1507).

3 'The Artist's Parents', 1806, in the Museum in Hamburg; reproduced in Rosenblum 1988: 38.

4 'Un coup c'était Cafougnette, y ren'tre dans une boucherie, puis y avait un grenier, alors lui y ren'tre dans l'grenier puis y voit un trous, y dit merde, qu'est-ce que c'est. Alors y prend sa bitte puis il l'enfonce dans l'trou. Alors v'la une femme et puis elle dit: si, si y'en a une. Alors "peut-être c'est la dernière" alors y prend, il l'coupe Zwitt. Alors y donne à la femme . La femme la mande et l'lendemain, elle revient et elle dit: - elle était bien bonne vot'saucisse, vou n'navez pas une autre et Cafougnette après y dit par l'trou, "quand er r'poussra' (Gaignebet 1974: 186–7).

9 Cannibalism qua capitalism

1 I employ the term 'ideologeme' in the sense defined by Fredric Jameson in his *The Political Unconscious*. According to Jameson, 'the ideologeme is an amphibious function, whose essential structural characteristic may be described as its possibility to manifest either a pseudoidea – a conceptual or belief system, an abstract value, an opinion or prejudice – or as a protonarrative, a kind of ultimate fantasy about the 'collective characters' which are the classes in opposition. This duality means that the basic requirement for the full description of the ideologeme is already given in advance: as a construct it must be susceptible to both a conceptual description and a narrative manifestation all at once. The ideologeme can of course be extended in either of these directions, taking on the finished appearance of a philosophical system on the one hand, or that of a cultural text on the other; but the ideological analysis of these finished cultural products requires us to demonstrate each one as a complete work of transformation on that raw material which is the ideologeme in question' (Jameson 1983: 87). Jameson's claim that the ideologeme is both a 'pseudoidea' and a 'protonarrative' holds considerable value for the analysis of cannibalism as an imagining of the 'other'. In colonial fiction and anti-semitic discourse, the cannibal is always imagined in relation to 'a conceptual or belief system, an abstract value, an opinion or prejudice', in short, a 'philosophical system' of the truly human. In both the fiction and the discourse, the 'conceptual description' of cannibalism is always eloquent of a narrative treatment of an ideal cultural solidarity: in the colonial world, this becomes the *laager* of 'white' colonials resolved to keep at bay the horde of ignoble savages; in the world of capitalist class relations where finance and mercantile capital are particularly singled out as wreckers of community, it becomes the fascist 'class fantasy' of war against 'the Jews', the 'savages' within the fold. The ideologeme is born, then, in a politics of Self and Other which invariably makes for 'system' and 'text'. In this respect, it seems a natural theoretical measure of

cannibalism as a literary and ideological motif. As regards the theoretical import of the term *ressentiment* in the endeavour to illuminate the logic of social divisiveness, it seems to me a useful concept, because it speaks to the pathologisation of a fantasy 'slave morality' – the sense in which racists and anti-semites will often claim (against verifiable reality) that they are the real victims of the insidious activities of 'blacks' and 'Jews'. Indeed, Nietzsche himself noted that '*ressentiment* ... this plant blooms best today among anarchists and anti semites – where it has always bloomed, in hidden places, like the violet, though with a different odor' (Nietzsche 1967: 73).

2 In *Capital Volume I*, Marx defines primitive accumulation as the 'starting-point' of 'capitalistic accumulation' proper. In social terms, it is 'nothing else than the historical process of divorcing the producer from the means of production' (1976: 875). Alienation, exploitation, and the fetishism of commodities follow in train. Marx noted that it 'was in fact the cheapness of human sweat and the human blood which were converted into commodities, which permitted the constant extension of the market; this was especially true of England's colonial market' (601). Thus, in the guise of colonialist depredations, primitive accumulation 'proclaimed surplus-value making as the sole end and aim of humanity' (706). Not the least of capitalism's barbarities is the violence that it visits upon the most defenceless members of the human community. A persistent theme in *Capital* is the exploitation of children in 'blood-sucking institutions' (598) – namely, factories and mills. Indeed, to this day 'the capitalised blood of children' (920) – as signified by child labour and infant mortality rates – forms an integral part of profit-making's daily diet of human misery.

3 Consider the episode in *Heart of Darkness* where a shed full of trade goods is consumed by an accidental fire. Marlow's summation of the affair is particularly instructive as regards the cultural logic of colonial pedagogy: 'A nigger was being beaten nearby. They said he had caused the fire in some way; be that as it may, he was screeching most horribly' (Conrad 1967: 253). Freud famously observed that the fantasy of 'a child is being beaten' is key to the inculcation of civilised values within the infant subject (Freud 1955). According to Freud, the fantasy ministers to the infant's fear of castration, brought on by the regime of the Oedipus complex. Now, in colonial pedagogy, the rhetoric of 'family' has the function of legitimating political authority over 'undeveloped races' (Moresby 1876: 102). As decreed by the colonial 'Oedipal' regime, the threat of castration (that is to say, annihilation) is generalised beyond the sexual realm (where 'white' women are wholly taboo) and explicitly takes in questions of work and obedience, conduct and propriety. The basic 'moral' scenario for colonial pedagogy is thus 'a nigger is being beaten'. Note that Marlow gets an appointment with the company because his predecessor 'had been killed in a scuffle with the natives' (217).

The dead captain had 'whacked [an] old nigger mercilessly' in a dispute over 'some hens' (217). The old man's son had killed the captain in the course of defending his father. In one respect, Conrad's novella is a reflection on the moral significance of making real the fantasy of beating 'niggers'.

4 Peter Hulme observes that in 'the discourse of savagery' gold was 'the pivotal term around which others clustered' (1986: 22). Hulme advances a symptomatic reading of Columbus' journal, in order to show how 'desire and fear, gold and cannibal' (41) conjoined to form a rhetoric of invasion, a way of viewing the Caribbean as a potential colonial space.

5 I must point out, however, that, as regards the critique of cannibalism as a racist slander, Marlow gives with one hand what he takes away with the other. Marlow asserts that cannibals are 'fine fellows in their place. They were men one could work with' (245). Yet at a later point in the narrative, he must needs ask himself: 'Why in the name of all the gnawing devils of hunger they didn't go for us ... Restraint! I would just as soon have expected restraint from a hyena prowling amongst the corpses of a battlefield' (252–3). That a trope of animality should naturally spring to Marlow's mind is proof positive of the real hold of colonial discourse on his narrative.

6 For a cogent discussion of 'dominant', 'residual', and 'emergent' as analytic terms, see Williams (1977: 121–8).

7 A striking instance of the metaphorical use of the Jew is seen in a famous passage from *Capital Volume I*: 'The capitalist knows that all commodities however tattered they may look, or however badly they may smell, are in faith and in truth money, are by nature circumcised Jews, and what is more, a wonderful means for making still more money out of money' (1976: 256). Here Marx satirises a brace of anti-semitic motifs: namely, the claim that Jews have a particularly offensive smell, and the claim that Jews are ubiquitous, and can only be known, in the last analysis, by the mark of circumcision. Marx employs the stereotype of the wily, 'scurvy' Jew to point out the genius of the commodity-form, its generation of money and power from mere matter. The aim of this analogy is surely to make plain the hypocritical investment in the Jew, which allows the Christian world to condemn Jewish money-lenders, but not the overall power of money. As George Mosse notes, Marx's 'argument [in 'On the Jewish Question'] was opposed to all racism, for it advocated complete assimilation, and the abolition of conflict between men' (1978: 155). For a well-considered account of Marx's complex relation to the Jews, I refer the reader to Gilman (1986: 188–209).

8 Compare Sartre's observation: 'If the Jew did not exist, the anti-semite would invent him' (Sartre 1973: 13).

9 Shylock, as instructive metaphor, appears often in Marx's writings. For example, Marx uses the proper name Shylock to indict the 'cannibalistic' who blithely philosophise against revolutionary struggle. The relevant passage reads as follows: 'There is a school

that justifies the abjectness of today by the abjectness of yesterday, a school which declares every cry of the serf against the knout to be rebellious as long as the knout is an aged, historical knout with a pedigree, a school to which history, like the God of Israel to his servant Moses, only shows its posterior. This school, the Historical School of Law, would have invented German history had it not itself been an invention of that history. It is a Shylock, but a servile Shylock that for every pound of flesh cut from the heart of the people swears upon its bond, its historical, Christian-Germanic bond' (Marx 1977: 65).

10 In the last analysis, the horrible torture of the accused brought the world into line with the fevered fantasies of the anti-semitic imagination. Po-Chia-Hsia notes that, as a result of being tortured, one of the defendants 'confessed to biting [the murdered boy]', another 'described a scene of jubilation, with stomping of feet and laughter; still others confessed to indecent and grotesque bodily gestures, exposing their penises and bare bottoms and sticking their tongues out, all done to scorn the Christian child' (88). The 'carnivalesque' scene conjured-up by the application of torture is, of course, a parable of misrule, of the devil at large in the world.

11 In this respect the comic economy of the drama has something in common with the renaissance politics of carnival. Carnival season was a time when anti-semitism might be given popular expression, in the form of carnival songs, effigies, and, of course, violent street assaults upon individual Jews. Indeed, François Laroque has noted that many of 'the cardboard ogres which paraded the streets may have been popularly interpreted as the grotesque caricatures of the Jews. This was probably encouraged by the phonetic proximity between the words carnival and cannibal which may have been a standard pun at the time' (Laroque 1983: 118). Looked at from this point of view, early modern drama is only a visual formalisation of prevailing cultural attitudes regarding Jews.

12 One area in which neo-nazism has increasingly been able to normalize its virulent anti-semitism is in the political controversy concerning abortion. Tom Metzger, leader of the California-based White Aryan Resistance, has gone on record as saying that 'Almost all abortion doctors are Jews ... Jews must be punished for this holocaust and murder of white children' (quoted in Burghardt 1995: 27). That such rhetoric cannot be dismissed as simply 'marginal' to the 'real' abortion debate is made amply plain by the sentiments expressed by Father Paul Marx, founder of Human Life International, an anti-abortion organisation. Marx has written that a large number of 'abortionists ... and pro-abortion medical professors ... are Jewish ... [A] segment of the Jewish community ... more or less led the greatest holocaust of all time, the war on unborn babies' (quoted in Burghardt 1995: 30). Thus in anti-abortion discourse, which leans heavily on anti-semitism, the vicious stereotype of the Jew as a ritual murderer of Christian children is once again made operative.

10 Consumerism, or the cultural logic of late cannibalism

1 One of the film guides (*Video-Hound's Golden Movie Retriever 1995*) at my local video store listed ninety-five items under the category of 'Cannibalism'. Most of these were low budget cult horror flicks with titles like *Cannibal Women in the Avocado Jungle of Death* (which came highly recommended by the store's teen-aged video clerk, who not only was very familiar with the 'cannibal genre' (!), but also did not find it in the least odd that I arrived at the store with a request for anything he had 'involving cannibals'). Interestingly, this list did not include vampire or werewolf (among Marx's favourite analogies for capitalists) movies, such as *Wolf* – which seem to me to deal (albeit ambivalently) with similar issues of 'dog eat dog' capitalism. If such films had been included, the list would be considerably longer.

2 Greenaway was trained as a painter before taking up film-making and a 'painterly' aesthetic has had a deep influence on all of his film work (see Denham 1993: 24).

3 Although the feast of human flesh has precedent in classical drama, it is only in the sixteenth century and after that such a feast became 'cannibalistic' (see discussion of Peter Hulme below), as in Greenaway's film, rendering his historical citation quite specific. For classical precedents, see Bowers (1940: 45 and *passim*). The principal early modern innovation in the revenge tragedy is to spectacularise violence. Whereas the classical precursors would have kept the more gruesome action (e.g. elaborate, drawn out murders, tortures, rape) off-stage, the Elizabethan and Jacobean playwrights did not hesitate to bring it on – and call attention to it (a practice Greenaway does not shy from). The commonplace in drama history is that Jacobean tragedy is 'darker' than its Elizabethan counterpart – that it seems less convinced of a redemptive order returned by the detour through violence – and this seems to be what Greenaway is getting at in his appeal to Jacobean drama.

4 Patricia Parker discusses the relation of copia to wealth in this way: 'Erasmus, for example, explains in *De Copia* – a work whose title already institutes a relation between rhetorical abundance and economic wealth – that the best way to amplify a discourse is to divide it into its separate parts, and directly invokes for this rhetorical enterprise the analogue of purposing to sell' (1987: 128). Terence Cave (1979) emphasizes the ways in which copia encouraged an understanding of prose as limitlessly extendible.

5 Examples of the cannibal figure referred to on this and following pages were culled from the following sources (a handful of its many, many appearances): Richard Acello, 'Smart and Final Seeks Jump Into Big Box Border Battle', *San Diego Daily Transcript* (December 1993), A1; Christopher Amatos, 'Applebee's Franchise Weighs Area Expansion', *Columbus Dispatch* (30 August 1993); Jessica Hall, 'Cannibalizing a Market', *Warfield's Business Record*, 9.45 (December 1993), sec. 1, p. 1; Tom Lowry, 'Local Biz Balks at Home Depot', *New*

York Daily News (2 November 1993), sec. 1, p. 27; Travis Poling, 'The New Fast Food Fix', *San Antonio Business Journal*, 8.44 (December 1993); Greg Heberlen, 'Eagle Profit Plunges', *Seattle Times* (December 1993), sec. D, p. 1; Sylvia Wieland Nogaki, 'Wholesale Competition', *The Seattle Times* (12 October 1992), sec. E, p. 1; Tina Cassidy, *Boston Business Journal*, 12.32 (5 October 1992), sec. 1, p. 9.

6 See, for example, Volosinov (1986). The struggle in cannibalism is, however, rather more complex than the simple 'class struggle' (23) theorised by Volosinov.

7 See: Marx's discussion of 'So-called Primitive Accumulation' (1990: 873–940); Foucault's supplement to Marx's discussion of primitive accumulation in *Discipline and Punish* (1979: 221) – his claim is that capital requires (in addition to the dispossessing of the worker-to-be) a transformation in subjectivity, an 'accumulation of men', which he describes as a 'political' process; and Richard Halpern's injunction to study the 'cultural' aspects of primitive accumulation in *Poetics of Primitive Accumulation* (1991).

8 This analysis is commonplace in part because it is so easily traced in the arguments for colonisation in early modern texts, as Todorov (1984) – among many others – has pointed out. Kirkpatrick Sale notes: 'reports of cannibalism provided the means of justifying the enslavement and deportation of those creatures so clearly beyond the pale of God's favor that they could rightfully by regarded as beasts' (1990: 134).

9 See Gramsci: 'in studying a structure, it is necessary to distinguish organic movements (relatively permanent) from movements which may be termed "conjunctural" (and which appear as occasional, immediate, almost accidental)' (1971: 177).

10 For example, to Dean MacCannell, all capitalists are 'metaphoric' cannibals – a state which he does not see as developmental progress (1992: 20). 'The cannibal (or the capitalist),' he argues, 'is *the one* that attempts to gobble up the other *one*, for gain we are told, but also to restore and literally to embody the impossible logic of singularity' (8). Later he refers to the capitalist-cannibal fantasy as one of 'a crude but effective method of producing capital gain through legalized murder, plunder, and/or inheritance, and compounding the gain by eating the dead' (53). What MacCannell's analogy (and others like it) fail to take into account, however, are the ways in which cannibalism and capitalism are incompatible.

11 See this volume's Introduction for discussion of the cannibalism debate initiated by William Arens's work.

12 Apparently it was of some interest, however. In the copy of the *Divers Voyages* (1582) once owned by Edmund Brudenell (one of the subscribers to the Gilbert expeditions for which the book was probably intended to attract interest), the entire 'Godliness is great riches' passage is underlined. My main point, however, is to suggest agreement with Edward Lynam's contention that, in general, Elizabethan interest in voyages 'was much more sluggish than would have been adequate to the Elizabethan achievement without the

work of Hakluyt' (1946: 18) – and that Hakluyt was willing to use a variety of means to accomplish these ends.

13 Resistance to the 'upstart' joint-stock companies by the established merchant community has been amply demonstrated by Robert Brenner's recent monumental *Merchants and Revolution* (1993). Not only was there resistance to changing old trading habits, but a general mistrust of travel and travellers persisted as well. David Cressy discusses state (and joint-stock company) attempts to control the flow of English people into North America to protect what were perceived to be financial and security interests. He points out that 'leaving England [in the seventeenth century] was not simply a matter of making a decision and raising the necessary cash. Prospective emigrants [as all travellers] needed permission to depart the realm' (1987: 130). It was into a situation such as this that books like Hakluyt's had to work not only to evoke the desire of investors to direct attention and resources in new directions, but also for the official sanctions to allow these shifts to occur.

14 As Derrida puts it: 'metaphysics consists of excluding non-presence by determining the supplement as simple exteriority, pure addition or pure absence. The work of exclusion operates within the structure of supplementarity. The paradox is that one annuls addition by considering it a pure addition. What is added is nothing because it is added to a full presence to which it is exterior' (1976: 167).

15 Both sides of Anderson's claim are exaggerated (land can be 'extended' by increasing its fertility, etc. and commodity production, as I shall indicate below, is subject to some limits), but his distinction between feudal and capitalist orientations is important and useful.

16 Marx's claim here can be supported with this observation by Peckham: 'it is well knowen, that sithence the time of Columbus his first discoverie, through the planting, possessing, and inhabiting those partes, there hath bene transported and brought home into Europe greater store of Golde, Silver, Pearle, and Precious stones, then heretofore hath bene in all ages since the creation of the world' (Hakluyt 1965: VIII, 96).

17 'I am not ignorant of Ptolomies assertion, that Peregrinationis historia [individual accounts of travels], and not those weary volumes bearing the titles of universall Cosmographie which some men that I could name have published as their owne, beying in deed most untruly and unprofitablie ramassed and hurled together, is that which must bring us to the certayne and full discoverie of the world' (Hakluyt 1907: 6).

18 The 1582 *Divers Voyages* is unpaginated, though signatures are marked. Beginning from the back of the title page (on which a list of geographers appears), the volume has 113 *printed* pages (i.e. blank leaves excluded).

19 Contrast Mullaney (1983).

20 On this influence of Gramsci on cultural studies, see Stuart Hall (1988). For a range of positions marking this shift in Marxism, see Hall and Jacques (1989).

21 This differs also from a case such as Jonathan Swift's 'A Modest Proposal' which uses cannibalism to distinguish an 'other' in the West, England as cannibal other to Ireland.

11 The function of cannibalism at the present time

1 See, for example, one sixteenth-century witness who qualified his own descriptions of frightening cannibal practices in America, by reminding his reader of horrors happening at home (in particular, the bloody wars of religion fought over the meaning of communion):

> It is possible to cite other examples of the cruelty of savages towards their enemies, but I believe that what I have said is enough to cause the hair to stand up from horror. It is profitable, nevertheless, upon reading about such barbarities, for the readers not to forget that which is practiced among ourselves ... [D]o we not encounter here, in Italy and elsewhere, persons bestowed with the title of Christians, who, not satisfied with killing their enemy yet eat their liver and heart? ... We should not, therefore, abhor too greatly the cruelty of the anthropophagous savages. There exists among us creatures so abominable, if not more so, and more detestable than they [i.e. the Indians] are, who only assault enemy nations on whom they take vengeance. It is not necessary to go to America, not to leave our [own] country, to see such monstrous things. (Jean de Léry quoted in Forysth 1985: 30)

As both Léry and Montaigne suggest, cannibalism begins at home. See also Arens (1979b: 78), who notes that sixteenth-century scholars debated the nature of the natives, in order to decide whether they were indeed Noble Savages, or simply subhuman beasts. His point that one learned debate over the fate of the Indians resulted in a decision 'to impose humanitarian limits on the character of colonial rule', which was literally 'academic' as the Spaniards took no 'notice of the debate among learned monks in Latin', is a sobering reminder of the restricted ability of critical interpretation to impose limits and create differences.

2 See especially MacCannell (1992), who reads cultural cannibalism as much more corrupt than natural, on the grounds that the literal is more honest and direct than the figurative. Extending Montaigne's logic, he sees indirection and the so-called sublimation of appetite found in society as a sign of deceit, arguing that the fact 'that cannibalism has transformed itself into a *metaphoric* cannibalism should not be greeted as a positive development' for 'it is precisely its metaphoric character that protects it from having to admit its own gruesome excesses, empowering it in ways that the original form of cannibalism could not imagine. Metaphoric or reflexive cannibalism, driven by the same desire for absolute domination and control, now armed with high technology, need never look its victims in the face, or, even if by chance it does, it need never acknowledge what it sees' (20). See also his claim that metaphors are

more subsuming than savages: 'The potential for evil and cruelty lurking unsaid in this statement [a figurative expression] is far greater than anything openly expressed by the old warriors' (4–7). For MacCannell, all metaphors of incorporation are insidious, giving away our modern 'cannibal consciousness'; see especially his chiding of Nancy Chodorow, who is generally 'a person of unimpeachable goodwill', for a lapse in judgment in using an image of consumption to describe psychic processes (67–8). Personally, I like figurative language and find it much less sinister than he suggests; given a choice, I would definitely prefer to be cannibalised metaphorically than literally.

3 Cannibalism often plays a role in such myths of progress and evolution from lower to higher, nature to culture, literal cannibalism to symbolic cannibalism. This provides a way of discussing the differences between cultures who practise real cannibalism, and those who have developed symbolic substitutes – such as the Christian act of communion. As the bloodthirsty battles over the meaning of the real presence of Christ's body in the Eucharist have suggested, however, even in this symbolic act the relation between the symbolic and the literal is unclear (see further Kilgour 1990: 15–16, 79–85). Peggy Reeves Sanday reads the function of ritual cannibalism itself as involving a comparable form of sublimation, as it transforms the purely physical into the symbolic (1986: 95–101). Inversely, Eli Sagan sees cannibalism as a failure to acquire the capacity for metaphorical thinking: 'The undeveloped imagination of the cannibal does not deal very adequately with metaphorical usage. He is compelled to take the urge for oral incorporation literally' (1974: 81).

4 See also Obeyesekere, who argues that the English obsession with cannibalism, fed on fairy-tales and accepted practices of survival cannibalism following shipwrecks, resurrected and reinforced native practices. He thus suggests that the English in one sense created Polynesian cannibals (1992b: especially 643–4; 650, 652–4).

5 Bob Balaban's film *Parents* plays on a similar collapsing of symbolic and literal cannibalism, which also takes a poke at Freud's theories of sexual development. Shot from the child's point of view, the film seems to present the boy's confused perception of the adult world, and of sex as cannibalism. The little boy sees his parents making love, and mistakes his mother's smeared lipstick for blood. From his perspective, parents are weird cyclops-like creatures, whose food must be rejected as through it they are trying to make him one of them, offering him strange cuts of meat that serve as his initiation rite into this dream '50s family. Thin and withdrawn, the little boy seems ghoulish and weird. We begin by believing that this is all his literalising cannibalistic and incestuous dark family romance about the adult world. In the end, however, as the movie takes a dramatically dark turn, his fantasies are realised: cannibalism is no metaphor here, but the literal truth about the basis of this family, which consolidates itself by eating the flesh of strangers.

6 See, for example, *Dracula*, which again uses how and what one consumes to define oppositions: the good guys eat normally (though with suspicously obsessive heartiness and frequency), while Dracula feeds perversely.

7 Freud's depiction of the relation between doctor and patient is a complex one. To cure the patient, the doctor must remain completely detached from her, observing her from a position of what Freud commonly describes as a scientific objectivity, which keeps the two completely separate (thus guarding too against the danger of the countertransference). Yet at the same time, the doctor must be able to sympathise with the patient in order to understand her; see also Day (1985: 186), who compares this delicate balancing act of objectivity and identification to that between the detective and his criminal.

8 See Harris (1988: 290, 325) for her meditations on her ancestors, as a doomed race of backward hillbillies from whom she needs to differentiate herself. Earlier, in her first encounter with one of Bill's victims, her background earns her a privileged status with the West Virginian police, who accept her as 'heir to the granny women, to the wise women, to the herb dealer, the stalwart country women who have always done the needful, who keep the watch and when the watch is over, wash and dress the country dead' (82). Her exploitation of her past here, and her 'special relationship' with the victim, enables her to enter the male realm from which she had just been excluded – by playing on her identification with the other women, she distances herself from them.

9 Laura Killian pointed out to me the precise nature of this analogue, in which difference again suggests identification.

10 The subtext of *Dracula*, with its perversion of religious sacraments, especially communion and marriage, is apparent again here.

11 The novel creates a similar effect by juxtaposing the final scene of Clarice's apparently innocent sleep, with a scene in which Lecter writes to her. While the letter reveals their geographic separation – we don't know where Lecter is now – it also implies their continuing communication and sympathy – suggested both by Lecter's proposing a pact with her: 'I have no plans to call on you, Clarice, the world being more interesting with you in it. Be sure you extend me the same courtesy' (366), and by his closing remark that, though they are in different places, 'Some of our stars are the same' (367).

12 Arens argues that the idea of cannibalism provides anthropology with what it needs to establish itself: a convenient way of marking the difference between the natural and the cultured. When a society relinquishes cannibalism it moves up one step in the great chain of progress. If, as Arens argues, there is no evidence that cannibalism as a ritual has ever occurred, suggesting that the taboo against eating human flesh is essential to humans rather than something acquired with culture, then the difference between nature and culture disappears – we are all equally natural or civilised.

13 Sexism and cannibalism go together, not only in our culture in which women are in numerous ways defined as 'consumers' as well as

'vamps'. For the traditional rumour that women are cannibals, see Arens (1979b: 26–7, 109–10). Where Arens sees charges of cannibalism as a sign of misogyny, Sanday argues that cannibalism is practised in misogynistic cultures in which the differences between the sexes are most extreme and rigid (1986: 12–13, 59–82).

14 One example of this in the cannibal controversy is Marvin Harris's 'cultural materialist' reading of the motives of cannibalism as economic rather than symbolic, reducing Aztec cannibalism to a response to a protein shortage (1977: 97–110).

References

Abler, Thomas S. (1980), 'Iroquois Cannibalism: Fact Not Fiction', *Ethnohistory*, 27(4): 309–16.

Abraham, Nicolas (1987), 'Notes on the Phantom: A Complement to Freud's Meta- psychology', *Critical Inquiry*, 13 (Winter): 287–92.

Adorno, Theodor and Max Horkheimer (1979), *Dialectic of the Enlightenment* [1944], trans. J. Cummings, London: Verso.

Alpers, Michael (1966), 'Epidemiological Changes in Kuru, 1957 to 1963', in D. Carleton Gajdusek, Clarence J. Gibbs, and Michael Alpers, eds., *Slow, Latent, and Temperate Virus Infections*, Washington, DC: U.S. Government Printing Office, pp. 65–82.

Alpers, Michael and D. Carleton Gajdusek (1965), 'Changing Patterns of Kuru: Epidemiological Changes in the Period of Increasing Contact of the Fore People with Western Civilization', *American Journal of Tropical Medicine and Hygiene*, 14: 852–79.

Ames, Nathaniel (1832), *Nautical Reminiscences*, Providence: William Marshall.

Anderson, Benedict (1991), *Imagined Communities: Reflections on the Origins and Spread of Nationalism*, revised edn., London: Verso.

Anderson, Perry (1974), *Lineages of the Absolutist State*, London: New Left Books.

Andrade, Ana Luiza and Graham Huggan, eds. (forthcoming), *Eating Dis-orders: Cannibalism in Contemporary Latin American Culture*.

Andrade, Joaquim Pedro de (1988a), 'Cannibalism and Self-Cannibalism', in Johnson and Stam, eds., *Brazilian Cinema*, pp. 81–3.

(1988b), 'Criticism and Self-Criticism', in Johnson and Stam, eds., *Brazilian Cinema*, pp. 72–5.

Andrade, Mário de (1978), *Macunaíma: o herói sem nenhum caráter*, ed. Telê Porto Ancona Lopez, Rio de Janeiro: Livros Técnicos e Científicos Editora.

Andrade, Oswald de (1972), 'Manifesto Antropófago', *Obras Completas*, vol. 6, ed. Benedito Nunes, Rio de Janeiro: Civilização Brasileira, pp. 11–19.

(1991a), *Estética e Política*, ed. Maria Eugenia Boaventura, São Paulo: Editora Globo.

(1991b), 'Cannibalist Manifesto' [1928], trans. Leslie Bary, *Latin American Literary Review*, 19, no. 38: 38–47.

Anon (1994), 'Cannibalism', *Encarta*, Redmond, WA: Microsoft Corp.

Ansión, Juan (1989), ed. *Pishtacos: de verdugos a sacaojos*, Lima: Tarea.

Anzieu, Didier (1989), *The Skin Ego: A Psychoanalytic Approach to the Self*, New Haven: Yale University Press.

Apuleius, Lucius (1988), *The Golden Ass*, trans. Robert Graves [1950], Harmondsworth: Penguin.

Arens, William (1977), Personal Communication. Correspondence with D. C. Gajdusek.

(1979a), 'Cannibalism: An Exchange', *New York Review of Books*, 26, no. 4, 22 March: 45–6.

(1979b), *The Man-Eating Myth: Anthropology and Anthropophagy*, New York: Oxford University Press.

(1990), '*Kuru* and Cannibalism: Practice or Preconception?', in Sir Burton G. Burton-Bradley, ed., *A History of Medicine in Papua New Guinea*, Kingsgrove, NSW: Australian Medical Publishing Co., pp. 151–64.

(1991), Personal communication. Correspondence with F. J. P. Poole.

(1995), Personal communication. Interview with Shirley Lindenbaum.

Aronowitz, Stanley (1990), *The Crisis in Historical Materialism*, 2nd edn., Minneapolis: University of Minnesota Press.

Atwood, Margaret (1987), *Bluebeard's Egg and Other Stories*, London: Jonathan Cape.

Augé, Marc (1972), 'Les métamorphoses du vampire d'un societé de consommation à l'autre', *Destins du cannibalisme: Nouvelle Revue de Psychanalyse*, no. 6: 129–48.

Aulnoy, Marie-Catherine d' (1892), *The Famous Tales of Madame d'Aulnoy*, trans. Anne Thackeray Ritchie, London: Lawrence and Bullen.

(1956), *Les Contes de Fées*, vol. 1, Paris: Mercure de France.

Baal, J. Van (1984), 'The Dialectics of Sex in Marind-anim Culture', in Gilbert Herdt, ed. *Ritualized Homosexuality in Melanesia*, Berkeley: University of California Press, pp. 128–66.

Bacon, Francis (1942), 'Of Riches', in his *Essays and New Atlantis*, Roslyn, NJ: Walter J. Black, pp. 146–51.

Bakhtin, Mikhail (1968), *Rabelais and His World*, trans. Helene Iswolosky, Cambridge, MA: MIT Press.

Balibar, Etienne (1995), *The Philosophy of Marx*, trans. Chris Turner, London: Verso.

Barker, Francis, Peter Hulme, and Margaret Iversen (1990), eds. *Uses of History: Marxism, Postmodernism, and the Renaissance*, Manchester: Manchester University Press.

(1992), eds. *Postmodernism and the Re-reading of Modernity*, Manchester: Manchester University Press.

(1994), eds. *Colonial Discourse / Postcolonial Theory*, Manchester: Manchester University Press.

Barnet, Richard J. (1994), 'Lords of the Global Economy', *The Nation* (December 19), 754–7.
Baudet, Henri (1988), *Paradise on Earth: Some Thoughts on European Images of Non-European Man*, Wesleyan, CT: Wesleyan University Press.
Beaver, Harold (1986), Introduction to Edgar Allan Poe, *The Narrative of Arthur Gordon Pym of Nantucket*, ed. Harold Beaver, London: Penguin.
Beer, Gillian (1978), 'Ghosts', *Essays in Criticism*, 28(3): 259–64.
Benjamin, Walter (1992), *Illuminations*, trans. Harry Zohn, London: Fontana/Collins.
Bergman, David (1991), 'Cannibals and Queers: Man-Eating', in his *Gaiety Transfigured: Gay Self-Representation in American Literature*, Madison: University of Wisconsin Press, pp. 139–62.
Bernardet, Jean-Claude (1978), *Trajectória crítica*, São Paulo: Polis.
Besson, Paul B. et al., (1979), eds. *Cecil Textbook of Medicine*, 15th edn., Philadelphia: W. B. Saunders Company.
Bhabha, Homi K. (1994), *The Location of Culture*, London: Routledge.
Blaine, James G. et al. (1892), *Columbus and Columbia: A Pictorial History of the Man and the Nation*, Richmond, VA: B. F. Johnson & Co.
Blakeslee, Sandra (1991), 'Heretical Theory on Brain Diseases Gains New Ground', *The New York Times*, October 8, pp. C1, C12.
Blaut, J. M. (1993), *The Colonizer's Model of the World: Geographical Diffusionism and Eurocentric History*, New York: The Guilford Press.
Bloom, Harold (1973), *The Anxiety of Influence: A Theory of Poetry*, New York: Oxford University Press.
Bober, P. P. and R. O. Rubinstein (1986), *Renaissance Artists and Antique Sculpture: A Handbook of Sources*, London and Oxford: Harvey Miller and Oxford University Press.
Bopp, Raul (1966), *Movimentos Modernistas no Brasil, 1922–1928*, Rio de Janeiro: Livraria São José.
Borges, Jorge Luis (1993), *Ficciones*, New York: Everyman Library.
Bosi, Alfredo (1979), *História Concisa da Literatura Brasileira*, São Paulo: Cultrix.
Boswell, James (1963), *Boswell: The Ominous Years, 1774–1776*, ed. Charles Ryskamp and Frederick A. Pottle, London: William Heinemann.
Bowden, Ross (1984), 'Maori Cannibalism: An Interpretation', *Oceania*, 55: 81–99.
Bowers, Fredson (1940), *Elizabethan Revenge Tragedy*, Princeton: Princeton University Press.
Bradbury, Malcolm (1959), *Eating People is Wrong*, Harmondsworth: Penguin.
Brady, Ivan (1982), 'The Myth-Eating Man', *American Anthropologist*, 84: 595–611.
Brathwaite, Kamau (1974a), 'Timehri', in Orde Coombs, ed. *Is Massa Day Dead?* New York: Anchor, pp. 29–46.
(1974b), *The Development of Creole Society in Jamaica 1770–1820*, Oxford: Clarendon Press.
(1984), *History of the Voice*, London: New Beacon.

Brenner, Robert (1993), *Merchants and Revolution: Commercial Change, Political Conflict, and London's Overseas Traders, 1550–1653*, Princeton: Princeton University Press.

Brooks, Peter (1994), *Psychoanalysis and Storytelling*, Oxford: Blackwell.

Brown, Elizabeth A. R. (1981), 'Death and the Human Body in the Later Middle Ages: The Legislation of Boniface VIII on the Division of the Corpse', *Viator*, 12: 221–70.

Brown, Paul (1994), 'Vertical Transmission of Prion Disease', *Human Reproduction*, 9: 1,796–97.

Brown, Paula and Donald Tuzin (1983a), 'Editor's Preface', in Paula Brown and Donald Tuzin, eds., (1983), pp. 1–5.

(1983b), eds. *The Ethnography of Cannibalism*, Washington, DC: Society for Psychological Anthropology.

Bucher, Bernadette (1979), 'Les fantasmes du conquérant', in Raymond Bellour, ed., *Claude Lévi-Strauss / textes de et sur Claude Lévi-Strauss reunis pour Raymond Bellour et Cathérine Clément*, Paris: Gallimard, pp. 321–59.

(1981), *Icon and Conquest: A Structural Analysis of the Illustrations of de Bry's 'Great Voyages'*, Chicago: Chicago University Press.

Burghardt, Tom (1995), 'Neo-Nazis Salute Anti-Abortion Zealots', *Covert Action Quarterly*, 52: 26–33.

Burroughs, Edgar Rice (1990), *Tarzan of the Apes* [1914], London: Penguin Books.

Bush, George (1991), 'The Possibility of a New World Order', *Vital Speeches of the Day*, 62 (15): 450–2.

Campbell, Mary (1988), *The Witness and the Other World: Exotic European Travel Writing, 400–1600*, Ithaca: Cornell University Press.

Campos, Augusto de (1978), *Poesia, Antipoesia, Antropofagia*, São Paulo: Globo.

Campos, Haroldo de (1992), *Metalinguagem & Outras Metas*, São Paulo: Perspectiva.

Candido, Antonio (1966), ed. *Presença da Literatura Brasileira*, 3 vols., São Paulo: Difusão Européia do Livro.

(1977), *Vários Escritos*, São Paulo: Duas Cidades.

Carter, Angela (1975), *The Bloody Chamber*, Harmondsworth: Penguin.

Cavalcanti, Waldemar (1929), *Leite Criôlo*, xv, 22/09/1929.

Cave, Terence (1979), *The Cornucopian Text: Problems of Writing in the French Renaissance*, New York: Oxford University Press.

Césaire, Aimé (1972), *Discourse on Colonialism*, trans. Joan Pinkham, New York: Monthly Review Press.

Cixous, Hélène (1976), 'Fiction and its Phantoms: A Reading of Freud's "Das Unheimliche"', *New Literary History*, 7(3): 525–47.

Clarke, Ben and Clifton Ross (1994), eds. *Voice of Fire: Communiqués and Interviews from the Zapatista National Liberation Army*, Berkeley: New Earth Publications.

Clunie, Fergus (1977), *Fiji Weapons and Warfare*, Suva, Fiji: Bulletin of the Fiji Museum.

Cohen, Margaret (1993), *Profane Illumination: Walter Benjamin and the Paris of Surrealist Revolution*, Berkeley: University of California Press.

Cohn, Norman (1975), *Europe's Inner Demons*, London: Paladin.

Cominas, E. D. et al. (1989), 'Kuru, AIDS and Unfamiliar Social Behavior-Biocultural Consideration in the Current Epidemic', *Journal of the Royal Society of Medicine*, 82: 95–8.

Conklin, Beth (1995), 'Thus are our Bodies, Thus was our Custom', *American Ethnologist*, 22: 75–101.

Connor, Steven (1989), *Postmodernist Culture: An Introduction to Theories of the Contemporary*, Oxford: Basil Blackwell.

Conrad, Joseph (1967), *Heart of Darkness*, in *Great Short Works of Joseph Conrad*, New York: Harper & Row.

Cook, Captain James (1961), *The Voyage of the* Resolution *and* Adventure *1772–1775*, ed. J.C. Beaglehole, Cambridge: Cambridge University Press.

Craft, Christopher (1984), '"Kiss Me with Those Red Lips": Gender and Inversion in Bram Stoker's *Dracula*', *Representations*, 8: 107–33.

Crain, Caleb (1994), 'Lovers of Human Flesh: Homosexuality and Cannibalism in Melville's Novels', *American Literature*, 66(1): 25–53.

Cressy, David (1987), *Coming Over: Migration and Communication between England and New England in the Seventeenth Century*, New York: Cambridge University Press.

Cunningham, Hilary and Stephen Scharper (1996), 'The Human Genome Project', *Indigenous Affairs*, 1/96: 54–6.

D'Anghera, Peter Martyr (1587), *De Orbe Novo*, ed. Richard Hakluyt, Paris: G. Auray.

Dante Alighieri (1958), *The Divine Comedy*, trans. John D. Sinclair, 3 vols., London: Bodley Head.

Day, William Patrick (1985), *In the Circles of Fear and Desire: A Study of Gothic Fantasy*, Chicago: University of Chicago Press.

De Certeau, Michel (1986), *Heterologies: Discourse on the Other*, trans. Brian Massumi, Minneapolis: University of Minnesota Press.

Defoe, Daniel (1975), *Robinson Crusoe* [1719], ed. Michael Shinagel, New York: W. W. Norton.

Deleuze, Gilles and Félix Guattari (1977), *Anti-Oedipus: Capitalism and Schizophrenia*, trans. Robert Hurley, Mark Seem, and Helen R. Lane, New York: Viking Press.

Delumeau, Jean (1989), *El miedo en occidente*, Madrid: Taurus.

Denham, Laura (1993), *The Films of Peter Greenaway*, London: Minerva.

Dening, Greg (1980), *Islands and Beaches: Discourse on a Silent Land*, Hawaii: University of Hawaii Press.

Derrida, Jacques (1976), *Of Grammatology*, trans. Gayatri Chakravorty Spivak, Baltimore: Johns Hopkins University Press.

(1991), 'Eating Well ...', in E. Cadava, P. Connor, J-L. Nancy, eds., *Who Comes After the Subject*, London: Routledge, pp. 96–119.

(1992), 'Force of Law: The "Mystical Foundation of Authority"', in D. Cornell, M. Rosenfeld, D. G. Carlson, eds., *Deconstruction and the Possibility of Justice*, New York: Routledge, pp. 3–67.

(1994), *Specters of Marx: The State of the Debt, the Work of Mourning, and the New International*, trans. Peggy Kamuf, London: Routledge.

Diapea, William (alias John Jackson) (1928), *Cannibal Jack: The True Autobiography of a White Man in the South Seas*, ed. James Hadfield, London: Faber and Faber.

Diaz, Bernal (1963), *The Conquest of New Spain*, trans. J. M. Cohen, Harmondsworth: Penguin.

Donald, James (1989), 'The Fantastic, the Sublime and the Popular, Or, What is at Stake in Vampire Films', in James Donald, ed., *Fantasy and the Cinema*, London: British Film Institute, pp. 233–51.

Douglas, Mary (1989), 'Distinguished Lecture: The Hotel Kwilu-A Model of Models', *American Anthropologist*, 91: 855–65.

Drake, Sandra (1986), *Wilson Harris and the Modern Tradition: A New Architecture of the World*, New York: Greenwood Press.

Dryden, John (1970), 'The Tempest, or The Enchanted Island' [1670], in *The Works of John Dryden*, vol. x, ed. Maximilian E. Novak and George Robert Guffey, Berkeley: University of California Press, pp. 1–103.

D'Souza, Dinesh (1995), *The End of Racism: Principles for a Multicultural Society*, New York: Free Press.

Eagleton, Terry (1995), *Heathcliff and the Great Hunger*, London: Verso.

Edgerton, Robert (1992), *Sick Societies: Challenging the Myth of Primitive Harmony*, New York: Free Press.

Edmond, Rod (1997), *Representing the South Pacific: Colonial Discourse from Cook to Gauguin*, Cambridge: Cambridge University Press.

Ellroy, James (1995), *American Tabloid*, London: Century.

Endicott, William (1923), *Wrecked Among Cannibals in the Fijis: A Narrative of Shipwreck and Adventure in the South Seas*, Salem, MA: Marine Research Society.

Erskine, John Elphinstone (1967), *Journal of a Cruise Among the Islands of the Western Pacific* ... [1853], London: Dawson.

Escalante, Evodio (1992), 'Texto histórico y texto social en la obra de Rulfo', in Juan Rulfo, *Toda la obra*, Madrid: Collección Archivos, pp. 561–81.

Fanon, Frantz (1967), *Black Skin, White Masks*, trans. Charles Markmann, New York: Grove Weidenfeld.

Farquhar, Judith and D. Carleton Gajdusek (1981), eds. *Kuru: Early Letters and Field-Notes from the Collection of D. Carleton Gajdusek*, New York: Raven Press.

Felix Bolaños, Alvaro (1994), *Barbarie y canibalismo en la retórica colonial: los indios pijaos de Fray Pedro Simón*, Bogotá: CEREC.

Ferguson R. B. and Whitehead N. L. (1992), eds. *War in the Tribal Zone: Expanding States and Indigenous Warfare*, Santa Fe: SAR Press.

Fletcher, John (1995), 'The Sea Voyage' [1622], in Anthony Parr, ed., *Three Renaissance Travel Plays*, Manchester: Manchester University Press, pp. 135–216.

Forbes, Jack D. (1992), *Columbus and Other Cannibals: The Wetiko Disease of Exploitation, Imperialism, and Terrorism*, New York: Automedia/ Semiotexts.

Formisano, Luciano (1992), 'Introduction', to *Letters from a New World: Amerigo Vespucci's Discovery of America*, ed. Luciano Formisano, trans. David Jacobson, New York: Marsilio, pp. xix–xl.

Forsyth, Donald W. (1985), 'Three Cheers for Hans Staden: The Case for Brazilian Cannibalism', *Ethnohistory*, 32.1: 17–36.

Foucault, Michel (1979), *Discipline and Punish*, trans. Alan Sheridan, New York: Vintage.

(1984), 'Nietzsche, Genealogy, History', in *The Foucault Reader*, ed. Paul Rabinow, New York: Pantheon, pp. 76–100.

Freud, Sigmund (1955), '"A Child is Being Beaten": A Contribution to the Study of the Origin of Sexual Perversions', in *The Standard Edition of the Complete Psychological Works of Sigmund Freud: Volume XVII (1917–1919) On Infantile Neurosis and Other Works*, ed. James Strachey, London: Hogarth Press, pp. 179–202.

(1959), 'The "Uncanny"' in his *Collected Papers*, ed. Ernest Jones, New York: Basic Books, pp. 368–407.

(1960), *The Ego and the Id*, trans. Joan Riviere, New York: Norton.

(1961a), *Beyond the Pleasure Principle*, trans. James Strachey, New York: Norton.

(1961b), *Civilization and Its Discontents*, trans. James Strachey, New York: Norton.

(1961c), *Three Essays on Sexuality*, trans. James Strachey, New York: Basic Books.

(1963), 'Analysis Terminable and Interminable,' in his *Therapy and Technique*, trans. James Strachey, New York: Collier, pp. 233–71.

(1965a), *New Introductory Lectures on Psychoanalysis*, trans. James Strachey, New York: Norton.

(1965b), *The Interpretation of Dreams*, trans. James Strachey, New York: Avon Books.

(1975), *The Psychopathology of Everyday Life*, trans. Alan Tyson, Harmondsworth: Penguin.

(1983), *Totem and Taboo*, London: Ark Paperbacks.

Friedlander, Saul (1992), ed. *Probing the Limits of Representation: Nazism and the "Final Solution"*, Cambridge, MA: Harvard University Press.

Gaignebet, Claude (1974), *Le Folklore obscène des enfants*, Paris: Maisonneuve et Larose.

Gajdusek, D. Carleton (1963), *Kuru Epidemiological Patrols from the New Guinea Highlands to Papua 1957*, Bethesda: National Institute of Health.

(1968), *New Guinea Journal October 2, 1961 to August 4, 1962. Part Two*, Bethesda: National Institutes of Health.

(1970a), 'Physiological and Psychological Characteristics of Stone Age Man', *Engineering and Science*, 33: 2b-33, 56–62.

(1970b), *New Guinea Journal June 10, 1959 to August 15, 1959*, Bethesda: National Institutes of Health.

(1971), *Journal of Expeditions to the Soviet Union, the Islands of Madagascar, la Reunion and Mauritius, Indonesia, and to East and West New Guinea, Australia and Guam to study Kuru and other Neurological*

Diseases, Epidemic Influenza, Endemic Goitrous Cretinism, and Child Growth and Development with Explorations on the Great Papuan Plateau and on the Lake Plain and Inland Southern Lowlands of West New Guinea, Bethesda: National Institutes of Health.

(1976), *Correspondence on the Discovery and Original Investigations on Kuru: Smadel-Gajdusek Correspondence, 1955–1958*, Bethesda: National Institutes of Health.

(1977a), 'Unconventional Viruses and the Origin and Disappearance of Kuru: Nobel Lecture, December 13, 1976', in W. Odelberg, ed. *Les Prix Nobel en 1976*, Stockholm: The Nobel Foundation, pp. 160–216.

(1977b), 'Unconventional Viruses and the Origin and Disappearance of Kuru', *Science*, 197: 943–60.

(1977c), Personal Communication. Correspondence with William Arens.

(1978), Personal Communication. Correspondence with William Arens.

(1979), 'Observations on the Early History of Kuru Investigation', in S. Prusiner and W. Hadlow, eds. *Slow Transmissible Diseases of the Nervous System*, vol. 1., New York: Academic Press, pp. 7–35.

(1981), *New Guinea, Philippine and Indonesia Journal, September 25, 1980 to December 20, 1980*, unpublished manuscript.

(1990), 'Subacute Spongiform Encephalopathies'. In B. N. Fields and D. M. Knipe, eds., *Field's Virology*, 2nd edn., New York: Raven Press, pp. 2,289–324.

Gajdusek, D. Carleton and V. Zigas (1957a), 'Degenerative Disease of the Central Nervous System in New Guinea', *The New England Journal of Medicine*, 257: 974–8.

(1957b), 'Kuru', *The Medical Journal of Australia*, pp. 745–54.

Galeano, Eduardo (1973), *The Open Veins of Latin America*, trans. Cedric Belfrage, New York: Monthly Review Press.

Garber, Marjorie (1985), ed. *Cannibals, Witches, and Divorce: Estranging the Renaissance. Selected Papers from the English Institute, 1985*, Baltimore: Johns Hopkins University Press.

Gautier, Theophile (n.d.), *Mademoiselle de Maupin*. New York: n.p.

Gelder, Ken (1994), *Reading the Vampire*, London: Routledge.

Gibbs, Clarence J. and D. Carleton Gajdusek (1965), 'Attempts to Demonstrate a Transmissible Agent in Kuru, Amyothropic Lateral Sclerosis, and other Subacute and Chronic Progressive Nervous System Degenerations of Man', in D. Carleton Gajdusek, Clarence Gibbs and Michael Alpers, eds. *Slow, Latent and Temperate Virus Infections*, Washington, DC: U.S. Government Printing Office, pp. 39–48.

Gil, Juan and Consuelo Varela (1984), eds. *Cartas de particulares a Colón y relaciones coetáneas*, Madrid: Alianza.

Gilkes, Michael (1975), *Wilson Harris and the Caribbean Novel*, London: Longman.

Gillies, John (1994), *Shakespeare and the Geography of Difference*, Cambridge: Cambridge University Press.

Gilman, Sander (1986), *Jewish Self-Hatred: Anti-Semitism and the Hidden Language of Jews*, Baltimore: Johns Hopkins University Press.

Girard, René (1977), *Violence and the Sacred*, trans. Patrick Gregory, Baltimore: Johns Hopkins University Press.
Glasse, Robert (1967), 'Cannibalism in the Kuru Region of New Guinea', *Transactions of the New York Academy of Sciences*, 29: 748–54.
Glasse, R. M. and Shirley Lindenbaum (1976), 'Kuru at Wanitabe', in R. W. Hornabrook, ed. *Essays on Kuru*, Faringdon, Berks: E. W. Classey Ltd., pp. 38–52.
Glissant, Edouard (1989), *Caribbean Discourse: Selected Essays*, ed. Michael Dash, Charlottesville: University Press of Virginia.
González, Eduardo (n.d.), 'Flesh-Eating and Ghost Text in Saer's *El entenado*', unpublished manuscript.
Gordon-Grube, Karen (1988), 'Anthropophagy in Post-Renaissance Europe', *American Anthropologist*, 90: 405–9.
Gramsci, Antonio (1971), *Selections from the Prison Notebooks*, trans. Quintin Hoare and Geoffrey Nowell Smith, New York: International.
Green, André (1972), 'Cannibalisme: réalité ou fantasme agi?', *Destins du cannibalisme: Nouvelle Revue de Psychanalyse*, no 6: 27–52.
Greenblatt, Stephen (1980), *Renaissance Self-Fashioning: From More to Shakespeare*, Chicago: Chicago University Press.
(1991), *Marvelous Possessions: The Wonder of the New World*, Chicago: University of Chicago Press.
Greene, J. (1615), *A Refutation of the Apology for Actors*, [by Thomas Heywood], London: W. White.
Griffin, J. A. (1971), 'Is a Cannibal a Criminal?', *Melanesian Law Journal*, 1: 79–81.
Grimm, Brothers (1975), *The Complete Grimm's Fairy Tales*, trans. Anon, London: Macmillan.
Guerra, Ruy (1988), 'Popular Cinema and the State', in Johnson and Stam, eds., *Brazilian Cinema*, pp. 101–3.
Guest, Harriet (1992), 'Curiously Marked: Tattooing, Masculinity, and Nationality in Eighteenth-Century British Perceptions of the South Pacific', in John Barrell, ed., *Painting and the Politics of Culture: New Essays on British Art, 1700 - 1850*, Oxford: Oxford University Press, pp. 101–34.
Hadfield, Rev. James (1928), 'Introduction', in Diapea (1928), pp. xi–xix.
[Hakluyt, Richard] (1966), *Divers Voyages*, Ann Arbor: University Microfilms.
Hakluyt, Richard (1907), *Voyages*, 8 vols., New York: Dutton.
(1965), *Principal Navigations*, 12 vols., New York: AMS.
Halberstam, Judith (1991), 'Skinflik: Posthuman Gender in Jonathan Demme's *The Silence of the Lambs*', *Camera-Obscura: A Journal of Feminism and Film Theory*, 27: 37–52.
(1993), 'Technologies of Monstrosity: Bram Stoker's *Dracula*', *Victorian Studies*, 36(3): 323–52.
Hall, Stuart (1988), 'A Toad in the Garden,' in Cary Nelson and Lawrence Grossberg, eds., *Marxism and the Interpretation of Culture*, Urbana: University of Illinois Press, pp. 35–74.
Hall, Stuart and Martin Jacques (1989), eds. *New Times: the Changing Face of Politics in the 90s*, London: Lawrence and Wishart.

Halpern, Richard (1991), *Poetics of Primitive Accumulation*, Ithaca: Cornell University Press.

Handlin, Oscar (1957), *Race and Nationality in American Life*, Garden City, NY: Doubleday.

Hannabus, Stuart (1989), 'Ballantyne's Message of Empire', in Jeffrey Richards, ed., *Imperialism and Juvenile Literature*, Manchester: Manchester University Press, pp. 53–71.

Harner, Michael (1977), 'The Ecological Basis for Aztec Sacrifice', *American Ethnologist*, 4: 117–35.

Harris, Marvin (1977), *Cannibals and Kings: The Origins of Culture*. New York: Random House.

(1995), *Cultural Anthropology*, New York: Harper & Row.

Harris, Thomas (1982), *Red Dragon*, New York: Bantam.

(1988), *The Silence of the Lambs*, New York: St. Martin's Press.

Harris, Wilson (1967), *Tradition, the Writer, and Society*, London: New Beacon.

(1970), 'History, Fable and Myth in the Caribbean and Guianas', *Caribbean Quarterly*, 16: 1–32.

(1983), *The Womb of Space: The Cross-Cultural Imagination*, Westport, CT: Greenwood Press.

(1985), *The Guyana Quartet* [1960], London: Faber and Faber.

Harvey, David (1990), *The Condition of Postmodernity*, Cambridge, MA: Blackwell.

Haynes, Jonathan (1986), *The Humanist as Traveler*, London: Associated University Press.

Helena, Lúcia (1994), 'Sobre a História da Semana de 22', in *História e Literatura: Ensaios*, Campinas, SP: Ed. da UNICAMP, pp. 101–28.

Herbert, T. Walter (1980), *Marquesan Encounters: Melville and the Meaning of Civilization*, Cambridge: Harvard University Press.

Herdt, Gilbert (1984), 'Ritual Homosexual Behavior in the Male Cults of Melanesia, 1862–1983', in Gilbert Herdt, ed. *Ritualized Homosexuality in Melanesia*, Berkeley: University of California Press, pp. 1–81.

Hesiod (1982), *Theogony*, trans. Dorothea Wender, Harmondsworth: Penguin.

Hides, J. G. (1936), *Papuan Wonderland*, London: Blackie and Son, Ltd.

Hill, Jonathan (1996), ed. *History, Power, and Identity: Ethnogenesis in the Americas, 1492–1992*, Iowa City: University of Iowa Press.

Hitler, Adolf (1943), *Mein Kampf*, trans. Ralph Manheim, Boston: Houghton Mifflin Co.

Hocart, A. M. (1929), 'Lau Islands, Fiji, Honolulu', *The Bernice P. Bishop Museum Bulletin*, 62: 203.

Hogan, Patrick (n.d.), 'Thinking Oppression: Cognitive Models for Race, Sex, and Other Status Categories', unpublished manuscript.

Holderness, Graham, Bryan Loughrey, and Andrew Murphy (1995), '"What's the Matter?": Shakespeare and Textual Theory', *Textual Practice*, 9: 93–119.

Hornabrook, R. W. (1976), ed. *Essays on Kuru*, Faringdon, Berks: E. W. Classey Ltd.

Howard, W. J. (1970), 'Wilson Harris's "Guiana Quartet": From Personal Myth to National Identity', *Ariel* 1(1): 46–60.

Huggan, Graham (1994), 'A Tale of Two Parrots: Walcott, Rhys, and the Uses of Colonial Mimicry', *Contemporary Literature*, 35(4): 643–60.

(n.d.), 'Cannibal Rights: Intertextuality and Postcolonial Discourse in the Caribbean Region', in Andrade and Huggan, eds. (forthcoming).

Hulme, Peter (1986), *Colonial Encounters: Europe and the Native Caribbean 1492–1797*, London: Methuen.

(1993), 'Making Sense of the Native Caribbean', *New West Indian Guide*, 67: 189–220.

(1994), 'Making No Bones: A Response to Myra Jehlen', *Critical Inquiry*, 20: 179–86.

Hulme, Peter and Neil L. Whitehead (1992), eds. *Wild Majesty: Encounters with Caribs from Columbus to the Present Day*, Oxford: Clarendon Press.

Indiana, Gary (1990), 'Peter Greenaway', *Interview*, 20.3: 120–1.

Jackson, John (1967), 'Jackson's Narrative' [1853], Appendix A in Erskine (1967), pp. 412–77.

Jackson, Rosemary (1981), *Fantasy: The Literature of Subversion*, London: Methuen.

James, C. L. R. (1963), *The Black Jacobins: Toussaint L'Ouverture and the San Domingo Revolution*, New York: Vintage.

James, M. R. (1915), *Ghost-Stories of an Antiquary*, London: Edward Arnold.

Jameson, Fredric (1983), *The Political Unconscious: Narrative as a Socially Symbolic Act*, London: Methuen.

(1991), *Postmodernism or, the Cultural Logic of Late Capitalism*, Durham: Duke University Press.

Janzen, Karen (1980), 'Meat of Life', *Science Digest*, Nov /Dec: 78–81, 121.

Jehlen, Myra (1993), 'History before the Fact; or, Captain John Smith's Unfinished Symphony', *Critical Inquiry*, 19: 677–92.

Jodelle, Étienne (1965), *Oeuvres complètes*, vol 1. Paris: Gallimard.

Johnson, Randall (1984), *Cinema Novo x 5: Masters of Contemporary Brazilian Film*, Austin: University of Texas.

(1987), 'Tupy or not Tupy: Cannibalism and Nationalism in Contemporary Brazilian Literature and Culture', in John King, ed., *Modern Latin American Fiction: A Survey* London: Faber, pp. 41–59.

Johnson, Randall and Robert Stam (1988), eds. *Brazilian Cinema*, Austin: University of Texas.

Julius, Charles (1981), 'Sorcery Among the South Fore, with Special Reference to Kuru' [1956], in Farquhar and Gajdusek (1981), eds. pp. 281–8.

Jung, C. G. (1970), *Mysterium Coniunctionis: An Inquiry into the Separation and Synthesis of Psychic Opposites in Alchemy*, Princeton: Princeton University Press.

Kant, Immanuel (1993), *Critique of Practical Reason*, ed. Lewis White Beck, trans. Lewis White Beck et al., New York: Macmillan Publishing Company.

Keesing, Roger (1981), *Cultural Anthropology*, New York: Holt, Rinehart and Winston.

Ketterer, David (1992), 'Tracing Shadows: Pym Criticism, 1980–1990', in Richard Kopley, ed., *Poe's Pym: Critical Explorations*, Durham: Duke University Press, pp. 233–74.

Kilgour, Maggie (1990), *From Communion to Cannibalism: An Anatomy of Metaphors of Incorporation*, Princeton: Princeton University Press.

Klibansky, R., Fritz Saxl, and Irwin Panofsky (1964), *Saturn and Melancholy: Studies in the History of Natural Philosophy, Religion and Art*, London: Thomas Nelson.

Klitzman, R. L., M. P. Alpers and D. C. Gajdusek (1984), 'The Natural Incubation Period of Kuru and the Episodes of Transmission in Three Clusters of Patients', *Neuroepidemiology*, 3: 3–20.

Koenigsberger, Dorothy (1975), 'A New Metaphor for Mozart's Magic Flute', *European Studies Review*, 5: 229–75.

Kolata, Gina (1986), 'Anthropologists Suggest Cannibalism Is a Myth', *Science*, 232: 1,497–500.

(1994), 'Viruses or Prions', *New York Times*, October 4, pp. C1; C12.

Koyre, Alexandre (1957), *From the Closed World to the Infinite Universe*, Baltimore: Johns Hopkins University Press.

Krabacher, Thomas (1980), Review of *The Man-Eating Myth*, *Human Ecology*, 8: 407–9.

La Bible des poètes. Metamorphoses (c. 1485), Paris: Antoine Verard.

La Bible des poètes. Metamorphoses (c. 1507), Paris: Antoine Verard.

Lacan, Jacques (1977), 'The Mirror Stage', in his *Ecrits: A Selection*, trans. Alan Sheridan, New York: W. W. Norton.

Lacey, R. W. and S. F. Dealler (1994), 'The Transmission of Prion Disease', *Human Reproduction*, 9: 1,792–6.

Laroque, François (1983), 'An Analogue and Possible Secondary Source to the Pound-of-Flesh Story in *The Merchant of Venice*', *Notes and Queries*, April, pp. 117–18.

Leach, Edmund (1966), *Rethinking Anthropology*, London: Athlone Press.

(1979), 'Long Pig, Tall Story: Review of *The Man-Eating Myth*', *New Society*, August 30: 467.

(1982), *Social Anthropology*, New York: Oxford University Press.

(1989), 'Writing Anthropology', *American Ethnologist*, 16: 137–41.

Leroux, Charles (1982), 'The Professor who was Consumed by Cannibalism', *Chicago Tribune*, April 13, Section 2, pp. 1, 4.

Léry, Jean de (1990), *History of a Voyage to the Land of Brazil*, trans. Janet Whatley, Berkeley: University of California Press.

Lestringant, Frank (1982), 'Catholiques et cannibales. Le thème du cannibalisme dans le discours protestant au temps des guerres de religion', in Jean-Claude Margolin and Robert Sauzet, eds., *Pratiques et discours alimentaires à la Renaissance*, Paris: G.-P. Maisonneuve et Larose, pp. 233–45.

(1994), *Le cannibale: grandeur et décadence*, Paris: Perrin.

Lévi-Strauss, Claude (1981), *The Naked Man*, trans. J. and D. Weightman, London: Harper and Row.

(1992), *Tristes Tropiques*, trans. John and Doreen Weightman, Harmondsworth: Penguin Books.

Leyda, Jay (1969), *The Melville Log: A Documentary Life of Herman Melville, 1819–1891*, New York: Gordian Press.

L'Héritier, Marie-Jeanne (1718), *Les Caprices du destin, or Recueil d'Histoires singulières et amusantes*, Paris: P. M. Huart.

Lindenbaum, Shirley (1979), *Kuru Sorcery: Disease and Danger in the New Guinea Highlands*, Palo Alto: Mayfield Publishing Co.

(1982), Review of *The Man-Eating Myth*, *Ethnohistory*, 29: 58–60.

(1990), 'Science, Sorcery and the Tropics: Review of Vincent Zigas, *Laughing Death*', *New York Times Review*, July 1, p. 12.

(1992), 'Knowledge and Action in the Shadow of Aids', in Gilbert Herdt and Shirley Lindenbaum, eds. *The Time of Aids*, Newbury Park, CA: Sage Publications.

Lipstadt, Deborah E. (1993), *Denying the Holocaust: The Growing Assault on Truth and Memory*, London: The Free Press.

Locke, John (1965), *Two Treatises on Government* [1689], ed. Peter Laslett, New York: New American Library.

Lukács, Georg (1971), 'Reification and the Consciousness of the Proletariat', in his *History and Class Consciousness*, trans. Rodney Livingstone, London: Merlin Press, pp. 83–222.

Lynam, Edward (1946), *Richard Hakluyt and his Succesors*, London: The Hakluyt Society.

Lyons, Paul (1996), 'From Man-Eaters to Spam-Eaters: Literary Tourism and the Discourse of Cannibalism from Herman Melville to Paul Theroux', in John Rieder and Larry E. Smith, eds., *Multiculturalism and Representation: Selected Essays*, Honolulu: College of Languages, Linguistics and Literature, University of Hawaii and the East-West Center, vol. 10, pp. 67–85.

Lyotard, Jean-François (1977), *Rudiments païens*, Paris: Points.

MacCannell, Dean (1992), *Empty Meeting Grounds: The Tourist Papers*, London: Routledge.

Malchow, H. L. (1996), *Gothic Images of Race in Nineteenth-Century Britain*, Stanford: Stanford University Press.

Marlowe, Christopher (1966), *The Jew of Malta*, New York: Hill & Wang.

Marx, Karl (1977), *Selected Writings*, ed. David McLellan, Oxford: Oxford University Press.

(1990), *Capital Vol. One*, trans. Ben Fowkes, Harmondsworth: Penguin.

Mascie-Taylor, C. (1993), *The Anthropology of Disease*, Oxford: Oxford University Press.

Mason, Peter (1990), *Deconstructing America: Representations of the Other*, London: Routledge.

Matthews, John, Robert Glasse, and Shirley Lindenbaum (1968), 'Kuru and Cannibalism', *The Lancet*, August 24, 2: 449–52.

Mayhew, Henry (1967), *London Labor and the London Poor*, 4 vols., New York: Augustus Kelley.

Mayne, Judith (1987), '*King Kong* and the Ideology of Spectacle', *Quarterly Review of Film Studies*, 1 (4): 373–87.

McElroy, Ann and Patricia Townsend (1989), *Medical Anthropology in Perspective*, Boulder: Westview Press.

McWatt, Mark (1985), 'The Two Faces of Eldorado: Contrasting Attitudes Toward History and Identity in West Indian Literature', in M. McWatt, ed., *West Indian Literature in its Social Context*, Barbados: UWI, pp. 33–47.

Melville, Herman (1972), *Typee* [1846], Harmondsworth: Penguin Books.

Mittelholzer, Edgar (1955), *My Bones and My Flute*, London: Longman.

Miyoshi, M. (1993), 'A Borderless World? From Colonialism to Transnationalism and the Decline of the Nation-State', *Critical Inquiry*, 19: 726–51.

Molotsky, Irwin (1997), 'Nobel Scientist Pleads Guilty to Abusing Boy', *New York Times*, 19 February 1997, p. 710.

Montaigne, Michel de (1928), *The Essayes of Michael Lord of Montaigne*, trans. John Florio, 3 vols., London: J. M. Dent.

(1988), *Les Essais*, 3 vols., ed. Pierre Villey, Paris: Quadrige/Presses Universitaires de France.

Moore, Richard (1972), *Caribs, Cannibals, and Human Relations*, Patchogue, NY: Pathway Publications.

More, Thomas (1992), *Utopia*, 2nd edn., trans. Robert Adams, New York: Norton.

Moresby, John (1876), *New Guinea and Polynesia: Discoveries and Surveys in New Guinea and the D'Entrecasteaux Islands, a Cruise in Polynesia and Visits to the Pearl-Shelling Stations in Torres Straits of HMS 'Basilisk'*, London: John Murray.

Moretti, Franco (1982), 'The Dialectic of Fear', *New Left Review*, 136: 67–85.

Morse, Richard M. (1995), 'The Multiverse of Latin American Identity, c.1920–c.1970', in *The Cambridge History of Latin America: Volume x: Latin America Since 1930: Ideas, Culture and Society*, ed. Leslie Bethell, Cambridge: Cambridge University Press, pp. 1–128.

Mosse, George (1978), *Toward the Final Solution: A History of European Racism*, London: J. M. Dent.

Mullaney, Steven (1983), 'Strange Things, Gross Terms, Curious Customs: The Rehearsal of Cultures in the Late Renaissance', *Representations*, 3: 40–67.

Naipaul, V. S. (1984), *The Loss of El Dorado* [1969], New York: Vintage.

Needham, Rodney (1980), 'Chewing on the Cannibals' [review of Arens' *The Man-Eating Myth*], *Times Literary Supplement*, January 25: 75–6.

Nietzsche, Freidrich (1967), *On the Genealogy of Morals and Ecce Homo*, New York: Vintage.

(1968), *The Will to Power*, trans. Walter Kaufmann and R. J. Hollingdale, ed. Walter Kaufmann, New York: Vintage Books.

(1990), *Beyond Good and Evil: Prelude to a Philosophy of the Future*, trans. R. J. Hollingdale, New York: Penguin Books.

Norris, Chris (1992), *Uncritical Theory: Postmodernism, Intellectuals and the Gulf War*, London: Lawrence and Wishart.

Nunes, Benedito (1979), *Oswald Canibal*, São Paulo: Perspectiva.
(1990), ed. *A Utopia Antropológica*, São Paulo: Globo.
Obeyesekere, Gananath (1981), *Medusa's Hair: An Essay on Personal Symbols and Religious Experience*, Chicago: University of Chicago Press.
(1992a), *The Apotheosis of Captain Cook: European Mythmaking in the Pacific*, Princeton: Princeton University Press.
(1992b), '"British Cannibals": Contemplation of an Event in the Death and Resurrection of James Cook, Explorer', *Critical Inquiry*, 18: 630–54.
Opie, Iona and Peter Opie (1974), ed. *The Classic Fairy Tales*, Oxford: Oxford University Press.
Ortiz De Montellano, Bernard (1983), 'Counting Skulls', *American Anthropologist*, 85: 403–6.
Osborne, Lawrence (1997), 'Does Man Eat Man?: Inside the Great Cannibalism Controversy', *Lingua Franca*, 7(4): 28–39.
Pagden, Anthony (1993), *European Encounters with the New World*, New Haven: Yale University Press.
Palencia-Roth, Michael (1993), 'The Cannibal Law of 1503', in Jerry M. Williams and Robert E. Lewis, eds., *Early Images of the Americas: Transfer and Invention*, Tucson: University of Arizona Press, pp. 21–64.
Parker, Patricia (1987), *Literary Fat Ladies*, London: Methuen.
Paz, Octavio (1959), *El laberinto de la soledad*, Mexico: Fondo de Cultura Económica.
(1981), *Los hijos del limo*, Barcelona: Editorial Seix-Barral.
Peck, James (1987), ed. *The Chomsky Reader*, New York: Pantheon Books.
Perrault, Charles (c. 1750), *The Famous History of Tom Thumb Wherein is declared His Marvellous Acts of Manhood Fulle of Wonder & Merriment*, London: Printed and sold in Aldermary Churchyard.
(1967), *Contes*, ed.Gilbert Rouger, Paris: Garnier.
(1977), *The Fairy Tales of Charles Perrault*, trans. Angela Carter, New York: Avon.
Piersen, William D. (1993), 'Why God's Black Children Suffer', in his *Black Legacy: America's Hidden Heritage*, Amherst: University of Massachusetts Press, pp. 3–34.
Pietz, P. W. (1985), 'The Problem of the Fetish, I', *Res*, 9: 5–17.
(1993), 'Fetishism and Materialism', in E. Apter and W. Pietz, eds., *Fetishism as Cultural Discourse*, Ithaca: Cornell University Press, pp. 119–51.
Plotinus (1964), *Enneads* in *The Essential Plotinus*, trans. Elmer O'Brien, Indianapolis: Hackett.
Po-Chia-Hsia, R. (1992), *Trent 1475: Stories of A Ritual Murder Trial*, New Haven: Yale University Press.
Poe, Edgar Allan (1971), *Tales of Mystery and Imagination*, New York: Dutton.
(1986), *The Narrative of Arthur Gordon Pym of Nantucket*, ed. Harold Beaver, London: Penguin.

Poole, Fitz John Porter (1983), 'Cannibals, Tricksters, and Witches', in Brown and Tuzin, eds., (1983b), pp. 6–32.

Portocarrero Maisch, Félix et al. (1991), eds. *Sacaojos: crisis social y fantasmas coloniales*, Lima: Tarea.

Pratt, Mary Louise (1992), *Imperial Eyes: Travel Writing and Transculturation*, London: Routledge.

(1994), 'Transculturation and Autoethnography: Peru 1615/1980', in Francis Barker, Peter Hulme, and Margaret Iversen (1994), eds. pp. 24–46.

Prusiner, Stanley (1982), 'Novel Proteinaceous Infections Particles Cause Scrapie', *Science*, 216: 136–44.

Prusiner, Stanley, D. Carleton Gajdusek, and Michael Alpers (1982), 'Kuru with Incubation Periods Exceeding Two Decades', *Annals of Neurology*, 12: 1–9.

Quint, David (1995), 'A Reconsideration of Montaigne's *Des Cannibales*', in Karen Ordahl Kupperman, ed., *America in European Consciousness, 1493–1750*, Chapel Hill: University of North Carolina Press, pp. 166–91.

Rama, Angel (1982), *Transculturación narrativa en América Latina*, Mexico City: Siglo XXI Editores.

Ramos, José Mário Ortiz (1983), *Cinema, Estado e lutas culturais (Anos 50/60/70)*, Rio de Janeiro: Paz e Terra.

Rawson, Claude (1978–9), 'Cannibalism and Fiction', *Genre* 10: 667–711, and 11: 227–313.

(1984), 'Narrative and the Proscribed Act: Homer, Euripides and the Literature of Cannibalism', in Joseph P. Strelka, ed. *Literary Theory and Criticism: Festschrift Presented to René Wellek in Honor of his Eightieth Birthday*, Bern: Peter Lang, II: 1,159–87.

(1992), '"Indians" and Irish: Montaigne, Swift, and the Cannibal Question', *Modern Language Quarterly*, 53: 299–63.

Rennie, Neil (1996), *Far-Fetched Facts: The Literature of Travel and the Idea of the South Seas*, Oxford: Oxford University Press.

Revista de Antropofagia (1975), complete facsimile edition, São Paulo: Abril.

Rigby, Nigel (1992), 'Sober Cannibals and Drunken Christians: Colonial Encounters of the Cannibal Kind', *Journal of Commonwealth Literature*, 27 (1): 171–82.

Riley, Thomas (1986), 'Existence of Cannibalism', *Science*, 232: 926.

Rivière, Peter (1980), Review of *The Man-Eating Myth*, *Man*, 15: 203–5.

Rocha, Glauber (1963), *Revisão crítica do cinema brasileiro*, Rio de Janeiro: Civilização brasileira.

Roediger, David (1991), *The Wages of Whiteness: Race and the Making of the American Working Class*, New York: Verso.

Root, Deborah (1996), *Cannibal Culture: Art, Appropriation, and the Commodification of Difference*, Boulder: Westview Press.

Rose, Gillian (1978), *The Melancholy Science: An Introduction to the Thought of Theodor W. Adorno*, London: Macmillan Press.

Rosenblum, Robert (1988), *The Romantic Child From Runge to Sendak*, London: Thames & Hudson.

Rowe, John Carlos (1992), 'Poe, Antebellum Slavery, and Modern Criticism', in R. Kopley, ed., *Poe's Pym: Critical Explorations*, Durham: Duke University Press, pp. 117–40.

Rulfo, Juan (1955), *Pedro Páramo*, Mexico City: Fondo de Cultura Económica.

Rushdie, Salman (1992), *Midnight's Children*, New York: Avon Books.

Saer, José Juan (1990), *The Witness* [1983], trans. Margaret Jull Costa, London: Serpent's Tail.

Sagan, Eli (1974), *Cannibalism: Human Aggression and Cultural Form*. New York: Harper Torchbooks.

Sahlins, Marshall (1978), 'Culture as Protein and Profit', *New York Review of Books*, 25, no. 18, 23 November: 45–53.

(1979), 'Cannibalism: An Exchange', *New York Review of Books*, 26, no. 4, 22 March: 46–7.

(1983), 'Raw Women, Cooked Men and other "Great Things" of the Fiji Islands', in Brown and Tuzin (1983), eds. pp. 72–93.

(1985), *Islands of History*, Chicago: University of Chicago Press.

(1995), *How "Natives" Think: About Captain Cook, For Example*, Chicago: University of Chicago Press.

Sale, Kirkpatrick (1990), *The Conquest of Paradise*, New York: Knopf.

Sanday, Peggy Reeves (1986), *Divine Hunger: Cannibalism as a Cultural System*, Cambridge: Cambridge University Press.

Sandison, Alan (1967), *The Wheel of Empire: A Study of the Imperial Idea in Some Late Nineteenth and Early Twentieth-Century Fiction*, New York: St Martin's Press.

Sandys, George (1970), *Ovid's Metamorphoses Englished, Mythologized and Represented in Figures*, ed. Karl K. Hully and Stanley T. Vandersall, Lincoln: University of Nebraska Press.

Sartre, Jean-Paul (1973), *Anti-Semite and Jew*, trans. George Becker, New York: Schocken.

Savigny, J.-B. Henry and Alexander Correard (1986), *Narrative of a Voyage to Senegal in 1816* [1818], Marlboro, VT: The Marlboro Press.

Schwarz, Roberto (1987), *Que Horas São?* São Paulo: Cia de Letras.

(1992), *Misplaced Ideas: Essays on Brazilian Culture*, ed. John Gledson, London: Verso.

(1994), 'Fim de Século', in *Folha de São Paulo*, 4 de dezembro: 'Mais!', p. 9.

Seale, R. (1987), 'Kuru, AIDS and Aberrant Social Behavior', *Journal of the Royal Society of Medicine*, 80: 200–2.

(1989), 'Kuru, AIDS and Unfamiliar Social Behavior', *Journal of the Royal Society of Medicine*, 82: 571.

Shakespeare, William (1970), *The Merchant of Venice*, Harmondsworth: Penguin.

Shell, Marc (1978), *The Economy of Literature*, Baltimore: Johns Hopkins University Press.

Sherman, Cindy (1992), *Fitcher's Bird*, New York: Rizzoli.

Silko, Leslie Marmon (1991), *Almanac of the Dead*, New York: Penguin.

Simpson, A. W. Brian (1986), *Cannibalism and the Common Law: The Story of the Tragic Last Voyage of 'Mignonette' and the Strange Legal Proceedings to Which It Gave Rise*, Harmondsworth: Penguin.

Smith, Adam (1986), *The Wealth of Nations: Books I–III*, Harmondsworth: Penguin.

Snead, James (1991), 'Spectatorship and Capture in *King Kong*: The Guilty Look', *Critical Inquiry*, 33 (1): 53–69.

Sorenson, E. Richard (1976), *The Edge of the Forest: Land, Childhood, and Change in a New Guinea Protoagricultural Society*, Washington, DC: Smithsonian Institution Press.

Staden, Hans (1929), *The True History of His Captivity, 1557*, trans. and ed. Malcom Letts, London: George Routledge & Sons.

(1963), *Zwei Reisen nach Brasilien, 1548–1555*, ed. Karl Fouquet, Marburg an der Lahn: Trautvetter & Fisher.

Stallybrass, Peter and Allon White (1986), *Politics and Poetics of Transgression*, Ithaca: Cornell University Press.

Stannard, David E. (1992), *American Holocaust: Columbus and the Conquest of the New World*, New York: Oxford University Press.

Steadman, L. B. and C. E. Merbs (1982), 'Kuru and Cannibalism?', *American Anthropologist*, 84: 611–27.

Strathern, Andrew (1993), *Landmarks: Reflections on Anthropology*, Kent, OH: Kent University Press.

Strathern, Marilyn (1980), Personal Communication. Correspondence with William Arens.

Sued Badillo, Jalil (1984), 'Los conquistadores canibales', *Homines*, 8(2): 69–80.

(1992), 'Christopher Columbus and the Enslavement of Amerindians in the Caribbean':, *Monthly Review*, 44 (3): 71–102.

Swift, Jonathan (1973), *The Battel of the Books* in *The Writings of Jonanthan Swift*, ed. Robert A. Greenberg and William B. Pyper, New York: Norton, pp. 373–96.

Taussig, Michael (1980), *The Devil and Commodity Fetishism in South America*, Chapel Hill: University of North Carolina Press.

Taylor, D. M. (1989), 'Bovine Spongiform Encephalopathy and Human Health', *Veterinary Record*, 125: 413–15.

Taylor, E. G. R. (1935), ed. *The Original Writings and the Correspondence of the Two Richard Hakluyts*, 2 vols., London: The Hakluyt Society.

Tharp, Julie (1991), 'The Transvestite as Monster: Gender Horror in *The Silence of the Lambs*', *Journal of Popular Film and Television*, 19(3): 109–13.

The Mighty Sparrow (1988), 'Congo Man', on *The Mighty Sparrow: Party Classics*, vol. 2, no. SCR 3247, Barbados: West Indies Records.

Thevet, André (1953), *Les Français en Amérique pendant la deuxième moitié du XVIe siècle. Le Brésil et les Brésiliens*, ed. Suzanne Lussagnet, Paris: Presses Universitaires de France.

Thomas, Julian (1886), *Cannibals and Convicts: Notes of Personal Experiences in the Western Pacific*, London: Cassell and Company.

Thomas, Keith (1971), *Religion and the Decline of Magic*, London: Weidenfield and Nicolson.

Thomas, Nicholas (1991), *Entangled Objects: Exchange, Material Culture, and Colonialism in the Pacific*, Cambridge, MA: Harvard University Press.

Thompson, Basil (1908), *The Fijians: A Study of the Decay of Custom*, London: Heinemann.

Tiffin, Helen (1987), 'Post-colonial Literatures and Counter-Discourse', *Kunapipi*, 9(3): 17–34.

Todorov, Tzvetan (1975), *The Fantastic: A Structural Approach to a Literary Genre*, trans. Richard Howard, Cornell: Cornell University Press.

(1984), *The Conquest of America*, trans. Richard Howard, New York: Harper Collins.

Turner, Patricia (1993), *I Heard it Through the Grapevine: Rumor in African American Culture*, Berkeley: University of California Press.

Vaz de Caminha, Pêro (1940), 'Carta do Achamento do Brasil' [1500], in *Os Sete Únicos Documentos de 1500, Conservados em Lisboa, referentes à viagem de Pedro Álvares Cabral*, ed. António Fountoura da Costa and António Baião, Lisbon: Agência Geral das Colónias, pp. 61–92.

Verne, Jules (1964), *Among the Cannibals* [1868], ed. I. O. Evans, London: Arco.

Vidal-Naquet, Pierre (1987), *Les assassins de la mémoire: 'Un Eichmann de papier' et autres essais sur le révisionnisme*, Paris: Editions de la Découverte.

(1992), *Assassins of Memory: Essays on the Denial of the Holocaust*, trans. Jeffrey Mehlman, New York: Columbia University Press.

Volosinov, V. N. (1986), *Marxism and the Philosophy of Language*, trans. Ladislaw Matejka and I. R. Titunik, Cambridge, MA: Harvard University Press.

Voltaire (1962), *Philosophical Dictionary*, trans. Peter Gay, New York: Harcourt.

Wachtel, Nathan (1994), *Gods and Vampires: Return to Chipaya*, Chicago: University of Chicago Press.

Walcott, Derek (1974), 'The Caribbean: Culture or Mimicry?', *Journal of Interamerican Studies*, 16: 3–13.

Warner, Marina (1994a), 'Cannibal Tales', in her *Managing Monsters: Six Myths of Our Time*, London: Vintage

(1994b), *From the Beast to the Blonde: On Fairy Tales and their Tellers*, London: Chatto and Windus.

(1994c), ed. *Wonder Tales*, London: Chatto and Windus.

(1995), 'Cannibals and Kings (On "King Kong, Eighth Wonder of the World")', in *Ape, Man, Apeman: Changing Views since 1600*, ed. Raymond Corbey and Bert Theunissen, Leiden: Department of Prehistory, Leiden University, pp. 354–63.

Wasserman, Renata (1984), 'Reinventing the New World: Cooper and Alencar', *Comparative Literature*, 36: 130–45.

Webb, Barbara (1992), *Myth and History in Caribbean Fiction*, Amherst: University of Massachusetts Press.

Weiner, James (1987), 'Cannibalism, Why Not', *Australian Natural History*, 22: 172–3.

Wey-Gómez, Nicolás (1992), 'Cannibalism as Defacement: Columbus's Account of the Fourth Voyage', *Journal of Hispanic Philology*, 16: 195–208.

White, Tim (1992), *Prehistoric Cannibalism at Mancos.* SMTUMR 2346, Princeton: Princeton University Press.

Whitehead, Neil (1990), 'The Snake Warriors - Sons of the Tiger's Teeth', in Jonathan Haas, ed. *The Anthropology of War*, Cambridge: Cambridge University Press, pp. 146–70.

Whitehead, Neil L. (1997), 'Monstrosity and Marvel: Symbolic Convergence and Mimetic Elaboration in Trans-cultural Representation. An Anthropological Reading of Ralegh's *Discoverie* ... ', *Studies in Travel Writing*, 1: 72–95.

Will, R. G. and J. W. Wilesmith (1994), Response to the article 'Vertical Transfer (sic.) of Prion Disease', *Human Reproduction*, 9: 1,797–800.

Williams, Eric (1984), *From Columbus to Castro: The History of the Caribbean* [1970], New York: Vintage.

Williams, Raymond (1977), *Marxism and Literature*, Oxford: Oxford University Press.

Williams, Thomas (1870), *Fiji and the Fijians*, London: Hodder and Stoughton.

Xavier, Ismail (1993), *Alegorias do subdesenvolvimento: Cinema novo, tropicalismo, cinema marginal*, São Paulo: Editora Brasiliense.

Young, Elizabeth (1991), '*The Silence of the Lambs* and the Flaying of Feminist Theory', *Camera Obscura: A Journal of Feminism and Film Theory*, 27: 5–35.

Youngs, Tim (1994), *Travellers in Africa: British Travellers, 1850–1900*, Manchester: Manchester University Press.

Zigas, Vincent (1990), *Laughing Death: the Untold Story of Kuru*, Clifton, NJ: Humana Press.

Zigas, Vincent and D. Carleton Gajdusek (1957), 'Kuru: Clinical Study of a New Syndrome Resembling Paralysis Agitans in Natives of the Eastern Highlands of Australian New Guinea', *The Medical Journal of Australia*, 11: 745–54.

Index